"THE SOUL EXCEEDS ITS CIRCUMSTANCES"

"THE SOUL EXCEEDS

ITS CIRCUMSTANCES"

The Later Poetry of Seamus Heaney

EDITED BY
Eugene O'Brien

UNIVERSITY OF NOTRE DAME PRESS

NOTRE DAME, INDIANA

University of Notre Dame Press
Notre Dame, Indiana 46556
www.undpress.nd.edu
All Rights Reserved

Published in the United States of America

Library of Congress Cataloging-in-Publication Data

Names: O'Brien, Eugene, 1958- editor of compilation.
Title: "The soul exceeds its circumstances" : the later poetry of
Seamus Heaney / edited by Eugene O'Brien.
Description: Notre Dame, Indiana : University of Notre Dame Press, [2016] |
Includes bibliographical references and index.
Identifiers: LCCN 2016032982 (print) | LCCN 2016041886 (ebook) | ISBN
9780268100209 (hardback) | ISBN 0268100209 (hardcover) |
ISBN 9780268100223 (pdf) | ISBN 9780268100230 (epub)
Subjects: LCSH: Heaney, Seamus, 1939–2013—Criticism and interpretation. |
Heaney, Seamus, 1939–2013—Literary style. | BISAC: LITERARY
CRITICISM / European / English, Irish, Scottish, Welsh. | LITERARY
CRITICISM / Poetry.
Classification: LCC PR6058.E2 Z886 2016 (print) | LCC PR6058.E2 (ebook) |
DDC 821/.914—dc23
LC record available at https://lccn.loc.gov/2016032982

∞ *This paper meets the requirements of ANSI/NISO Z39.48-1992*
(Permanence of Paper).

To Seamus and Marie Heaney

"To school the intelligence and make it a soul"

And to the memory of our colleague

Elmer Kennedy-Andrews

CONTENTS

ABBREVIATIONS

Chapters 4, 10, and 11 use the pagination of the Farrar, Straus and
Giroux editions. The rest of the chapters use the pagination of the
Faber editions of the collections.

AH	*Anything Can Happen*	MV	*The Midnight Verdict*
B	*Beowulf*	N	*North*
BT	*The Burial at Thebes*	OG	*Opened Ground*
CP	*Crediting Poetry*	OL	*An Open Letter*
CT	*The Cure at Troy*	P	*Preoccupations*
DC	*District and Circle*	PD	*Place and Displacement*
DD	*Door into the Dark*	PPP	*Place, Pastness, Poems*
DN	*Death of a Naturalist*	PW	*The Place of Writing*
EL	*Electric Light*	RP	*The Redress of Poetry*
FK	*Finders Keepers*	SI	*Station Island*
FW	*Field Work*	SL	*The Spirit Level*
GT	*The Government of the Tongue*	SS	*Stepping Stones*
		ST	*Seeing Things*
HC	*Human Chain*	WO	*Wintering Out*
HL	*The Haw Lantern*		

ACKNOWLEDGMENTS

The idea for this book came as I was compiling a bibliographic entry for the Oxford Online Bibliography project on Seamus Heaney. Having written three books on Heaney, I felt that I was *au fait* with all of the work done on him and was quite surprised that his later work was critically underanalyzed. It was with this in mind, and on something of a whim, that I sent off a series of e-mails to the major scholars who have written on Heaney over the years, suggesting a book on Heaney's later poetry. It was gratifying to note that the replies were positive, and the process began. So, my first thanks is to my cocontributors. I think it is fair to say that they are the major figures in Heaney studies, and it has been a joy to work with them. Reading the essays was instructive, and together these essays make a significant contribution to the study of one of the greatest poets in the language. The essays were a pleasure to read and required little or no editing—the project was a joy. The University of Notre Dame Press was also a joy to work with, with readers seeing the value of the work, and with an affirming editor in Stephen Little, whose enthusiasm for the project was heartening. Elisabeth Magnus did a wonderful job copyediting what is a large book, and the finished product is cleaner, sharper, and more coherent thanks to her work. Rebecca De-Boer was a careful, organized, and very supportive editor whose work on processing the manuscript has improved it immeasurably.

However, in all joy there is sadness. In the compiling of this book, Seamus Heaney died, and the world is the poorer for his absence. I think he would have liked this book, and it is my hope that the scholarship contained here does justice to the texts that are analyzed and studied, and to his complex and sustaining view of the place of the aesthetic in our lives as human beings. His daughter Catherine, with whom I have worked on this and another book, has been the soul of courtesy and help, and it has been a pleasure working with her (I promise to stop bugging her with questions now). A further shock to the system came with the news of the death of one of our contributors, Elmer Kennedy-Andrews. Elmer was a fine scholar and a lovely man, and he, and his work, will be missed. It was a pleasure to meet and work with someone whose writing on Heaney I had long admired.

Personally, I must thank my colleagues in Mary Immaculate College, and our president, Professor Michael Hayes, who has inaugurated an Institute for Irish Studies and who is a strong supporter of the work being done in the college in Irish studies. The new structures have made Mary Immaculate College a sustaining environment for the work that I do, and I am grateful for this. I would like to offer special thanks to Professor Mick Healy, associate vice president for research, for his support and his help in the preparation of this book. My own colleagues in the Department of English Language and Literature, by their efficiency and hard work, have allowed me the time to work on this project, and I thank them: Linda McGrath, John McDonagh, Maria Beville, Marita Ryan, Anne O'Keeffe, Kathryn Laing, Deirdre Flynn, Margaret Healy, Joan O'Sullivan, Eóin Flannery, and Donna Mitchell.

Finally, my wife Áine has always been the main supporter of my work, and her conversation, questions, comments, and encouragement have been invaluable as ever. My children, Eoin, Dara, and Sinéad, have been a source of fun, joy, and laughter in the process of writing this book, and I thank them for making my life better and brighter through their presence. A lot of this book was edited at home, and Áine, Eoin, Dara, and Sinéad are integral parts of it, however hauntological those parts might be.

It is my contention that the later poetry of Seamus Heaney is among the finest to be written in the English language, and the aim of this book was to help to demonstrate this to be the case. It is up to others to decide whether the book succeeds in this aim or not; for me, the pleasure has been in its construction and execution, and I am now more convinced than ever of the value of a poetry that very definitely allows the soul to exceed its circumstances.

Introduction

Eugene O'Brien

The death of Seamus Heaney in August of 2013 was the passing of one of the most revered literary figures in the world. Encomia to his life and art, his humility and generosity, his sense of the ethical and the aesthetic, have resounded throughout the global media. He has been that rare phenomenon, an artist who is popular among audiences as well as being studied to the very highest level within the academy. Indeed, he has been seen as a national poet, though the term has not been used as often as one might think, and there are reasons for this. Moynagh Sullivan notes that the "very notion of a national poet in Ireland initiates a crisis because it involves a denial of the boundary that separates the island" and that such terms need to be used with nuance and care as they involve "questions of nation and representivity" (2005, 451). Such have been the conditions within which Heaney was writing that people in Northern Ireland have felt "compelled to murder one another or deploy their different military arms over the matter of nomenclatures such as British or Irish" (*P*, 56), so issues of national, political, and cultural representivity have long been problematic in an Irish literary context.

Given the complex nature of identity in Northern Ireland, and given that this is no mere academic issue—some 3,600 people were killed over the thirty years before the peace process—it is all the more remarkable that Seamus Heaney was able to become so eminent a poetic voice in the anglophone world, and indeed in the world as a whole. Over fifty books and collections of essays have been written on his work, and a bibliography compiled by Rand Brandes and James Durkan (2008) includes some two thousand entries. To offer another collection of essays on his work would seem to be a task that is in need of justification, but in terms of the material covered in this book such justification is relatively easy. The vast majority of the published books deal with what might be termed Heaney's early and middle poetry. Though his canon comprises thirteen complete collections, the last five have received comparatively little attention, and this is especially true of the final three books. This means that, while Heaney's reputation remains secure, the style, progression, and development of his later work have not been widely analyzed, nor have the developments in tone, style, imagery, symbol, and allusion that can be seen to come to fruition in these books. In a sense, the standard view of Heaney is of someone almost frozen in time, as a type of static poetic presence who reached a certain poetic standard and then remained there. However, even at the level of practicality, this is an oversimplification.

The man who wrote *Death of a Naturalist* in 1966 was a lecturer in English at St. Joseph's College of Education, in Belfast, and was someone who had left Ireland only to go on a trip to Lourdes and to work in a summer job in the passport office in London (*SS*, xxii). The man who wrote *Human Chain*, some forty-four years later, was a Nobel Prize winner and a former professor in Oxford and Harvard who was feted throughout the world and who had been a professional poet and academic for many years. Ongoing exposure to the work of other poets, and also to writings about the work of poets, would have been a strong influence on his development, and Heaney has long been one of the best critics and aesthetic thinkers writing in the anglophone public sphere. It is often forgotten that he has four weighty collections of essays on poetry and the aesthetic to his name: *Preoccupations* (1980); *The Government of the Tongue* (1988); *The Redress of Poetry* (1995); and *Finders Keepers* (2002). This huge disparity in life and literary experience necessitates a detailed reading of his later poetry in order to come to some understanding of just how his work progressed and in what directions it developed.

It is the contention of this book that the later poetry of Heaney comprises some of the greatest collections of lyric poetry in the English language. It deals with structures of feeling and nuanced expressions of emotion, mood, attitude, and perspective, and it sheds clear light on what it means to be a human being in the Ireland, and the world, of the late twentieth and early twenty-first centuries. It is also the work of a man who has grown older, who has seen more of the world, and who has thought about the feelings and experiences of his own life, his own country, and the role of poetry in such a life. As he has evocatively put it:

> Poetry, let us say, whether it belongs to an old political dispensation or aspires to express a new one, has to be a working model of inclusive consciousness. It should not simplify. Its projections and inventions should be a match for the complex reality which surrounds it and out of which it is generated. *The Divine Comedy* is a great example of this kind of total adequacy, but a haiku may also constitute a satisfactory comeback by the mind to the facts of the matter. As long as the coordinates of the imagined thing correspond to those of the world that we live in and endure, poetry is fulfilling its counterweighting function. It becomes another truth to which we can have recourse, before which we can know ourselves in a more fully empowered way. (*RP*, 7–8)

This is just one example of a very sophisticated theory of poetry and its role in the aesthetic, ethical, and political spheres in which people have their being. A "working model of inclusive consciousness" is a resonant phrase as a descriptor of the mode of being of poetry, and the idea that poetry "should not simplify" is embodied in much of Heaney's later writing. This is a body of work that is in need of serious and sustained critical investigation, and this book will be the first step in this necessary academic task.

The ascription of the adjectives *early* or *late* to any writer's work is necessarily arbitrary, as the points of transition between one period and another are, by nature, permeable and subjective. In this book, the later Heaney is seen as comprising the following books: *Seeing Things* (1991); *The Spirit Level* (1996); *Electric Light* (2001); *District and Circle* (2006); and *Human Chain* (2010). Of course, the case could be made for taking the last three or four books instead, but as Geoffrey Bennington has put it, "Saying that there is no secure starting point does not mean that one starts at random. You always start somewhere but that somewhere is never just anywhere" (Bennington and Derrida 1993, 22). The starting point of this collection is that these later books can be grouped in terms of style, theme, approach, and intertextuality. They develop themes that were apparent in Heaney's earlier work, but they also break with these themes in terms of addressing issues that are radically different from those of the earlier collections. It is possible to see the middle period as a type of hinge, or what Jacques Derrida might term a *brisure*, meaning a "joint" or "break" but also a "hinged articulation of two parts of wood- or metal-work. The hinge, the *brisure* [folding-joint] of a shutter" (Derrida 1976, 65), in that it is open to both the early themes of ground, soil, memory, and rootedness and the later themes of space, air, and literature. This middle section could be seen as a break from the earlier themes or as a point of articulation from these to the later ones, "as a *brisure* can indicate a crack or a break as well as a hinge or a joint" (Robert 2010, 29), but in either case there is agreement that thematic focus changes in the later books, and it is this change, and these books, that are the focus of our investigations in this study.

The chapters in this book are all written by acknowledged experts on Heaney's work, from both sides of the Atlantic, and they combine the work of bright new scholars in the field with that of some of the pioneering figures in the area of Heaney studies. While Heaney's earlier books are not examined here, they are a necessary context for understanding his later development. The later poetry of Heaney does not appear, fully formed, ex nihilo; it is preceded by his earlier work.

In this introduction, I briefly trace the trajectory of Heaney's poetry from the early to the later books in order to bring out continuities and discontinuities. Perhaps the most overt break in style, to use Helen Vendler's (1995) term, is the shift from an artesian to an aerial imaginative structure. The earlier Heaney was someone who looked to the ground, both literal and metaphorical, to understand himself, his society, and his unconscious. In "Digging," a poem that has been seen to have something of "the authority of an *ars poetica*" (D. Lloyd 1993, 21), Heaney spells out his artesian imagination and the direction in which his early poetry will be directed:

> But I've no spade to follow men like them.
>
> Between my finger and my thumb
> The squat pen rests.
> I'll dig with it.
>
> (DN, 14)

Critical commentary on the poem has recognized its importance in Heaney's imaginative teleology. Andrew Waterman sees the poem as a personal artistic manifesto that claims continuities and analogues between Heaney's own writing and the "manual skills and livelihoods of his forebears" (1992, 12). Neil Corcoran, having noted the centrality of the pen/spade metaphor, speaks of a "willed continuity between spade and pen" (1998, 51), while Elmer Kennedy-Andrews observes the poet celebrating the diggers' "intimacy with the land" and sees Heaney as attempting to replicate this artesian experience in his writing as he "delves into his experience to produce poems" (1988, 38–39). Michael Parker suggestively argues that the "gun, like the pen, triggers feelings of unease. Its presence indicates that the young man's duel with his father is not yet resolved, nor the struggle against competing cultural expectations" (2012, 330), suggesting a deeper familial tension at work in the poem.

   This artesian aspect of Heaney's writing was to become a thematic constant in his earlier books, with his physical digging becoming transformed into a metaphorical probing of the unconscious of the self. In the final poem of his first book, "Personal Helicon," this connection between digging and writing is again foregrounded:

Now, to pry into roots, to finger slime,
To stare, big-eyed Narcissus, into some spring
Is beneath all adult dignity. I rhyme
To see myself, to set the darkness echoing.

(DN, 57)

Robert Buttel (1975, 48) cites the poem's dedicatee Michael Longley in seeing the poem as "both credo and manifesto," while Blake Morrison (1982, 19) sees the "narcissistic self-consciousness" that is clear from the closing stanza of the poem as an indication that "the business of writing is indeed a major theme of his work." Elmer Kennedy-Andrews sees the core of the poem as enacting a version of Jacques Lacan's mirror stage, since here language disrupts the symmetry between the subject and the image, and since language in the poem, rather than describing a prior meaning, "is primary, and meaning, far from preceding language, is an effect produced by language" (1988, 25). In both of these poems, language is a seminal and forceful subtheme, and this will endure throughout Heaney's poetry.

One could see the early Heaney as very much probing his "door into the dark," and in *North* (1975) the darkness moved from the personal to the political as the Jungian ground of the bogs of Ireland morphed into a tribal unconscious which attempted to give voice to the atavisms that spawned a thirty-year conflict between notions of Irishness and Britishness, notions of republicanism and unionism, and notions of nationalism and loyalism. In this collection, Heaney, clearly aware of the complexities of the title, attempts to recontextualize Northern Ireland in a far less binary manner. He locates the opening of the book in an imagined "North" that includes the world of the Vikings and Norse mythology. This gave rise to some criticism, with Edna Longley wondering about the connection between the "not very Nordic North of Ireland" and poems about "fertility rites and capital punishment in prehistoric Denmark" (1986, 159). A number of critics saw this book as mired in the past, with Heaney being termed a "laureate of violence" (Carson 1975, 183).

However, what Heaney was offering here was a recontextualization of the Northern Irish situation. Rather than accepting fixed frames of identity from the Irish/British adversarial opposition, he suggestively proposes a reinterpretation of that past in terms of another construction that is also based on history. Viking invasions took place in Ireland over a period of some four hundred years. These "neighbourly, scoretaking / killers" (*N*, 23) came to raid and stayed to trade. Many Irish cities, Dublin and Limerick, for example, were founded by the Vikings, and there is much archaeological evidence of their presence in early Ireland. Their pattern of intermarriage and interaction with the native Irish has many similarities with that of the later Norman, and still later English, settlers. In terms of their influence on a native culture, it seems, the Vikings have as much right to be seen as seminal and originary as have the Catholic nationalist and Protestant loyalist traditions. Clearly, for Heaney, "The connection between language and reality is plural and in no way confined to the nationalist republican paradigm" (E. O'Brien 2003, 135).

I would argue that the Viking theme provides Heaney with a lever that will facilitate the process of "unrooting" his psyche from the "memory incubating the spilled blood" (*N*, 20) and of imposing some form of plurality on the place, instead of allowing the place to be the ground of his ideas. Magdalena Kay correctly points to a dichotomy in *North* when she adverts to a choice Heaney must make between a desire for immersion in identity and a more detached attitude to the signifiers of identity. The speaker of the poems must choose between surrender and control, "and these choices correspond to a metapoetic dichotomy between conceptions of the poet as receptacle for inspiration (*vates*) and poet as creator (*makar*)" (2010, 88). For Kay, there is a subtler dialectic at work in this book than was generally seen at the time.

The atavism voiced in *North* was something of a surprise in the Irish public sphere of the time. Whatever feelings might have been expressed in private, one of the linguistic consequences of the violence was, ironically, an overt self-censorship in middle-class Northern Irish discourse. Rationally, in a public sphere that had grown increasingly politically correct, the voices of atavism were seldom heard, and Heaney, as a poet, parodied this in *North*: "One side's as bad as the other, never worse" (*N*, 57). However, in Part One of the book, Heaney speaks with the voice of the unconscious and with a strong resonance of atavism and of racial and sectarian embedded feeling. As Henry Hart maintains, what makes Heaney's "bog poems so ethically dubious are his personae who

identify with the romantic dead with nothing less than erotic passion"
(1989, 404), and some of the language and imagery of these poems is
stark in the extreme. Reading P. V. Glob's *The Bog People* (1977) provided
Heaney with sustaining metaphors for symbolizing the long-buried, but
still potent, sectarian and religious hatred that erupted on the streets of
Belfast and Derry in 1969.

These symbolic bog people allowed him to follow the Yeatsian ex-
ample of writing in a public crisis by "making your own imagery and
your own terrain take the colour of it, take the impressions of it" (Heaney
1979b, 13). This is precisely what Heaney does in his bog poems—he
tells a truth about the Troubles in a way that is inclusive of the compli-
cated different reactions of consciousness. This volume definitely does
not simplify. Glob argued that a number of the Iron Age figures found
buried in the bogs were "ritual sacrifices to the Mother Goddess" (*P*,
57). For Heaney, the notion of these people as bridegrooms to the god-
dess, as sacrifices that would ensure fertility in the spring, was symbolic
of an "archetypal pattern," and he tells of how the photographs in the
book fused with photographs of contemporary atrocities in his mind.

Thus in "Punishment" he parallels the fate of the Windeby Girl,
who was punished for adultery in Iron Age Germany by being bound,
tied to a "weighing stone," and drowned, with that of young Catholic
girls who dated British soldiers and who were tied to railings and cov-
ered in tar. As Hart has noted, the poet expresses an almost erotic attach-
ment to the Windeby Girl as he tells of how the "wind / on her naked
front" blows "her nipples / to amber beads" (*N*, 37), and in the closing
stanza he explains the reasons for his inaction, admitting that he is some-
one "who would connive / in civilized outrage yet understand the exact /
and tribal, intimate revenge" (*N*, 38). In this poem, which serves as a
synecdoche of the modus operandi of *North* as a collection, there is a
split perspective: that of the rational, twentieth-century educated sensi-
bility and that of an atavistic and emotional Jungian group identity. It is
not a case of either/or but of both/and. Heaney contains within himself
both perspectives, and the poems in this book, and indeed the collection
as a whole, give clear voice to the different attachments that run through
his consciousness.

Now that this book can be read at a temporal and political remove,
as the violence in Northern Ireland has been largely, if not totally, ended

thanks to the peace process, this complex and nuanced perspective can be seen as offering as rounded an image as possible for the conflicted and contrary sense of political engagement and civilized distance that Heaney must have felt at this time. Richard Rankin Russell makes the telling point that critics have not accorded *North* the recognition that it deserves in "Heaney's developing concepts of artistic fidelity and cultural reconciliation, instead focusing mostly on its at times divisive politics" (2010, 214). There is a fusion and an oscillation between conscious attitudes and unconscious pulsions, and interestingly, when speaking of the genesis of his poem "Undine" in *Door into the Dark* (*DD*, 26), Heaney explains the poetic thinking behind such a process. He stresses that it was the "dark pool of the sound of the word" itself that first spoke to his "auditory imagination" (*P*, 52), and he goes on to suggest how the sound of the word unites "primitive and civilised associations" and is almost a poem in itself: "*Unda*, a wave, *undine*, a water-woman—a litany of undines would have ebb and flow, water and woman, wave and tide, fulfilment and exhaustion in its very rhythms" (*P*, 53). What is interesting here is that for Heaney a poem is a structure of unification of the primitive and the civilized, of the unconscious and the conscious, and this notion of a mediation or transformational fusion of disparate discourses is at the core of his view of poetry as a discourse that "should not simplify."

Citing Wallace Stevens, Heaney states that the nobility of poetry "is a violence from within that protects us from a violence without. It is the imagination pressing back against the pressure of reality" (*RP*, 1), and this pressing can change the shape of that reality. Therefore, to read *North* politically is to do a generic disservice to poetry, a point tellingly made by Helen Vendler, who notes that "since no lyric can be equal to the whole complexity of private and public life at any given moment, lyrics are not to be read as position papers" (1998, 7). Heaney, through his poetry, was offering an imaginative response, as opposed to a political solution, to the stark reality of Northern Ireland during the dark years of violence.

Michael Molino would agree with Vendler's position, as he states that between 1968 and 1972 Heaney developed a "polyphonic voice that displaced the political and cultural antagonisms endemic to his country and relocated them in a realm of reflexive, historical linguistics." Molino goes on to note that Heaney's writing at this time "circumvented the political/poetic dilemma with a poetry whose vernacular problematic addressed old antagonisms in an innovative way" (1993, 181). This innovation was to become a central factor in Heaney's aesthetic, and it would be further progressed in his next collection, *Field Work* (1979).

Writing about the deaths of real, contemporary people in *Field Work* allowed Heaney to discuss how death can affect the individual who has been exposed to it. Without the communal security blanket of tribal bonding, such violent deaths have a chilling effect on the individual. "The Strand at Lough Beg" refers to Colum McCartney, "a second cousin" of Heaney's who was "shot arbitrarily" as he was "coming home from a football match in Dublin" (Heaney 1979b, 21). At the end of the poem, Heaney imagines himself washing the dead body with "handfuls of dew" and dabbing it "clean with moss" before plaiting "Green scapulars to wear over your shroud" with rushes that grow near Lough Beg (*FW*, 18).

Another elegy, "Casualty," describes a fisherman, Louis O'Neill, who used to come to Heaney's father-in-law's public house in County Tyrone:

> He was blown to bits
> Out drinking in a curfew
> Others obeyed, three nights
> After they shot dead
> The thirteen men in Derry.
> (*FW*, 22)

As Daniel Tobin argues, the poem "recognizes that the individual's freedom and compassion originate in an inner demand more powerful than the tribal call" (1998, 155), and this is a pivotal point in the development of Heaney's aesthetic. Here is a rhetorical and ethical swerve from the funerals of the thirteen who were killed by the British army on Bloody Sunday, January 13, 1972, in the Bogside area, in Derry, and from the almost tribal reaction of nationalist Ireland:

> Unrolled its swaddling band,
> Lapping, tightening

Till we were braced and bound
Like brothers in a ring.
                                        (*FW*, 22)

In many ways the perspective of Part One of *North* was from the inside of that ring as Heaney tried to voice the intensity of tribal and sectarian feeling that was a fact of life in Northern Ireland. The focus on the individual is programmatic here, as Heaney is gradually bringing his aesthetic lens to bear on the individual, and it is on the individual consciousness and indeed unconscious that his later books will focus.

This probing of individual experience can be traced to the elegies in *Field Work*, and the facticity of a life ending becomes more central than the politics of the polis or the community. Heaney expresses this point clearly in *The Government of the Tongue*: "Here is the great paradox of poetry and of the imaginative arts in general. Faced with the brutality of the historical onslaught, they are practically useless. Yet they verify our singularity, they strike and stake out the ore of self which lies at the base of every individuated life. In one sense the efficacy of poetry is nil—no lyric has ever stopped a tank. In another sense, it is unlimited" (*GT*, 107). Heaney's later poetry will be a sustained exploration of this singularity of experience, and the increasing number of poems about individuals, especially elegies on the deaths of the famous and those known only to the community within which they lived, are a metonym of this increased concern for the lived human life in all of its complexity, nuance, and value. From this point onwards, as Bernard O'Donoghue avers, "Heaney's writing is increasingly linked to this kind of self-commentary" (2009, 5).

In *Field Work*, there is also a change in the type of stanzaic structure and rhythm that is used. There is a more self-conscious sense of the structure of the line and of experimentation with different poetic forms in this book, with the "Glanmore Sonnets" standing out as a set piece that places Heaney firmly within the English and European poetic traditions by his use of this most poetic of constructions. Tobin notes that "the sonnets are little fields where art and nature inform each other" because "just as the world becomes transfigured through its connection with art, so art itself becomes fully empowered through its connection with the earth" (1998, 156).

His point is well taken, as poetry as a form of communication between self and other is enunciated in the opening line: "Vowels ploughed into other: opened ground" (*FW*, 33). Seeing Glanmore as a "hedge-school" (*FW*, 34), Heaney finds time to write about himself and his rural surroundings. We have already noted his view that it was the similarity between Glanmore and Mossbawn that allowed him to write about the place in which he was living. Here, he concentrates on personal and marital growth, going on to implicitly compare himself and Marie, his wife, to "Dorothy and William" Wordsworth (*FW*, 35) and to discuss the etymological associations of "boortree" and "elderberry" (*FW*, 37). This poem heralds a preoccupation with language in all of its variety, a preoccupation that registers the connection between this and his "first place," Mossbawn (*P*, 18).

As with Wordsworth, Heaney's reaction to nature is mediated through language, and indeed the very fact that Wordsworth and Dorothy, while brother and sister, are mentioned as a literary couple implies that this response to nature will be literary in tenor and in tone, seeing a cuckoo and corncrake, for example, at twilight as "crepuscular and iambic" (*FW*, 35). Indeed, he places himself and Marie in the context of other literary couples in the final sonnet: "Lorenzo and Jessica in a cold climate / Diarmuid and Grainne waiting to be found" (*FW*, 42). These couples, one Shakespearian from *The Merchant of Venice* and the other Irish from the *Fiannaíocht* cycle of tales, serve to foreground the literary nature of their rural idyll. The gradual movement from poems of earth and myth to poems that have an intertextual relationship with works of European literature was begun in *North* and has been continued in *Field Work*. The effect of this referencing of the word as opposed to the physical world is to recontextualize references to territory, a point that has been made by Andrew Auge, who, following the thought of Deleuze and Guattari, speaks of a nomadic style of writing that attempts to deterritorialize language. This style of writing no longer attempts to "be saved by culture or by myth" but instead takes on the more difficult struggle involved in "transferring one's allegiance from the familiar pieties and identities of the past to the unknown and as yet unimagined possibilities of the future" (2003, 270–71).

Auge correctly identifies Heaney's change of poetic stance, a process that comes to full fruition in the later books. It could be signaled in the second terms of the following progression: from earth to air; from "we" to "I"; from myth to imagination; from experience to literary allusion; from English vernacular to classical frame of reference; from Ireland to the world; from politics to ethics; and from past to future. The later books will focus on the second terms of these binaries as they immerse themselves in the literary and poetic contexts within which the author has himself been immersed in a lifetime of writing, thinking, and feeling about the word and its effects on the world, and vice versa.

The ever-increasing range of classical references in Heaney's work is a stylistic trope that is seen at its strongest in the later Heaney, and this is typified by his extensive use of the elegy in these books. Elegy is a classical genre that can often seem overburdened with its classical and literary inheritance. However, as Heaney has noted in terms of inheritance, "whatever is given // Can always be reimagined" (*ST*, 22), and his own reimagining of this genre in his later books is based on a fusion of the classical and the familial and local inheritances of his own experience. Meg Tyler sees Heaney's inheritance as enabling rather than disabling because it provides "him with distance from the 'significance' of his work. His rural ancestors have freed him from the noose that seems to hover above the heads of those writers burdened by the past" (2005, 134). By working in tandem with the classical tradition of Greece and Rome in these books, Heaney is using literary versions of the past to proclaim a more optimistic future. His decision "to work within institutionalized forms in English and Latin poetry is, in a way, a decision to work against meaninglessness or nihilism" (Tyler 2005, 170).

In *Station Island*, Heaney's questioning of the role of art in a political situation, and by extension of the role of the aesthetic with respect to the political, is being teased out all the time, and the consistent references to Dante underscore this questioning process. Whereas in *North* he used his art to utter the concerns of his tribe, in this section he attempts to transform that consciousness through a focus on his own growth. This is the driving force behind the central sequence of this book, namely the poems that make up "Station Island" itself. In this sequence, the self is haunted by ghosts, memories, specters, images from both his personal and his literary and historical contexts: "The central section of *Station Island*—which is much the longest single volume of Heaney's—shares the volume's title, describing a Dante-influenced purgatorial pilgrimage to Lough Derg in County Donegal, a demanding penitential programme that Heaney undertook three times when he was young. The question of guilt is obviously central here as the narrator/poet encounters figures from his own past life and the literary past" (O'Donoghue 2009, 6–7). The mode of pilgrimage allowed Dante to use the journey metaphor to catalog changes and developments in himself; for Heaney, this would prove to be a potent symbolic avenue through which he could explore the "typical strains which the consciousness labors under in this country . . . to be faithful to the collective historical experience and to be true to the recognitions of the emerging self" (Todorov 1988, 18–19). In his doorway into the dark, he probes the givens of history and the past; in his doorway into the light, he can choose and create the spectral figures of a personal aesthetic history.

These ghosts act as mirror images or refractions of aspects of his own personality, and they engage him in a dialectical series of conversations that urge him to focus more on the singular than on the plural. Thus Simon Sweeney, who is a combination of "a traveller" and a neighbor of Heaney's called "Charlie Griffin," who is remembered as "roaming the hedges with a bowsaw, cutting branches and dragging them home for firewood" (*SS*, 240), urges Heaney to "stay clear of all processions" (*SI*, 63). The second ghost is the writer William Carleton, who wrote *The Lough Derg Pilgrim* in 1828. Heaney notes that he was one of the possible guides through the whole sequence, and his reasons for this are significant: "He was a cradle Catholic, a Northern Catholic, a man who had lived with and witnessed the uglier side of sectarianism, but still a man who converted to the Established Church and broke with 'our tribe's complicity'" (*SS*, 236). In this way, Carleton embodies the individual who is guilt-stricken and torn between personal and communal demands. Heaney, in section II, has Carleton call himself a "traitor" and give the advice that "it is a road you travel on your own" (*SI*, 65), terms that illustrate the guilt associated with leaving a communal identity.

Carleton's advice to the poet is to "remember everything and keep your head" (*SI*, 66). Patrick Kavanagh, a poet who exerted a strong early influence on Heaney, and who also wrote about Lough Derg, appears in section V. His comment is similarly scathing: "Forty-two years on / and you've got no farther" (*SI*, 73). All three figures voice Heaney's frustration that parts of his psyche have not yet outgrown the societal and religious givens of his culture.

As the sequence comes to its climax, another literary specter gives the final piece of advice. As Stephen Regan has observed, it is "James Joyce rather than Dante who provides artistic sustenance," and it is the arch-individualist himself who "tells the poet, 'What you must do must be done on your own,' and all the signs are that Heaney has since reaffirmed his belief in lyric intensity and concentration" (2007, 21):

> Keep at a tangent.
> When they make the circle wide, it's time to swim
>
> out on your own and fill the element
> with signatures on your own frequency.
>
> (*SI*, 93–94)

Perhaps the most important aspect of this sequence is that it allows Heaney to speak through the personalities of others; through these encounters with different ghosts he is able to give voice to doubts and uncertainties using these personalities, and the focus has firmly turned to the individual self and to the experience and agency of that self.

In his next book, this focus is more overt. The epigraph to *The Haw Lantern* demonstrates the transforming power of language: "The river-bed, dried-up, half-full of leaves. / Us, listening to a river in the trees" (*HL*, vii). This image is more complex than it seems on first reading: does he mean the sound of wind in the trees is like a river, or does he mean that the rustling of the leaves in the riverbed is like a river in the trees, or does he mean both at the same time? In a book where presence and absence interact in a dialectical fashion, and where there are a number of ponderings on the nature of selfhood and of agency, this epigraph sets the tone, as it develops the ghostly images of the "Station Island" sequence.

Here, the notion of the "I" that we saw being unfolded or unwound in the last books is further developed as different aspects of his individuality are afforded "second thoughts" (*HL*, 4), an image from the poem "Terminus," where the complexity of identities that cohere in his own selfhood is expressed in the telescoped line: "Baronies, parishes met where I was born," with its juxtaposition of the British political term *baronies* with that of the Irish Catholic *parish*. For Heaney, selfhood and identity, like the image of the riverbed in the trees reflecting the one on the ground, are complex and reflective and refractive of different contexts of sociopolitical identity: "I grew up in between" (*HL*, 5).

In his essay "From the Frontier of Writing," he eschews the use of the "I" in a manner that makes it very different from an analogous poem in *Field Work* entitled "The Toome Road." In both poems there is an encounter with the British army, but in "The Toome Road" there is a palpable antagonism: "How long were they approaching down my roads / As if they owned them?" (*FW*, 15). Here place is seen in terms of a dialectic of ownership; however, in the latter poem, the focus is on "the tightness and nilness around that space" (*HL*, 6). Instead of the certainties of place, there is the "nilness," but also the undefined nature of "space": it is hard to quarrel about the ownership of "nilness," and it is as if the idea of space has cleared out all of the possessive antagonism of the earlier poem.

Another nil space is found in the sonnet sequence "Clearances," which deals with the death of Heaney's mother. In the emblematic third sonnet, he speaks of recalling how, while "the others were away at mass," he and his mother peeled potatoes in "silence": "I was all hers. . . . Never closer the rest of our lives" (*HL*, 27). In sonnet 7, his mother's death is described in terms of its effect on those in the room with her:

> That space we stood around had been emptied
> Into us to keep, it penetrated
> Clearances that suddenly stood open.
> High cries were felled and a pure change happened.
>
> (*HL*, 31)

Here, in his mother's death, the importance of space and absence as sources and as necessary aspects of identity are made clear. Heaney's own pure change is very much the sense that presence is connected with absence and that place is haunted by space. In the final sonnet of this sequence, he speaks of a chestnut tree that had been planted in the year he was born by his aunt Mary, whose "affection came to be symbolized in the tree"; whereas the rest of the garden was mature, "the chestnut tree, on the other hand, was young and was watched in much the same way as the other children and myself were watched and commented upon, fondly, frankly and unrelentingly" (*GT*, 3). What is most significant here is that the connections with the tree are all metaphors for the connection with his aunt; it is as if the tree is an organic symbol of the connection between them. The tree was subsequently cut down, and in this sonnet he speaks of

> . . . walking round and round a space
> Utterly empty, utterly a source
> Where the decked chestnut tree had lost its place
> In our front hedge above the wallflowers.
>
> (*HL*, 32)

Instead of lamenting the absence of the tree, or feeling a sense of loss, the speaker of the poem looks to that "pure change" of which the earlier sonnet spoke, as the "deep planted and long gone" tree, the poet's "coeval" chestnut, has transformed but endured. The symbol of "deep planted" immanence has become transformed into a resonant symbol of the transcendent, as its "heft and hush become a bright nowhere, / A soul ramifying and forever / Silent, beyond silence listened for" (*HL*, 32). The use of the word *ramifying* is significant, as it suggests the complexities of the transcendent, or the subdivisions and extra consequences; etymologically, it derives from Medieval Latin "*ramificare*," meaning "to form branches." So even in the "nilness around that space," the original branches are both present and absent, with the images of the real foliage being spectrally mimicked by the imagined ones in the "bright nowhere" of the space of the tree. At this juncture, the tree "is transformed from a place that is written about into the space where writing takes place" (E. O'Brien 2002, 147): it is "utterly a source."

Here the dialectic between the place of the rooted tree and the space that it once occupied is a crucial trope of *The Haw Lantern*, as is indicated by the mirroring of the river and the trees in the epigraph. This book paves the way for what I term the later Heaney, where there is a more nuanced and complex relationship between issues of self and other, text and context, and ethics and aesthetics. The notion of the soul as branching ever outwards and engaging with complexities is an image that can act as a metonym for the poetic thought that is at work in the later books. In this collection, the chapters will look at how Heaney faces issues of mortality and also at the desire for transcendence. They will examine the style of these books and discuss how it is often both literate and literary, though at the same time remaining accessible and profound. Chapters will also discuss Heaney's use of translation; his sense of what might be termed a ramified Irishness and transnational identity; his specific sense of the numinousness of objects and of life as a gift; and his highly complex sense of space and the spatial.

One of the interesting things about this collection is how so many of the writers involved see Heaney's work as transcending, to greater or lesser degrees, the mire of the political. A confluence of ideas here present Heaney as a writer who, even in his earlier stages, was looking toward something transcendent and more ethically utopian. This is not to say that the chapters on his later writing will share a single purpose, but they share a core view of Heaney as stressing the literary over the actual and of looking at the interstices and the positions of liminality and complexity in almost every situation. His use of literary reference in the later books is an example of this, as he seeks literary avatars against whom he can bounce his own ideas and with whom he can enter into a form of aesthetic and ethical dialogue. In his later work, his fondness for Latin and his ongoing literariness come to the fore, with the number of classical references to Greek and Roman literature multiplying as the books develop.

PART ONE: HEANEY AND DEATH

The subject of death pervades *Human Chain*, and Andy Auge's chapter shows how Heaney's figurations of a posthumous existence in this book are evocatively indeterminate: a reflected shadow of a solar eclipse, a mote of dust adrift in a sacral space, a kite that breaks free and is declared a "windfall," or, more overtly, "a not unwelcoming emptiness." Equally significant is how these poems undercut the rigid binary oppositions of life and death, presence and absence, being and nothingness. In that regard, the citations and transpositions of book 6 of Virgil's *Aeneid*, most notably in the sequences "Album," "The Riverbank Field," and "Route 110," establish how the dead and the living, the past and future, as Robert Pogue Harrison states, "copenetrate and codetermine each other," and Auge concludes with a discussion of how the image of Aeneas carrying his father Anchises, which is echoed in Heaney's frequent references to his father in his last debilitated days, serves as an emblem of what Jacques Derrida referred to as "survival," the obligation of the living to bear the dead within themselves.

Magdalena Kay looks at Heaney's musings on death across a number of his later books. She begins by looking at his "Clearances" sequence in *The Haw Lantern* and progresses to *Seeing Things*, which steps into the realm of emptiness and virtuality most deliberately. Although bookended by Dantean scenes, the volume explores underworlds and otherworlds in ways that are often abstract, unconventionally figurative, and sometimes riddling. Kay suggests that if the noumenal and absolute can be accessed only through the phenomenal and circumstantial, and if we accept a certain randomness to inform the process, then what is given can be endlessly reimagined—and reimagine Heaney does. Her reading of this process of reimagining culminates in the striking minimalism of "A Herbal," in which Heaney surprisingly rejects the abstract and mediatory function of symbol in order to insist upon the physical immediacy of image. This turn allows for an unusual relation to the realm of emptiness, one unburdened by pathos, in which what is usually ponderous becomes light as air.

Helen Vendler examines Heaney's treatment of death in his 1991 forty-eight-poem sequence entitled *Squarings*, later published in *Seeing Things*. Her reading traces the impetus for this sequence back to the fact that Heaney's parents had both died within two years: Margaret Heaney in 1984 (when the poet, born in 1939, was forty-five), and Patrick Heaney in 1986. In *Squarings*, the impact of those deaths has deepened to redefine their son's world. The parents are no less significant dead than alive; time has taken on in their absence a stasis from which it cannot now recover. This chapter will analyze the sequence and will discuss its significance in the later aesthetic thought of Seamus Heaney. The world asks to be reconstituted anew, with vacancy and invisibility, rather than presence and solidity, as its atmosphere. Vendler concludes with a discussion of the "overture" to *Squarings*, its harrowing first poem, which confronts the moment after death (when, in Christian belief, the soul undergoes the "particular judgment"—the divine judgment on its individual life, consigning it to heaven or hell).

PART TWO: HEANEY'S LATER STYLE

In "The Golden Bough" Heaney translates from book 6 of Virgil's *Aeneid*: "So from the back of her shrine the Sybil of Cumae / Chanted fearful equivocal words and made the cave echo / With sayings where clear truths and mysteries / Were inextricably twined." This translation incorporates the kind of self-referential elements that recur in Heaney's later volumes—in particular the word *equivocal*. Michael Molino examines the use of the term *equivocal* (*aequi* ["same" or "identical"] *vocal* ["voice" or "sound"]), which has a complicated etymology that refers to voice or sound interpreted in various ways. Molino sees this term as manifesting the performative opportunities of identical sound in which understanding and meaning vary with the hearing, interpretation, or predisposition of the listener. Heaney's translation calls attention to greater possibilities for the listener rather than any limited intent of the speaker. For the poet, it is the difference between Sybil and Aeneas, from being the prophet forced to reveal a certain path to being one of many travelers seeking a world of possibilities.

Neil Corcoran's chapter characterizes some features of "late style" in Heaney under the aegis of some theorizing about the idea of "late style," notably by Edward Said. It examines some of Heaney's critical essays and reflections in *Stepping Stones*, with a view to establishing both his interest in the late style of other poets and his sense of what constitutes late style and of what its deficiencies and rewards might be. Crucial in this regard are his views of Wordsworth, Yeats, and Eliot, as well

as the critical and poetic relationship between Eliot and Yeats, which of-
fers a view of lateness in poetry and a style appropriate to it. Heaney's
relevant accounts of Robert Lowell, Patrick Kavanagh, W. H. Auden,
and Dylan Thomas are also considered. The chapter concludes with a
discussion of Helen Vendler's view of the "breaking of style" in Heaney,
suggesting rather a consistent remaking of it, and of Derek Mahon's
poem "Autumn Skies" addressed to Heaney, which appears to support
this view.

Meg Tyler's chapter explores the formal concerns and patterns in
District and Circle and *Human Chain*. In *District and Circle*, almost two-
thirds of the poems are sonnets or approximate sonnets. In a few of these
fourteen-line poems, Heaney upsets our rhyming expectations by plac-
ing some rhyming pairs at the beginning rather than at the end of the
line. A Petrarchan rhyme scheme haunts "A Shiver," with the octave and
sestet mirroring the contraction and release of the muscular system. The
chapter examines how this poem deconstructs the expectations of such
almost physical release. In *Human Chain*, on the other hand, none of the
poems is fourteen lines long. The absence of the sonnet is pronounced,
yet there are poems here that could be seen to converse, subtly, with the
sonnet tradition; the sonnet is the ground against which they can be
seen. The chapter considers the ways in which Heaney's engagement
with and avoidance of the sonnet form has changed over the years.

PART THREE: TRANSLATION AND
TRANSNATIONAL POETICS

Fueling and enriching his own imaginative labors, translation has been
at the core of Heaney's work and has extended his reach and grasp in
time and space, bearing him away from and back to his own spatial and
temporal points of origin. His translations have been generally faithful
to the source texts but also divergent from their sources, taking creative
liberties in order to experience "a new lease of freedom" and forge stron-
ger links with the larger body of his writings. Michael Parker's chapter
focuses on both kinds of "translation" in *Human Chain*, which pays trib-
ute to the multiple literary traditions on which Heaney draws (Latin,

English, Irish, French, and Italian) in the quest to journey back to a past "long since vacated / Yet returnable to." It includes detailed readings of his versions of Eugene Guillevic's "Herbier de Bretagne" and Giovanni Pascoli's "L'aquilone," as well as "Route 110" and "Hermit Songs," inspired respectively by Virgil's *Aeneid*, book 6, and medieval Irish poetry.

Heaney's transnationalism is obviously partly a locational matter—given his "lighthouse-keeping" at Harvard for over thirty years until 2007, his tenure at Berkeley in the 1970s, his time spent at Oxford as professor of poetry, and his global travels as a poet—and partly a matter of his reading of and interest in the classics and eastern European poetry and literature. Both of these sources allow him to establish some perspective and distance from his immediate existence and in ways draw him away from it. Through looking at the influences of classical and eastern European literature, Elmer Kennedy-Andrews examines how Heaney becomes not only a poet of Ireland but also a poet of the world and then, having established the mature Heaney's global reach, shows how in these last five collections the "appetites of gravity" return him to his beloved "first place" of childhood as a way of understanding and coming to terms with the horror and uncertainty of the contemporary world. This arc is traced through an analysis of poems from all five books.

It has been commonly said and felt since the sudden death of Seamus Heaney that people have felt unmoored or unsupported in various ways: that a kind of underwriting that he represented is suddenly gone. One of the most striking things about his writing career has been a steadiness of affiliation: a clear-eyed fearlessness in choosing a line, debating it, and sticking to it. In the later poetry, he was ready to mix a more challenging temper ("Weighing In" and so on) with the more equable positions associated with him (ideals like balance and redress). But his combativeness—an unlikely term for him—is always positive. Bernard O'Donoghue looks at the way Heaney has taken up cudgels for different poets and perspectives, such as poetry in Irish (Eoghan Rua Ó Suilleabháin, for example) and medieval writing in English (*Beowulf* and Henryson), and how he finds a place for these within a wider cultural world, linking them to eastern European writing, the *Aeneid*, and things further afield. The effect of his interventions has been to cosmopolitanize areas that have traditionally been seen as marginal, and this is just one reason why his death represents the removal of a significant nurturing influence for a particular area within poetry in English.

PART FOUR: LUMINOUS THINGS AND GIFTS

The idea of poetry as a gift is as ancient as poetry itself. For the Greeks and the cultures they influenced, poets supplicated the Muses for the gift of inspiration and paid tribute to their inspiriting benefactors in their poems. Henry Hart looks at how aspects of "gift theory," which Heaney articulated in his early poetry and prose, are developed in his later poetry. Heaney compares the redemptive gift-exchange ceremony at the heart of Christianity with Greek mystery cults (Heaney calls the church at Lourdes "the Eleusis of its age") and ultimately with poetry. In many of his later poems, most notably "The Settle Bed," "The Rain Stick," "Whitby-sur-Moyola," "An Architect," "The Sharping Stone," "Helmet," "The Conway Stewart," and "The Gift of a Fountain Pen," Heaney writes about poetry as a gift, worries that he has betrayed his poetic gift by devoting too much time to what he calls "community service," laments the various ways his gift has been commodified, and struggles to achieve a judicious balance between his poetic gift and his political responsibilities.

In his chapter, Richard Rankin Russell uses a combination of what Bill Brown and others call "thing theory," along with theories of memory, drawn from the work of Edward Casey, Paul Ricoeur, and Sarah Ahmed, to think about how Heaney's objects become "sticky," or full of affective value. Interested from the beginning of his career in the emotional stickiness of things, Heaney began working out a theory of objects and their emotive power in his essay "Place, Pastness, Poems: A Triptych." There, Heaney suggests that Thomas Hardy's poem "The Garden Seat" implies how a "ghost-life . . . hovers over some of the furniture of our lives . . . the way objects can become temples of the spirit" (*PPP*, 30). Ricoeur's articulation of memory's ability to thrust us forward into the future as it simultaneously leads us into the past helps us understand the peculiar sense of presentness that Heaney's lovingly caressed, long-contemplated objects acquire in his later volumes.

Shortly before the publication of *Field Work* (1979), Seamus Heaney wrote to Brian Friel that he "no longer wanted a door into the dark" but "a door into the light." That turning toward the light heralded a new preoccupation with clarity, vision, and self-definition in poetry, but it also had a far-reaching political significance, ushering in a decisive reconsideration of the role of the poet in a time of violence. It anticipated the brightening and lightening of *Seeing Things* (1991), with its willingness to credit marvels and its spirited determination to move from the murderous to the miraculous. His 1982 essay "The Main of Light" also sanctioned a poetry of epiphany and lucent affirmation. The publication of *Electric Light* (2001) confirmed the direction Heaney's work had been taking toward light-filled vistas of the imagination. As well as considering the "main of light" in *Seeing Things* and *Electric Light*, this chapter will explore the symbolic and mythic patterns of light in *District and Circle* (2006) and *Human Chain* (2010).

PART FIVE: USUAL AND UNUSUAL SPACES

The use of feminine imagery and gendered poetic dynamics has long been commented on by critics and readers of Heaney's work. The chapter by Moynagh Sullivan explores how one of Heaney's later collections, *Seeing Things*, a volume more noted for being about his father, reveals in fact the shape of the mother, and argues that this shapeliness is key to the stretch and touch of Heaney's work. Heaney's work explores aspects of femininity and feminine creativity in very powerful ways, and indeed his great popularity may in large part be due to the ways in which his work can be said to be implicated in the creative and psychic realm of what philosopher, psychoanalyst, and artist Bracha L. Ettinger calls the matrixial realm. Ettinger's work proposes a parallel psychic dimension, the matrixial borderspace, which is closely tied but not reducible to late prenatal experience, and which provides the means for artistic connection along the borderspaces of ourselves—and connection and touch is what Heaney's work has been most famous for, at least outside the academy.

Central to his achievement, and central to his technique, is Heaney's belief that "the redress of poetry" happens when a poet interposes "his or her perception and expression" with such concentration that "the conditions" become transfigured in the poem. Daniel Tobin's chapter explores how Heaney's tack of imaginative transfiguration negotiates the shift in emphasis from poems whose passages seek the transcendent in "searches, probes, allurements," as he writes in "Station Island," to poems that scan the immanent in memory and the objects of memory, in elegy—in "air from another life and time and place," as he writes in "A Kite for Aibhín." In doing so, the essay draws on studies examining the figural imagination by Erich Auerbach, Owen Barfield, Nathan Scott Jr., and Richard Kearney. In the end as at the beginning, Heaney's transfigurative poetics takes "a stand against nothingness," and he continues to embrace a vision of poetry as nothing less than "a ratification of the impulse toward transcendence."

Rand Brandes focuses on the notion of revelation and reverie in Heaney's later poetry. For him, the starting point is Gaston Bachelard's *Poetics of Reverie* where he argues: "The being of reverie crosses all ages of man from childhood to old age without growing old. And that is why one feels a sort of redoubling of reverie late in life when he tries to bring the reveries of childhood back to life" (1969, 102); this happens "literally" in the rebirth/resurrection of Michael in "The Blackbird of Glanmore" and more figuratively in "A Kite for Aibhín." The essay uses these two poems as touchstones and launchpads for a more general discussion of the role of the child in the final two volumes (ruminating on old age) and a few uncollected poems. The child here is something closer to the "child function," as Brandes echoes Foucault's construction of the "author function." The analysis utilizes some unpublished and uncollected materials related to these two poems. For instance, in the blackbird poem, "Hedge-hop, I am absolute / For you" follows an imaginative thread from Shakespeare, to T. S. Eliot, to Ted Hughes. While the first two influences have been noted (or at least Shakespeare), bringing Hughes into the equation adds a new level of complexity and poignancy to the poem and volume.

The book concludes with my own chapter, which looks at language as polysemic: "Words themselves are doors; Janus is to a certain extent their deity, looking back to a ramification of roots and associations and forward to a clarification of sense and meaning." Writing in *Preoccupations*, Heaney gestures toward a fundamental trope in his aesthetic thinking. His work will probe the interstices of past and future; material and spiritual; immanent and transcendent. This trope, which can be found in his earlier work in embryo, is fully realized in his later poetry. Tracing this in the later books, and comparing his work to that of Jacques Derrida and Martin Heidegger, this chapter demonstrates how, in Heaney's later writing, the door always stands open, and this openness is to other cultures, other visions, other choices, and to a sense of the common humanity that connects victims of violence in ancient Greece and contemporary Northern Ireland. The connection with other languages and literatures is another example of how Heaney's later poetry inhabits the space created by the opening of the doors of the heart and the soul.

PART ONE

HEANEY AND DEATH

> lifetime, then the deathtime: reticence
> Keeping us together when together,
> All declaration deemed outspokenness.
> —Seamus Heaney, "The Lift"

CHAPTER ONE

Surviving Death in Heaney's *Human Chain*

Andrew J. Auge

On Easter Saturday, April 11, 2009, as part of RTÉ's celebration of Seamus Heaney's seventieth birthday, the radio presenter Marian Finucane interviewed Heaney. Over the course of the program, she questioned him about what thoughts of death had arisen in the aftermath of his stroke in 2006. After initially demurring, Heaney preceded to indicate that he no longer accepted the traditional Catholic beliefs in the particular judgment and an eternal heavenly reward and that he believed that death meant "extinction" (Waters 2010, 116). Those offhand comments sparked outrage from the Irish cultural commentator John Waters. After acknowledging the potential nuances of this position, Waters ultimately insisted that Heaney's response was intentionally provocative, that he had leveraged "the weight of his poetic 'office' to make a reinforcing point on behalf of the prevailing culture . . . denying something that for many people is of momentous importance: the idea of eternal life" (2010, 118). Waters then mocked Heaney for the superficiality and incoherence of his thinking on this topic and on the general role of religion in contemporary Irish society. Whatever guarded praise of Heaney's poetry Waters offered in this essay was offset by its title, which consigned the Nobel Prize winner's oeuvre to "the poetics of nothing-ness" (2010, 115).

Such fulminations might have been avoided had Waters taken the trouble to read the full expanse of Heaney's poetry or, in lieu of that, his prose reflection on the poet's responsibilities with regard to the subject of death, "Joy and Night: Last Things in the Poetry of W. B. Yeats and Philip Larkin," collected in *The Redress of Poetry* (1995). There he would have found that his accusation that Heaney is a purveyor of "the poetics of nothingness" not only misrepresents Heaney's thoughts on mortality but also anachronistically ignores the realities of modern secularity, where, as Heaney paraphrases the Catholic poet Czesław Miłosz, "No intelligent contemporary is spared the pressure exerted . . . by the void, the absurd, the anti-meaning." Facing death, the modern poetic imagi-nation is, Heaney asserts, always caught in a "stalemate between the death-mask of nihilism and the fixed smile of a pre-booked place in paradise" (*RP*, 153). For Heaney, merely dwelling within the tensions of this dialectic is not sufficient: the poet's task is to negotiate a settle-ment that at least tentatively enacts an "outfacing [of] the inevitable" rather than a hopeless acquiescence to it (*RP*, 147). He delineates these alternatives by pitting the facile negation of Larkin's "Aubade" against the hard-wrung affirmations of Yeats's "A Cold Heaven" and "Man and the Echo." It is the later poem, written when Yeats was on the cusp of death, which for Heaney manifests the transformative power of poetry, its ability to hew a shard of meaning from a stony silence. However, despite the sense of creaturely sympathy evoked at the end of Yeats's poem by the cry of a stricken rabbit, the confrontation with death staged in "Man and the Echo" is, as the title suggests, solitary. In that regard if not others, it typifies Yeats's quest in his late poems to cultivate a hard-edged masculine aloofness that outfaces death's nullity (Ramazani 1990, 145–50). Here, as elsewhere, the contrast between Heaney and his pre-cursor is illuminating. In Heaney's last published book of poems, *Human Chain* (2010), it is not heroic self-sufficiency but human connections—the bonds of care and love linking the living and the dead—that allow death to be faced, withstood, and survived.

To understand this difference better, we might consider Yeats's reso-lute grappling with mortality in light of the most significant modern philosophical analysis of the role of death in human existence. In book 2 of *Being and Time*, Martin Heidegger establishes death as foundational for human existence—as *Dasein*'s most integral and intimate possibility. When mortality is no longer regarded as a distant terminus but is accepted to be ever-present as the fatal condition that occasions all of the self's projects, it becomes a bounding line that gathers human being into an individualized totality. In Heidegger-speak, this being-toward-death means embracing mortality as the "ownmost nonrelational possibility not to be bypassed" (Heidegger 1996, 232). That is to say, the human being who authentically confronts death recognizes that it "does not just 'belong' in an undifferentiated way to one's own Da-sein [being], but it *lays claim* on it as something *individual*" (1996, 243). Jahan Ramazani discerns in what he calls Yeats's "self-elegies" something akin to this Heideggerian posture: an unflinching approach to death that triggers a process of self-recapitulation and thereby consolidates the self into a distinctive "aesthetic whole" (1990, 163–64). It is precisely this narrow emphasis on being-toward-death as an individuating project that has disturbed some of Heidegger's more recent philosophical interlocutors, most notably Simon Critchley and Jacques Derrida. Their correctives to Heidegger deserve further attention, since, as I hope to show, they point toward something distinctive in Seamus Heaney's approach to death in *Human Chain*.

In characterizing death as "nonrelational," Heidegger asserts that we never truly participate in the death of others but are merely off-stage spectators of their ordeal. Certainly, the deaths that we witness, especially of those closest to us, remain fundamentally enigmatic, closed off to any efforts to comprehend them. However, Heidegger pushes this too far when he claims that "we do not experience the dying of others in a genuine sense. . . [but] are at best always just 'there' too" (1996, 222), or so Simon Critchley suggests when he insists, *pace* Heidegger, "that death is first and foremost experienced in a relation to the death or dying of the other and others, in being-with the dying in a caring way, and in grieving after they are dead" (2008, 144). Derrida in *Aporias* makes the same point more succinctly when he insists that being-toward-death ultimately means acknowledging "the death of the other in 'me'" (1993, 76). For Derrida, this experience of bearing traces of dead others and bequeathing traces of our passing selves to others constitutes the act of survival. Like the related Derridean motif of the specter, survival undermines the familiar binary oppositions of self and other, presence and absence, life and death, being and not-being. Perhaps for that reason, Derrida in one of his last public statements identified survival as "an originary concept that constitutes the very structure of what we call existence" (2007a, 50). In that final interview he insisted that life is nothing more, nothing less than survival, literally the act of "living on"— that is, living upon the remnants of other lives as well as living through the remnants of ourselves incorporated by others (2007a, 26). Survival is then manifested, not just through mortality, but in mundane acts of departure or passing on. For instance, the act of writing whereby one's own words are ceded to others signifies for Derrida "at once my death, either to come or already come upon me, and the hope that this trace survives me" (2007a, 32). Yet mortality remains for Derrida the boundary by which survival is ultimately defined. The traces of the dead survive only if those who remain are willing "to carry both the other and *his* world, the other and *the* world that have disappeared" (2005, 148). This unappeasable responsibility exceeds the traditional Freudian notion of mourning, whereby the death of the loved one is eventually resolved through the "idealizing introjection" of the lost other into the self. The melancholy that prohibits this and that Freud identifies as pathological is regarded by Derrida as "*necessary*," for it acknowledges that these lingering traces of the dead can never be fully assimilated or subsumed but will continue to haunt the survivors who carry them (2005, 160–62).

The extent to which these contrasting philosophical approaches to death parallel the differences between Seamus Heaney's and W. B. Yeats's culminating responses to morality is strikingly evident in Heaney's revision of one of Yeats's privileged figures for death: the image of the empty coat upon a hanger. That image anchors Yeats's late poem "The Apparitions," where each stanza concludes with the refrain: "*Fifteen apparitions have I seen; / The worst a coat upon a coat-hanger*" (1965, 352; italics in original). This skeletal simulacrum encountered in solitude elicits from the aging poet an intensification of mood, a meditative self-concentration: "When a man grows old his joy / Grows more deep day after day, / His empty heart is full at length." An earlier variant of this figure in "Sailing to Byzantium"—"An aged man is but a paltry thing, / A tattered coat upon a stick, unless / Soul claps its hands and sings" (Yeats 1965, 193)—epitomizes the solitary soul's power to override mortality through artistic creation. Heaney humanizes this image by restoring it to its actual mundane context. In "The Butts," the empty coat is his father's suit jacket hanging in the wardrobe. Whereas in the past it was raided for the loose tobacco left in its pockets, in more recent times it yielded "nothing but chaff cocoons" (*HC*, 13). Those husks of detritus serve as a metonym for the frailty of the father's body, in his last days carefully tended by his children, who must reach beneath

> Each meagre armpit
> To lift and sponge him,
>
> One on either side,
> Feeling his lightness,
> Having to dab and work
>
> Closer than anybody liked
> But having, for all that,
> To keep working.
> (*HC*, 13)

This move from a generic empty coat on a hanger to the unclothed body of one's father marks the distance between Yeats and Heaney on this crucial issue. It is the difference between a poet who confronts death in the solitary recesses of his own consciousness and one who addresses it through an intimate encounter with the dying other. While the unnerving task of washing a moribund parent lacks the grandeur of Yeats's staged confrontations with his own imagined cadaver, Heaney invests this act with a matter-of-fact dignity. He casts the process of "being-with the dying in a caring way" and "grieving after they are dead," to quote Critchley again, as strenuous labor. It is precisely this hard work that makes death, and its survival, tangible.

The title poem of *Human Chain* sharpens this insight by rendering death as a physical jettisoning of the body that paradoxically binds us to others, by forging from the discarded mortal coil a link that connects even the most distant members of the human race. This point is made deftly through a sequence of three loosely concatenated scenes: the all-too-familiar televised image of sacks of flour being passed by aid workers to a starving Third World crowd; the poet's recollection of lugging bags of grain during the harvests of his rural youth; the shuffling off of the body in death. Heaney reverts here and frequently throughout this volume to the twelve-line structure that he first employed in the *Squarings* sequence of *Seeing Things*, capitalizing once more upon this form's fluidity and its drift toward a culminating flash of insight. Beyond a shared sense of a sudden unburdening, the scenes each spotlight the human body's vulnerability. And the hyphenated phrases—"hand-to-hand," and "eye-to-eye" (*HC*, 18)—describing the close coordination involved in conveying the bags of grain stress how those corporeal limits necessarily connect us to one another. While the passage of the bags of grain yields something substantive, that is not the case with the passing on of the human body itself. The poem's conclusion evokes that difference through the abrupt sundering of syntax.

> Nothing surpassed
>
> That quick unburdening, backbreak's truest payback,
> A letting go which will not come again.
> Or it will, once. And for all.
>
> (*HC*, 18)

The stanzaic enjambment implies that only an abyssal emptiness awaits human beings as they pass beyond life into death. But the subsequent chiasmic rime riche, the kind of aural flourish so characteristic of Heaney, casts the "unburdening" of the body in death in more ambivalent terms: as both welcome release from and meager recompense for the pain endured in life. It is the final caesura, though, that justifies this poem's position as the volume's signature work, for it augments death's finality by gesturing toward the binding power of its universality.

Several other poems from *Human Chain* echo the figuration of death established in the title poem, employing the well-worn trope of death as release into an unfathomable domain. Heaney has always wielded such elegiac motifs with an ambidextrous flexibility that balances "the claims of both consolation and skepticism, transcendence and realism" (Ramazani 1994, 358). However, here, even more than he had previously done, Heaney imbues them with a provocative open-endedness. Consider, for instance, the volume's last poem, "A Kite for Aibhín," an adaptation of "L'aquilone," by the fin de siècle Italian poet Giovanni Pascoli. Heaney's version concludes by paralleling the departure of the human spirit in death with the ascent of a kite that eventually breaks free from its string:

> the kite a thin-stemmed flower
> Climbing and carrying, carrying farther, higher
> .   .   .   .
> Until string breaks and—separate, elate—
>
> The kite takes off, itself alone, a windfall.
>
> (*HC*, 85)

What is most striking about Heaney's adaptation is how it radically re-arranges the original to fashion this conclusion. In the more precise translation of Pascoli's poem that Heaney produced for an Italian colleague, a variant of the above passage appears near the middle of the poem, where the "you" addressed is subsequently identified with a schoolmate of the Italian poet who died young, with his childlike notions of death intact: "You over whom I shed *my* tears and prayed, / You were lucky to have seen the fallen / Only in the windfall of a kite" (Morisco 2013, 42). The conclusion of Heaney's adaptation garners even more significance when it is juxtaposed with his midcareer poem "A Kite for Michael and Christopher" (*SI*, 44), where the anticipated collapse of the kite in the woods signals death's eventual felling of the body. In "A Kite for Aibhín," Heaney employs the equivocal word *windfall* to present death not as exclusively destructive, as he had done in the earlier poem, but also as a bit of good fortune, a blessing. That attitude is no longer tarnished by naïveté, as in Pascoli's original, but is invested through its culminating position with the mature poet's authority.

In two of the formal elegies that appear in *Human Chain*, Heaney elaborates on the postmortem realm into which the dead are delivered, deepening its penumbra of mystery. "The Door Was Open and the House Was Dark" is dedicated to David Hammond, the Belfast musician and media impresario who was one of Heaney's oldest friends. As the poem's speaker ventures into the now abandoned house of his dead friend, its silence nearly overwhelms him until he accommodates himself to this space where "there was no danger, / Only withdrawal, a not unwelcoming / Emptiness" (*HC*, 82). The negative formulation qualifies but does not cancel out the benign aura bestowed upon the vacancy that follows death. This ambivalence intensifies with the metaphor that renders this space into "a midnight hangar // On an overgrown airfield in late summer" (*HC*, 82). The scene encapsulates the desolation of death. But its identification with a site that could be either a terminal destination or a point of embarkation and with a transitional time on the cusp of harvest season tempers the gloom with a tincture of hopeful anticipation. "Death of a Painter," dedicated to the Welsh-born artist and County Wicklow resident Nancy Wynne-Jones, enacts a series of metaphorical transitions through which the dead woman is integrated into the space that she previously observed from a distanced perspective. The poem plays off the revisionary impulse that, as Helen Vendler has noted, is so central to Heaney's poetic consciousness (1998, 10). Its shifting figurations are negated almost as soon as they are asserted— that is, until the final unchallenged image, borrowed from "Patience," a late fourteenth-century poem ascribed to the Pearl Poet: "And now not a butterfly but Jonah entering / The whale's mouth, as the Old English says, / Like a mote through a minster door" (*HC*, 60). In this terminal metaphor, where the minster door is the entryway to a cathedral, the void becomes a vast sacral space into which the deceased, albeit reduced to the merest particles of being, are subsumed.

"Slack," another poem that invokes the idea of death as release, redirects the passage of the dead from an ulterior otherworld back to the domain of the living. In that regard, its trajectory more closely reflects the volume's dominant tendency to dwell less on the unfathomability of postmortem existence than on the traces that the dead leave in this world. Slack, as the poem notes, refers to the coal grounds added to the hearth fire to extend its burning. This use of slack to "bank the fire" elicits an allegorical maneuver from the poet, who casts it as "a check on Mammon" and "keeper of the flame" (33). But here more than anywhere else in the volume, Heaney privileges the auditory powers of the poetic imagination over its penchant for symbolism, relishing the object for the sounds it generates: "*Slack schlock / Scuttle scuffle / Shak-shak*" (*HC*, 33). At the end of the poem's second section, though, he synthesizes sound and symbol as exquisitely as in the bog poems of *North* or the poems on archaic things from *District and Circle*. When the burnt-out coal grounds are transmogrified into a "cindery skull / Formed when its tarry / Coral cooled," the assonantal and alliterative couplings in that last clause offset the fear aroused by this memento mori (*HC*, 34). The poem's final section compounds this with clustering rhymes—"its violet blet / its wet sand weight"—that vivify the slack's evocation of a decomposing human corpse (*HC*, 34). The aural pleasure generated by these passages, however, does not seem sufficient to justify the speaker's declaration of "*Catharsis*" (*HC*, 34) as he remembers pouring out the coal grounds. The sudden appearance of this freighted term from the classical lexicon appears unwarranted or overblown. Certainly, the dumping and burning of coal detritus does not accord with a process of purification—the etymological root of *catharsis*. Nevertheless, the identification of its symbolic analogue, the disposal and cremation of the corpse, with this term is perhaps more apposite given Aristotle's association of the deaths staged in Greek tragedy with a cathartic release from pity and fear. Another context—implicit in this poem but overtly foregrounded in others— offers further validation for this proclamation. For as Robert Pogue Harrison notes, in the ancient world, and particularly in classical Roman society, the hearth and its fire were identified with the ancestral dead, the household deities known as *lares*. Through this "sacred fire . . . the dead maintained a presence among the living" (2003, 38). Such an intimation of postmortem survival in the intimate recesses of those who live on alleviates the terror aroused by death.

   This Roman lens predominates in the three poems from *Human Chain*, including two longer sequences, which employ book 6 of Virgil's *Aeneid* as a source text. Extending back to his schooldays at St. Columb's College, Heaney's fascination with this central section of the *Aeneid* was so profound that as he was writing *Human Chain* he confessed his desire to translate that entire book on its own, to complete what he began in "The Golden Bough," the translation of book 6, lines 98 through 148, that inaugurates *Seeing Things* (*SS*, 296, 440). In lieu of that fuller and more formal translation, Heaney proffers in these poems multiple citations and allusions. These effectively transpose Aeneas's journey into the underworld with Heaney's experiences in rural County Derry growing up with and then ultimately away from his parents as he leaves home and they age. The central presence of the *Aeneid* in this volume corroborates the line of argument pursued in this essay. For Virgil's masterpiece is, among other things, an epic of survivorship. Beginning with the flight of war refugees from Troy, led by Aeneas bearing his father Anchises upon his back; reaching its apex in the underworld encounter where Aeneas futilely seeks to embrace the specter of Anchises and is consoled with a vision of the noble dead who will be reborn as his successors; ending with a reference to the "Shades below" (book 12, line 1270; Mandelbaum 1971, 336)—the *Aeneid* is, as Lawrence Lipking asserts, "a haunted work" (1981, 81). It is not just the spectral presence in the *Aeneid* of the Homeric epics that justifies Lipking's claim but also the fact that Virgil's hero is haunted by his responsibilities as a survivor, his obligation to continue bearing his father and the world he embodied even after they have disappeared.

In the first of these Virgilian poems, "Album," Heaney evokes and clarifies this dilemma of survival that we all share with Aeneas. Employing his now familiar twelve-line form, this sequence begins with three retrospective images of the poet's parents that appear to be as randomly arranged as the photographs in an old family album. However, their portending of death and its aftermath connects them at a deeper thematic level. Thus in the first section Heaney envisions his parents standing on a hill near their home in Mossbawn, looking down at church spires in the nearby village of Magherafelt. The scene is imbued with an aura of absence and loss as its site—"Grove Hill before the oaks were cut" (*HC*, 4)—is identified with the empty space left by the felled chestnut tree that culminates "Clearances," Heaney's elegy for his mother. For the parents at least, the prospect of a heavenly afterlife, signaled by the upward-pointing church spires toward which their "steady gazing"

(*HC*, 4) is trained, provides consolation in the face of death. Heaney offers an alternative perspective in the next section, which focuses upon his separation from his parents as a young adolescent when he entered boarding school at St. Columb's, an event cast throughout this volume as proleptic of the final separation of death. If the motto of St. Columb's College—"*Seek ye first the kingdom*" (*HC*, 5)—confirms the parents' outlook in the previous section, a poem attributed to the college's namesake and cited in this section shifts the focus of those departing from what lies ahead to what has been left behind. Thus, in "Colum Cille's Greeting to Ireland," the saint actually bids farewell to his native land as he readies himself to journey from Howth to Iona. When he turns "a grey eye . . . [to] look back upon Erin" (*HC*, 5), the line echoed in this section and more fully rendered in "Colum Cille Cecinit" (*HC*, 72–73) from later in the volume, Colum Cille registers in poignant detail the features of the Derry homeland that he is leaving forever (Meyer 1913, 85). Similarly, from the poet's viewpoint, it is the parents' departure from their son, their shared sense of loss, rather their prior hopes of gaining a heavenly kingdom, that inextricably binds them together.

The poem's third section envisions the parents' wedding dinner from the spectral perspective of the unborn poet but then points to their relationship's ultimate dissolution via references to future unobserved anniversaries and a final evening journey. The littoral setting for the dinner, the insistence upon the poet's "ineluctable" (*HC*, 6) yet invisible presence, the intermingling of birth and death—all of these features call to mind "Proteus," the third section of Joyce's *Ulysses*. Nevertheless, the poem's paralleling of the prenatal and the postmortem more strongly echoes Virgil's evocation of the rebirth of the souls of the noble dead in *Aeneid* book 6, a scene that Heaney directly presents at the conclusion of his other two Virgilian poems. Only in "Album," however, does he recapitulate the poignant preceding episode where Aeneas fails three times in his attempt to clasp his father's ghost. Thus the penultimate section of "Album" focuses upon three putative embraces between the poet and his father. The first is only optative, a desired but unfulfilled opportunity to hold his father before his departure to St. Columb's; the other two involve acts of carrying his father when he was debilitated, first by drink and then by his imminent death. The juxtaposition of these Virgilian acts—the phantom embrace, the bearing of the dying father—points toward Derrida's central insight concerning the survival of the dead. The living have a responsibility to bear the dead within them, yet they can never encapsulate or encompass the deceased other. To authentically bear the dead requires forsaking the temptation to bury them within oneself and submitting instead to the interminable process of "carrying without appropriating to oneself" (Derrida 2005, 161).

This Derridean connection deepens in the poem's final section. There the aging father's reanimation in the aftermath of his young grandson's sudden embrace triggers an epiphany in the poet:

> Coming as great proofs often come
> Of a sudden, one-off, then the steady dawning
>
> Of whatever *erat demonstrandum*.
> Just as a moment back a son's three tries
> At an embrace in Elysium
>
> Swam up into my very arms, and in and out
> Of the Latin stem itself, the phantom
> *Verus* that has slipped from "very."
>
> (*HC*, 8)

Just as the ghost of Anchises can never be grasped by Aeneas, so too does the specter of Heaney's father, dead for over twenty-five years, remain inapprehensible to his son. However, while his deceased father lacks the presence of a subsistent object, he is not absent. Heaney's culminating etymological metaphor, in a manner akin to Derrida, associates the survival of the dead with the phenomenon of the linguistic trace (Derrida 2007a, 26, 32). Tellingly, this trace is the Latin word for "true" undergirding the commonplace English adjective *very* that superfluously emphasizes a present actuality. In a similar manner, the poem implies, the dead hover in the consciousness of the living, infusing gravity and depth into the lightness and superficiality of everyday existence.

This interconnection of the dead and living expands in "Route 110," Heaney's most extensive adaptation of *Aeneid* book 6. There the overarching presence of this masterwork of a "dead" language heightens, like a noonday shadow, the mundane events of Heaney's life. The poem's Virgilian refractions range from obvious to subtle. Thus in sections ii and iii, a younger Heaney rushing through Smithfield Market in Belfast, clutching the used copy of Virgil's *Aeneid* book 6 that he has just purchased and boarding a crowded bus, is cast as one of the ghostly horde struggling to board Charon's ferry across the Styx. In section v, a neighbor's homing pigeons serve as a counterpart to the doves of Venus that led Aeneas to the Golden Bough, while foil-encased oak stalks substitute for the mythic talisman itself. Similarly, in sections vi and vii, the familiar Irish routine of waking the dead—in this case, a young man lost at sea—recovers its sacral status when it is linked to the ritual burial of Misenus, another victim of Triton's fury, that Aeneas must perform before entering the underworld. The adolescent poet's spurning of a girlfriend becomes in section viii a less traumatic analogue of Aeneas's betrayal of Dido, who rejects her former lover when he encounters her in the first precinct of the underworld, the Fields of Mourning inhabited by those "whom bitter love consumed with brutal waste" (book 6, line 584; Mandelbaum 1971, 147). The dark undercurrents of Virgil's masterpiece fully surface in section ix, where Heaney revisits the bleak period of the Troubles. His lingering outrage over the innocent victims destroyed by this sectarian violence is accentuated by another Virgilian parallel. While the dead paramilitaries of both sides are "laid // In war graves with full honours" (*HC*, 56), like the military heroes of the Trojan War who occupy a prominent position in the underworld, those whose bodies were so decimated by bombs that they were merely "accounted for and bagged / behind grief cordons" (*HC*, 56) cannot rest in peace but remain restive, like the unburied dead of Virgil's Limbo, until their loss is duly acknowledged. A lighter note returns in section x, where a sports day in Bellaghy is comically elevated into the athletic contests of Elysium, with the piped-in voice of the American crooner Slim Whitman replacing Orpheus's transcendent singing. All of these Virgilian adaptations reward the kind of detailed attention that critics such as Michael Parker have bestowed upon them (2013, 374–86). But it is the last two sections of this poem—whose twelve-part structure reiterates that of the *Aeneid* as well as its own twelve-line stanzaic form—where the themes we have been explicating come to a head.

The border between life and death blurs without entirely disappearing in section xi, where the Moyola blends, as it does in the previous poem, "The Riverbank Field," into the Lethe. Fishing in the gloaming, the speaker loses his ordinary perceptual hold on the world. Things flow in and out of the shadows, like the otter that may only be "a turnover warp in the black // Quick water" (*HC*, 58). This stanzaic enjambment evokes and then subverts the hard-and-fast division of the quick from the dead, as does the speaker's liminal position on the shifting ground of the riverbank. The culminating Virgilian allusion reminds us that we, the living, already dwell among specters:

> as if we had commingled
>
> Among shades and shadows stirring on the brink
> And stood there waiting, watching,
> Needy and ever needier for translation.
>
> (*HC*, 58)

At one level, the passage reflects the desire of those poised on the precipice of life to be finally delivered or carried over—the Latin root of *translate*—to the domain of the dead. However, the more commonplace meaning of *translation* as the conversion of one tongue into another suggests another reading: if the living wish to avoid being suspended in a vacuous present, they must communicate with the specters of the dead. The central sequence of *Station Island* and many other Heaney poems testify to his success in conducting what Henry Hart refers to as "ghostly colloquies" (1992, 159). But the final section of "Route 110" implies that authentic communing with the dead, as opposed to those prior exercises in poetic ventriloquism, requires a more primal way of speaking, one that is less semantic than somatic, that relies not on concepts but on affective resonances.

Just as book 6 of the *Aeneid* culminates with the dead souls gathered on the far bank of the Lethe awaiting their rebirth, so too does the conclusion of Heaney's poem imbricate death and birth. Recalling a time in the past when flowers were brought into the house to greet the mother and her newborn baby, he fashions his own Virgilian bouquet:

So now, as a thank-offering for one
Whose long wait on the shaded bank has ended,
I arrive with my bunch of stalks and silvered heads

Like tapers that won't dim
As her earthlight breaks and we gather round
Talking baby talk.

(HC, 59)

Given this ending and the poem's apparent dedication, along with the last poem in this volume, to a new granddaughter, "Route 110" seems to follow a well-traversed path in seeking consolation for the death of one's parents or oneself in the birth of a new generation. Such sentiments, although clearly present here, are complicated by the way in which Heaney conflates arrival and departure. It is not just the soon-to-be-born but also the dying who await their transition, and for whom earthlight will "break," not by bursting open, but by shattering into darkness. Similarly, when those who remain gather around the one who has just departed, they find themselves tongue-tied in their grief, struggling for words that would allow them to articulate the inexpressible. In inviting us to consider the discourse of mourning as another form of "baby talk," Heaney reminds us that the specters of the dead are reanimated not by a controlling medium that coerces them into speaking but rather by the mere act of loving acknowledgment.

Virgil's vision of the transmigration of souls captivated Heaney enough to generate two redactions in *Human Chain*. Its status there is more than just poetic device but less than mystic credo. It allows Heaney to posit an ongoing intercourse between the living and the dead without having to commit himself to a definitive position on the possibility or the nature of postmortem existence. Nevertheless, regardless of his attraction to Virgil's account of reincarnation, Heaney rejects the Platonic disdain for corporeality and exaltation of the immaterial that underlies it (Luck 1973, 148; Feeney 2000, 108–10). As Stephen Heiny demonstrates, Heaney's translated excerpt from *Aeneid* book 4 in "The Riverbank Field" omits the sections where this Platonism is most overt (lines 724–47) and accentuates Virgil's reference to the bodily nature that these reincarnated souls resume (Heiny 2013, 309). This is especially evident, Heiny notes, in the poem's conclusion. There Heaney converts Loeb's more literal translation, describing how these souls "conceive desire to return again to the body" (Heiny 2013, 309), into an urgent craving to be restored to corporeality: "memories of this underworld are shed / And soul is longing to dwell in flesh and blood / Under the dome of the sky" (*HC*, 47). For Heaney, the imminent prospect of death eventuates, not in a Platonic detachment from the material world, but in a wistful savoring of its beauty. Thus, in "The Baler" (*HC*, 24–25), the deadening mechanical sound of freshly mown hay being gathered and packaged triggers no intimations of a grim reaper on the horizon. Instead, it conjures up an idyllic scene of hay gathering from the poet's youth. Against this gleaning from the harvest store of memory, the poem juxtaposes the posture of Heaney's friend and portraitist Derek Hill, who on the verge of death turns his back on the splendor of the sunset.

It is not surprising then that in "Loughanure," an elegy for the painter Colin Middleton, Heaney assays more thoroughgoing forms of survival than the tenuous traces described in previous poems. In section ii, these traces take the form of the Middleton painting of the eponymous northwest Donegal landscape that hangs in the poet's house and the painter's "remembered stare" (*HC*, 62) when he visited and gazed at his handiwork. These lingering vestiges of the painter's life pale by comparison to the more substantial conceptions of postmortem existence envisioned by Plato and Dante: "Who watched immortal souls / Choose lives to come according as they were // Fulfilled or repelled by existences they'd known" (*HC*, 62). When Heaney in the next two sections considers his own variants of these classical notions of the afterlife, one pagan, the other Christian, he finds them both unviable. In section iii, the brash rhyming of baptismal "font" and "fontanel" (*HC*, 63) marks the primacy in the young poet's consciousness of the Christian belief in a heavenly kingdom while hinting toward its subversion. That happens via a reversal of this transcendental aspiration. The existential vertigo once induced by this childhood belief in higher plane of reality becomes an artistic strategy, the inverted perspective of the painter who would "spread his legs, bend low, then look between them / For the mystery of the hard and fast / To be unveiled" (*HC*, 63). The prospect of a heavenly kingdom is literally overturned. No longer an end in itself, it becomes merely a means for restoring the wonder of mundane reality. Similarly outdated is the traditional Celtic notion of a faery world that Heaney first encountered during adolescent visits to the Gaeltacht and that he revisits in this poem's penultimate section. Lacking native fluency in Irish, deficient in his second-hand knowledge of its mythology, he finds himself unable to access this indigenous avenue of transcendence.

In the poem's fifth and final section, Heaney places himself in the vicinity of Loughanure, the anglicized version of the Irish *Loch an Iub- hair*, the actual landscape painted by Middleton. Having traded repre- sentation for reality, Heaney considers yet another simulacrum of this temporal world. The all-encompassing vision of "a world restored com- pletely" (*HC*, 65) dwarfs the faded copies of reality evoked by notions of a Celtic otherworld or a Christian heaven. The concept referenced here, gnostic in its origins and cultivated by Russian Orthodox thinkers, is *apokatastasis*, which "promises a return of the entire universe in its ideal state, snatched from the jaws of change and death" (Fuit 1990, 82). This archaic idea was brought back into circulation by Czesław Miłosz, one of Heaney's poetic masters. Elaborating on its use in his poem "Bells in Winter," Miłosz indicates that "apokatastasis tends to mean that no detail is ever lost, no moment vanishes entirely. They are all stored somewhere and it's possible to show that film again, to re-create a reality with all those elements restored. . . . Its meaning is that of a restoration of all moments in a purified form" (Czarnecka and Fuit 1987, 246–47). If Miłosz is ambivalent about claiming this as a belief, Heaney refuses to go even that far. Not only does he declare his disbelief in this concept, but also he disassociates himself from any nostalgic longing for a para- disiacal alternative to this world. And he follows that by gently mocking Miłosz's esteemed idea:

> . . . I drive unhomesick, unbelieving, through
> A grant-aided, renovated scene, trying
>
> To remember the Greek word signifying
> A world restored completely. . . .
>
> (*HC*, 65)

While *apokatastasis* denotes a cosmic refusal to forget even the most minute detail, Heaney in the poem cannot even remember the term itself. While it promises an absolute restoration of the past, the poem proffers only a government scheme to renovate a long-neglected and overlooked landscape. Yet in his dismissal of this idea Heaney validates its underlying assumption: that even the most trivial things manifest a distinctive particularity, a *haecceity* in the philosophical parlance of Duns Scotus, worthy of preservation (Kearney 2006, 133–34).

Hannah Mhór's turkey-chortle of Irish,

The swan at evening over *Loch an Iubhair*
Clarnico Murray's hard iced caramels
A penny an ounce over Sharkey's counter.
(*HC*, 65)

The artful interweaving of sounds here—the near rhyming of "Mhór" and the first syllable of "chortle," of "*Loch an Iubhair*" and "counter," the chiasmic reverberations between "Clarnico" and "iced caramel," the onomatopoeic evocation of the guttural phonemes of Irish—makes these otherwise contingent moments memorable. While they are not subsumed into the film vaults of eternity to be replayed on an endless loop, these ephemeral traces of the poet's experience still haunt, however intermittently, the memories of his readers.

The cover of the Faber and Faber edition of Heaney's *Human Chain* bears an illustration from an illuminated manuscript of Dante's *Paradiso* of Christian philosopher-saints in the heavenly sphere of the sun, linked hand to hand. That image recasts the bonds forged by human frailty evoked in the volume's title poem into a supernal ring generated by spiritual wisdom. In canto 10 of the *Paradiso*, where the aforementioned scene occurs, the pilgrim Dante is uplifted by the radiant singing of these blessed souls. The reader who, primed by this cover image, opens Heaney's book expecting some echo of this beatific Christian afterlife will be disappointed. *Human Chain* provides no transcendent music, no celestial harmonies, to console us in the face of death. However, neither does it leave us stranded in the eternal silence of the void that so terri-fied Pascal. What it offers instead is a terrestrial space resonant with the susurrations of spectral voices. Nowhere is that more evident than in "Canopy," written over a decade earlier but included here for the first time in a volume of Heaney's poetry. Occasioned by the British artist David Ward's May 1994 public art piece *Canopy: A Work for Voice and Light in Harvard Yard*, the poem accurately registers most of the in-stallation's essential features: "Voice-boxes in the branches / Speakers wrapped in sacking," emanating "speech-gutterings, desultory // Hush and backwash and echo" (*HC*, 44). But it omits one important detail. In Ward's installation, the voices murmuring from the burlap-covered tape recorders high in the trees belonged to Harvard students and professors, who speaking in various languages either read passages from Italo Calvino's *Invisible Cities* or shared vignettes about their own sense of place (Temin 1994). In the poem, the voices in the trees are entirely dis-embodied, their provenance obscured. This allows Heaney to naturalize them—"antiphonal responses / In the congregation of leaves," "a wood that talked in its sleep"—and thereby enact the long-standing Romantic project of giving voice to the earth itself (*HC*, 44). But the poem's last three stanzas restore a human dimension to these voices through an allusion to the "wood of the suicides" (*HC*, 45) in canto 13 of Dante's *Inferno*. There, petrified into trees, the suicidal dead remain silent, speaking only when one of their branches is broken. By contrasting the emanations that he hears from the trees in Harvard Yard to Dante's reti-cent dead, Heaney imparts a ghostly quality to these ramifying whispers.

In "Canopy," though, it is love, rather than misery, that inflects these spectral voices. The claim that they exert upon their hearers is exempli-fied through another arboreal image: "As if it were mistletoe / Taking tightening hold" (*HC*, 45). *Viscum album*, the botanical name for the European variant of mistletoe, is best known as a holiday decoration that demands that those in its proximity kiss one another. A parasite that draws food and water from its host trees, *Viscum album* is metaphorically associated with the Golden Bough in the *Aeneid* and thus has long been regarded as its prototype (Mandelbaum 1971, 140; Freeman 1918, 28–29). All of these features make this image an apt hieroglyph for

Heaney's conception of the afterlife of the dead. Heaney's figurative branch of mistletoe inverts Virgil's, for it marks not the entry of the living into the underworld but the encroachment of the dead into the realm of the living. These dead, as Heaney has repeatedly shown in in *Human Chain*, require our love, and only if we respond to that imperative and grant them sustenance will they survive.

CHAPTER TWO

DEATH AND EVERYMAN

Imagining a "Not Unwelcoming Emptiness"

Magdalena Kay

Does the imagination dwell most upon the death of one's body or one's mind? If its belief in the afterlife is strong, then the latter may appear gloriously oxymoronic, a concept that smacks of materialist disbelief. Rather than death, say transformation; rather than dying, say beginning a passage through new territories of feeling and understanding. But what if the imagination is torn between mourning the dying animal of the body—one's own, a parent's, a friend's, an artist's—and hearkening to the promise of renewed life elsewhere?

The tradition of classical lament, in which a grieving singer "communalizes" emotion, is the basis for modern elegies written in the wake of political violence.[1] Violent and untimely, death is often caused by political aggression and reprisal in Seamus Heaney's early poetry, and the murdered dead creep back into waking life. There are also unpolitical passings, but death is often a communal matter. Something new happens in 1987 when Heaney's mother is commemorated in "Clearances": her beautifully envisioned homecoming is balanced, in this world, by unexpected silences and clearings. Death will always be a matter for ethical meditation for Heaney, but it also becomes a matter of seeing out from the tragic moment, of crediting its transformative possibilities as well as acknowledging its tragic heft.

From this moment on, death is more often personal than communal. The "space emptied / Into us to keep" (*HL*, 31) when a dear one dies cannot be understood in political or religious terms. One does not draw lessons from such intimate grief. *The Haw Lantern* (1987) begins Heaney's step into the (unpolitical) realm of emptiness most deliberately accomplished in *Seeing Things* (1991), affecting all his work thereafter. As he reconsiders the Catholic roots of his imagination, his poems range among different stores of tales and images used to understand and possibly mitigate the tragic fact of death. *Seeing Things* is bookended by Dantean scenes, but its exploration of underworlds and otherworlds is often abstract, riddling, and unconventional. If the noumenal and absolute can be accessed only through the phenomenal and circumstantial, and if we accept a certain randomness to inform the process, then what is given can be endlessly reimagined. This process of reimagining culminates in the variousness of *Human Chain* (2010), Heaney's last volume, in which the poignantly autobiographical "Chanson d'Aventure" (*HC*, 14–16) is counterpointed by the minimalism of "A Herbal" (*HC*, 35–43), where the physical immediacy of image takes precedence over the mediatory function of symbol. Our materiality is reckoned with and finally accepted; the "untranscendent music" (*DC*, 51) with which the meditative poet comes down to earth must be heard, held in the mind, and sung proudly in the face of "a not / Unwelcoming emptiness" (*HC*, 82).

How to write about states of absence or, more hearteningly, clearance is the major question behind *Seeing Things*. Heaney's figurations of absences and otherworlds are at their most experimental in this volume. His need to "credit marvels" (*ST*, 50) results in poems such as "The Pitchfork," which skirts the absurd as it imagines its titular object taking flight "Evenly, imperturbably through space, / Its prongs starlit" (*ST*, 23). Risky, to be sure, in its attempt to lead from the burnished grain of the actual to an "imagined perfection" (*ST*, 23); it is followed by "The Settle Bed," in which a "nonsensical vengeance" of furniture comes tumbling from heaven onto our disbelieving heads. Such poems

seek to conquer the weight of mortal physicality and symbolic meta-
phor itself so that our minds learn that "whatever is given / Can always
be re-imagined" (ST, 29). A particular metaphor may command emo-
tion and attention but ultimately belongs to the given world; the world
of imagination and abstraction surrounds and blankets it and can always
find images adequate to its need for grounding. A paradox ensues: the
amazingly free progress of objects into an otherworld is seen raptur-
ously, but the speaker himself is happy to dwell in a world with concrete,
tangible markings. Heaney's home ground, poetically speaking, is con-
crete; this complicates his attraction to the abstract noun and his desire
to account for states of disembodiment, even of transcendence. When
it comes to mourning, it is imperative to honor a real, concrete human
being. Heaney's early elegies most always offer a setting in which to
commemorate a lost life, yet his desire to believe in the Christian after-
life pulls the gaze toward what can only be imagined. Although Heaney's
faith in such a world wavers and diminishes, his desire to contemplate its
possibility stays intense, and the question of belief is never fully settled.

Jahan Ramazani sees Heaney as Yeats's "inheritor" (1994, 335, 337–
38), but Yeats's obsessive systematization of mystical belief bespeaks a
need for certainty that Heaney appears not to have (Ramazani 1990,
158). Death can be accepted but not transcended, and Yeats's heroic ef-
fort is alien to Heaney. Lack of certainty brings fear, though, and this
very human fear that cognitive closure cannot be achieved permeates
Heaney's meditations and evocations of death, often voiced by a child-
persona whose fear is based on a primal understanding of death as fi-
nality. The boat that "dipped and shilly-shallied / Scaresomely" during a
Sunday outing does not transport the Heaney family into the under-
world, but its instability causes the poet to envision another boat, swim-
ming "far up" above the first and enabling a new vision of the mortal
world (ST, 16). The poet's imaginary creation of a second plane of expe-
rience, one enabling deeper vision and more poignant affection (as he
"loved in vain our bare, bowed, numbered heads") (ST, 16) than ordi-
nary experience, is an areligious means of affirming the existence of a
plane of being above the mortal world. This does not exempt him from
mortality but affirms that one type of perspective—sublunary, earth-
bound, timebound—can itself be reimagined.

Hence, his father's early brush with death in the same poem impels the poet to reach tentatively forward into what "might . . . still be happily ever after" (*ST*, 18). This longitudinal perspective reveals a fear that our chance to establish emotional intimacy is given only for the span of an earthly life, even as the desire for a "happily ever after" makes us imagine its infinite extension. The poet wants to believe that nothing is lost in the transition between the past and the "ever after," that the human space emptied by death is given to us to keep, that there is no emotional obstruction imperiling such a connection between the living and the dead. He wishes to fill the unbounded space of the future, but here Heaney struggles against himself: part of him feels liberated by the prospect of "unroofed scope" (*ST*, 55) while the other needs to "batten down," "dig in," and contain earthly life while it is still present in all its sensually concrete particulars (*ST*, 56). These are two distinct responses to finality and modes of approaching the emptiness outside one's body, which existed prior to it and will outlast it. In poem sequences such as *Squarings*, the poet refuses to relinquish the consolation of presence in his exploration of absence.

What can survive death? Perhaps nothing. Heaney's cold heaven is as piercing and wintry as Yeats's, as the remains of human life give way to bare walls, empty hearths, and puddled water "where the soul-free cloud-life roams." This chilly picture merely makes us see the "old truth dawning: there is no next-time-round" (*ST*, 55).[2] Philip Larkin would recognize this scene, even though Heaney resists Larkin's bleak "Aubade," which must be reckoned with as "the definitive post-Christian English poem, one that abolishes the soul's traditional pretension to immortality" (*RP*, 156). Although he suggests that its lyrical craftsmanship works against the poem's nihilism, Heaney finally cannot accept poetry that is not "on the side of life" (*RP*, 158). Larkin's poem "does not hold the lyre up in the face of the gods of the underworld" and thus shirks the "spiritual intellect's great work" (*RP*, 158).

Where does this leave us with the first "Squaring"? Despite its denials, its wintry light and puddled ruins do not deny sensual knowledge—as Larkin's moonscape draws its power from visceral apprehension as well as complex comprehension—but the first-person singular with which we associate Heaney is absent. "Squarings" are not abstract *sensu stricto*—

they almost all represent embodied experience—but their brevity (twelve lines each) and their tendency to use minimal syntactic units ("Roof it again. Batten down. Dig in. / Drink out of tin") (*ST*, 56) are innovations that distance these poems from Heaney's fully embodied first-person mode, and their minimalism will find an echo later, in "A Herbal." This minimalism is well suited to the uncannily disembodied perspective that is present here, and it often relies on the second-person pronoun (which will also reappear in "A Herbal"). In *The Redress of Poetry*, Heaney affirms that "consciousness can be alive to two different and contradictory dimensions of reality and still find a way of negotiating between them" (*RP*, viii). It can reconcile its pragmatic, earthly identity with attunement to a disembodied, spiritual dimension—yet Heaney's imagery often suggests that the latter is less a part of life than of death. This is still "reality"—perhaps too much so—but until *Human Chain* it will be held quite separate from what he elsewhere calls soft-mouthed life. After *Seeing Things*, Heaney's work tries to reconcile the notion of death as disembodiment and clearance with the possibility (probability?) that the prospect of "unroofed scope" will not be brightened by notions of transcendence or roofed, as it were, by the chance to live again. That one can consciously accept the presence of marvels in everyday life does not quite brighten the image of life ever after: it is, rather, becoming "focused and drawn in by what barred the way" (*ST*, 22).[3] Just as a hospital patient can see "deeper into the country" than one would expect, so a focus on the empirical world—solid yet marvelous—allows us to see speculatively into an ideal world, to picture it in terms we can understand. Yet what if "lightening" does not occur in the soteriological sense that Heaney suggests, as the "phenomenal instant when the spirit flares / With pure exhilaration before death," illuminated by the possibility of salvation (*ST*, 66)? Several poems in the "Squarings" and "Lightenings" sections of *Squarings* experiment with this possibility. The poet maintains a pose of conjecture until he allows anguish to have its say: in the moment where he turns Henry Vaughan's initial affirmation—"They are all gone into the world of light"—into a question, his hardest work begins (Witherspoon and Warnke 1982, 985–86).

Neither Vaughan's nor Heaney's poem is strictly elegiac—"they" remain unspecified. The religious doubt that overwhelms the poet, though, is directly connected to personal grief: If death may signify terminal confinement of the body without subsequent resurrection of the soul, then how, Vaughan asks, can we resist total despair? If the mortal "world of thrall" is our final resting place, if our sense of solitude is not brightened by the certainty that those we loved—siblings, spouses—have been enlarged into the space of a better world, however mysterious, then what pleasure can our continued existence bring? His poem describes a downward arc from the brightness of remembrance and certainty to doubt. Heaney attempts stoicism: perhaps "sheer forms" crowd into heaven after death; perhaps they do not. This speaker is "well prepared // For the nothing there—which was only what had been there" (*ST*, 104). His pose of toughness, of long-held doubt rather than tremulous faith, differentiates his poem from his predecessor's—after all, if there is "nothing" in the afterlife then we are simply left with the known world, "what had been there" all along. Heaney knows the feeling of being "ungratified" by a reality harder and darker than what we feel we have been promised. Thus he amends his initial metaphor: rather than the disappointment of an empty fishing line, the sense of disbelief is rather like finding the line snapping, breaking, and drifting away, leaving us shocked and bereft.

If time seems out of joint in the instant the mourner feels himself losing touch with the world from which so many have gone, then time and space can be reimagined so that apparitions of "the nearly blessed" stand their ground in an unchanging landscape (*ST*, 102). Heaney's return to the substantial in *The Spirit Level* responds to a need to "Secure / The bastion of sensation" (*ST*, 56) and reaffirm its rightful value. Things—rain sticks, spirit levels, mint, iron weights—do not need to be etherealized in the same way that pitchforks and settle beds were in *Seeing Things*. Perhaps the prospect of an empty heaven is too much to bear or is inimical to Heaney's poetic of sensual affirmation. Perhaps the experiment with dematerialization has been finished; *The Spirit Level* signals a return to materiality and to story-based lyric. When death enters the poetic landscape, it does so as it has before, in archaic, often Homeric terms ("Damson") (*SL*, 15) or documentary ones with a strong underswell of pathos ("Keeping Going") (*SL*, 10). The power of allegory is reaffirmed as a concrete visualization of what can only be imagined ("St Kevin and the Blackbird") (*SL*, 20), while the imaginary realm is populated by specific presences.

The form of the "Squarings" suits them to the provisional and paradoxical nature of their images, which do not quite settle into traditional symbols. A similar quality will come up in certain poems in *Human Chain*, but after *Seeing Things* Heaney's poems reestablish a more traditional symbolic footing. Hence, "A Call," a poem that reaches into allegory not to provide resonance to the real but to play out an imagined scene, presents a modern morality play. Unlike the "virtual" poems of *Seeing Things*, it does not turn outward to imagine absences and hereafters. A telephone call—often interpreted as one to Heaney's father, though the relationship described could be friendly or filial—begins with the companion being called inside, out from the garden where he is playing the part of benevolent reaper. As the poet listens to the unattended telephone recording the "amplified grave ticking of hall clocks," envisioning "mirror glass and sunstruck pendulums," this eerily liminal moment inspires the poem's allegorical leap: "if it were nowadays, / This is how Death would summon Everyman" (*SL*, 53). His next impulse—accorded an outriding line at the end of what could be a sonnet—is to make an admission of love, venturing out from the accepted domain of masculine emotional stricture.

But "nowadays" we rarely think that we are called by outside forces, and the poem's experiment with allegory reveals both its anachronism and the power of its stark abstraction. Just as the sonnet breaks its third and ninth lines, sets off an unrhymed couplet, and tacks on a surprised outrider, refusing conformity with either Petrarchan or Shakespearean models, so the abrupt entrance of allegory, and the equally abrupt step into almost-inappropriate emotional conduct, refuse to naturalize the poem's imagined ruptures. Its relatively abstract treatment of death hearkens back to *Squarings*, while its realistic details—recorded dialogue, vivid imagined scenes—firmly embody a situation whose embodiment had seemed so tenuous in "All gone . . ." (*HL*, 3). Yet this interlocutor is not Everyman; the poet's familiarity with his actions, house, and garden demonstrates that Heaney is a poet not of allegorical personification but of specific reference. Good and evil cannot be neatly kept apart, as in medieval allegory; throughout his life, however, Heaney is attracted to the traditional notion of a final account, a last look at the shape of one's life.

Is the last look ever truly final, though? "A Call" is emotionally and generically striking, but its vision of death as a sudden rupture is not the vision that rings truest to Heaney's eschatological imagination. Its tableaux reflect in a literary hall of mirrors, as do so many of Heaney's poems on death, but he is more apt to credit metaphors of passage, transformation, or linkage (as Kevin finds himself "linked / Into the network of eternal life" in "St Kevin and the Blackbird") (*SL*, 20) than those of absolute finality. It is part of his deeply ingrained Romanticism: in Heaney's own words, "I am a child of Romanticism as much as anything else and so the idea of the poem as an imaginative journey, as the crossing of some border into an elsewhere, that idea is very deeply laid down. . . . You get 'carried away,' 'transported'" (Morgan 2008). This clarifies the work he expects a poem to do, and moments when imaginative links are lost—like a caught line snapping—are poetically unhelpful, at worst destructive. Heaney glories in the crossing of borders, the simultaneous vision of several strata of reality, and while this is surely due to his early love of the Romantics, it is also due to his childhood Catholicism.

This may be his "anything else," though the offhanded phrase also gestures toward his generation's influence by the knowing, this-worldly Movement of the 1950s, which took its bearings from the Georgians more than from the Romantics. Poets such as Heaney and Ted Hughes worked in their own way and interpreted the twentieth century differently from the Movement poets. Even within the Northern Irish literary scene, Heaney felt his difference from ambitious coevals such as Derek Mahon and Michael Longley (Parker 1993, 53).[4] His comment also urges readers to link his Romanticism—as he construes it above—with his religious feeling, which he has always affirmed to be imaginatively meaningful. Opposed to the sociological manner of discussing Northern Irish Catholicism is a "purely religious, transcendental" way of describing its effect: "Growing up with the idea of God in his eternal present around and about and above you everywhere, . . . of sanctifying grace, a universe shimmering with light," builds up a "luminous private world" (Heaney 2002b, 84). Of course Heaney feels "an imperative to secularize

[him]self and put the test on all this stuff" as a university student and after (Heaney 2001b, 24), but even this conscious effort is noteworthy. His experiments with an areligious perspective have a significant amount at stake. To give up on "a universe shimmering with light" in favor of "soul-free cloud-life" and "the nothing there" is not only an intellectual but a creative loss; the "old truth dawning: there is no next-time-round" displaces the old truth of faith, as remorseless temporality takes the place of an "eternal present" that blankets and buffers the soul.

This issue will need to be worked through, yet *Electric Light* focuses on the individual elegy more than on matters of faith or evocations of death. When the latter appears, it does so with subtle humor: the portentously titled "Bodies and Souls" (*EL*, 73–74) begins lightly, likening passage to the afterlife to following a school caretaker as "he does his rounds," sorting and cleaning. Not only is this personification radically dissimilar to the invisible, medieval Death of "A Call," but the poem is built on a different premise: the afterlife can be metaphorized in a direct, personal manner that keeps one foot on Heaney's home ground while it evokes the insubstantial. This poem does not wish to contemplate "starlit and absolutely soundless" space; nor does it depart from the retrospective mode. Although gentle skepticism imbues its metaphorical presentation, this is not its main subject. "It wasn't asphodel but mown grass" that schoolboys play on after "night prayers" that have failed to transport them away, but the Greek underworld, just like the Christian afterlife, is held in the mind as the poet's temporal and spatial distance proves illusory: "The older I get, the quicker and the closer / I hear those laboring breaths and feel the coolth" (*EL*, 73). As the poem moves into and out from metaphor, it becomes more difficult to classify: As retrospective? As allegory?—Perhaps as meditation, even, inasmuch as Louis Martz (1954, 15) defines it as an act undertaken with the goal of entering a state of devotion, in which the mind turns toward spiritual matters? This perhaps overstates the case, given the deftness of Heaney's loose blank verse, but the speaker's personal stake in his imagery allows us to recognize its place in sequence with poems such as "Clearances," *Squarings*, and "A Call," all of which consider one's own place in their tableaux, whether as one of the bereaved, surrounded by dissonance as they "face the exercise" (*EL*, 73) of grief, or as one of many sportsmen who feels the night's chill coming ever closer.

The line connecting him to an ever-living past never snaps, however. Heaney's late poetry refuses to deny the weight of the imagery it often treats skeptically—Homeric and Christian allegorical situations maintain their power. The traditional elegy, too, maintains its relevance and resonance. *Electric Light* contains a number of elegies for fellow poets (Ted Hughes, Joseph Brodsky, and Zbigniew Herbert) even while death itself is rarely spoken of, and the process of mourning is not considered at nearly the same level of pathos or detail as it is in "All gone. . . ." A certain etiquette seems to govern the "public" elegy—though several public figures were also Heaney's personal friends—according to which the life and gifts of the deceased are the elegy's primary foci. The difference between public honor and private mourning (or anticipation of mourning, as in "A Call") is great. "Public" poems are outward gestures, and they transition from anecdotes about the life of the deceased to the commemorative moment of the present. They insist that the deceased is not an Everyman but a flesh-and-blood figure whose achievements are the elegist's main concern.

When a loss occurs inside the poet's family circle, Heaney's poems take a different form: more searching, more questioning, less certain of their own stance vis-à-vis the event, they put Heaney's foundational sense of "God in his eternal present," omnipresent in a "universe shimmering with light," to the test. The poet fills clearances with images of the marvelous, endlessly reimagined and cognitively mysterious. It may appear perverse that deep losses would occasion such bold explorations, but given their tremendous effect upon the poet, we may understand the need to appraise and explore one's own understanding of the undiscovered country in which so many loved ones reside. This country may even resemble the known world uncannily, and the living may be seen to inhabit both realms at once:

> The automatic lock
> Clunks shut, the blackbird's panic
> Is shortlived, for a second

I've a bird's eye view of myself,
A shadow on raked gravel

In front of my house of life.
(*DC*, 76)

This is not to argue that Heaney has stopped believing that there is a definite crossing between life and death. Yet "The Blackbird of Glanmore" insists upon interconnection more than his *Squarings* did and effaces the boundary between what is given (i.e., phenomenal) and what is imagined (i.e., nonempirical). The bird may have presaged the early death of his brother, Christopher; it is continuously present around the poet's house, and who is to say whether its presence may, once again, be ominous? The speaker's temporarily disembodied view reveals a photographic negative of himself, a shadow where he had been assured of his solid, active presence.

Instead of confessing fear, he makes a surprising admission: "It's you, blackbird, I love" (*DC*, 75). But a blackbird is not a nightingale, and its connection to a childhood trauma that is neither easeful nor painless blackens it further. The subterranean Keatsean feeling of this line casts Heaney back to his schooldays, when the odes were especially inspiring, but such retrospective gestures do little to redress the darkness of a presence that is, nonetheless, not unwelcoming. Is death something to be wished for or to be banished? Is it right to be half in love with a specter that summons the memory of other, beloved shades, never mind a proleptic view of one's own passing? Such a poem exists in a rich referential field, but when it comes to imagining one's own death or summoning that of a loved one, its code of images must come from one's own memory bank as well as from art, and the fit (or misfit) between literary history and personal feeling is not foreseeable.

At times, *District and Circle* may emphasize a "traffic in recognition" in its eponymous sonnet sequence, but the volume also questions patterns and certainties and seeks to credit "the nonce / and happenstance, / the *Who knows* / and *What nexts* / and *So be its*" (*DC*, 45). Its evocations of underground passages ("District and Circle") (*DC*, 17), resurrections ("The Tollund Man in Springtime") (*DC*, 55), and unexpected losses ("On the Spot") (*DC*, 54) are extremely various in approach and tone. The portentous quiet of "The Blackbird of Glanmore" has little in common with the hissing apocalyptic winterscape of "In Iowa" (*DC*, 52). Christianity offers the poet a storehouse of words and images rather than a trusted belief system in several poems, which handle the heft of biblical language and tales in order to strengthen their evocative intensity ("In Iowa"), offer alternatives to "black and white" morality ("To George Seferis in the Underworld") (*DC*, 20), or bring together pagan and Christian ceremonies ("I was like turned turf in the breath of God," utters the Tollund Man, resurrected into a "virtual city" of the modern mind) (*DC*, 55). Pre-Christian tales of the underworld still hold their sway over a poet who recognizes Charon at an entrance to the London Tube, though the "District and Circle" (*DC*, 17–19) sequence is a highly humanized, allegorical vision that takes medieval as well as classical literature as its background for a contemporary subway journey (in the wake of the 2005 London bombings); its allegorical surreality is reminiscent of "A Call." Despite their dramatic chiaroscuro and structural variety, the sonnets of "District and Circle" emphasize the communal nature of the underground passage, unlike "The Blackbird of Glanmore," where the sudden specter of one's own, individual, demise appears. "District and Circle" offers comfort in numbers; "The Lift" movingly places an elegy for a favorite aunt in an entire landscape of grief, summoning "Whole requiems at the sight of plants and gardens" (*DC*, 43). Although we receive no glimpse of a Christian afterlife here, "The Lift," like "District and Circle," keeps within a human-centered universe (unlike, eventually, "A Herbal"). Their communal quality does not diminish the pathos of such poems, but it calls forth a question: at some point in this volume so fixated on the final passage, the issue of individual belief and self-placement must be broached, as it was in "Bodies and Souls" in *Electric Light*.

"Like everybody else" (*DC*, 47), Heaney happily participated in a religion that thrived on the very communal nature of its rituals. "Out of This World" (*DC*, 47) does not disclaim the (seemingly) miraculous or life-affirming nature of Catholicism, but the poem forces serious reconsideration of its exact effect upon the poet's language and worldview. It is unclear who is speaking to whom in its first section—is this Heaney to Czesław Miłosz (for whom this is a memorial), or is the shared nature of this experience being emphasized, in which one celebrant, like so many others, "receive[s] the mystery" of holy Communion while slowly doubting in the truth of religious miracle ("The loss occurred off stage"; *DC*, 47)? Heaney knows that loss of faith is common, and he is not prepared to overdramatize and aggrandize his own experience of it. He also knows that this experience binds him closely to another poet from a conservatively Catholic, rural hinterland, one for whom the matter of faith was a constant subject of meditation, debate, and rethinking. Miłosz, too, has written about the nature of sacral time, including the curious timelessness of *kairos* that Heaney's speaker feels so acutely when he opens his eyes after giving thanks and feels "time starting up again" (*DC*, 47).

Yet the poem does record a loss. Its refusal to "disavow" the language of belief—"words like 'thanksgiving' or 'host'"—makes us realize what a complex matter Heaney's (and, for that matter, Miłosz's) Catholicism is.[5] Far from being simply a dogma subject to acceptance or denial, it is an experiential, imagistic, and linguistic field of force that deepens language itself, which has a sacral dimension to one raised in a religious culture.[6] At times, however, the question of how far one culturally particular word usage involves him in a belief system is pressing. Refusal to disavow Catholicism is not the same as full acceptance of it. The punning title "Out of This World" lightens the poem's meditative mood by hinting that the serious matter of faith may be reimagined and viewed from many perspectives (as the tripartite poem makes clear);[7] it also points to the unknowable space beyond this world, a space that each religion populates with its own images. "The Lift" gestures toward a non-Christian future in its awareness, during a funeral procession, of "open air, and the life behind those words / 'Open' and 'air.'" However, open air cannot sustain a grieving nephew, whose mind veers back to his beloved aunt's death agony, finally finding solace in the natural world's participation in his grief, not in openness and emptiness. The bleakness of a fully desacralized perspective is hard to take at such a moment.

A further question presents itself: Do we need faith to fully appreciate beauty? If one suffers a loss of faith, will the language, imagination, and heart undergo restrictions that may prove ruinous for the creation of an art that relies on language? This is the major question of Heaney's late work. "Out of This World" refuses to work against the gravity exerted by sacral language, yet its second section ("Brancardier") disparages the superficial and bureaucratic aspects of Catholicism that may cause faith to waver. "You're off" (*DC*, 48), it begins, as a remembered journey to help bear stretchers in Lourdes winds its way through quatrains whose embraced rhymes sound less solemn than the blank verse of the poem's first section ("*'Like everybody else . . .'*") (*DC*, 47). The anguish of Vaughan's phrase becomes a casual admission of forgetting ("*Rue de quoi?* All gone"); the "Mystic- // al Body" that serves as "the Eleusis of its age" is broken between stanzas, "not what was meant to be," like the underground "acoustic" intended to reinforce it (*DC*, 49). The communal ritual holding together the faithful is threatened by *chronos*—the poem's initial almost-sonnet breaks its eighth line between "time starting up again" and its admission of loss of faith—and, in "Brancardier," is cluttered and diminished by its association with this-worldly *realia* (canteens of Lourdes water, religious kitsch). Can this type of Catholicism nourish the poet as he contemplates death, and can its mythos match Homer or Virgil's pagan evocations? The inclusiveness of Heaney's personal iconography should not distract us from the tests to which he puts his own religious background.

Excerpted from the catechism, the necessity of renunciation ("*Q. Do you renounce the world? / A. I do renounce it*") (*DC*, 50) is obviously antipathetic to Heaney and to the indirectly elegized Miłosz, and the bare wallsteads and "soul-free cloud-life" of the first "Squaring" are the visual effects of renouncing a faith that populates and irradiates a universe that would otherwise be empty, seen as a ruined hearth. The rough pentametric quatrains of the poem's third section ("Saw Music") refuse to renounce either representations of divinity (painter Barrie Cooke's "godbeams"), the "untranscendent music" of a beggar playing a greased saw, or Miłosz's desire to touch "'what cries out to be expressed'" yet refuses representation (*DC*, 51). They make a grand attempt to hold heaven and earth in one glance, to unite elegy with celebration. This time there are no broken lines, and an addition to the last stanza deftly affirms the capacity for body and art to dwell "out of this world" while firmly within it. There is no need to renounce mundane reality, which is capacious enough to quell one's desire for the ineffable ("'what cries out to be expressed'") with the "untranscendent music" of the everyday.

Even if "Out of This World" illustrates the sufficiency of the mundane when brought into direct juxtaposition with the "tremor and draw" of the sacral, the question of whether we still persist in "harking to the promise" of Christian salvation (*ST*, 66) at the moment of death may remain. Heaney's elegized figures are not transported beyond this world in these late volumes, but the radiance of a Christian heaven is not fully renounced. The problem of finding language and imagery adequate to the material fact of death without viewing our embodiment as a matter of stark brutality is not resolved in *District and Circle*. It is connected to the lingering question of temporality: If the deceased lies "coffined" while the rich music of life continues around him, is this not a mostly tragic view of death as terminus? Without a salvific notion of the afterlife, the materiality of death becomes an overwhelming fact. For one of Heaney's temperament, the existential and even aesthetic comfort of a "cosmos ashimmer with God" (Heaney 2001b, 24) surrounding the deceased cannot easily be rejected: a parallel—not necessarily compensatory—vision must be established.

Likewise, the ethical conundrum of unaccountability, of freedom to pass through life with no final judgment of one's actions, is not merely abstract but personal: *Human Chain*, another elegiac volume, grapples with the mystery and insufficiency of embodiment, both one's own and the embodiment of those one loves, and where this leaves us at moments of finality. The death of Heaney's father comes back to haunt the volume, as the son must struggle with the inability of love to find expression in physical affection (as with a reticent father), though often it must (as with one's wife). When the body suffers, previous expressions of love may require modification: one may endure "love on hold, body and soul apart" (*HC*, 14), or the purely physical must take the place of language, as when a child carries and bathes his elderly father, having to work "closer than anybody liked" (*HC*, 13), knowing what depths of feeling lie behind such uncomfortable actions.

This focus on the body underscores the fact that modern elegists do not tend to believe in "successful" mourning or, for that matter, perfectly sufficient expressions of love. When the notions of appropriate judgment and a benevolent heaven are put into doubt, the question of how to adequately mourn the dead, to liberate oneself from morbid melancholy or excessive grief, becomes unanswerable. Particularly to a poet raised as a believer, it is not easy to entrust the beloved deceased to a questionable future. Ramazani points out that several modern and contemporary poets—Heaney among them—have "reclaimed compensatory mourning by subduing its promise" (1994, 31), refusing the "orthodox consolation" of an imagined rebirth or, perhaps, even the consolation of claiming special grandeur for the deceased (1994, 4). Although Ramazani's division of "melancholic" and "compensatory" mourning has a solid psychoanalytic basis, such terms still reveal their insufficiency, especially when the problem of a Catholic poet's growing agnosticism troubles the notion of compensation.

Heaney's personal iconography may be extraordinarily various and changeable, but the conundrum motivating *Human Chain* is fundamental: "Love's mysteries in souls do grow / But yet the body is his book." The epigrammatic passage from John Donne's "Extasie" accompanies a meditation that becomes wrenching in its application: if, as Donne (1994, 48–50) argues, the body enlarges the soul and serves as a means for revealing love, then the experience of physical breakdown forces one to reckon with the status of the soul. In "Chanson d'Aventure," the still-reliable outside world is described by Heaney in sturdy Anglo-Saxon terms reminiscent of "The Settle Bed," as the poet is "strapped on, wheeled out, forklifted, locked / in position . . . , / Boneshaken" (*HC*, 14). Instead of ascending to an affirmation of imaginative capability, though, the poem swoops and dips, creating unrhymed verbal echoes ("our gaze ecstatic and bisected") (*HC*, 15), combining stoicism with pathos. Both gently comical and confessional, it gains intensity in its address to the poet's wife, connecting Donne with Keats ("Apart: the very word is like a bell") (*HC*, 15) and with Heaney's own previous work. If a medieval *chanson d'aventure* typically involves an unexpected encounter, here it would be an encounter with death itself. This tragic adventure brings death close while human love tries to assert its continuity, the lovers' gaze "ecstatic" yet "bisected" by illness, danger, and fear. This may well be how Everyman is summoned, and the embarrassed failure to assert love at the end of "A Call" is rectified as, years later, husband and wife remain unparted, "Everything and nothing spoken, / . . . no transport / Ever like it" (*HC*, 14).

Even in the midst of direct physical suffering, the imagery of "Clearances" and *Seeing Things* returns, and a pure change happens: instead of metaphorizing the end of life with images of stasis ("sunstruck pendulums" in "A Call"), school after hours ("Bodies and Souls"), or a poet "coffined" amid brightness ("Out of This World"), the eponymous poem of *Human Chain* reintroduces an image of unburdening, "A letting go which will not come again. / Or it will once. And for all" (*HC*, 18). Heaney is still attracted to the image of souls reinhabiting "second bodies," yet *Human Chain* also includes a supernatural Celtic landscape lit by "weird brightness" beyond death ("Wraiths") and questioning of an all-too-empty perspective: "So this is what an afterlife can come to? /. . . / This for an answer to Alighieri?" (*HC*, 62). The volume offers no firm decision as to what happens after "letting go." When the futility of calling a name and expecting silence is accepted, though, a strange peacefulness descends: "here there was no danger, / Only withdrawal, a not unwelcoming / Emptiness" (*HC*, 82). This night-piece derives its title and ambience from Wallace Stevens's "The House Was Quiet and the World Was Calm," where the scene's "quiet was part of the meaning"—here, perhaps, all of the meaning. Its form, however—almost terza rima, almost a sonnet—also summons that of Shelley's "Ode to the West Wind," yet the voice, tempo, and perspective of Heaney's poem could not be more different. While Heaney's obituary for David Hammond (the poem's elegiac subject) emphasizes his ability to embody "a one-man peace process," the poem casts itself beyond politics (Heaney 2008a). The formal echo of Shelley does not reinforce a political commitment, even to peace, but insists that although darkness may be final it does not pose danger, is not unwelcoming.

"The Door Was Open . . ." ends in "late summer" (*HC*, 82) and this paradoxical promise of bounty connects it to the innovative "Herbal." Death's clearances now resemble gaps in late summer overgrowth rather than barren or abstract, affectless spaces in which we must assume a mind of winter:

Everywhere plants
Flourish among graves,

Sinking their roots
In all the dynasties
Of the dead.

(*HC*, 35)

"A Herbal" resists the symbolic mode so central to post-Romantic poetry after Yeats, rejecting the abstract and mediatory function of symbol for the physically immediate image. Its landscape is material and impersonal: plants that sink into "all the dynasties" of the dead do not individuate. Not every poem about death is an elegy or a eulogy. Although "A Herbal" focuses on the senses, its affective work is muted as biological life acts upon itself with no figure to mourn, and as the central mystery of death is materialized. It is a physical fact, a phenomenon, and a fait accompli.

"A Herbal" is a new accomplishment, one marked by a lack of affect and individuation and a focus upon sensation. Sensation can be less individual than feeling, even if post-Romantic poets usually unite the two. Is "graveyard grass" (*HC*, 35) different from any other? Surely, it matters what psychic history this material covers or stands in for; Heaney's elemental world is traditionally associated with precise human histories. Here, the speaker is not fully individuated—his character is far more hidden than in most of Heaney's work. Death is not associated with solitude or exceptionalism. It is not a tragic event impinging upon particular persons but is both abstract (not imagined as a concrete, singular event) and utterly physical.

The poem holds itself aloof from the literary tradition that nourishes Heaney's work, which is a type of minimalism extending the more obvious formal minimalism of its short, heterometric lines, microstanzas, and copious white space. Although a translation of Eugène Guillevic's "Herbier de Bretagne," Heaney's "Herbal" does not undertake a translational "raid" or echo his literary ancestors. Most surprising is its break with the Romantic tradition and the verse patterns (pentameters both sonorous and sly, sonnets of all kinds, tercets variously rhymed) that have formalized most of Heaney's evocations of the final journey. Likewise, the poem privileges image over symbol. Heaney's work after *Seeing Things* frequently reconfigures its relation to the symbol, starting with the provisional, paradoxical images of *Squarings*, so often subject to interrogation. Symbolic dramas rely on some certainty in the poet's control over the relationships the poem vivifies. In *Squarings*, the speaker is not confident he possesses it; in "A Herbal," he does not seek it.

As the poem moves from quickly drawn scene to scene, so death is not proud, and neither is the poet. "A Herbal" does not celebrate the completed arc of one life because it refuses such totalizing ambition. If the Yeatsian symbol relies for its potency upon representativeness, the new Heaneyan image relies for its acuity upon singularity. "To crush a leaf or a herb / Between your palms" (*HC*, 41) is not a metaphorical act. Its emotional effect is unrepeatable and resistant to philosophy. It is marked by neither modernist irony nor Romantic natural supernaturalism. The poem's images are involved in a spiderweb of contingencies: grass, bells, leaves, and stones shift their resonance as the poem enacts myriad minor dramas, pushing against our expectations of breadth or height, expansiveness or epiphany.

Heaney breaks with the tradition of the Romantic image as articulated by Frank Kermode, seeking neither epiphany nor supernatural vision but penetration to the core of material reality. If there is metaphysics here, it results from the naive stoicism with which the physical world—no "meta" about it—is made immediate. He takes this technique from Guillevic, whose "Herbier" evokes a worldview formed by local rocks and stones and trees; he favors the third-person *on*, which Heaney renders as "you," allowing his vision to ring true to any life. The poem surprises by the embodied yet generic nature of its speaker—Heaney may be hiding his self, perhaps as a counterweight to the intensely personal poems. Perhaps there are limits to confession and self-revelation, and there is a therapeutic value to viewing the self, or "you," as Everyman, the death of one as the death of any.

In their own casual idiom, Heaney's lines view communion with the earth as movement and change. When we bring ashes to ashes, earth to earth, we may not rest in peace but participate in a Heraclitean flux. Hence he adds the search for "an elsewhere world" to the poem's end, to signify not homecoming but a journey onward, outward. This is the great recognition of "A Herbal":

> On sunlit tarmac,
> On memories of the hearse
>
> .   .   .   .
>
> The dead here are borne
> Toward the future.
>
> .   .   .   .
>
> Where can it be found again,
> An elsewhere world, beyond
>
> Maps and atlases . . . ?
>
> (*HC*, 43)

The poem answers its own final question.

If "A Herbal" is centered by recognition of the continuity between life and death, decay and flourishing, memories of funeral rites and journeys into the unknown, does this invalidate the elegiac project altogether by evading the reality of death and grief? One could hardly accuse Heaney of evasion, but the vision of "A Herbal" is surprisingly bright, and the darkness of "The Door Was Open" is "not unwelcoming." The poet's acceptance of emptiness, however, does not signal lack of grief or a morbid metaphysical turn. Heaney insists that continuing life can be embraced without disclaiming grief—which, in turn, is not debilitating. Vaughan's previously questioned line—"All gone into the world of light?"—can now be affirmed, and the pathos of a fishing line snapping, severing the dead from the living, can be reimagined, as what was once given can be "found again."

The pull of Catholicism, seen as the "tremor and draw" of hidden water in "Out of This World," is curiously bypassed. We are enclosed by air instead of water, a material landscape rather than an emblematic one; the primum mobile here is earth itself. The landscape of Guillevic's "Herbier," like that of Heaney's "Herbal," excludes human speech and contains its own drama (Winspur 2004, 55–68), even as human presence is necessary for the lyric—and certainly for Heaney, who insists upon the physical presence of a singular subject even as its particular history is temporarily hidden. Perhaps this is how Death summons Everyman— by cutting him loose from the history, politics, familial ties, and stories constituting the substance of the self. The turn from symbolic emblems to physical things that survive death or even take sustenance from it—as plants flourish among graves—is accomplished by this summons. As we leave behind the subjective self, we also leave behind pathos. The poem's minimalism enables the potentially ponderous to become light as air: "The dead here are borne / Towards the future" (*HC*, 38). There is new beauty in this view of death as entrance into the unknown, a new verbal space we cannot know, not an underworld but, more radiantly, "an elsewhere world, beyond // Maps and atlases."

NOTES

1. See Nagy (2010, 13–45). As the lyric has come to be associated with personality rather than community, so our modern understanding of elegy has been modified, yet this ancient paradigm has not lost its relevance. Abbie Potts, for example, insists upon the personal journey the elegist undertakes toward anagnorisis, toward revelation (1967, 2, 10, 38–39).

2. Heaney had been working on a selection of Yeats's verse when this poem "came through unexpectedly" (Heaney 1997b, 108).

3. The Hopkinsian language of "Field of Vision"—the woman looks out on "sycamore trees unleafing / And leafing" (*ST*, 22), like an older incarnation of Margaret from "Spring and Fall," educating her visitor rather than being educated by him—hints at spiritual import in the natural scene. It is hard, however, to conjoin a fundamentally sacramental view of nature with the possibility that it may be "soul-free"; one feels the imaginative effort in Heaney's late work.

4. At a gathering with Mahon and Longley, Heaney declared, "I'd like to write like you boys, but I have to do my own thing." This could be a reaction to their own literary-historical self-identifications, to their Protestantism, or simply to the fact that Mahon and Longley were fast friends; I suspect this is indeed a poetic and cultural statement asserting the difference of his vision (Parker 1993, 53).

5. I have developed this idea further within *In Gratitude for All the Gifts* (Kay 2012).

6. Peter McDonald points out how much attention has been paid to Northern Irish poets' backgrounds but how little it is brought to bear on formal analysis of their actual work (Christopher Ricks and Edna Longley are obvious exceptions here). It is especially surprising given, as McDonald writes, "how often, and how explicitly, the poets themselves have given critics their cue" (2012, 479). Heaney gives plenty of cues: "Prayers were a form of poetry in my generation. . . . In the very fabric of ordinary daily life there was a linking of language to transcendence" (2000c, 84).

7. Heaney's punning has frequently been remarked upon; Stan Smith writes of his "habit of ringing all the possible changes on an equivocal word or phrase" (1997, 223–51).

CHAPTER THREE

SQUARINGS

Helen Vendler

In 1991, four years before he was awarded the Nobel Prize for Literature, Seamus Heaney published, in the volume called *Seeing Things*, a forty-eight-poem sequence under the title *Squarings*. These poems conduct a meditation on invisible things—sound rising in a Roman amphitheater, the conjectured sight lines imagined by a boy aiming his marble, the ghost of the poet's father called to mind by the words he used to say. The poems bring up visible things, too, but portray them as frozen, drawn out of time. Verbs drop out, and we see motionless nouns:

> Whitewashed suntraps. Hedges hot as chimneys.
> Chairs on all fours. A plate-rack braced and laden.
> The fossil poetry of hob and slate.
>
> <div align="right">(<i>ST</i>, 69)</div>

Things are silent, poised, stilled. And even when an action is permitted, it is often filtered through memory and becomes an action halted in time. "You watched" (*ST*, 64) (the poet says to himself, dwelling on suspended moments of the past), or "You squinted out from a skylight of the world" (*ST*, 57). When the present intrudes in *Squarings*, the poet is often pausing, usually to reflect on what he must do next: "Relocate the bedrock in the threshold. / Take squarings from the recessed gable pane" (*ST*, 56).

What is the source, and what is the object, of this poetry of the invisible, the still, the suspended, the pausing-for-thought? Heaney's earliest poetry had exulted in the solid and the eminently visible: the "sloped honeycomb" of a thatched roof (*DD*, 20), the shaped pats of butter at the end of churning day. And Heaney's middle-period poetry had recorded, with high-voltage verbs, the effects of sectarian violence in Northern Ireland:

> I see him as he turned
> In that bombed offending place,
> Remorse fused with terror
> In his still knowable face,
> His cornered outfaced stare
> Blinding in the flash.
>
> (*FW*, 23)

What has happened to make Heaney turn toward the stopped and the invisible? And what does the new "square" shape of these poems offer him as a form?

The shortest (if incomplete) answer to the first question is that Heaney's parents had both died within two years: Margaret Heaney in 1984 (when the poet, born in 1939, was forty-five); Patrick Heaney in 1986. There are elegies for both parents in *The Haw Lantern* (1987), the volume immediately following their deaths, but in *Squarings* the impact of those deaths has deepened to redefine their son's world. The parents are no less significant dead than alive; time has taken on in their absence a stasis from which it cannot now recover. The world asks to be reconstituted anew, with vacancy and invisibility, rather than presence and solidity, as its atmosphere. The "overture" to *Squarings*, its harrowing first poem, therefore confronts the moment after death (when, in Christian belief, the soul in the afterlife undergoes the "particular judgement" [*ST*, 55]—the divine judgment on an individual, consigning the soul to heaven or hell). Heaney is no longer a believer. He sees the site of the particular judgment as an abandoned house, with its roof gone, a rain puddle where its hearth fire was, and nothing in the puddle reflection of the winter sky but the "soul-free cloud-life." At this crumbling ruin of a family dwelling stands "a beggar shivering in silhouette," the poet's surrogate in deprivation:

> Shifting brilliancies. Then winter light
> In a doorway, and on the stone doorstep
> A beggar shivering in silhouette.
>
> So the particular judgement might be set:
> Bare wallstead and a cold hearth rained into—
> Bright puddle where the soul-free cloud-life roams.
>
> And after the commanded journey, what?
> Nothing magnificent, nothing unknown.
> A gazing out from far away, alone.
>
> And it is not particular at all,
> Just old truth dawning: there is no next-time-round.
> Unroofed scope. Knowledge-freshening wind.
>
> (ST, 55)

In this poem, desolation is total—the bleak shell of the house, the extinguished hearth, the shivering beggar. Yet at the same time, the world is as beautiful as ever: the winter light causes shifting brilliancies, the clouds roam above, the puddle is bright, the absence of a roof enables a sight of the scope of the sky, and the wind gusting through the doorway refreshes knowledge. *Squarings*, taken as a whole, says: Death is; Life is. Or, Life is; Death is. These uncompromising clauses are not joined by a "yet" or a "however" or "on the other hand." The two truths have no synthesizing or unified being within a single larger sentence. Each is absolute. The beggar shivers. The "knowledge-freshening" wind brings a new truth to the mind.

The eternally incompatible presence of the two truths—of life, of death—is one Heaney rescues from the Irish Annals. As the monks at Clonmacnoise are at prayer, a strange ship enters through the roof and sails through the air above them in the church, but its anchor catches on the altar rail. A sailor descends on a rope to try to release the anchor, but in vain. The monks look at him, bewildered, but the abbot, seeing the plight of the sailor, intervenes:

> "This man can't bear our life here and will drown,"

> The abbot said, "unless we help him." So
> They did, the freed ship sailed, and the man climbed back
> Out of the marvellous as he had known it.
>
> (*ST*, 62)

For us the otherworld ship represents "the marvellous," but for the denizens of the upper air it is our world that is the wonder; each world poses a danger to the other. The earthly air of the monks is a threatening sea to the sailor from otherwhere. Each atmosphere has its claim, depending on our vantage, to become the marvelous. Heaney can retell such a legend only by presenting it as a legend. If the poem had not begun with "The Annals say," Heaney would be the naive prolonger of the miracle. As it is, he is the rescuer of an unverifiable but imaginative fable, voicing it in a further version of the single stopped moment.

Such moments of vision are both recognized and demystified by Heaney. The atmosphere of death can flagellate the living world itself, as Heaney discovers leaving his father's deathbed:

> That morning tiles were harder, windows colder,
> The raindrops on the pane more scourged, the grass
> Barer to the sky, more wind-harrowed,

> Or so it seemed.
>
> (*ST*, 91)

What at first manifests itself as a realistic exterior narrative is, by Heaney's self-correction, transformed to an interior one. The qualifying demurrer "or so it seemed" arises from the son's chastened memory of his father's plainspokenness, which would reprove such emotional fantasies of a harshly augmented world. The father's "plain, big, straight, ordinary" house enters the poem as a "rebuke to fanciness." Yet even this sturdy house is affected, within the son's mind, by the memory of his father's fatal illness:

> The house that he had planned
> "Plain, big, straight, ordinary, you know,"
> A paradigm of rigor and correction,
>
> Rebuke to fanciness and shrine to limit,
> Stood firmer than ever for its own idea
> Like a printed X-ray for the X-rayed body.
>   (*ST*, 91)

The house, now emptied of its owner, is both solidly itself and yet also, now, an invisible paradigm, a Platonic form of Patrick Heaney's integrity in life and his suffering in death. Once again, in *Squarings*, life and death stand side by side as the visible house and the invisible X-ray, both true.

In his investigation of the coexistence of the visible and invisible, Heaney remembers how Thomas Hardy, as a child, lay flat on the ground amid a flock of sheep, pretending to be dead, "experiment[ing] with infinity" (*ST*, 60). Much later, "at parties in renowned old age," Hardy sometimes "imagined himself a ghost / And circulated with that new perspective" (*ST*, 61). Like Hardy, Heaney "experimented with infinity" even in childhood. The adult poet tells of "One hot summer afternoon" in wartime, when American soldiers were billeted in an aerodrome near the Heaney farm. The child withdraws from the farm routine, passing into the epiphanic world of pure receptivity: "I was seraph on gold leaf," he says of the suspended moment when time came to a halt as he stood on a railway, hearing around him not only rustic sounds but also the sights and sounds of military preparation: "larks, / Grasshoppers, cuckoos, dog-barks, trainer planes / Cutting and modulating and drawing off" (*ST*, 70). It was a time "marked by assent and by hiatus" (*ST*, 70), a form of eternity within time itself. Such seraphic occasions recur often in *Squarings*, as the poet recalls talismanic moments of arrested time. In one he watches his father's silent and gratified contemplation of a home-cured flitch of bacon (*ST*, 71); in another he is a child nestling with his mother and her sisters in a meadow-stranded boat (*ST*, 63); in yet another he comes "face-to-face" with a startled fox on a roadway (*ST*, 83). Each of these recollected instants has symbolic power: the father treasuring the bacon from his own pigs is the essence of farm economy; the moment with his mother and aunts reassures the child of his safety; the encounter with the fox reminds the poet of his link to the animal world.

When *Squarings* turns to inquire about its own efforts to recapture the stilled past, it recalls memory advice from the Renaissance: if you want to remember things or people, you should erect a mental house or city and place the memories—according to some order—in the various niches of this theater of the mind; you will then be able to retrieve them without difficulty. Such a stationing of memories in an ordered space is *Squarings*'s own figure for itself:

> Memory as a building or a city,
> Well lighted, well laid out, appointed with
> *Tableaux vivants* and costumed effigies—
>
> Statues in purple cloaks, or painted red,
> Ones wearing crowns, ones smeared with mud or blood:
> So that the mind's eye could haunt itself
>
> With fixed associations and learn to read
> Its own contents in meaningful order.
> Ancient textbooks recommended that
>
> Familiar places be linked deliberately
> With a code of images.
>
> (*ST*, 75)

We recognize the furnishings of Heaney's Catholic childhood, no longer sacred, no longer bearing their proper names, but merely inventoried as "statues in purple cloaks," just as the dramatis personae of the Northern Irish troubles appear in the equally anonymous (because abstracted) statues "smeared with mud or blood." The coded images that link Heaney's "familiar places" were amassed almost unconsciously in his earlier poems narrating the processes of making butter or collecting blackberries. Now his life is commanding him to look back and "read . . . in meaningful order" the import of his past. As he does so, the past eerily foretells the future: "You knew the portent / In each setting, you blinked and concentrated" (*ST*, 75). Reviving past life with the benefit of hindsight, the poet recognizes that apparently casual experiences and events of his youth were actually "portents" of what he would become.

It is precisely the concentration of the poems of *Squarings* that gives them their tense compression. What is it about Heaney's twelve-line form that makes it an apt set of "rooms" ("stanzas") for his theater of memory? The English douzain has usually been printed (by Yeats for instance) as a single unbroken twelve-line stanza. In Heaney's adaptation, the douzain is broken into four equal tercets, separated by white space. A tercet is a "naturally" unstable form by comparison to a quatrain; a four-line passage seems finished, while a three-line one seems incomplete. The great poet of tercets, Dante, encourages his lines to run on and run over; in imitation of him, later poets writing in tercets (Shelley, Stevens) have often conceived of the form as a fluid one, spilling down the page. Yet the form has another potential, exploited by all its poets: a tercet can be a powerfully monumental object on a page, especially when each of its lines is end-stopped. Heaney is well aware of the power of one-line tercet-sentences to isolate individual statements:

> Running water never disappointed.
> Crossing water always furthered something.
> Stepping stones were stations of the soul.
> (*ST*, 90)

Even two end-stopped lines in sequence have an epigrammatic effect: "How habitable is perfected form? / And how inhabited the windy light?" (*ST*, 78). Such distinct lines, such pointed questions, stop a poem in its tracks, and Heaney—by inserting such end-stopped lines or such burdened questions—gives his short poems the weight usually associated with longer meditations. Such a gravity accompanies the "squaring" in which Heaney interrogates his powerful predecessor in the poetry of death, W. B. Yeats. The poem poses eight questions, each bearing a different significance, before it arrives at its explanatory conclusion:

> Where does spirit live? Inside or outside
> Things remembered, made things, things unmade?
> What came first, the seabird's cry or the soul
>
> Imagined in the dawn cold when it cried?
> Where does it roost at last? On dungy sticks
> In a jackdaw's nest up in the old stone tower
>
> Or a marble bust commanding the parterre?
> How habitable is perfected form?
> And how inhabited the windy light?
>
> What's the use of a held note or held line
> That cannot be assailed for reassurance?
> (Set questions for the ghost of W. B.)
>
> (*ST*, 78)

Large concepts and categories of the spirit and its posthumous habitation underlie this "philosophical" poem, which disparagingly and ironically presents itself as a school exercise of "set questions." Heaney glances, in sequence, at the body (a thing unmade by death); memory (lost things remembered); art (made things); symbolic replacement of the real (soul and seabird); isolation (the jackdaw's dungy nest in the Miłoszian tower); posthumous fame (the petrified marble bust); and the felt presence of the absent dead (imaginable only as presences inhabiting the windy light). The questions of the habitation of the spirit move on from those of location and priority to ones more urgent for the artist, as the simple "live" in "Where does spirit live?" takes on abstract Latinate form: "How habitable is perfected form? / And how inhabited the windy light?" Can human beings find solace in art; can the spirit take up residence there? And finally, what is the use of a musical note or a held line of verse if we cannot, when we are grief-stricken or fearful, "assail" it—almost assault it—demanding reassurance?

Addressing the shades of the Gore-Booth sisters, Yeats imagines their posthumous existence: "Dear shadows, now you know it all" (1965, 236). Does "the ghost of W. B.," then, know the answers to metaphysical questions? Heaney leaves his queries vibrating, unsolved, in the air. We notice that each of the unanswerable questions "violates" the boundaries of the line-form except for the two central epigrammatic ones earlier quoted, each of them commanding a single end-stopped line. Heaney poses in these two questions the kernel of the whole poem: How habitable is art? By whom is the light inhabited? Art and the dead become the riddles besetting and perplexing the poet.

Heaney's four-part "squarings" have something in common with Shakespeare's four-part sonnets: just as the three quatrains and the couplet of a Shakespearean sonnet can be set in different relation to each other—augmenting, or correcting, or comparing, or contrasting, or ironizing one part in the light of another—so Heaney's tercets can buttress, or quarrel with, or qualify, or query each other. One tercet can be abstract, another sensuous; one plainspoken, another alive with metaphor; one static, another stormy; one colloquial, another meditative. The white space between the tercets can be a hinge on which the poem turns; conversely, it can become an obstruction that the poem must overcome; or it may simply afford a pause before the next venturing thought.

The European sonnet is very satisfying, since it implies, by its very asymmetry, that the shorter six lines can resolve the preceding eight, just as the Shakespearean sonnet implies by its closing couplet that the quatrains' engagements can somehow be summed up, or capped, or ironically dismissed. On the page, a pentameter sonnet is longer than it is wide, a rectangle. Heaney's square poems—as broad in their roughly pentameter lines as they are long in their twelve-line form—are indeterminate in implication; they have no formal solution implied in their shape, as sonnets do. Sometimes open-ended, sometimes "closed," they

can leave their questions disturbingly unsolved or momentarily equili-
brated. But in either case, each squaring melts as the next comes into
view: there is no narrative binding the squarings together, no march of
logic entailing a particular order. They possess, intrinsically, the uncer-
tainty of chance and the unforeseeability of Fate: in the later Heaney,
death has begun to live inside the spirit.

An example of the unresolved can be seen most painfully as Heaney
reexamines the case of the crucified "good thief" to whom Jesus prom-
ises heaven. But is the thief "translatable," in modern minds, into the
promised bliss? As Heaney's squaring closes, the thief's cosmic agony re-
mains unassuaged:

> so body-racked he seems
> Untranslatable into the bliss
>
> Ached for at the moon-rim of his forehead,
> By nail-craters on the dark side of his brain.
>   (*ST*, 66)

Yes, there has been the promise—"*This day thou shalt be with Me in
Paradise*" (*ST*, 66)—but it has not yet been fulfilled for that crucified
brain. The suffering forehead, symbolically monumentalized as the
moon, shows only the dark side of the brain, cratered by the nails from
which the good thief hangs. Nonetheless, the brain is still aching for that
afterlife; faith and hope hover as possibility.

But the poet's internalizing of the deaths of his parents forbids
sentimentalizing their future. A bleak vacancy attends Heaney's re-
writing of Vaughan's religious statement placing the vanished dead in a
celestial world: "They are all gone into the world of light." The poet
echoes his predecessor:

> *All gone into the world of light?* Perhaps
> As we read the line sheer forms do crowd
> The starry vestibule. Otherwise
>
> They do not.
>   (*ST*, 104)

Thereupon, Heaney proceeds to shorten Vaughan's visionary line to two words, changing the meaning of "all": *All gone*. That flat admission feels, he says, like a fishing line snapping, as the whole effort and hope of the cast is brought to nothing:

> Although in fact it is more like a caught line snapping,
> That moment of admission of *All gone*,
>
> When the rod butt loses touch and the tip drools
> And eddies swirl a dead leaf past in silence
> Swifter (it seems) than the water's passage.
>
> <div align="right">(<i>ST</i>, 104)</div>

Heaney's incomparable gift for imaginative analogy appears here. As the masculine energy of the taut fishing line is vacated, the successive verbs convey movements of the mourning heart through the felt drooping of rod and line and leaf—a line snapping, a rod butt losing touch, a dying tip drooling, a dead leaf swirled downstream almost before the eye can register it. Even the untrustworthiness of perception, "seeming," is given its due; death "seems" to carry away the fallen leaf with a speed faster even than the current of time itself.

As the line snaps binding the parental generation to the filial one, Heaney sets up, against his desolation, remembered joys of both the sensuous and the imagined. Joys, too, inhabit rooms in the theater of memory and are as undeniable in their plenitude as mourning is in its emptiness. Among the joys are landscape, music, companionship, and sexual energy. These all have their discourses and their symbols in Heaney's recollection: a road where moonlight wakened the river, and "silver lamé shivered on the Bann" (*ST*, 108); the music of a fiddle heard across stone-walled fields (*ST*, 106); an evening climb in Rome with friends that will close in conviviality (*ST*, 98); an uninhibited rope-man on fair days commending his rope ("how thick it was, or how long and strong") as he "menaced" the local farmers with his lawless "freedoms" (*ST*, 74).

The loftiest of the poems of joy in *Squarings* celebrates a moment in which the bowl of sky and the bowl of ocean, untroubled by any presence other than the poet's own, are in perfect equilibrium. This is the Platonic moment of "perfected vision":

Deserted harbour stillness. Every stone
Clarified and dormant under water,
The harbour wall a masonry of silence.

Fullness. Shimmer. Laden high Atlantic
The moorings barely stirred in, very slight
Clucking of the swell against boat boards.

Perfected vision: cockle minarets
Consigned down there with green-slicked bottle glass,
Shell-debris and a reddened bud of sandstone.

Air and ocean known as antecedents
Of each other. In apposition with
Omnipresence, equilibrium, brim.

(ST, 80)

We feel implications here of an exquisite arranging hand (not super-
natural but natural) that has "consigned" each thing to its place, estab-
lishing an untroubled congruence of the organic with the inorganic in a
"bud" of sandstone. Instead of having to choose between ocean and air,
as in "The annals say," we enter a paradoxical succession in which air and
ocean can each be an "antecedent" of the other; an expansion of the self
turns human presence into a natural "omnipresence"; and the percep-
tual moment is so full that "equilibrium" spills over into "brim." These
impressions are drawn out so finely by the diction that the poem barely
seems to move as it glides from awareness to awareness, from height to
depth, from air to ocean.

On the other hand, for all Heaney's commitment in *Squarings* to the
conceptual and the absent and the invisible, he will not take up any per-
manent station in the natural sublime. The joys enumerated in *Squar-
ings* include the most ordinary pleasures of boyhood, ranging from the
exciting apprehension of the sinister reek and shine of rat poison on
moldy crusts of bread (xvi) to the kinetic exhilaration of plotting moves
at marbles:

Squarings? In the game of marbles, squarings
Were all those anglings, aimings, feints and squints
You were allowed before you'd shoot, all those

Hunkerings, tensings, pressures of the thumb,
Test-outs and pull-backs, re-envisagings[.]

(*ST*, 57)

The "glad animal movements" (Wordsworth) of what Heaney names
"the muscles' outreach" (*ST*, 57) in the marble-playing boy are as yet
not visible but are purely mental: "feints" and "re-envisagings" play a
more memorable part in the happiness of recollection than the actual
outcome of play. And the boy lives on in the man, who, when he drives
under a canopy of old fir trees, experiences this passage through tree life
not merely as a visual phenomenon but as an invisible physical sensation
replacing the reality of the car:

You drive into a meaning made of trees.
Or not exactly trees. It is a sense
Of running through and under without let,

Of glimpse and dapple. A life all trace and skim
The car has vanished out of. A fanned nape
Sensitive to the millionth of a flicker.

(*ST*, 89)

Why does a poet write this kind of poetry—a poetry of inciden-
tal moments, of sensations so evanescent as to be almost indescribable,
of glimpse and dapple, of flickers on the nape of the neck? These are
hardly the usual subjects of male poetry. Heaney's sequence omits those
consequential actions—military, exploratory, amorous, vocational—that
usually populate poems of masculine life, and though *Squarings* owes
a debt to Wordsworth's revivifying "spots of time" and to Hopkins's
joyous "dappled things," it sets its memorial moments in a more lowly
world, that of his parents—a world that includes the rope-man, the rat
poison, and a folk ritual mingling superstition and belief (St. Brigid's

Day; *ST*, 88). Wordsworth's sacred moments are no longer Heaney's atmosphere: he now inhabits a different sort of philosophical ambience, a more everyday one associated with the Chinese poet called "Cold Mountain." Heaney's *hommage* to Cold Mountain, like the douzain of the memory-city, is one of the self-admonitions concerning poetic discourse that we find scattered throughout *Squarings*. Just as the memory city recommended order, so the stoic poems of Cold Mountain recommend plain speech:

> The poems seem
> One-off, impulsive, the kind of thing that starts
> *I have sat here facing the Cold Mountain*
>
> *For twenty-nine years*, or *There is no path*
> *That goes all the way*—enviable stuff,
> Unfussy and believable.
>
> (*ST*, 97)

Squarings, when it appeared in *Seeing Things*, was a shock to Heaney's readers. The Keatsian Heaney of the earliest books, the Joycean Heaney of the autobiographical *Station Island*, the domestic Heaney of *Field Work*, had not by any means disappeared entirely from either the volume or the sequence. Nevertheless, *Squarings* shows us a Heaney chastened by parental death into a loss so deep that its only measure is the equal depth of life. The elemental facts of death and life demand from the poet both the bleakly factual and the impulsively imaginative. It is only by doing "one-off" poems that Heaney can catch the unpredictable and almost inarticulable vicissitudes of feeling that follow on loss. The short douzains, one after another, track motions that Heaney names—in the four subheadings of his sequence—"Lightenings," "Settings," "Crossings," and "Squarings." The "lightenings" of deaths are burdens too; places are settings, yes, but deaths are "settings" as well; life and death are mutual crossings, each the antecedent of the other; and "squaring" these events in verse gives decisive aim and form to emotions otherwise uncapturable.

We see many things in *Squarings*, but most of all we behold the effect—enlarging both death and life—of the disappearance of an un-questioned and elemental reality present from the poet's birth. When the parental roof vanishes and the fire in the hearth goes out, the son has no choice, as he stands, a shivering beggar, but to acknowledge in this unroofed scope an unprecedented and knowledge-freshening way of seeing things. The geometrical symmetry of the poems' form and the mathematical neatness of their grouping—forty-eight poems of twelve lines each, clustered in four sets of twelve—embody the equilibrium of mind and heart that the stricken son seeks to attain, inhabiting a space balancing the current of time and the stillness of perfected perception, the dispossession of mourning and the stopped memories of joy.

PART TWO

HEANEY'S LATER STYLE

> I affected epaulettes and a cockade,
> wrote a style well-bred and impervious
> to the solidarity I angled for,
> and played the ancient Roman with a razor.
> —Seamus Heaney, "Wolfe Tone"

CHAPTER FOUR

The Freed Speech of "Equivocal Words"

Seamus Heaney's Door into the Light

Michael R. Molino

Those signing the Good Friday Agreement "recognize[d] the birthright of all the people of Northern Ireland to identify themselves and be accepted as Irish or British or both, as they may choose" (Northern Ireland Peace Agreement 1998, "Constitutional Issues," 1, iv). Fintan O'Toole immediately pronounced that such language evidenced a transition toward postnationalism in which "it is people who identify themselves, not governments or tribes who tell them who they are. That nationality is a matter of choice, not of inescapable destiny" (1998a, 16). The day after the Agreement was signed, Seamus Heaney described the "evolutionary" document as "a set of structures and a form of words which have the potential to release all sides from their political and historical entrapment" (1998b, 57). Of course, O'Toole likewise understood that nuanced notions of identity and transformation could not take hold without a vital and informed civic culture willingly unshackled from the very political and historical entrapment Heaney identified: "Unless newly fashionable words like 'equity' and 'respect' are given real economic and social substance, we will be left with nothing to stand on but the rough fragments of demolished ideologies" (O'Toole 1998b, 14).[1]

Heaney's optimism in 1998 stands in counterpoint to sentiments he expressed in his 1995 Nobel lecture, "Crediting Poetry," where he laments a sort of spirit-draining repetitiveness to the violence and oppression against which he has struggled to find a place for his poetic voice: "After 1974, however, for the twenty long years between then and the ceasefires of August 1994, such a hope [a balance between promise and violence] proved impossible. The violence from below was then productive of nothing but a retaliatory violence from above, the dream of justice became subsumed into the callousness of reality, and people settled in to a quarter century of life-waste and spirit-waste, of hardening attitudes and narrowing possibilities that were the natural result of political solidarity, traumatic suffering and sheer emotional self-protectiveness" (*CP*, 17). Heaney's later career, as we have conceived it here, spans a period a few years preceding and the fifteen years following the Good Friday Agreement. If his early poetic career entailed a search for "images and symbols adequate to our predicament" (*P*, 56), then Heaney's later poetic endeavors could be described as the search for fragile yet sustaining lyric moments of recollection and expectation recurrent and necessary to make the dream of civil change real. This contemporary Irish lyric poet selected the ancient Roman epic poet Virgil as his guide during this transition, with book 6 of Virgil's *Aeneid* marking the passages and labors required for such a dream to enter the physical world.

In an interview, Dennis O'Driscoll asked Heaney why he had not engaged in a "poetic remaking" of *Beowulf* as part of his translation. Heaney provides a rather surprising response:

> I did not know or love *Beowulf* enough to remake it. If it had been a poem I'd internalized and lived with long and dreamily there might have been a chance of doing what I'd done with *Buile Shuibhne* in "Sweeney Redivivus" or have done, more recently, with *Aeneid* VI in "Route 110." I like that book of the *Aeneid* so much I'm inclined to translate it as a separate unit, as Sir John Harington did in the seventeenth century. But in the case of *Beowulf*, I only really got to know and love it page by laborious page as I translated. (*SS*, 440)[2]

Many critics described Heaney's translation of *Beowulf* as a form of cultural appropriation, taking possession of the English language in a manner that closes a linguistic circle first identified by Stephen Dedalus after his conversation with the dean of studies in *A Portrait of the Artist as a Young Man*. Terry Eagleton is a particularly clear example of such praise, calling Heaney the "erstwhile outsider [who] . . . has now placed himself boldly at the *fons et origo*, claiming the tongue as always-already his own from the outset," and concluding, "It might be argued that Heaney's anxious need for this move to be legitimated is a sign of the cultural colonization it aims to overcome. Yet having reversed his cultural dispossession, he then reverses the reversal" (1999, 15–16). Despite such vaunted success and literary pedigree, Heaney expresses a kinship with book 6 of Virgil's *Aeneid* resembling his connection with *Buile Shuibhne*. Of course, Heaney throughout his career inclined toward the relationship between the civic and the mythic, especially the mythic violence that staggers the civic order, and all three works have that in common.

The connection with Virgil's epic had a long incubation period. Mary Francis Williams in her article "Seamus Heaney's *Exposure* and Vergil's *Aeneid*" explores Virgilian influences in the final poem of Heaney's *North*. Williams finds the first reference, apropos a poet like Heaney, in the poem's landscape setting: "The poem begins with a Virgilian mention of trees, a recollection of those famous woods where Aeneas found the golden bough in book 6 of the *Aeneid* (6.187–188), the same woods which Dante recalls in the beginning of the Inferno" (1999, 245). Bernard O'Donoghue in similar fashion reveals the influence of Greek and Latin classics on Heaney's poetry, especially the later poetic works. Referring to Heaney's volume *Electric Light*, O'Donoghue states, "In Northern Irish terms it is at first reading a peace process book, and Heaney is trawling though the classics for the texts that lend themselves to that; clearly, a great epic of civil war like the *Aeneid*, even if is to result in the *pax Romana*, does not suit" (2009, 113). This point is well taken with regard to the entire epic work. Yet Heaney in his interview with O'Driscoll suggests a hospitality and familiarity found in *Aeneid* 6 but absent from *Beowulf*. The stand-alone translation of *Aeneid* 6 will remain incomplete, but its influence helps provide some shape to an analysis of Heaney's later career. The critical, interpretive issue is one of intersections or relationships rather than parallels or equivalencies.

In his article on the Good Friday Agreement, Heaney asserts that it is through "the creative spirit, in the realm of glimpsed potential rather than intransigent solidarity, that the future is shaped" (1998b, 57). Virgil is a kindred spirit in such glimpses. Heaney's, albeit incomplete, poetic reimagining of *Aeneid* 6 is more than a political allegory where Heaney stands in for Aeneas or the Irish stand in for the Trojans. Heaney's creative spirit finds in Virgil a way of respecting the past while looking to the future. My intention is to identify Heaney's fascination with book 6 of the epic in an effort to show how that individual book allows Heaney the opportunity to consider the prospect of a peaceful, civic society for the first time released from its "political and historical entrapment." I take Heaney at his word in his Nobel lecture that for years he strained as one under "some dutiful contemplative pivoting his understanding in an attempt to bear his portion of the weight of the world, knowing himself incapable of heroic virtue or redemptive effect" and that some alternative was eventually demanded of him by his own creative spirit (*CP*, 19–20). Heaney turned to a variety of classical and modern mentors, ranging from Ovid and Dante to Mandelstam and Miłosz, who broadened his sense of resilience and inspiration in the face of suffering. I believe, though, that during this transition *Aeneid* 6 acted as a literary antecedent elegantly attuned to Heaney's imagination at a time when that imagination attuned itself to a world of possibility it dared not consider before.

Heaney's sense of familiarity with *Aeneid* 6 probably stems in part from recurring traits in his and Virgil's poetry. *Aeneid* 6 abounds with images of passages and openings—gateways, doors, thresholds, and mouths that act as passageways and barriers, invitations and hindrances, entities in themselves and the space to which they give access. Mouths are passageways of speech, song, prayer, and prophecy, but also the place where eating is transformed into aggressive, violent consumption. Spaces of passage and speech recur throughout Heaney's canon, with the two often found together, as with the "dark drop" and the "darkness echoing" of "Personal Helicon" (*DN*, 57). With the two together, the poem then renders, not a specific or single event in a present moment, but the longing for a continued experience attuned to both the physical and spiritual. The echo in "Personal Helicon" reverberates until it reaches

Rosie Keenan, the blind neighbor of the Heaneys who set the lonely silence ringing with her piano playing and singing. Heaney remembers the young woman in "At the Wellhead" and recalls reading one of his poems to her that featured the family well, presumably "Personal Helicon," to which the young woman claims, the impossible becoming possible, that she "can see the sky at the bottom of it now" (*SL*, 77).

The interconnection here points to another parallel trait. Oppositions at work in *Aeneid* 6 resonate with Heaney's natural inclination toward multiple perspectives. The virtually simultaneous sense of possession and loss, including the lingering connection with that which is absent, certainly connects Heaney with *Aeneid* 6. Of course, in this book, Aeneas's journey takes him into the underworld, and Heaney has ventured into the darkness before. Such journeys place the living and the dead in a space commonly reserved for the dead alone and thus allow corporeal body and shade to interact in ways impossible in the physical world except, perhaps, through poetic musings. Just as the poet visitor to the underworld can encounter or envision the soul in transition from its former to its eternal self or souls destined for the physical world, the poet can mourn the past while recognizing that the future springs in part from it.

"Two Lorries" provides a good example of counterparts that span time and physical dimension, interconnected as coal and ash are one and different, with images and characters from Heaney's childhood woven together with those on May 23, 1993, when an IRA car bomb devastated the Magherafelt business district, killing eleven people. The poem enacts both memory and vision as Heaney first recalls his "nineteen-forties mother" in the past deflecting the palaver of a cheeky coalman making a delivery in his lorry and then envisions her as a ghost abroad in "a time beyond her time" (*SL*, 17). Film acts as a fancy man's flirtatious lure to the exotic escape of the motion pictures in the memory but switches to the film of destruction running on the nightly news after another lorry "groans into shot" (*SL*, 17). The bus on the 110 route, later to continue its journey in *Human Chain*, rolls by in the past, never to return to the Ulster bus station obliterated in the present. Coal bags morph into body bags, while shopping bags and tally bags occupy a space at home both then and now. The poem does not render diptychlike counterpart images of stark violence, as Heaney does, for instance, in "The Tollund Man," where the sacrifice then and the optative sacrifice now appear with equal horror in their context. In "Two Lorries," the space vacated by the bomb's blast is quickly filled by the residents of Magherafelt working to reconstitute the world turned to ash. The "payload" does its damage, but the coalman, or some counterpart of his, is "plying his load" in an effort to restore order. The coalman, "filmed in silk-white ashes," "heft[s] a load" (*SL*, 14) of the destroyed Magherafelt and, shuttling between worlds, returns as Mrs. Heaney's charmer. Also in contrast to "The Tollund Man" and other earlier poems, "Two Lorries" does not pivot exclusively on the poet's anguished uncertainty about his obliged response to violence. The poet stands in as the one who remembers and as the one who envisions, but others respond and take action and, implicitly, resume the lives they had. The bombers instigate a moment of chaos, but the citizens create and reestablish the order that defines Magherafelt, then and now.

The oppositions at work in *Aeneid* 6 extend to the world of possibilities. What is possible in the physical world may not be so in the spirit world, as with the three poignantly failed embraces between father and son in *Aeneid* 6. The desire to make tangible what is not does not diminish the significance of the desire. Aeneas's encounter with his father in *Aeneid* 6 reflects a level of intimate attachment lacking in his encounter with his mother elsewhere in the *Aeneid*. Aeneas's parallel encounters with his parents highlight the potent relationship between material and spirit worlds. His exchanges with his father, Anchises, which Heaney has translated in part, reveal not only a potent kinship between the generations but the ideals and challenges of creating a civil society. Venus, in contrast, offers all the intimacy and philosophical subtlety of a military supply sergeant. Conversely, what is conceivable in the nonmaterial world, such as the ideal of a lasting peace, falls prey to a multitude of corrupting influences in the material world, making all efforts to forward a civil society a process of recurring imperfections, but nonetheless spurred on by the desire for the ideal. The father figure helps clarify the important difference between material and spiritual in such a way that incompatibilities do not result invariably in separation or exclusion.[3] Heaney's beautiful poem "The Harvest Bow" reveals the way what is and what is not, what did and what did not happen, lead to an intimate connection among memory, imagination, and hope. Here the living son, recalling the still-living father, remembers what was and knows what could be, "Gleaning the unsaid off the palpable" (*FW*, 58). A poem such as "The Harvest Bow" points the way toward like-minded poems in Heaney's later volumes where the distinct yet collaborative elements of the material and spiritual worlds are found in ordinary things like the glint of a straw bow, the sound of a rain stick, or the smell of mint. Such poems punctuate the angry poems of *The Spirit Level* and, at times, enter late, like the dove rising and ever rising in "The Flight Path" (*SL*, 22, 26).

Heaney recalls three embraces of his father in the intricately crafted "Album" from his collection *Human Chain*. The three embraces in *Aeneid* 6 fail because the human son cannot cling to his father's shade; in Sarah Ruden's translation,

> Three times he tried
> To throw his arms around his father's neck,
> Three times the form slid from his useless hands,
> Like weightless wind or dreams that fly away.
>   (Virgil 2008, 137)

Heaney's embraces, each occurring at different stages of life, encompass the hypothetical or longed-for, the clumsy and embarrassing, and the compassionate—variations on embraces between physical men that nonetheless fail because of useless hands or exist as little more than weightless dreams. The poem as a whole entails five twelve-line sections in which Heaney looks back on a past whose echo is fading in present memory to such a point that verb tenses change from the certainty of the past tense to the conditional "as it must have been" or "Could have been" (*HC*, 4). In this recollection, individualized images of events linger amid an elliptical story, each standing out from memories forgotten as "all the anniversaries of this / They are not ever going to observe" (*HC*, 5). Heaney recalls three imperfect embraces of his father in part 4 but lovingly observes recurring successful embraces between grandfather and grandson in part 5. What may fail between two generations does presume future failure as well. More important, though, is the "steady dawning" that the elusive moment, the longed-for capture of spirit by body, is more than just an elusive dream. The gesture itself, frail and flawed as it may be, is nonetheless rooted in something true:

> an embrace in Elysium
> Swam up into my very arms, and in and out
> Of the Latin stem itself, the phantom
> *Verus* that has slipped from "very."
>
> (*HC*, 7)

The word *very* may be an exsanguinated descendant, a throwaway word today barely connected to the truth, but the connection is there to be discovered as the love of a father and son can flow in and out of Heaney's "very arms."

Beyond recurring poetic traits that reveal his acute sensitivity to *Aeneid* 6, Heaney has translated portions of the book and written variations on others. Heaney begins *Seeing Things*, for instance, with a translation of lines 98 through 148 from *Aeneid* 6, which he titles "The Golden Bough." The setting is one attuned to Heaney's canon: the earth, the mythic underworld, and the voices that echo through and from it. In Virgil's epic, the Trojans have arrived at what will be their home and eventual glory, but they face a future fraught with conflict. Aeneas seeks direction into the spirit world and insight as to his fate from the Sybil. Of course, this is not Heaney's first encounter with the ancient oracle. Heaney entered the Sybil's cave in "Triptych" from *Field Work*, where he beseeched the oracle: "'What will become of us?'" (*FW*, 13). The three poems—"After a Killing," "Sybil," and "At the Water's Edge"—capture, in the aftermath of Bloody Sunday, the "predicament" not only of a poet striving for poetic inspiration but of all citizens of Northern Ireland trapped in a cycle of violence. This cycle seems so ingrained, so much part of the Irish collective memory, that each new act recalls earlier acts as if the landscape is haunted by "unquiet founders." Such hauntings make any prospect of a civil society seem but a dream that the island's inhabitants have no right to entertain: "Who dreamt that we might dwell among ourselves?" (*FW*, 12). The speaker longs for a civil society attuned to a natural order, not the "neuter original loneliness" or the "comfortless noise" of a land "flayed and calloused." The Sibyl projects an imaginable change in "form," and the protest marchers' "scared, irrevocable steps" that conclude the third poem may be an early sign of that change. Heaney's choice of *irrevocable* plays off the spatial and the temporal, the connection between sound and action, with the marchers' movement as sign of belief and hope. The word acts as a premonition—a vision, not received from the oracle, but fashioned from the human imagination—that once uttered even as a dream may attain the same level of potency in the collective memory as that which "hatched" those "unquiet founders." Images and references from "Triptych" recur with variation in Heaney's later poems that likewise allude to Virgil's *Aeneid*: the child as representative of the polis and the anticipation of a brighter future, the landscape as an Irish Elysium, and the journey spanning Northern Ireland and the memory that links generations. I shall return to these references later in the discussion of "Route 110" and "The Riverbank Field."

Heaney once again enters the Sibyl's cave in his translation from the *Aeneid* 6 that begins *Seeing Things*:

> So from the back of her shrine the Sybil of Cumae
> Chanted fearful equivocal words and made the cave echo
> With sayings where clear truths and mysteries
> Were inextricably twined.
>
> (ST, 5)

This translation incorporates the kind of self-referential elements that recur in Heaney's later volumes—in particular the word *equivocal*, which, earlier in his career, Heaney and his critics used as an indictment of his purported uncertainty, evasiveness, or insincerity. The word, though, placed in the context of Sybil's cave within Aeneas's story, suggests possibilities of knowledge and insight. The original Latin reads:

> Talibus ex adyto dictis Cumaea Sibylla
> horrendas canit ambages antroque remugit,
> obscuris vera involvens: ea frena furenti
> concutit, et stimulos sub pectore vertit Apollo.
>
> (Virgil 1951, 444)

The Sybil sings from her shrine the fearsome enigmas that boom out from her cave, obscuring truth in darkness. Heaney translates *ambages* not as "ambiguity" or "enigma" or "mystery," as other translators have, but as "equivocal." The passage details the problem of truth and the challenge for those eager to speak that which is true. Of course, *ambages* exists in English only in archaic form, having not taken root in English as it did in French. Its meaning then as now signifies a winding way or indirect procedure, a long story, a circumlocution or evasion, or ambiguity. The sense of mystery surrounding any interpretation of the truth recurs in the line that follows as "obscuris vera involvens," often translated in aphoristic form as "truth enveloped in obscurity."[4]

Rooted more firmly in English than *ambages*, the word *equivocal* (*aequi*, "same" or "identical"; *vocal*, "voice" or "sound") has a complicated etymology that refers, not just to double-talk or intentional ambiguity, but to a voice or sound interpreted in various ways. The term manifests the performative opportunities of identical sound in which understanding and meaning vary with the hearing, interpretation, or predisposition of the listener—a message interpreted differently by different listeners. Heaney's translation calls attention to greater possibilities for the listener rather than any limited intent of the speaker, and it by implication suggests counterpart interpretations in which the various meanings exist in relationship to one another. The one who speaks equivocal words may seem inscrutable to someone eager for a single, preferred meaning. The one who interprets equivocal words envisions possibilities not available in unequivocal words. For the poet, it is the difference between Sybil and Aeneas, between being the prophet forced to reveal a certain path and being one of many travelers seeking a world of possibilities.

Heaney wrote a short essay for Amnesty International titled "Anything Can Happen," which acts as the preface to a series of translations of Horace's *Odes* 1.34, with "Parcus deorum cultor" submitted as "Horace and the Thunder."[5] The poem, whose opening line repeats the title of the essay, is translated into English by Heaney and translated into twenty-three other languages by an equally varied number of writer-translators. In this essay, Heaney makes the case for poetry's importance at times of violence and uncertainty when it appears in the most negative sense that indeed anything can happen—referencing the terror attacks on September 11, 2001, directly but many others as well by implication:

> The indispensable poem always has an element of surprise about it. Even perhaps a touch of the irrational. For both the reader and the writer, it will possess a soothsaying force, as if it were an oracle delivered unexpectedly and irresistibly. It will arrive like a gift from the muse or, if you prefer, the unconscious. If poetry has a virtue [in the face of terror and destruction], it resides in its ability to bring us to our senses about what is going on inside and outside ourselves. As human beings, we crave this realization. (*AH*, 13–14)

The poem, then, is the sight of the equivocal, where meaning surprises and reveals with equal measure. Heaney here is poetically and politically far removed from the drive for "images and symbols adequate to our predicament."

Heaney continues with Virgil's sixth book in an issue of *Modern Poetry in Translation* dedicated to "Freed Speech" (Heaney 2009c, 57), in which he translates lines 77 through 97, titled "Three 'Freed Speeches' from *Aeneid* VI." What exactly is "freed speech"? According to David and Helen Constantine's editorial introduction to the issue, the process of translation moves a poem from the rules governing one language to the rules governing another, and in that process "The effect of the poem is *enlarged* . . . given its liberty . . . [introduced into] a new land to run free in" (2009, 1). Heaney's translations from *Aeneid* 6 satisfy that definition. However, Heaney's freed speech requires breaking free from or resisting containment as part of its creation and expression. Freed speech occurs as part of a passage through, one without any guarantees about the destination or outcome—a passage through the familiar, through the uncertainty and doubt, through the fear, and through the barriers (real or implied) of everyday experience and common speech. It occurs at the moment linking voice or word and action where, as Heaney reveals in his poem "From the Frontier of Writing," "Suddenly you're through, arraigned yet freed" (*HL*, 6). The three translations from *Aeneid* 6 Heaney offers in *Modern Poetry in Translation* represent just such moments of passing through.

The first of the three translations, "Aeneas," begins as Aeneas witnesses Apollo's domination of the Sybil. The section emphasizes the need not merely to bear witness to this struggle for control but to muster the conviction to plead one's case and stand ready for the necessary action to follow. Aeneas makes his plea for his people as a group cast off from Troy's "name and fame," "the last of its relicts" (Heaney 2009c, 59). The choice of *relicts* suggests that Aeneas in his description looks backward—his people as *remnants*, or *relics*, or *widows*—and forward—as a group living in a vastly changed environment, as one survived and surviving. Aeneas's plea may be cloaked in the language of supplication, fortune, fate, and divination, but the identification of his people evokes an ecology of evolutionary adaptation.

For her part, the Sibyl in the second translation enacts a sort of verbal version of the frontier of writing. Her words, pointing toward the future, echo forth as a result of her resistance to Apollo's inexorable efforts to control and dominate her body and mind. At the moment of greatest thrashing, the "tunnel-mouths" open "of their own accord" and release the prophecy that reinforces the command to persevere: "Whatever disasters befall, do not flinch / Go all the bolder to face them" (Heaney 2009c, 60). The third translation, "Anchises," continues the relationship between domination and choice. This passage comes from the end of book 6 and the second of two speeches of father to son. This speech seems the least hospitable to an Irish poet of all the passages Heaney translated. Anchises concedes the arts and sciences to other cultures in favor of Roman command in the arts of war and governance. If both speeches are read in tandem, though, then one finds that for Anchises humans, limited as they are, are prone to fight and kill as well as create. In his earlier speech, which Heaney does not translate here, Anchises explains the struggle between the material and the spiritual, with matter imposing corrupting limitations on the spirit. Nonetheless, humans respond to possibilities that can in turn forward humanity, envisioning a dream as destiny. Flawless peace may exist only in the spirit world, and efforts toward such in the material world fall short of the ideal. However, those invariably unsuccessful efforts give life its transcendence, coming as they do out of the interaction between the two. Anchises uses contrasting verbs in Heaney's translation when he presents the role of those who must "impose," "justify," "spare," and "crush." Anchises's speeches are discursive rather than poetic, instructive rather than visual, with an emphasis, not surprisingly, on explanation and itemization over the imaginative. Hope emerges from the preponderance of evidence brought forth as Anchises lists the great and the powerful who will rule Rome. Virgil does not reveal Aeneas's immediate response to his father's words. One must infer that his increased sense of purposeful resolve in subsequent books reflects his conviction that his father's words are destiny.

Like James Joyce before him, Heaney recognized that beyond his translation or allusions to a classical antecedent he could use Aeneas's journey as a counterpart to his own story. The counterpart gives shape to the story and creates moments of intersection and parallel but does not act as a schematic to follow toward a common end. Thus Heaney occupies multiple selves in "Route 110," his streamlined version of *Aeneid* 6. He is the poet-creator, a latter-day Virgil "shortcutting" his way through the epic to reach the lyric core he wants to tell. He is also the autobiographical self, telling a story that begins in his youth when he purchased a copy of *Aeneid* 6 in a used bookshop. Heaney thereby assumes the Aeneas role in a story that partially echoes that of the classical counterpart. He is also the hopeful grandfather welcoming a granddaughter into the world of the living. These various selves lend the poem a sense of time looking backward and forward at an expectant moment when new life enters the world. Heaney alerts the reader to consider Virgilian parallels in the first sentence when he purchases a copy of *Aeneid* 6 from a dusty, decaying bookshop in the Smithfield Market. Parallels or variations on book 6 recur throughout the poem so frequently, particularly in the early sections, that the reader is tempted to engage in a direct translation of modern events into classical analogues. The poem, though, is about Heaney's experience that, in his own retrospection, gravitates toward a partial reading/telling that parallels Aeneas's journey.

Direct references to Virgil begin with the book's purchase. In section 2, both Lake Avernus, at one time considered an entrance point to the underworld, and "Charon's barge" mark the beginning of a journey across Northern Ireland, "Cookstown via Toome and Magherafelt," and into Heaney's memory (*HC*, 50–51). Heaney has a little fun amid the direct references. After acknowledging that the once foul-smelling but song-filled pet shop is now silent and "birdless," Heaney makes his way through the market's bustle with "my bagged Virgil," as if the book were a hunter's valued quarry. "Virgil's happy shades" begin section 10, but most of the references to the *Aeneid* occur intertwined in Heaney's personal experience. The shopgirl, emerging out of the "Classics bay," sells him a copy of book 6 and unwittingly predicts Heaney's future. McNicholl's pigeons stand in for Venus's doves. Michael Mulholland's wake recalls the spirits awaiting transport. Mr. Lavery, "blown up in his pub" among other unnamed victims, resembles the bludgeoned warrior Deiphobus along with unnumbered casualties of battle. The reference to the betrayed Dido reveals Heaney's use of his Virgilian parallel. Section 8 begins with the moment Aeneas sees his former lover and recognizes his culpability in her demise. Heaney uses a portion of lines 524 and 525 from Robert Fagels's translation but reverts to his own words in the enjambment. Fagels's translation reads: "as one when the month is young may see or seem to see the new moon rising up through banks of clouds" (Virgil 2006, 346). Heaney removes any doubt of perception and poignantly represents the memory of the young girl's face as fading from sight as the moon disappears and daylight breaks: "*As one when the month is young sees a new moon* / Fading into daytime" (*HC*, 55). Heaney then quickly departs, leaving the young girl, "her hurt still new," in the distance as he speeds away down "pre-Trouble roads" (*HC* 55). The scene combines innocence lost, a fugitive escape, and impending political turmoil on the near horizon.

The shade of James Joyce gave farewell instructions to the pilgrim Heaney at the end of "Station Island," advice Heaney certainly seems to have followed in the latter portion of his career, seeking and crediting "echo-soundings, searches, probes, allurements" (*SI*, 94). Joyce's presence in "Route 110" is less overt but thoroughly at home in Heaney's imagination. The scene in the bookshop that begins the poem recalls the tenth section of the "Wandering Rocks" episode in *Ulysses* where Leopold Bloom peruses books in a seedy bookshop—waited on by a shopkeeper with breath reeking of onions, who bundles a stack of books, "hugged them against his unbuttoned waistcoat and bore them off behind the dingy curtain" (Joyce 1986, 193). Bloom buys the breathless

Sweets of Sin for Molly, to which the shopkeeper gives his confirmation, "That's a good one" (1986, 194). His prized classic safely ensconced in its "brown paper bag," Heaney hurries through the jostling market, "Parrying the crush . . . / Past booths and the jambs of booth with their displays" (*HC*, 50). The scene resembles the young boy's market excursions in "Araby," where his impassioned longing for Mangan's sister must be held secure and protected against a hostile and corrupt world: "We walked through the flaring streets, jostled by drunken men and bargaining women, amid curses of laborers, the shrill litanies of shop-boys who stood on guard by barrels of pigs' cheeks, the nasal chanting of street-singers, who sang a *come-all-you* about O'Donovan Rossa, or a ballad about the troubles in our native land. These noises converged in a single sensation of life for me: I imagined that I bore my chalice safely through the throng of foes" (Joyce 1976, 31). The boy at the beginning of his life has embarked on a journey. He envisions himself here as priest in a Eucharistic processional and later as a questing knight, his life before him and his expectations limitless. The boy represents early life, young and earnest, eager for the journey and the treasured prize, life's first epiphanic letdown still ahead. Bloom at midlife stands virtually static amid the momentum of city life. "Wandering Rocks" teems with life: birth and death, church and state, feast and famine, history and revolution, true and false charity, art and commerce. The episode's nineteen sections are woven together as narratives intersect and overlap, characters encounter and knock into one another. In the central tenth section, Bloom examines plates of fetuses in the womb that resemble the organs of slaughtered animals and recalls the pregnant Mrs. Purefoy, whose child will be heralded into the world in a subsequent episode.

Books intrigue and play a key part in the life of each of the three central figures: Heaney with Virgil, of course, though Heaney expresses his devotion to variety of literary ancestors in "Hermit Songs" as well; the boy in "Araby," who finds among books owned by the house's former inhabitant copies of *The Abbot*, *The Devout Communicant*, and for variety *The Memoirs of Vidocq*; Bloom, who contemplates *The Artful Disclosure of Maria Monk*, Aristotle's *Masterpiece*, and von Sacher-Masoch's *Tales of the Ghetto* (presumably *Stories from Polish Ghetto*). Heaney has chosen a different classical ancestor as the pretext for his poem, but one that likewise negotiates the underworld and winds through the obstacles of the physical world. It is helpful also to remember that Joyce dedicated an entire episode of his novel to an event hardly mentioned in the *Odyssey*. When given the choice to navigate his ship through the hazards of the Wandering Rocks or to snake between the contrasting hazards of Scylla and Charybdis, Odysseus opts for the monster and the whirlpool. Joyce, on the other hand, knows that his fellow Irish negotiate opposing forces and meandering obstacles on any given day and that in such meandering one finds the full variety of life.

In a much more direct reference, Heaney varies upon the opening line of D. H. Lawrence's poem "Bavarian Gentian," converting the affirmative grasp of the flower-torch in Lawrence's poem to a negative "reach me not a gentian but stalks" of oats that, wrapped in foil from candy bars by McNicholl's wife, light his way into the "age of ghosts" at the poem's midpoint. The poem's final sections are announced as "age of births" where one guest arrives with "fresh-plucked flowers" (*HC*, 59) and Heaney arrives with the same stalks and "silvered heads" of oats as a gift to his granddaughter, the Anna Rose of the dedication, who has just left the banks of the River Lethe and entered the world of the living. Heaney mentioned his fascination with Harington's seventeenth-century stand-alone translation of book 6. Harington takes some license in his translation. Beyond cultural transgressions in which Virgilian idealism colludes with Machiavellian politics and the city of Romulus and Augustus conflates with the city of popes, Harington shows returning souls eagerly moving toward their physical form on the banks of the Lethe and in the process "learning to forget," a fascinating variation on Virgil's *immemores*. Harington's oxymoron ironically characterizes those already living in post–Good Friday Northern Ireland more than it does the new inhabitants of the land. The living must learn to forget if they are to make their newly devolved legislature, judiciary, and police function as agents of a civil society. The Heaney clan greet newborn Anna Rose, her grandfather ready with his "thank-offering" (*HC*, 59), and speak in baby talk, the language of a new day.

Heaney ignores some events from *Aeneid* 6 in "Route 110," choosing instead to break some out as separate poems. He also avoids all reference to Aeneas's exit from the underworld through the Gate of Ivory, the passageway whereby false dreams enter the world above. Heaney apparently is at this point willing to leave the question of governance to others and accept what he has to offer to his granddaughter and the world. Of course, all hope must face the realities of those bent on resistance and destruction. Those, too, Aeneas sees on his journey of the underworld. Just months before his death, Heaney admitted to the *Times* of London reporter Erica Wagner that age-old divisions and the symbols and pageantry keeping them alive are resistant to change and new beginnings: "'There's never going to be a united Ireland, you know,' he says plainly. 'So why don't you let them fly the flag?'" (Heaney 2013d, T2, 2). The spiritual world of poetry allows humans to see things beyond what ordinary sensibilities permit; these are glimmers and possibilities that escape capture the way a spirit father pours through the embrace of physical son, but they are, like the word *very*, rooted in *verus*. "The Riverbank Field" offers an Irish variation on classical landscape where Heaney admits he will "confound the Lethe in Moyola" and envisions a peaceful world of ordinary life that parallels the Elysian Fields where Aeneas witnesses former soldiers immobilize their weapons and release their war horses unharnessed to graze in green pastures, taking the joy now in peace that they once took in battle. Once again, in Virgil's version, Anchises tells his son that these are souls for whom another body and another opportunity at life await. Heaney ends the poem "'in my own words'" (*HC*, 46), knowing the soul's desire to experience the fullness of life in the physical world.

Heaney takes a journey into the underworld in *District and Circle*, a collection of distant memories and farewells. Death and the separation it brings loom over most of the poems in the collection. The title, evoking intersection lines on London's Underground, also suggests a border or boundary that surrounds and defines Heaney's life. The last poem in the collection enacts an out-of-body experience as Heaney, believing he was about to die, takes a bird's-eye view of himself splayed out on the gravel drive as thoughts drift into the past and dwell on death. He recalls his younger brother Christopher, whose name can still not be mentioned, and the moments that provoked the painful "Mid-Term Break" (*DN*, 28), from *Death of a Naturalist*. In contrast, *Human Chain* ends with a poem dedicated to another granddaughter. The movement downward and into the past is reversed to an upward, hopeful perspective as the young child, her life still before her, takes joy in the movement of a soaring kite that is at first tethered and then free, just like young Aibhín's birthright as a citizen of Ireland.

NOTES

1. Social and political scientists have analyzed the Peace Agreement and the challenges facing its implementation. A few are listed here in chronological order: J. Lloyd (1998); Stevenson (1998); Carey (1999); S. Dunn (1999); K. Williams and Jesse (2001); Hayward and Mitchell (2003); Gilligan (2003; see also essays by Jarman, McAuley, Shirlow, Tonge, and Wolff from this same issue); Muldoon et al. (2007); White (2007); Doran (2010); Patterson (2012); Schwartz (2012); Rolston (2013).

2. Heaney is referencing Harington (1991).

3. I am not asserting an allegorical parallel between Aeneas's parents and Heaney's own parents. Heaney's poems that reference his mother are filled with love and understanding, albeit unspoken at the time, as we see in the sequence "Clearances."

4. Sarah Ruden translates the line as "Her fearsome, truth-entangling riddles" (Virgil 2008, 120). Frederick Ahl translates the line as "Fearsome, ambiguous words . . . // roll[ed] up the truth in obscurity's riddles" (Virgil 2007, 131).

5. Heaney reprints the poem in *Human Chain*.

CHAPTER FIVE

HAPPENING ONCE FOR EVER

Heaney's Late Style

Neil Corcoran

Seamus Heaney is of course a major critic as well as poet; and, as with most good poet-critics, his criticism offers evidence of a high degree of self-definition or self-identification. It chances—although this is not just chance—that essential essays of Heaney's concern three poets in whom the idea of lateness is, in fact, critical, poets in whom lateness constitutes a form of crisis: Wordsworth, Yeats, and Eliot. Heaney's essays do not dwell on this crisis, but they do uncover in these poets forms of what he calls "exemplary" behavior; and implicitly the example is one that the poet Seamus Heaney is himself attending to as well as identifying. It seems clear that these poets might also prove exemplary, in negative as well as positive ways, for a poet bound, in the title of a well-known late poem, to the task of "keeping going." One major signal of lateness in Heaney is retrospect, and I shall examine in this essay some ways in which this affects the poems; but a crucial way in which it has affected our sense of Heaney more generally is the retrospective book *Stepping Stones*, published in 2008, a collection of interviews with his friend Dennis O'Driscoll, a book manifestly evolved in place of an autobiography and one that itself acted as the "initial inspiration" (*SS*, viii) for some later poems, in both *District and Circle* and *Human Chain*. In a passage in its "Coda," the book also has illuminating and relevant things to say about Wordsworth, Yeats, and Eliot.

Wordsworth, Heaney says, suffered an appalling "loss of grip," even though he remained capable of the "marvellous rally" of "Extempore Effusion," his poem in memory of James Hogg (*SS*, 466). Eliot perpetrated "alibis in the theatre" (*SS*, 466)—by which Heaney must mean, I think, that Eliot's poetic drama was not really poetic; many critics think of course that it was not really dramatic. "Alibis" is a harshly negative judgment, implying presumably that Eliot is to be blamed for knowingly duping his audience, or possibly himself, into thinking that he was still capable of producing genuine poetry. Yeats, on the other hand, Heaney says, conventionally enough, proved in his magnificent late work the close affinity between creative and sexual excitement: although it is hardly possible to believe that Seamus Heaney, a poet of sustained marital and domestic love, could ever have found, or have wished to find, a way of emulating such excitement, however much he may have admired or envied its poetic consequences. In *Stepping Stones*, Yeats also becomes, however, together with Shakespeare, Wallace Stevens, and Czesław Miłosz, one of a group of exemplars in whose late work "you sense an ongoing opening of consciousness as they age, a deepening and clarifying and even a simplifying of receptivity to what might be awaiting on the farther shore. It's like those rare summer evenings when the sky clears rather than darkens. No poet can avoid hoping for that kind of old age" (*SS*, 466). As it has turned out, Seamus Heaney had only five years or so to live after those words were published: so, as things go nowadays, he had no real "old age." Even so, I think they apply to those aspects of his late style that I intend to discuss in this essay; and I would like their own clarifying eloquence to stand over what I say.

In his critical prose Seamus Heaney frequently distinguishes various stages or phases in the careers of poets, and, in so doing, he discovers lateness as both gain and loss. In Robert Lowell's last book *Day by Day* Heaney identifies intimations of mortality "when a sad, half-resigned autumnal note enters" (*P*, 223), and, in one of his acute and captivating metaphoric scherzos, he figures Lowell's career as a brilliant geology, moving from the igneous to the sedimentary (*GT*, 129). In Patrick Kavanagh, a major exemplar for the younger Heaney, he finds a wholly new orientation in the later work, in which the idea of place shifts from documentary, realist geography to luminously transfigured image, the poet occupying a site "where the mind projects its own force" (*GT*, 5)—under which rubric we are surely being almost directed to read the luminous projections of the mind in relation to place in Heaney's sequence "Squarings" in *Seeing Things*. In Auden, on the other hand, Heaney finds even in "The Shield of Achilles" too equably composed a maturity: Auden's melodiousness and his impassiveness are "the result of the kind of synoptic wisdom which this poet settled into and settled for" (*GT*, 111). Although I would myself dispute this judgment, it is clear that, for this poet-critic, to settle into and to settle for—the postures of both comfort and concession—are being divined in order that they may be avoided.

Dylan Thomas died when he was only thirty-nine, so he did not really have a "late" phase in the conventional sense; but given that a large amount of his work was drafted, if not completed, before he was twenty, thirty-nine might well be accounted late for so compositionally peculiar a poet. In a strikingly, even willfully unconventional reading of Thomas's famous villanelle "Do Not Go Gentle into That Good Night," Heaney reads the form's reflexiveness as appropriate to a reflexiveness in its feeling. Thomas's villanelle, he says, is not just a son comforting a father but "the child poet in Thomas himself comforting the old ham he had become; the neophyte in him addressing the legend; the green fuse addressing the burnt-out case" (*RP*, 139). This is one of the few places in Heaney's criticism where an invocation of Harold Bloom's axioms of misreading seems appropriate. This is partly because Heaney astonishingly, even distressingly, fails to honor the poem's self-lacerating filial feeling, which is very inadequately represented by the word *comfort*. In what sense can you be said to be "comforting" a dying father by instructing him, possibly against his will, to rage against the dying of the light? The reading may, as Terence Brown has suggested, have been influenced by the closeness of the death of Heaney's father to his writing of the essay in 1986; but the only way I can really account for so unsympathetic a misreading from so humanely sympathetic a poet and critic is to presume that Dylan Thomas, as the burnt-out old ham soon to die an

ignominious death in an America that had taken this "Celtic" poet per-
haps too warmly to its heart, is being strongly—too strongly—identified
as an antiexemplar, an instruction in how not to do it (T. Brown 2009,
45–54). *Neophyte* is a word with strongly Catholic connotations: "a newly
ordained priest, the novice of a religious order" is the first definition in
the *Oxford English Dictionary*. What term could be less appropriate to
the chapel-background Welsh nonconformist Dylan Thomas? But what
term would be more appropriate to the young Seamus Heaney, educated
largely by Catholic priests and thereby inevitably invited to consider a
vocation to the priesthood?

Heaney's reading of "Do Not Go Gentle" also seems to me,
though, to be influenced by Patrick Kavanagh's very ambivalent attitude
to Dylan Thomas—Heaney actually deploys the caustic Kavanagh term
buckleppin (*P*, 126) during the course of the essay—and swayed to some
degree by a memory of the poem "Famous Poet" by Ted Hughes, an
early influence on, and a subsequent mentor of, the poet Seamus Heaney,
and a defender of the poetics of Dylan Thomas. Published in Hughes's
first book, *The Hawk in the Rain*, in 1957, that poem, in what we must
assume to be tyro—or "neophyte?"—self-admonition, as well as satire,
evokes the spectacle of a self-created "monster" born out of the readi-
ness to satisfy an admiring audience's demand for the virtuosic but hol-
low repetition of favorite effects. This wrecked monster is imagined,
undoubtedly with some melodrama but also memorably, as "a Stego-
saurus, a lumbering obsolete / Arsenal of gigantic horn and plate / From
a time when half the world still burned, set / To blink behind bars at the
zoo" (Hughes 1957, 18). "Famous Poet," "Famous Seamus": the poet
whose very name was long ago made to rhyme with fame, even as the
rhyme also harmonizes "fame" with "shame." Heaney must have loathed
this glibly offensive chime, first sounded, it seems, by Clive James; but
he must have been aware of the dangers of having been so often set, or
of having voluntarily so often set himself, behind the bars of the zoos of
contemporary media and academic attention. How does such a poet
survive, in his poetry?

In *The Breaking of Style* Helen Vendler (1995) suggests that Heaney's
stylistic changes can be identified in relation to the prominence of parts
of speech: adjectival first, then verbal, then nominal, then adverbial.

There is perceptive truth in this, but it seems to me that continuities rather than fractures of style are more apparent in this poet and that he does not therefore very easily fit any theory of stylistic breakage. Particularly when we remember the astonishing discontinuities in the careers of two earlier major Irish poets, Yeats himself and Louis MacNeice, we may feel that Heaney does not so much break as consistently remake a style. It is as though—to adapt one of his own metaphors, in a way almost irresistible when writing about this poet—a constant Heaney signal is being transmitted on different frequencies. In his book *An Autumn Wind* (2010), Heaney's friend Derek Mahon has a triptych of poems called "Autumn Skies," written as tributes to his fellow Northern Irish poets John Montague, Michael Longley, and Heaney himself. The poems engage in an element of affectionately subdued, admiring pastiche that perhaps involves just a hint of competitive joshing too. The poem for Heaney is (therefore?) called "A Country Kitchen," and it ends with the most Heaney-like lines Seamus Heaney never wrote. They memorably and with almost apothegmatic force make the point about style that I am trying to make here:

> The world of simple fact
> gleams with water, yields
> to the plough. A gull-race
> follows the working tractor.
> *Quidditas*: the used fields
> of Ulster and ancient Greece;
>
> and always the same river,
> the oracle and universe
> with no circumference,
> that infinite resource.
> If a thing happens once
> it happens once for ever.
>   (Mahon 2010, 40–41)

You cannot step into the same river twice, says Heraclitus: but you can step into it once for ever, says Derek Mahon when he thinks of Seamus

Heaney. And Mahon's collocation of "Ulster and ancient Greece" makes the classicist connection that is so much a signature of late Heaney too. Even more particularly, in an act of testimonial deference, Mahon's poem may make the Virgilian connection that is so prominently inscribed in that signature, notably so in *Seeing Things* (1991), *Electric Light* (2001), and *Human Chain* (2010), because its terms appear to be foreshadowed by a verbal gesture at the end of the closing poem of the triptych "Seeing Things."

The poem remembers a nearly fatal accident Heaney's father once had while plowing on the riverbank close to the family home and farm. The father manages to return home, however, the poem says, "undrowned" (*ST*, 8), a nonce word of a kind found frequently in Philip Larkin, formed by a prefix of cancellation, and here invented for the proximity to disaster, the appalled sense of the possibility only just avoided. The poem closes as the son comes upon his father:

> That afternoon
> I saw him face to face, he came to me
> With his damp footprints out of the river,
> And there was nothing between us there
> That might not still be happily ever after.
>   (*ST*, 8)

"I saw him face to face" echoes a renowned verse from St. Paul to the Corinthians: "For now we see through a glass, darkly; but then face to face: now I know in part; but then shall I know even as also I am known." St. Paul is talking about meeting God in an afterlife; Heaney is talking about a return to the ordinary temporal life of a beloved father who has just almost been killed. The degree and extent of the intimacy and permanence of the new knowledge between father and son brought by the accident, however, take on an almost religious solemnity by means of the allusion, in which it is the return to the world that is itself, as it were, read as a form of transcendence.

Another allusion is at work here too, though. The poem "Seeing Things" begins with the memory of a panic-stricken family boat trip from Inishbofin to the mainland, in which the boat's pilot is referred to as "our ferryman." This makes him a type of Charon, the ferryman in Virgil's account of Aeneas's descent into the underworld to meet his dead father Anchises in book 6 of the *Aeneid*. The volume *Seeing Things* is itself prefaced or introduced by "The Golden Bough," Heaney's version of fifty lines of *Aeneid* 6, in which the Sybil, who eventually accompanies Aeneas to the underworld, tells him that to get there he must first pluck the bough that will act as his entrance pass. When Aeneas does eventually meet his father, he meets him, in Robert Fagles's translation, "face-to-face" (Virgil 2006, 186). Heaney's vivid, even visionary evocation of a father returned alive to a son in a moment of newly radiant understanding flickers therefore with the literary recall of the father lost to, but briefly rediscovered by, Aeneas in the Elysian Fields. When Aeneas moves to embrace Anchises there, he finds, in some of the most memorable lines of the *Aeneid*, that there is nothing to embrace:

> Three times he tried to fling his arms around his neck,
> three times he embraced—nothing . . . the phantom
> sifting through his fingers,
> light as wind, quick as a dream in flight.
>
> (Virgil 2006, 205)

Heaney recalls this moment more substantially in the sequence "Album" in *Human Chain*. The poem is a further evocation of his father and also of something that was only ever with difficulty permitted to come between them, given the norms of repression and hesitation in Irish men of that generation: that is, an embrace. Heaney, remembering three attempts to hug his father, also remembers Virgil:

> Just as a moment back a son's three tries
> At an embrace in Elysium
>
> Swam up into my very arms, and in and out
> Of the Latin stem itself, the phantom
> *Verus* that has slipped from "very."
>
> (*HC*, 8)

The Latin "*verus*": true, real, proper, right. The phantom Anchises sifts or slips through Aeneas's fingers when the poet reads *Aeneid* 6; and the poet's recalled father slips back into his poem by means of a slippery etymology evoked as the transposition into language of pure bodily sensation, exactly the transcription of which this poet is such a past master. And that sensation itself—"swam up into my very arms"—takes on a painfully charged significance from the fact that in several other poems in *Human Chain* this poet, Seamus Heaney, recalls temporarily losing all sensation in one of his arms as a consequence of the stroke he suffered in 2006.

Seamus Heaney is one of the masters of modern elegy; he extends the resources of elegy, sometimes by dint of questioning its consolatory motives. Indeed, thinking of such poems as "Casualty" and "The Strand at Lough Beg" in *Field Work* (1979), we could say that Northern Ireland hurt Heaney too early into elegy by killing friends and relatives in reprisals or sectarian atrocities. In late Heaney, elegy remains prominent—so prominent, indeed, that almost the whole of the second part of *Electric Light* (2001) is composed of elegy, as is a great deal of *District and Circle* (2006). Many of these are elegies for poets. It is a truism, and, we might say, a generically scandalous one, that elegy cannot but be narcissistic too. In mourning the dead poet, the elegist is also inevitably preoccupied self-interestedly with his or her own mortality and with the making of the poem for which the death is the dreadful opportunity. These narcissisms are, in my view, self-reflexively included and diverted by Heaney in the *Field Work* poems and their successor, "Station Island." There, in the absorbing, unremitting dialogue with itself represented by Heaney's work, Heaney has the victim of sectarian assassination in "The Strand at Lough Beg" return to accuse him of now of making him, as it were, the victim of the aesthetics of elegy: "You saccharined my death with morning dew" (*SI*, 83).

Heaney's late elegies for poets are not always comparably self-doubting or self-critical. Among those elegized or addressed in commemorative poems are Ted Hughes, Joseph Brodsky, Zbigniew Herbert, Sorley MacLean, Pablo Neruda, George Seferis, Czesław Miłosz, and W. H. Auden. These are not negligible figures: they constitute, indeed, an international modern pantheon; and it is hard not to feel that there is an element of elegiac surplus in Heaney's so studiously giving himself to such commemorative responsibilities. It is also hard not to feel that some elegies are more the consequence of expectations held of this outstanding contemporary poet and Nobel Prize winner than of genuinely deep feeling on his part. To paraphrase Samuel Johnson on Milton's "Lycidas," "Where there is leisure to respond to expectation there is little grief" (1975, 88). Sometimes, too, the elegies run the risk of self-approval or self-regard, since the act of writing elegy necessarily implies that the elegist is of the company of those he presumes to elegize. We need not at all doubt this in the case of this elegist to wonder nevertheless whether it is to the benefit of the poetry that the elective affinities should be so prominently displayed.

When T. S. Eliot writes, fascinatingly and self-involvedly, about late Yeats, he identifies possible pitfalls for the poet as he ages: one is "becoming dignified" (1957, 257). Eliot may have discovered his alibis in the theater, but he did stop writing poems very early, so in his poetry, if not necessarily in his literary and social criticism or his drama, he does not run these risks. In my view, there is something a little dignified in some of the poetry of *Electric Light* and *District and Circle*, when the Nobel Prize–winning poet parades himself too obviously *as poet*. Heaney's personal decency of temperament and his manifest human generosity—so often and rightly commented upon at the time of his death—and his frequent registering of something like humility before the major literary achievements of others may have desensitized him to the risk. This is the one place in his work where it seems to me that a self-corrective analysis dramatized in his work years earlier seems at least to whisper at the edge of earshot when the Joycean figure conjured by "Station Island" admonishes the poet that "you lose more of yourself than you redeem / doing the decent thing" (*SI*, 93).

Although *Human Chain* contains its share of elegy and commemoration, the elegies are not for poets; so the volume signally cuts itself clear of the dangers I am presuming to suggest here. It is also a volume in which the elegiac is richly dispersed in various ways, and in which Virgil becomes a kind of allusive twilight illumination of elegiac mood and mode—like those rare summer evenings when the sky clears rather than darkens, it may be.

The poem "Seeing Things" ends on the riverbank, and in "Album" the first scene of possible paternal embrace is also the riverbank:

> Were I to have embraced him anywhere
> It would have been on the riverbank
> That summer before college, him in his prime,
>
> Me at the time not thinking how he must
> Keep coming with me because I'd soon be leaving.
> That should have been the first, but it didn't happen.
>
> (*HC*, 7)

"Album" is a poem in which Heaney charts the things that did not happen between this son and his parents, and does so with a great ache of longing and loss consequent on the parents' now having left forever. But the poet attempts to redeem this loss by retrospectively reading himself back into some of the circumstances of his parents' lives, putting himself there before his own birth at their wedding meal and even imagining the moment of his own conception. When his parents leave him in boarding school for the first time he watches them walking together down the school drive:

> I stood on in the Junior House hallway
> *A grey eye will look back*
> Seeing them as a couple, I now see,
>
> For the first time, all the more together
> For having had to turn and walk away, as close
> In the leaving (or closer) as in the getting.
>
> (*HC*, 5)

These lines, extraordinarily simple in diction, as much of *Human Chain* is, pivot about the participial "Seeing" and the present indicative "see," between the delicate, preverbalized quiver of recognition and comprehension by the child in the past and the exercise of firm retrospective judgment in the poet's, and the poem's, present moment. What he now sees with the eyes of his mind, presumably after years of meditation on the moment, is different from what he was able to see then with his eyes alone. The line "*A grey eye will look back*" is Heaney's own translation from the Irish of Colum Cille, as it figures in the poem "Colum Cille Cecinit" later in *Human Chain* (*HC*, 72–73), so the present recognition is bolstered or possibly even enabled by what has happened to this poet in literature as well as in life, by his ability newly and differently to contextualize his experience.

The delicacy and tact of the perception, which involves grateful acknowledgment and deep affection along with the grief of absence—temporary in the child's life, permanent in the adults'—are beautifully complemented by the punctuation of the final line. The parentheses—those marks of both inclusion and exclusion—which enclose the words "or closer" in fact hold the words not closer to but farther apart from the other words in the line; and those are the words for the parents' leaving and getting of the child who became the poet. The parentheses refuse to intrude any closer on the act being brought to mind and brought to language, even while making it clear nevertheless that the act has been pondered, as have the more inhibited sexual mores of a previous generation. So the act of salvage that memory and retrospect represent must include also the sad incommensurability of the experience of different generations, and the knowledge that you must first become your parents in order to understand them.

Many of the poems of *Human Chain* are poignant exercises in the repercussions of such comings and leavings and gettings; but they also know what one of them calls, after the Catholic phrase for damnation, "the pain of loss" (*HC*, 11) involved in forgetting and forgetfulness, when age takes away what we hopelessly try to recall, "as the memorable bottoms out / Into the irretrievable," as the poem "In the Attic" puts it (*HC*, 84). This is an experience all the more painful, we must assume, for a poet with the astonishing powers of recall apparent elsewhere in Seamus Heaney's work and known to anyone who ever had a literary conversation with him, that great testimony to the potential of verbal memory.

"Album" may well also, in its consummate simplicity, define a moment of originary trauma for this poet, whose work so frequently seems earthed in one form or another of homesickness, driven by the desire for irrecoverable origins in place, family, locale, and language itself. This could well be the ultimate place Seamus Heaney's poetry comes from, its bedrock of primal, imaginatively initiatory separation. In Heaney's work, homesickness is, we might say, a permanent condition; and the poetry is the tenting of the wound.

The riverbank setting of "Album" and the approach the poem makes toward a dead father, the filial posture it assumes and enacts, propose *Aeneid* 6 as the literary or imaginative origin for these settings of Heaney's, their foundational myth. Other poems in *Human Chain* too, notably "The Riverbank Field" and the long sequence "Route 110," make specific allusion to Virgil. In *Stepping Stones* Heaney says that *Aeneid* 6 is a poem he "internalized and lived with long and dreamily" (*SS*, 440), and he tells us that he considered translating it as a separate unit, as Sir John Harington did in the seventeenth century. Of course he has now done so. "The motifs of Book VI," he says, "have been in my head for years—the golden bough, Charon's barge, the quest to meet the shade of the dead father" (*SS*, 389). In fact, there is also another, more peculiar motif in *Aeneid* 6 that is vital to the poems of *Human Chain*. Just before Aeneas meets his father, he sees the spirits of the blessed thronging the riverbank of Lethe. They include warriors, priests, and poets, and Orpheus himself is there. Anchises explains to Aeneas that after years of punishment for their sins these souls are destined to return to the world after drinking the waters of Lethe in order to forget their previous existence. This appears to be a purely Virgilian invention that blends the Stoic doctrine of the *anima mundi* with Platonic and Orphic-Pythagorean elements. It was deeply influential on Dante, which is one of the reasons he had Virgil accompany the journeying poet of the *Commedia*; and in *Seeing Things* Heaney accompanies his opening translation of part of *Aeneid* 6 with a concluding version of the passage from canto 3 of the *Inferno* in which Virgil and Dante are ferried across the Acheron by Charon.

In *Human Chain* Heaney newly and surprisingly adapts the motif of the souls waiting on the riverbank of Lethe. "The Riverbank Field" crosses another memory of Heaney's first place, using specific place-names—"Moyola," "Back Park," "Grove Hill," "Long Rigs," "Upper Broagh"—some of which are also invoked elsewhere in his work. "I'll confound the Lethe in Moyola" (*HC*, 46), the poem says; and "The

Riverbank Field" does indeed "confound" Broagh with the Elysian Fields, superimposing them in an act of translation that becomes literally Heaney's own translation of several lines of *Aeneid* 6, as he reads himself perhaps into the Orphic role:

> All these presences
> Once they have rolled time's wheel a thousand years
> Are summoned here to drink the river water
>
> So that memories of this underworld are shed
> And soul is longing to dwell in flesh and blood
> Under the dome of the sky.
>
> (*HC*, 46)

The piercing quality of this derives from the intensity of this poet's desire to return their bodies to the "passing spirit-troops" (*HC*, 46) of his own remembered familial and neighborhood dead; from his ability to remember them but also from his desire to "re-member" them, to give them back their bodies, at least in the transformative language of his poetry. The naming of places—first places, primal and primary places— also carries a marked Dantean resonance, since in the *Commedia* the named places of the dead are consistently identified and frequently carry strong ethical implications.

"There is no next-time-round" (*ST*, 55), Heaney writes in "Squarings"; and *Stepping Stones* ends with his assent to Wordsworth's axiom that it is on this earth that "we find our happiness, or not at all" (*SS*, 475). Which is one reason, Heaney says there, for "keeping going" (*SL*, 10). A poet needs whatever motivation or impulsion he or she can get for *that* in advancing age, but Heaney's convinced certainty about the lack of an afterlife as he expresses it here seems to me relatively unusual for an Irish Catholic of his generation, and particularly for one who appears to have practiced his religion well into his maturity. As late as 1978, when he was nearing forty, Heaney was, for instance, contributing an article called "The Poet as a Christian" to an Irish theological periodical (1978, 603–06). More usual, in my experience, is a varyingly insecure agnosticism sometimes even articulated as a kind of bereavement, as it is for instance, very capably, in a well-known poem by Dennis O'Driscoll called "Missing God" (2002). Heaney appears to suffer no comparable sense of loss or grief, at least in his poetry. The matter is discussed with equanimity in *Stepping Stones*; and equanimity is also the keynote of the tripartite poem "Out of This World" in *District and Circle*.

Written in memory of Czesław Miłosz, the sequence opens with a poem in quotation marks, which presumably intend that we read it as vocalized on behalf of the recently dead Polish poet. Inevitably, however, it appears self-referential for this living poet too:

> There was never a scene
> when I had it out with myself or with another.
> The loss occurred off-stage. And yet I cannot
> disavow words like "thanksgiving" or "host"
> or "communion bread." They have an undying
> tremor and draw, like well water far down.
>
> (*DC*, 47)

On the stage of Heaney's own poetry there does remain in his repeated evocations of the dead an intensity arguably still religious in ways deriving from both the forms and the feelings of a now formally rejected Catholicism; and to be conscious of "what might be awaiting on the farther shore," whatever the degree of metaphoricity this may be thought to carry, is to be possessed of a religious consciousness. In *Human Chain*, however, these forms and feelings are transposed, or translated, into the Virgilian in a way that makes late Heaney an exercise not only in lateness but in venturesome new development too, advancing an image and embracing a scope of Virgil beyond the translation of *Seeing Things* and beyond the politically inflected eclogue translations and imitations of *Electric Light*.

The sequence "Route 110," dedicated to a new grandchild, Anna Rose, consists of twelve twelve-line poems divided into tercets, so it formally recalls the shapes and structures of *Squarings*. Like many of the poems in that sequence, it offers meditations on moments, details, episodes of a life that have now become, in memory, forms of epiphany. Unlike *Squarings*, though, this sequence shapes its moments of recall to a Virgilian pattern, moving from the first poem's recollection of the poet's purchase of a used copy of *Aeneid* 6 in Belfast's Smithfield Market to the final poem's celebration of the granddaughter's birth as the ending of her "long wait on the shaded bank" (*HC*, 59), her transformed return to the world from the waters of Lethe. In poem II the racks of suits in Smithfield Market, once worn by the recently dead, sway "Like their owners' shades close-packed on Charon's barge" (*HC*, 49). In poem III a bus journey from Belfast—"Cookstown via Toome and Magherafelt" (*HC*, 50)—also takes on the aspect of Charon's ferry across the Acheron, when the bus driver separates and directs his passengers as Charon does there. In poem V the doves of Venus, sent by Aeneas's mother, in the *Aeneid*, which lead Aeneas to the Golden Bough, metamorphose into the pigeons of a family, the McNicholls, recalled from childhood, with their "votive jampot" (*HC*, 52) containing, in place of the gentians of Virgil's Elysium, foil-wrapped oat-heads from the local fields.

In poem VII, the poet figures himself returning from a wake in a "corpse house" at which rounds of cigarettes have been smoked, "my clothes as smoke-imbued / As if I'd fed a pyre" (*HC*, 54). Poem VIII appears to deal, strikingly and for the only time in Heaney's poetry, with what appears to have been the guilty or remorseful breaking off of a relationship with an early girlfriend, recalling "her hurt still new" (*HC*, 55); it opens with a translation of a line from the most famous and emotionally draining episode in *Aeneid* 6, when Aeneas meets Dido, who reproachfully shuns him; she is first seen through the misty shadows of Hades, "*As one when the month is young sees a new moon*" (*HC*, 55), and Heaney recalls the relationship in chapter 2 of *Stepping Stones* (*SS*, 45, 406). In poem X, the riverbank with its shades and the arch-poet Orpheus weaving among them is said to be "not unlike a sports day in Bellaghy," and in poem XI an evening's fishing, once more on "the riverbank field," is read under a Virgilian rubric:

> as if we had commingled

> Among shades and shadows stirring on the brink
> And stood there waiting, watching,
> Needy and ever needier for translation.
>   (*HC*, 58)

The poem's supposition ("as if") makes the need for translation—the neediness, rather, because this is clearly a driven urgency, a hunger—literally, first of all, that of the shades to return to the world as they wait on the banks of Lethe. Figuratively though, it is the poet's need, or neediness, to keep translating himself and the world of his sympathetic affections, which constitute his poetic *donnée*, into the art of poetry—to *keep* translating them, to find new ways of "keeping going." "Route 110" manages this by translating the poet's place of origin into Virgilian episode, moment, vignette; which is why, in poem IV, at a wedding in "a small brick chapel" on "Etruscan slopes" Heaney represents himself as "the one there most at home" (*HC*, 51). The translation of Virgil to Bellaghy, as of a young Seamus Heaney to Tuscany, produces a perfect fit, both literary and topographical.

It is possible for this kind of neediness to result in something over-schematic in poetry, bending or coercing original experience to classical parallel; and the double negative of the phrase "not unlike a sports day in Bellaghy" risks bathos, its hesitant, double-negative simile alerting us to all the ways in which the fields of a Bellaghy sports day might be thought in fact to differ from the Elysian Fields. That the overschematic is not an issue in the sequence, however, has to do with the way Virgil is reconstituted in it quite differently from the way he is constituted elsewhere in English literary (and political) history. When Heaney says that he has lived "long and dreamily" (*SS*, 440) with *Aeneid* 6, *dreamily* is a word that accurately fits the way Virgil is configured in "Route 110"; and the word is virtually glossed by some passages of Virgilian attention in *Stepping Stones*. The classical poet becomes in the sequence an almost half-conscious reverie of restoration and return, a rhyme of origin and end, the textual place long meditated to which present poetic consciousness is liable to lapse and relapse. Virgil becomes also a mode of honorific recognition quite at variance with his reception into English cultural history as the epic-heroic poet of martial valor and public-school spirit. If poetic power is involved in Heaney's turn to Virgil—and it is, in various senses—it is power being wielded on behalf of the powerless, of those disregarded by history who are now being given names that will survive in poems. In the terms of "Anything Can Happen," in *District and Circle*, these are poems in which "those overlooked" actually do become "regarded" (*DC*, 13). Heaney's Virgil is therefore not, at least in the terms in which it is offered, T. S. Eliot's Virgil as the "universal classic" (Eliot 1957, 130), nor is he the Virgil *anima naturaliter Christiana* defined and celebrated in Eliot's essay "Virgil and the Christian World" (1957, 126).

There, Eliot admires Virgil as the poet of the "noble . . . ideal of Empire," and he does so in large part because, he reminds us, the Roman Empire became the Holy Roman Empire. Yet Eliot also celebrates the way Virgil's imperial ideal is affirmed by the *Georgics*, by the intelligence conveyed in that poem that "his devotion to Rome was founded on devotion to the land; to the particular region, to the particular village, and to the family in the village" (1957, 126). Heaney would not have had to read far into Virgil to find himself there. Heaney's Virgil is the Virgil not of *imperium* but of the local and the regional, and the poet of the shadowy underground, of the only vaguely perceived, the hinted-at, the twilight. He is a Virgil who comes in from the edge and stands at the margins: on the riverbank field, in the secondhand market, in the queue at the bus stop, in the country kitchens and wake-houses and sports fields of country people. This is an intensification, almost a setting into a different dimension, of the Virgil of "Bann Valley Eclogue" in *Electric Light*, where he is called "my hedge-schoolmaster Virgil" (*EL*, 11)—and so not just a countryman but a countryman of Seamus Heaney's, since the hedge-schoolmasters were those who ran clandestine schools for Irish Catholic children during penal times. Heaney's Virgil is eminently fit to take his place beside those other re-creations or reimaginings of Virgil in modern English-language poetry: in Thomas Hardy, T. S. Eliot, and Robert Lowell.

Seamus Heaney opens a posthumously published essay, an outstanding one, on Ted Hughes like this:

> Once upon a time there was a poet, born in the north of his native
> country, a boy completely at home on the land and in the landscape,
> familiar with the fields and rivers of his district, living at eye level
> with the wild life and the domestic life. Educated first in local
> schools, he proved himself a gifted son and was chosen for further
> education in the great centers of learning in the south. There, as he

mixed with the intellectual and social elite of that time and place, his extraordinary linguistic powers flourished and his first collection of poems gained him immediate notice and respect in the literary world. . . . Then, as he grew in achievement and reputation, his social circle widened and his sense of poetic destiny deepened. . . . His reading voice was bewitching, and all who knew him remarked how his accent and bearing still retained strong traces of his north-country origins. (Heaney 2013e, 221)

Heaney's audience, hearing this at the opening of the talk from which this essay derives, would of course have assumed that he was talking about Ted Hughes. Not so. What he has just said, Heaney says, "contains all the received truths about the historical and creative life of Publius Vergilius Maro, better known as Virgil, who was born on his father's farm near Mantua in northern Italy in 70 B.C." (2013e, 222). As of Virgil, so of Hughes. And—the reader must be thinking, and Seamus Heaney writing this must have intended the reader to think—*mutatis mutandis*, so also of Seamus Heaney, in what he is inventing here as a triple poetic-historical rhyme.

The idea of the return to the father and the trope of translation itself are both foreshadowed, not with specifically Virgilian reference, but still with classical reference, in "The Blackbird of Glanmore" (*DC*, 75–76), the closing poem of *District and Circle*. It is once more a poem of retrospect and return. Heaney returns to his home in Glanmore, the scene of two sequences of sonnets earlier in his career, "Glanmore Sonnets" (*FW*, 33–42) in *Field Work* and "Glanmore Revisited" (*ST*, 31–37) in *Seeing Things*. He returns to the figure of himself as the driver of a car, which features in such outstanding earlier poems as "Westering" (*WO*, 79–80), "The Tollund Man" (*WO*, 47–48) and "Postscript" (*SL*, 70). He returns to the subject matter of "Mid-Term Break" (*DN*, 28), one of the best-loved poems in his first book *Death of a Naturalist* (1966), a poem about the tragic accidental death of his young brother Christopher. He returns to the ornithological imagery of several early Irish poems that he has translated, including the long poem *Sweeney Astray* (1983d) and its autobiographical offshoot "Sweeney Redivivus" (*SI*, 97–119) and his sharp, haikulike version of "The Blackbird of Belfast Lough." And he

returns also to some lines of *The Cure at Troy*, the version of Sophocles's
Philoctetes that he published in 1991. The poem's returnings or homings,
its comings and goings, its leavings and gettings and gatherings, rhyme
arriving with leaving, literally so in its opening verse; and "The Black-
bird of Glanmore" steadies itself into, rather than against, the knowl-
edge that the habit of arriving and leaving will ultimately be broken by
the final leavetaking of all, when the self eerily or uncannily becomes its
own shadow:

> On the grass when I arrive,
> Filling the stillness with life,
> But ready to scare off
> At the very first wrong move.
> In the ivy when I leave.
>
> It's you, blackbird, I love.
>
> I park, pause, take heed.
> Breathe. Just breathe and sit
> And lines I once translated
> Come back: "I want away
> To the house of death, to my father
>
> Under the low clay roof."
>
> And I think of one gone to him,
> A little stillness dancer—
> Haunter-son, lost brother—
> Cavorting through the yard,
> So glad to see me home,
>
> My homesick first term over.
>
> And I think of a neighbour's words
> Long after the accident:
> "Yon bird on the shed roof,

Up on the ridge for weeks—
I said nothing at the time

But I never liked yon bird."

The automatic lock
Clunks shut, the blackbird's panic
Is shortlived, for a second
I've a bird's eye view of myself,
A shadow on raked gravel

In front of my house of life.

Hedge-hop, I am absolute
For you, your ready talkback,
Your each stand-offish comeback,
Your picky, nervy goldbeak—
On the grass when I arrive,

In the ivy when I leave.
                    (*DC*, 76–77)

This is one of the great glories of late style in Seamus Heaney, a poem
of intensely simple lyric concentration, limpidity, and lucidity. The word
heartbreaking is easily overused and abused, and I have never myself, to
the best of my knowledge, used it in my critical writing; but this poem
is heartbreaking.

   The eeriness of its effect has to do with the poet's representation of
himself as isolated and haunted by memories of his family dead, of both
the father and the son who has long since "gone to him," and as—not
comforted, exactly, but steadied by his taking in of, and poetic address to,
the blackbird. It has to do with the neighbor's words, which seem more
the product of quasi-Shakespearian or classical foreknowledge than of
local superstition, although the local dialect—"yon bird," repeated—
contributes powerfully to the occult effect, so that the blackbird of
Glanmore seems a beneficent substitute for the bird of ill omen. It has

to do also with the poem's strange form, in which the trimeter varies to both dimeter and tetrameter across six verse lines, one of which is separated off from—isolated from—the others to look like refrain on the page, although it is not: the only lines actually repeated are the first and final lines of the opening verse, which form the fifth and final, separated, line of the final one, as if to point the endlessness, the eternal repetition, of human arrival and departure themselves.

Formally too the poem's initiating six verse lines rhyme, or off-rhyme (arrive/life/off/move/leave/love), in a way that creates the expectation that the subsequent verses will rhyme too. But they do not, apart from a few muted, minor-key echoes (heed/translated; him/home; dancer/over; words/bird; lock/panic; myself/life; talkback/comeback) until the final two lines off-rhyme in the way they have in the opening verse also. They are separated there but come together here; and the rhyme is the poem's point, as it draws together arrival and departure in the sad, irresolute chiming of "arrive" and "leave." The effect of the combination of rhyme, off-rhyme, and variant meter is altogether one of irresolution and also of a simplicity of means to get a very strange thing said, as the poet has a sudden momentary vision of himself absent from himself, as a bird might see him, only "A shadow on raked gravel." The eeriness of the perception is set into high relief by its sharing the same brief verse space with the richly aural, assonantal specificity, so characteristic of this poet, of the automatic car lock that "Clunks shut." It is very much the house of life that enables such sensuous linguistic re-creation; but this is the house that the poet momentarily sees himself leaving, just as he has earlier recalled its opposite, in his translated phrase, "the house of death." The "panic" in this verse is the blackbird's, not the poet's; even so, it is his contemplation of the blackbird's panic that produces the poet's vision.

The poem's paradoxical mood, caught between a steadying of the self in the face of death and a longing for death, is itself concentrated into the paradoxical phrase for the dead brother, "A little stillness dancer." What is a "stillness dancer," and why is the noun being used adjectivally? It is, I take it, an image for the way the brother, once watched in vividly immediate, unforgettable life "cavorting" through the family yard as he sees his presumably adored eldest brother for the first time in

months, has, after his death, remained in that brother's—this poet's—
mind almost in the form of a cinematic freeze-frame, his dancing forever
stilled by the fact of his death but forever present also to the eye of the
poet's mind and imagination. Transformed into stillness by death, the
little stillness dancer thereby goes on doing what the blackbird does in
the poem's opening verse, "Filling the stillness with life." "Little stillness
dancer" is a beautifully tender phrase for the astonishment of permanent
recall. Giving the impression that it comes almost out of nowhere, it is
also however a phrase that itself recalls another poem: the third part of
T. S. Eliot's "East Coker"—"So the darkness shall be the light, and the
stillness the dancing" (1963, 186). In Eliot, the line is part of a passage
dealing with mortality and those Christian virtues of faith and hope that
may respond to, or even counter, the melancholy of mortality. "The
Blackbird of Glanmore" has no such assurance or expectation; but for its
readers as well as for its poet the poem, the rich fruit of late style, is itself
a steadying resource.

CHAPTER SIX

"The Whole of Me A-Patter"

Image, Feeling, and Finding Form in Heaney's Late Work

Meg Tyler

In "Feeling into Words" (*Preoccupations*), Heaney wrote of "Digging" that he felt he had "let a shaft down into real life" (*P*, 42). The afterlife of an image often sets not just a poem but also a feeling in motion for Heaney. Think of his early poem "Mossbawn: Sunlight," where love is

> like a tinsmith's scoop,
> sunk past its gleam
> in the meal-bin.
>
> (*N*, 9)

What makes the image and the poem radiate (radiant) is the light that is no longer visible, and through this imagined, lost "gleam" Heaney takes account of a feeling. A parallel movement occurs in later poems where he tries to get at the source of his unease. I would like to think about how this happens in "In Iowa," a poem that deepens for me, like the snow it describes, every time I read it:

In Iowa once, among the Mennonites
In a slathering blizzard, conveyed all afternoon
Through sleet-glit pelting hard against the windscreen
And a wiper's strong absolving slumps and flits,

I saw, abandoned in the open gap
Of a field where wilted corn stalks flagged the snow,
A mowing machine. Snow brimmed its iron seat,
Heaped each spoked wheel with a thick white brow

And took the shine off oil in the black-toothed gears.
Verily I came forth from that wilderness
As one unbaptized who had known darkness
At the third hour and the veil in tatters.

In Iowa once. In the slush and rush and hiss
Not of parted but as of rising waters.

                                        (*DC*, 52)

We imagine Heaney driving back from a poetry reading in Iowa City
in unrelenting weather. As we all know, driving in a storm is anxiety-
making. Heaney, ever attentive at the level of the image, looks through
his windshield, under assault from hail and sleet, and sees the figure of a
mowing machine. The snow that has begun to obscure it makes it into
something other. Its otherness leads him to reach past what he sees to
what he knows is there, an imagined and unseen "shine," which the
white covering has removed from the "black-toothed gears." For a mo-
ment, like the speaker, we imagine the white against the black, frozen
water against oil, which then leads us to think about the separation of
things, for instance, like the sprinkling of holy water and the anointing
of holy oil, restoratives. The small detail that catches his attention here,
the oil covered by snow, feeds into a burgeoning sense of dread.

    The image of the shining oil-covered gears covered by snow trig-
gers a feeling in him that he wants to get to the source of. The image
finds an echo of sorts in the wipers that try to clear the windscreen by
parting the sleet and snow and muck, as the flood waters fail to part but

instead would cover the dirty and sinful earth. The sonnet, at its turn, grows dark, and the poem becomes one of foreboding, without reassurance of redemption. How is it that he gets so much out of the image of a shine that can no longer be seen? Unlike "Mossbawn: Sunlight," this lost light brings no memory of love. What it erupts into is apprehension; his experience of such disquiet cannot help but be charged by his familiarity with the history of religion, with sectarian and historical violence, and he also knows that such things rarely end well. The wipers' "absolving slumps and fits" make us think of a priest's equally mechanical arm, forgiving sins. When the elements are fierce, wipers rarely do what they need to, and in fact, they can sometimes make vision worse. They attempt to clean but never can, like a gesture of absolution. The sonnet moves from storm to apocalyptic vision. The image affects his thinking and feeling, his attention goes to this process, and he tries to work it out formally in the sonnet. Structurally, "In Iowa" promises what is expected. Divided into three quatrains and a closing couplet, the poem in outward form is a Shakespearean sonnet, but the rhyme pattern suggests an Italian or Petrarchan sonnet in the first and third quatrains: *abba cded fggf hh*. The outward structure, however, belies the irresolution of the content.

What guides the movement of the sestet (the aftermath of the image) is never fully resolved. The frustration of expectation (don't sonnets try to work things out?) contributes to the power of feeling, the residual unease. Notice also the shift in ground from octave to sestet, from Iowa, land of the Mennonites, to the Middle East, the Promised Land. Here, there is no parting of the Red Sea for Moses's tribe but rather a deluge, and a cleansing that wipes the earth clean of its people.

A similar tracking of emotion in another sonnet in *District and Circle*, "Out of Shot," travels as far in scope and imagining as "In Iowa":

> November morning sunshine on my back
> This bell-clear Sunday, elbows lodged strut-firm
> On the unseasonably warm
> Top bar of a gate, inspecting livestock,
> Catching gleams of the distant Viking *vik*
> Of Wicklow Bay; thinking *scriptorium*,

Norse raids, night-dreads and that "fierce raiders" poem
About storm on the Irish Sea—so no attack
In the small hours or next morning; thinking shock
Out of the blue or blackout, the staggered walk
Of a donkey on the TV news last night—
Loosed from a cart that had loosed five mortar shells
In the bazaar district, wandering out of shot
Lost to its owner, lost for its sunlit hills.

                                                    (*DC*, 15)

The gleam of the "tinsmith's scoop" and the "shine off oil" on gears transmute into the imagined gleam from a word, of "the distant Viking *vik*," set in motion by the shimmering of Wicklow Bay on a sunny day. In each of these poems, an image begins a series of associations, all connected to a growing apprehensiveness. This "age of anxiety" arises from the impact of external violence, which is no longer confined to his island or to history books; the violence now rains down from the air, and it can happen anywhere, a "shock / Out of the blue."[1] *District and Circle*, written in the wake of 9/11 and the invasion of Iraq and Afghanistan, cannot shake this feeling. Heaney conveys this sense of ominousness in poems that wear as their husks a form that traditionally offers resolution, making the contrast that much greater between what cannot be solved and a form that superficially suggests it can be.

"Out of Shot" begins not in a snowstorm or in Iowa but in County Wicklow, the sun warming both the speaker's back and the "top bar of a gate" as he inspects livestock. He tracks his physical sensations and thoughts to get at why he feels unsettled when for other reasons in this moment he might be perfectly content. The light this time comes from a word in the past connected to the present glimmer of the water, the *vik* or *wic* of Viking in Wicklow Bay.[2] The shift in thought to the Vikings then leads him to think of poems about their violent raids on monasteries, and to remember that the monks felt relief when they saw a storm on the way—the storm offering reprieve from attack, the shock of an attack on a clear day, "out of the blue." This then calls forth what he saw on TV the night before, "the staggered walk / Of a donkey," "Loosed from a cart that had loosed five mortar shells" planted by insurgents, in a busy pedestrian area in Iraq. The donkey is shell-shocked and bewildered from the explosions. The poem begins in a deliberation on an image, and that deliberation leads to a groundswell of association, not into a clearing but to confusion and sadness. By the poem's end, Heaney is rather like the donkey, struggling to get his bearings. As "In Iowa," the sonnet leaves us in a much less settled place than where it began.

Note that a semblance of a Petrarchan rhyme scheme appears in "Out of Shot" in the octave: *abba abba* (*rima baciata*). Heaney then loosens or slackens the sonnet's rhyme scheme; the Petrarchan tightness gives over to what might initially seem a random sequence, but which actually sounds deliberate, with several of its concluding phonemes (k-k-k-k) sounding like a child's imitation of machine-gun fire. Gerard Manley Hopkins thought that by running the "rhymes of the octet into the sestet a downright prolapsus or hernia takes place, and the sonnet is crippled for life" (Abbott [1935] 1972, 35); one could argue that a kind of disabling takes place in "Out of Shot."[3]

The dislocation described at the poem's close significantly finds complement in the most notable rhyming pairs, which meet each other not at the lines' ends but at the beginnings or in midline:

> Loosed from a cart that had loosed five mortar shells
> In the bazaar district, wandering out of shot
> Lost to its owner, lost for its sunlit hills.
>
> (*DC*, 15)

Heaney insists upon our noticing the double-ness of "loosed" and "lost" and the allusion to Yeats's 1921 "The Second Coming" rings out, "bell-clear": "Mere anarchy is loosed upon the world, / The blood-dimmed tide is loosed, and everywhere / The ceremony of innocence is drowned" (Yeats 1965, 186).[4] Heaney intends to evoke Yeats's poem with its invocation of Bethlehem, the other location of a donkey in the Jesus story. "The Second Coming" ends in the oracular question, one that could as easily be posed today, as the TV news reports more and more unleashed aggression: "what rough beast, its hour come round at last, / Slouches towards Bethlehem to be born?" Once again, "passionate intensity" is being mistaken for wisdom. Wars on terror, after all, are never really "new."[5] Heaney's "Out of Shot" leaves us with the sense of something being dangerously out of balance, not entirely unlike the cryptic close of Yeats's "The Second Coming."

Yeats's structuring devices are perhaps not far from mind in "A Shiver," the second poem in the volume, which describes on the surface the force with which an unnamed figure (a laborer? Heaney's father?) uses a sledgehammer. The question mark at poem's end shifts the sonnet away from any expectation of resolution; it also recalls the question mark at the close of "Leda and the Swan," another poem about force. Both question what good can come from force ("Did she put on his knowledge with his power / Before the indifferent beak could let her drop?"). Here is "A Shiver":

> The way you had to stand to swing the ledge,
> Your two knees locked, your lower back shock-fast
> As shields in a *testudo*, spine and waist
> A pivot for the tight-braced, tilting rib-cage;
> The way its iron head planted the sledge
> Unyieldingly as a club-footed last;
> The way you had to heft and then half rest
> Its gathered force like a long-nursed rage
> About to be let fly: does it do you good
> To have known it in your bones, directable,
> Withholdable at will,
> A first blow that could make air of a wall,
> A last one so unanswerably landed
> The staked earth quailed and shivered in the handle?
>
> (*DC*, 5)

The question mark takes the inwardness of a sonnet and pushes it awkwardly outward, as if toward a listening audience. The privacy of the sonnet has been reconfigured. Who is this "you," we wonder? Anyone who experiences the physical and psychological effects of force? Both "A Shiver" and "Leda and the Swan" have at their center a kind of violence, and both puzzle over the consequence. The punctuation weakens any sense of resolution toward which the form itself aims.

As in "Out of Shot," a Petrarchan rhyme scheme haunts this poem, and in a traditional Petrarchan sonnet the octave and sestet often find complement in contraction and release of the muscular system. The one builds up pressure, the other releases it. The physical release narrated in "A Shiver," however, is not necessarily liberating. The only line that ends with a verb appears midpoem: "rest." Arrested motion is what a poem is, like a bronze sculpture of a warrior from the Greco-Roman era. The martial comparison might be apt; in describing the user's stance, his "locked" knees, Heaney refers to the *testudo* (Latin for "tortoise"), the formation used by Roman legions during battles, where the men would close up all gaps between each other and grab their shields at the sides. The image resonates. The word that closes the octave, "rage," rhymes perfectly with "cage" (line 4), and although used as a noun here, it quivers with the force of a verb as it enjambs the line and leads to "About to be let fly." Heaney links sounds by repeating the suffix (-able) in "directable" and "Withholdable." As in "Out of Shot," Heaney upsets our acoustic expectations here, reversing the normal ordering. A matching rhyme-partner appears as the first word in the next line rather than as the last.

Unlike the early "Digging," "A Shiver" does not reflect on and celebrate different but companionable forms of labor. ("A Shiver" also seems a clear descendant of Hopkins's description of "Harry Ploughman," who is "all quail to the wallowing o' the plough") (Hopkins 1961, 108). Similar to "Digging," where Heaney describes the pen "as snug as a gun" (*DN*, 13), an intimation of violence occurs. Heaney's poem begins with an observation about the impact of a sledgehammer against a stake, but it becomes a meditation on the exertion rather than the keeping in check of will. In any case, the end result is an earth that quails and shivers (enacted in the form of these jarring poems).

The sonnet forms in *District and Circle* act as membranes between the poet and the external world. The form is where he tries to work things out. However, the poems intimate that the sonnet closes too soon for the scope of the subject matter. There is something potentially too tidy about the form, too jewel-like in its perfection, in its insistence on resolution and completion. Having worked in the form for so many years, Heaney realizes its limitations; the sonnet is too complete and, at the same time, given the subject matter he tries to contain in it, leaves us with a feeling of incompletion. The force and briskness of earlier sonnet endings—"Where small buds shoot and flourish in the gap" (*FW*, 37)—is no more. The more recent poems end in incomplete or run-on sentences, in questions, as if even grammar cannot withstand the weight of present dysfunction. However, Heaney often leaves the ending couplets of many of these sonnets intact, but intact with sounds that jar or fall dissonant on the ear. To complement the interior discomfort the poems attend to, he upsets our rhyming expectations. Sound and not structure becomes an echo of the sense.

Take *District and Circle*'s third poem, "Polish Sleepers," for instance. It was first published in the *New Yorker* in 2005 and was revised substantially for the book publication. The original published version of the poem reads:

When they'd been block-built crisscross and four-squared
We lived with them and breathed pure creosote
Until they were laid and landscaped in a curb,
A molded verge, half-skirting, half-stockade,
Soon fringed with hardy groundcover and grass.
But as that bulwark bleached in sun and rain
Our gravel darkened and a tarry pus,
Imagined yet pervasive, reeked and ran
Like the breathing, bleeding bad in Dante's wood,
Unsettling, bearing forward into the garden
What I couldn't hear in the forties when I lay
Listening for what might come down the line . . .
Each deadlit, boarded, languid, clanking wagon.
And afterwards, *rust, thistle, silence, sky.*

(Heaney 2005b, 79)

The sonnet, a fortress in itself, turns on the idea of fortification. However, the "bulwark" made of railroad ties from Poland brings with it a dark history. Thinking about the railroad ties and where they come from leads Heaney first to the self-murderers turned into trees of Dante's *Inferno*, another wood that oozes "a tarry pus," and then to the cattle cars full of families, heading to their final destination. Glanced at here also is the poet's childhood, as he was "listening for" coming trains, ignorant of the unmitigated violence across the water.

For publication in the volume, Heaney relieves the poem of some of its direct associations:

> Once they'd been block-built criss-cross and four-squared
> We lived with them and breathed pure creosote
> Until they were laid and landscaped in a kerb,
> A moulded verge, half-skirting, half-stockade,
> Soon fringed with hardy ground-cover and grass.
> But as that bulwark bleached in sun and rain
> And the washed gravel pathway showed no stain,
> Under its parched riverbed
> Flinch and crunch I imagined tarry pus
> Accruing, bearing forward to the garden
> Wafts of what conspired when I'd lie
> Listening for the goods from Castledawson . . .
> Each languid, clinking wagon,
> And afterwards, *rust, thistle, silence, sky*.
>
> $\qquad\qquad\qquad\qquad\qquad\qquad$ (*DC*, 6)

Both versions attend to the way that historical violence bleeds into the present. In the final version, the "pus" is still "imagined" but Dante's suicides have been removed. Even the fortress of the sonnet can contain only so many complex and vast griefs. What changes cosmetically between versions is the first syllable from "When" to "Once," the hyphenation of some words, and the anglicizing of others. The first six lines are essentially the same, as is the final line. However, the next seven abandon direct references. The railroad ties sleep, but not quietly. In them are submerged memories of rage, now just something verged on, not quite manifest.

The visible structure of a sonnet has itself been a triggering image for Heaney for decades. Of other sonnets, each sonnet is in some respects a reflection—reflection in the physical sense of returning an image or energy, turning it back, and in the sense of mental or spoken thinking on a subject. Heaney's early sequence of the Glanmore Sonnets from *Field Work* (1975) converses consciously with tradition. Written in the wake of reading Robert Lowell's *Notebook*, these poems were quietly aware of the collection of blank verse by Heaney's American elder. Asked by Dennis O'Driscoll if the later Lowell sonnets influenced his own Glanmore sequence, Heaney responded: "Not that I'm aware of. I remember sending some of them to him after we'd spent time at the Kilkenny Arts Week in the summer of 1975. I was very conscious of how correctly iambic [my poems] were in comparison to his own much lumpier ingots, and indeed he implied in a letter to me that they could do with a bit of knocking about, but I was delighted when he said of them in general that they 'seemed to have come through a grief'" (*SS*, 216). Heaney did not immediately take Lowell up on this "bit of knocking about." Only decades later do we find sonnets such as "Out of Shot," "In Iowa," and "A Shiver," where the "correctly iambic" gives over to the crafting of verbal structures that do not sound much like sonnets, even though two-thirds of the poems in *District and Circle* are fourteen-liners. These "lumpier ingots" of Heaney's are a long way from the goldsmith soldering and other arts of his earlier sequences.

Heaney's memory of Lowell's comments reveals his awareness of the formal limitations of the structures he was working in, forms that could be too "correct" and needed "a bit of knocking about." In the correspondence between Heaney and Lowell about the Glanmore sonnets, from a letter of September 1975, Lowell's response was:

> I've read the sonnets a good many times. Two that I like best are "The Train" and "A Drink of Water." . . . Sonnets seem in two ways perhaps the wrong form for your sequence. First the somewhat too full-dress, particularly the final couplet; then the whole sequence makes me think of Wordsworth, and that something that goes so well should have gone even farther. At worst, you should [be] able to mine many poems out of your many strong lines—perhaps in quatrains, or more drastic changes. I've been so long netted in my own unrhymed sonnets that I'm no judge. (S. Hamilton 2005, 641–42)

Lowell noticed a feeling of incompleteness: "Something that goes so well should have gone even farther." The "too full-dress" of the sonnet did not seem like the right armor for Heaney's poems. Lowell did not, however, see the sequence in its entirety—the final collection of ten poems that immediately follows an "Elegy" to Lowell in *Field Work*. Fortunately, Heaney (as Christopher Benfey has pointed out) followed "Lowell's example rather than his advice" (2008, 129).

What happens to the sonnet form in *Human Chain*? What happens to the play of thought ignited by an image? Much has already been written about these poems by a number of good critics, some of whom focus heavily on the references to Aeneas's meeting of his father in the Virgilian afterlife. And this revisitation of family connectedness and sentiment powerfully informs *Human Chain*. Minute attention to an image followed by a tracing of feeling, and a wish to somehow get at the source of the feeling, continue here. The poems resonate with the unsaid, as ever, and the sounds are rich and varied. However, there are no visible sonnets. The poem that sets the volume in motion, "Had I not been awake," is charged by a specific if not concrete image:

Had I not been awake I would have missed it,
A wind that rose and whirled until the roof
Pattered with quick leaves off the sycamore

And got me up, the whole of me a-patter,
Alive and ticking like an electric fence:
Had I not been awake I would have missed it,

It came and went so unexpectedly
And almost it seemed dangerously,
Returning like an animal to the house,

A courier blast that there and then
Lapsed ordinary. But not ever
After. And not now.

(*HC*, 3)

The dread that accrues in *District and Circle* finds a way into these poems too. This time, the "wind" brings it, and it is a wind he would not have

noticed if he had "not been awake." Heaney's keen awareness of felt
sensations (and one imagines, the relief in still having them) leads him
to think of the afterlife of the stroke and the gust of wind. The imagi-
nation reshapes things as omens, just like the neighbor who spied the
"blackbird" before his little brother was killed many years ago: "I never
liked yon bird." The suddenness of the wind's arrival, its hasty departure,
brings foreboding into the poem. Notice how the attention in the poem
moves from "wind" to "leaves" on the roof to his body's alertness. Next
we get the image of an animal returning to the house (to find what?
him?), and then, spookily, the images cease. The syntax becomes choppy;
the future is intimated, and although it is unspecific we sense it is not
good. The wind has borne a message, a "courier blast" that quickly
"Lapsed ordinary"; but the poet's awareness and way of experiencing the
suddenness of the wind, of a shock "out of the blue," has changed things
utterly. There is no return to the ordinary in this sense. Notice how the
poem is twelve lines long, written in tercets, but with no suggestion of
closure. As Heaney leaves behind the room of the sonnet, we wonder
what will come next, if he will return. The door is left ajar, as it were.

The sudden sense of departure and its aftereffects recurs in the
third-to-last poem, which has at its center a door. The image of the door
sets off a chain of associations (and maybe these associations are another
kind of human chain, one that connects us to each other) in Heaney and
in the reader familiar with his work. The title, "The Door Was Open
and the House Was Dark," immediately brings to mind the title poem
for Heaney's second book, *Door into the Dark* (from the sonnet "The
Forge," "All I know is a door into the dark"; *DD*, 19). The childhood
fearfulness and amazement in "The Forge" have given over to a sorrow
and a silence. The poem is dedicated "In Memory of David Hammond":

> The door was open and the house was dark
> Wherefore I called his name, although I knew
> The answer this time would be silence
>
> That kept me standing listening while it grew
> Backwards and down and out into the street
> Where as I'd entered (I remember now)

The streetlamps too were out.
I felt, for the first time there and then, a stranger.
Intruder almost, wanting to take flight

Yet well aware that here there was no danger,
Only withdrawal, a not unwelcoming
Emptiness, as in a midnight hangar

On an overgrown airfield in late summer.

(HC, 82)

The silence that keeps him "standing listening" also "grew / Backwards and down and out into the street," and the silence triggers memory.[6] He feels like "a stranger. / Intruder almost, wanting to take flight" from the house of his friend. Like the wind in the opening poem, he wants to take flight, and we suspect that what he instinctually moves away from is the presence of death. The hand of Heaney's friend, David Hammond (with whom he and Michael Longley toured Northern Ireland in 1968, to perform "Room to Rhyme"), can "be clasp'd no more."

Like others in *Human Chain*, the poem is divided into tercets. It draws, however, on a (faint) traditional sonnet rhyme scheme, then falls short one line: *abcb ded fgfh ii*. If I had to plot which line of the fourteen had been omitted I would say it was line 7 or 8. The poem closes with a rhyming couplet, the two lines split from each other by a white space. Heaney uses exact rhyme and off-rhyme to create, as he says elsewhere, "the virtue of a slight dissonance." The first six lines are heroic. The first two are steadily iambic (and the last six lines are more or less ten syllables too). Line 7, however, extends only to six syllables, and it is here where I believe a kind of turn takes place, a shifting of the weight: the streetlamps too were out.

The poem is clearly not a sonnet, but I would suggest that the sonnet is the ground against which it can best be seen. Not only does the poem register the silence that falls after the singer's death; it is also a kind of elegy for Heaney's relationship with the form. If the sonnet is a mirror into the self, perhaps the mirror has grown dark, or he no longer looks into it for light. The second half of the poem begins conceptually with "I felt, for the first time there and then, a stranger." His experience with the form he has been working in for decades is no longer familiar; the form no longer suffices.[7]

In a review of *Human Chain*, Colm Tóibín (2010) suggests that "the verse structure Heaney seems most at home with here is the one most used in *Seeing Things*: it contains four stanzas of three lines per stanza, a sonnet without the couplet. This system offers a sort of looseness, a buoyancy, a refusal to close and conclude; it means that the endings of these poems can have a particular pathos, a holding of the breath." Outward form does not necessarily reflect inner. In subtle ways, "The Door Was Open and the House Was Dark" echoes (or reflects) moments from other Heaney sonnets. The emptiness and openness described at the close:

> Only withdrawal, a not unwelcoming
> Emptiness, as in a midnight hangar
>
> On an overgrown airfield in late summer
> (*HC*, 82)

are reminiscent of the end of the "Clearances" sonnet sequence when he writes of his "coeval / Chestnut from a jam jar in a hole,"

> Its heft and hush become a bright nowhere,
> A soul ramifying and forever
> Silent, beyond silence listened for.
> (*HL*, 24–33)[8]

We know that for Heaney silence is a generative space, as is the act of listening into it.[9]

So does the sonnet have a silent presence in *Human Chain*? In some of the poems, there is a gleam of the resilient form, which is suggestive rather than substantial, like the scoop "sunk past its gleam / in the meal-bin" or the imagined shine of the oil on gears now covered by snow. Heaney uses full stops only twice in "The Door Was Open"—once at the close of line 7 and again at the end.[10] Heaney finds a way to have a dramatic pause midline that is not marked by punctuation. We see this in lines 4 and 6—in "That kept me standing listening while it grew." The phrase "standing listening" is akin to a compound verb; the *–ing* participles, not divided by a conjunction, link the two as if they described one activity. In the sixth line—"Where as I'd entered (I remember now)"— he uses the parenthetical to create a modulation in tone, an aside, to give pause—which is a different way to give pause than by using a graphic mark like a comma. We are prepared for the pause by the slight hesitation we encounter when we move our eyes to the next line and read "Where as" (two distinct words) instead of "whereas," which we might have anticipated given the appearance of "Wherefore" a few lines earlier. As John Lennard (1991, 98) points out in his book *But I Digress: The Exploitation of Parentheses in English Printed Verse*, there is something mirrorlike about the image of the two parentheses. The act of reflection is contained within graphic marks that look as if they reflect each other. Are these small acts of mirroring a way of reimagining the work a sonnet traditionally performed, that of self-reflection?

As this recollection comes over him, the poem experiences a turn. The pace starts to slow, and the closing image is of the "midnight hangar" in "an overgrown airfield," where once there was activity: landings and takings-off. The phrase "(I remember now)" acts as a hinge for the poem, a recalling of once seen images. The "streetlamps too were out" introduces another kind of remembered or imagined light, whose shine cannot be seen. Somehow, the presence of the imagined light hovers around this poem, just as some elements of the sonnet seem to.

"The Baler," a poem of twenty-four lines on page 24 of *Human Chain*, also calls directly on memory, on reflection. "The Baler" returns us to the image of farm machinery and the idea of making bales, objects that are temporal, easy to dismantle, quick to disintegrate. At the same time, the baler gathers from the earth what is fertile and forces it into a structure, cylindrical or rectangular in shape. Sound, textures, light, farm implements, art, good friends, the realization that the end is drawing near—"The Baler" reflects on all these aspects. In addition, the image of farm machinery once again generates the thinking. The poem is clearly not a sonnet, but it does follow what might be called sonnet thought. Just as sound (or silence) features prominently in the Hammond elegy, so too do sounds (and the memories they mirror) collect and emerge as a chief concern of "The Baler":

> All day the clunk of a baler
> Ongoing, cardiac-dull,
> So taken for granted
>
> It was evening before I came to
> To what I was hearing
> And missing: summer's richest hours
>
> As they had been to begin with,
> Fork-lifted, sweated-through
> And nearly rewarded enough
>
> By the giddied-up race of a tractor
> At the end of the day
> Last-lapping a hayfield.
>
> But what I also remembered
> As woodpigeons sued at the edge
> Of thirty gleaned acres
>
> And I stood inhaling the cool
> In a dusk eldorado
> Of mighty cylindrical bales
>
> Was Derek Hill's saying,
> The last time he sat at our table,
> He could bear no longer to watch
>
> The sun going down
> And asking please to be put
> With his back to the window.
>
> (*HC*, 24–25)

The lines vary in length from five to ten syllables ("The sun going down" is the shortest line, reflecting the shortening of day and the life of his friend). The first four stanzas are a Heaney-like version of the closing stanza in "To Autumn." The sounds of the season bring on an awareness of the ephemerality of things. Just as Keats asked, what kind of music is appropriate for the dying season, and by extension for one who is dying young, so too does Heaney ask, what kind of music is appropriate for me ("thou hast thy music too"), thinking how close he might be to life's end? What kind of form?

Instead of the images of autumn that set Keats's thought in motion, and later, the bleating of lambs and the wailful choir of gnats as his ear rather than his eye attends, we have the cardiac-like clunk of the baling machine and the whir of a tractor—farm machinery rather than Keats's description of nature overbrimming. This focus on the machinery of harvest, along with the mention of "cardiac-dull," heightens awareness of the fragility of the human machine itself.

Although no deliberate rhyming patterns appear in "The Baler," there is a quiet weaving together of sounds: "clunk" gives over to "cardiac," the softly fricative "fork-lifted,"[11] the "last-lapping" of a tractor, assonance in line sixteen's "stood" and "cool," and, at poem's close, "please to be put." The sounds of the words themselves have less resonance than the memory of sounds that the clunk of the baler inspires. Even the phrase about the "woodpigeons" suing at the edge of thirty gleaned acres is a memory of their cooing before it becomes a memory of their courting (and in "sueing" I hear Keats's "rosy hue").

In this poem there are no swallows twittering but "woodpigeons" sueing (courting, wooing). Unlike "To Autumn," however, which begins with what autumn looks like and closes with its sounds, "The Baler" provides an almost mirror reversal: it opens with sounds and closes with the emphasis on sight. (Here I think of the almost-mirror reversal of "loosed" and "lost" in "Out of Shot.") The golden fields at dusk ("dusk eldorado") recall the painter Derek Hill's remark that he would rather not see them and be reminded of what he is about to lose, or where he is about to go: through a door into the dark.[12]

In both poems, the speaker reckons with a moment of heightened consciousness, when awareness dawns. In "The Baler," the speaker "came to / to what he was hearing"; he creates a mirror image in the enjambing of lines 4 and 5: "Came to / To what I was hearing"—but neither the sense nor the sounds—the stress pattern—are the same. Recall how in "The Door Was Open" his awareness grows as he is "standing listening" (and again in "Polish Sleepers" when he recalls "listening for" what was coming down the line).

When we listen, we are as aware of what we do not hear as of what we hear. In a BBC 4 radio talk, "Young and Old," Christopher Ricks discusses Shakespeare's sonnet 73 and its relationship to Keats's "To Autumn." "To Autumn" calls upon spring and summer but never mentions winter; it only intimates its coming. Ricks (2010) says that sonnet 73 "does not say 'old' or 'age' not because it is a dramatization of being in denial but because one does well to look at the eclipse of one's hopes—or at any rate, some of them—out of the corner of one's eye or though smoked glass or the help of a mirror of some kind. We have art that we may not perish over the truth."[13] In Heaney's elegiac poems, every figure of speech reveals or half-conceals the truth within. Neither "The Door Was Open" nor "The Baler" mentions Heaney's recent scrape with fate (as recounted in other poems in the volume: "Chanson d'Aventure," "Miracle," "Human Chain"); yet this experience is very present here, seen through "the help of a mirror" of some kind (which is the poem).

Ricks speaks elsewhere of the sonnet's "stoic acknowledgment and elegant armor." Heaney avoids, as Lowell recommended, "the somewhat too full-dress" of the sonnet in this last volume, but he manages to retain a quiet acceptance of what it is, in lighter formal garments. The visible ambition of the sonnet is left behind in these poems, but its impression remains, even if it is only on the inner eye, so to speak. The seeking of resolution, the finding of a form to express or contain the broad scope of a grief, is not as much of a concern, we suspect. At the same time, we are newly haunted by what else Lowell said, namely that Heaney certainly seems "to have come through a grief."

The "Door Was Open" and "The Baler" record the act of coming-to, and in this they mirror each other, an act to which he will perforce return, trying to stave off a return of what "came and went so unexpectedly," a stroke, but not of luck. Last, something must be said of the remarkable image that closes "The Door Was Open and the House Was

Dark," an image that lingers as much as the unseen gleam with which we began:

> Only withdrawal, a not unwelcoming
> Emptiness, as in a midnight hangar
> On an overgrown airfield in late summer.
>
> (*HC*, 82)

The "not unwelcoming emptiness" has a presence granted to it through the comparison to "a midnight hangar / On an overgrown airfield in late summer." Why is the emptiness "not unwelcoming"? Because within the confines of the form, now silent, there linger memories of activity, of construction, of a kind of home. And the hangar itself is surrounded by a fertile world, the tall grasses of late summer, untouched by mowing machine. The "overgrown airfield" also contrasts with the usual trimness of a sonnet, its stereotypical tidying couplet. The last two lines rhyme, but they are divided by a white space. Both "The Door Was Open" and "The Baler" close with images of endings, setting suns, late summer. Life's experience brims over the bounds of the sonnet, the edges of the meal-bin, just as the grass in the airfield will eventually obscure from view what Paul Keegan calls the tiny landing strip of the poem.

NOTES

1. In a 2006 National Public Radio interview, Heaney commented that what distinguished the *District and Circle* poems from earlier ones was the fact that we live in "a new age of anxiety," echoing Auden's 1948 baroque eclogue about life during wartime.

2. See the etymology of Viking n. in the *Oxford English Dictionary*.

3. I have written at length about "Out of Shot" elsewhere (Tyler 2008).

4. Yeats (1983, 187). Heaney's sonnet also reminds me of Wordsworth's "Sonnet in the Pass of Killicranky, an Invasion Being Expected, October 1803" ("Like a whirlwind came / The Highlanders, the slaughter spread like flame"), and his "October, 1803" closes with "I tremble at the sorrow of the time" (Wordsworth 1994, 175–76).

5. I think it is worth mentioning that the words *loosed* and *lost* also appear in the King James version of Matthew, in a passage that concerns, among other

things, the teaching and practice of forgiveness on earth. In Matthew 18:16, Peter asks Jesus: "How oft shall my brother sin against me, and I forgive him? till seven times? Jesus saith unto him, I say not unto thee, Until seven times: but, Until seventy times seven." Later, Matthew 18:27 reads, "Then the lord of that servant was moved with compassion, and loosed him, and forgave him the debt." While *loosed* suggests emancipation in Matthew, the word harbors, as it were, a darker kind of freedom in the poems by Yeats and Heaney.

6. As others have noted, the door opens onto literary memory as well, to the haunting lines of Tennyson's *In Memoriam A.H.H.* (section 7; Tennyson 1901, 12):

> Dark house, by which once more I stand
> Here in the long unlovely street,
> Doors, where my heart was used to beat
> So quickly, waiting for a hand,
>
> A hand that can be clasp'd no more—

7. Heaney composed approximately sixty-eight sonnets over his lifetime.

8. The final sonnet, 8, of "Clearances," has a Shakespearean rhyme scheme in the octave and something akin to a Petrarchan in the sestet: *abab cdcd eee ggg*.

9. The "heft and hush" of the final "Clearances" sonnet return us to—or reflect—the "Glanmore Sonnets," "where small buds shoot and flourish in the hush."

10. This is a familiar move for Heaney, who in the past has criss-crossed the traditional gestures of a sonnet by breaking it clean in two, 7 and 7 instead of 8 and 6, or instead of 4 and 4 and 4 and 2.

11. "Forklifted" appears ten pages earlier in "Chanson d'Aventure" as Heaney describes himself being placed in the ambulance after the stroke: "Strapped on, wheeled out, forklifted, locked / In position for the drive."

12. The remark is cited in the poem itself, *The Baler*: "And asking please to be put / With his back to the window" (*HC*, 24).

13. Ricks is quoting Nietzsche: "We have art so that we may not perish of the truth."

PART THREE

Translation and
Transnational Poetics

I lift my eyes in a light-headed credo,
Discovering what survives translation true.
　　　　—Seamus Heaney, "Remembered Columns"

CHAPTER SEVEN

"Renewed, Transfigured, in Another Pattern"

Metaphor and Displacement in Seamus Heaney's *Human Chain*

Michael Parker

> The serious writer of verse must be prepared to cross himself with the best verse of other languages and the best prose of all languages.
> —T. S. Eliot, "A Review of *Georgian Poetry, 1916–17*"

> The purpose of poetry is to remind us
> how difficult it is to remain just one person,
> for our house is open, there are no keys in the doors,
> and invisible guests come in and out at will.
> —Czesław Miłosz, "Ars Poetica?"

In the opening paragraph of his study into Northern Irish poets and their relationship with other literatures, Rui Carvalho Homem points out how the terms *translation* and *metaphor* have frequently been viewed as closely aligned, not least because "their respective etymologies, Latin and Greek . . . lend them a common meaning of 'displacement' or 'transport'" (2009, 1). Translation has been a staple feature of Seamus Heaney's literary activity for almost four decades, since he recognized early the value of reading and displacing himself in other cultures as a means of self-renewal, of enriching and extending the reach of his own compositions.[1] Each Heaney collection since *North* (1975) has included at least one translated poem, and from the late 1980s onward the poet regularly produced versions of longer and even whole works, reflecting the diversity of historical periods and cultures attracting his attention. Some, like *The Cure at Troy* (1990) and *The Burial at Thebes* (2004), were the result of specific commissions; others, like the Ovid and Merriman translations in *The Midnight Verdict* (1993), Jan Kochanowski's *Laments* (1995), *Beowulf* (1999), Leoš Janáček's *The Diary of One Who Vanished* (1999), an unpublished rendering of Virgil's *Aeneid*, book 6 (2007), and Robert Henryson's *The Testament of Cresseid* (2009), were undertaken at the behest of particular individuals or simply from an impulse of delight.[2]

Conscious that translation can only aspire to offering "a various, differentiated living equivalent to the original" (Constantine 1999, 14), Heaney varies considerably in his practice, as my analysis of four poems from *Human Chain* sets out to show. At times he keeps close to the "foreign" text, though even then he is inclined to "Derrycize" the original by, for example, altering the locations and metaphors. Thus Eugene Guillevic's references to the Brittany coast are edited out from Heaney's version of "Herbiers de Bretagne," and he shifts the setting of Giovanni Pascoli's "L'aquilone" from Urbino to Anahorish. On other occasions, as can be seen in the "Route 110" sequence, he departs radically from the source text, riffing on themes, images, and motifs from Virgil's *Aeneid*, book 6, making his own music by engaging in what Roger Garfitt has termed "the appreciative plunder" (1979, 2) to which poets often resort. Such readings—or "misreadings," as Harold Bloom has it (1973, 29–30)[3]—spark "an imaginative ignition, a release of new energy in an independent creation" (Garfitt 1979, 2).

Rereading *Human Chain*, one is forcibly struck by the skill with which Heaney has orchestrated and structured the volume, the generosity with which he embraces forebears and contemporaries in life, literature, and fine art. Whereas its opening movement frequently summons formative presences from English tradition, dominating its central and closing sections are translations—in the broadest sense—from French and Latin, Irish and Italian, which reflect the capaciousness of his cultural vision.

Occupying nine pages midway through the volume, "A Herbal," a rendering of Eugene Guillevic's "Herbier de Bretagne," allows Heaney's persona to train his poetic eye at what thrives at ground level and below ground.[4] Hardly surprisingly, given its roots in another time and culture, it differs significantly in form from *Human Chain*'s other lyrics. Yet while its component elements—the nineteen sections, stanzas, and lines—fluctuate in length, its concerns relate closely to those running throughout the volume. Weighed in the balance against the irrepressible natural world is frail humanity, all too conscious of its uncertain place on earth.

Vegetation's mastery is established from the outset of "A Herbal," underscored by the strategic placing of and stress in the initial adverb, the sole adjective, and the two verbs:

Everywhere plants
Flourish among graves,

Sinking their roots
In *all* the dynasties
Of the dead
    (*HC*, 35; italics mine).

Personification is used to reiterate this superiority, plants being credited with a "lush / Compliant dialect," grass with the ability to articulate their stance on the planet's mutability; their hippie-like advice to us is to "Go with the flow." Beneath this show of acquiescence, the speaker detects a resistant strain, which aligns the plant world with the *human* repressed; shrubs, like broom and gorse, reject any "settlement," while the grass "takes issue" and alternately "sets its face" to and "turns its back" (*HC*, 36) on the wind.

As the sequence unfolds, human subjects come increasingly to the fore. When in poem 8 Heaney refers to "sunlit tarmac," "memories," and "the hearse" (*HC*, 38), it seems probable that he is recalling his own experiences of walking the Wood Road, Bellaghy, to attend family and neighbors' funerals, since these images are entirely absent from the Guillevic. Yet the scene transcends its origins, and the reader is more likely to be left meditating on what "future" the dead are being "borne" toward. Is it simply physical decay or a "crossing" of some kind, "a transition" (Heaney 2009b)? Subsequent lyrics exhibit nature's responsiveness to death. Hearing a funeral bell, "The grass is all a-tremble," while the evergreen broom provides "company" and "sings" (*HC*, 38–39) to those in its midst.

Later sections in "A Herbal" may at first seem naive, but theirs is an innocence, like Blake's, steeped in experience. They explore children's close encounters with their physical environment, how these help shape identity. In contrast to his predecessor in *Death of a Naturalist*, for whom blackberries possessed a Eucharistic sweetness, the persona here insists on their primal taste, their origin in earth and stone: "There was slate / In the blackberries, / A slatey sap" (*HC*, 39).[5] After the fruit, the fall. Anxieties perturb the growing consciousness, with the realization that "Malignant things" exist, such as rats, nettles, unkind people. In Guillevic's poem, the threats are far more dramatic; he refers to vipers, rather than rats, "awaiting us," and bramble bushes that "Déchiraient les yeux" (tear at the eyes; Guillevic 1979, 203). Heaney's evocation of the child's exaggerated but very real dread quickens the readers' own recollections of when they too were at their most vulnerable. This only abates with the discovery of remedies at hand, how dock leaves neutralize "vicious stings" and how crushing an herb "between your palms" releases a balm enabling you to breathe again. Here, as in the four preceding lyrics, Heaney deploys second-person pronouns to increase our identification with the speaker.[6]

This strategy features for the last time in section 17, which adopts at its opening an informal, conversational style. Once more alliteration ("j," "n," "b," "t," "ð," "ʒ," "k"), and assonance ("ɪ," "ə," "u") are used effectively:

If you know a b*i*t
*A*bout the un*i*verse

It's because *you*'ve taken *it in*
Like that.

> (*HC*, 42)

Understanding the world necessitates intense scrutiny and self-scrutiny, facing up to the dark recesses within the earth and self, "the rat hole" masked by "vetch and dock," as Heaney has it. His imagery again diverges sharply from Guillevic's, which urges us rather to look closely "into the rock / into the unknown plant / that pushed against it" (Guillevic 1979, 210). Where the poets of "Herbier" and "A Herbal" are as one, however, is in their emphasis on the necessity of getting down, literally and metaphorically, to earth level. Where the French poet speaks of laying your cheek "on the lichen," his Irish *confère* proffers the more awkward, less comfortable option of resting one's head "Against the rush clump" (*HC*, 42).

In creating his own distinctively poignant ending, Heaney shifts Guillevic's litany to the flowers of his native region, reinstalling it as a prelude to his final section. A childhood spent between contrasting phenomena ("clear blue and cloud," "haystack and sunset sky," "oak tree and slated roof") is lauded for the diversity of experience it afforded. Foundational to their sense of identity, each poet's lost, first locale maintains an existence in memory, serves as a verifying source:

> I was there
> Me in place and the place in me.
>> (*HC*, 43)

> J'existais. J'étais là.
> Je servais de lieu.
>> (Guillevic 1979, 209)

That this originary state of total integration might be regained in some future location is posited in the closing couplets. In imagining such an "elsewhere," Heaney's narrator dismisses flat, manmade texts like maps and atlases that seek to represent vastness. Instead he conceives of an intimate, small-scale, fertile space, where "all is woven into / And of itself," like a nest (*HC*, 43),[7] like the intricate artifact he has just set before us.

Offspring of his translation of the *Aeneid*, book 6, "The Riverbank Field" and the "Route 110" sequence illustrate a very different species of translation, in which Heaney wryly recreates momentous incidents from his earlier years that mirror episodes in Virgil's epic. First appearing together in a Gallery Press limited edition of 2007 (Heaney 2007b), these lyrics constitute one of *Human Chain*'s most significant acts of commemoration and a further attempt to conjoin, or rather reconcile, the conflicting "voices of my education" (*P*, 35). While in its 2007 manifestation the past, the object of its journeying back, was described as "long since vacated / Yet returnable to" (Heaney 2007b, 23), the absence of these lines from the text in *Human Chain* indicates that Heaney had second thoughts about the viability of that Gatsbyesque claim.

For "The Riverbank Field" and the twelve-part "Route 110," he employs the tercet form favored by Dante, though not his *terza rima*. Self-reflexive elements are much to the fore in the prelude poem, where the poet puts to the proof translation's mediatory potential. That he is engaged in a dialogical exchange across time is apparent from the opening stanza, in which we encounter three participants—a first-person narrator, an unnamed translator, and an initially unidentified writer.[8] Requisitioning phrases and sentences from Virgil and from Loeb, which delineate the appearance and nature of the underworld, Heaney celebrates and elevates names, places, and spirits from his natal terrain. When in line 3 he asserts that he will "confound Lethe in Moyola" (*HC* 46), he invokes two meanings of the verb. In a sense, he is damning the river of oblivion, constructing an intricate verbal device as a stay against the erasure of personal memory that must inevitably come. He "bares the device," signaling how he intends to mix up features from the classical text ("the retired vale," "the sequestered grove," river and riverbank, those "peaceful homes") with ones from "where he started" (Eliot 1970, 197); in so doing, he prepares the ground for "Route 110"'s multiple acts of translation—temporal, spatial, linguistic, intellectual, cultural, psychological, cultural, political.

Though testimony to its author's recurring impulse to perceive "similarity in dissimilars" (Aristotle 1941, 1479), at the same time "The Riverbank Field" alerts us to differences and differentiation.[9] In stanzas 3 and 4, its narrator acknowledges limits to his conceit:

Moths then on evening water
It would have to be, not bees in sunlight,

Midge-veils instead of lily beds.

(*HC*, 46)

Within its opening line, there is a reminder of the instability of literary texts and how they can exist in plural and contested versions. Heaney alludes there to "what Loeb gives as," an acknowledgement of preexisting, established authorities that his translation will not only sit alongside but conceivably contend with; unlike the "virgin grass" mentioned on line 12, he is not unaffected by footprints that have gone before. From line 17 onwards, however, he determines to "continue. . . . In my own words," to set out his own path through the source text. This initial, selective delve into Virgil closes with Anchises's explanation that some human beings spend a thousand years stranded in the afterlife before being permitted "to dwell in flesh and blood" again "under the dome of the sky" (*HC*, 47).[10]

The opening stops on "Route 110" transport readers very much back down to earth. Poems I and II re-create the multifarious, at times unprepossessing sights and smells of Belfast's Smithfield Market, where the poet first acquired a secondhand copy of *Aeneid* book 6 from a stall. Although after a fifty-year lapse the speaker cannot recall the stallholder's face, what survives in the memory is her soiled shopcoat and, in particular, the "marsupial vent" (*HC*, 48) where she keeps her change. Whereas for her the Virgil may be merely a commodity, another sale, for him it is one of the most precious texts in literary history, an access point to other worlds. Poem I's closing stanza conveys vividly the mustiness then and remoteness now of late 1950s Belfast, achieving this effect by coining an ambivalent compound noun ("Dustbreath"), deploying two archaisms ("bestirred," "deckle"), emphasizing how the atmosphere that filled "the cubicle mouth" was—like Virgil's lyrical spirit—something he could not avoid inhaling.

Succeeding poems trace how the speaker negotiates his way from the market to the bus station to pick up the Magherafelt-bound route 110 bus, which will take him back to Bellaghy. To consolidate the Virgilian parallels and enhance the scene's dramatic impact, Gresham Street's

bustling crowds are compared to the throngs Aeneas observes "stream-
ing" toward the Acheron, hoping for a crossing (Virgil 1916, 555, line
305). Subsequently, poem II's depiction of secondhand suits and coats
swaying on racks puts him in mind of spirits "close-packed on Charon's
barge" (*HC*, 49), since most of their former owners are almost certainly
dead. Poem III incorporates and modifies an epic simile from the same
section of Virgil's original, where milling souls are compared to migrat-
ing seabirds.[11] For Heaney, passengers at the bus station resemble "agi-
tated rooks" circling "a rookery" where the inspector "ruled the roost"
(*HC*, 50). Following his enumeration of route numbers, the Saturday
shoppers disperse in all directions, not to "sunny lands" (Virgil 1916,
555, line 312), but to what were then still homely, peaceful towns.

However, before journeying back to South Derry, where six of the
sequence's eight remaining poems are set (V–VIII and X–XI), Heaney
represents translations of another kind in poem IV, as a result of rooting
around Smithfield's bargain stalls. Both purchases he makes—a heavy
winter coat and a light, loose-fitting summer suit—transform him in ap-
pearance and mood. To convey the greatcoat's weight and discomfort, he
deploys a run of compound adjectives and alludes to materials (coal,
tarpaulins, slate) associated with the railway, an industry his grandfather
McCann knew well (Heaney 1989a, 7). Despite being chafed by the
coarse fabric, he delighted in the gothic look the coat lent him when
making late night social calls, the "dismay" on his hosts' faces opening
their doors to this "creature of cold blasts and flap-winged rain" (*HC*,
51). Magically, stanzas 3 and 4 carry the narrator "up and away" to
southern climes, or, more specifically, to Virgilian territory. Kitted out
in a loose, light suit—gray like the doves that guide Aeneas to the
Golden Bough (Virgil 1916, 544, 547, lines 191–92)—he accompanies
some "tanned ex-pats" on an excursion to a hilltop oratory.[12] Once there
he senses his distinctness from his non-Catholic companions, character-
izing himself as "the one ... most at home" (*HC*, 51), a far less emphatic
claim than that voiced in the *Riverbank Field* version, where he speaks of
himself as "the only one at home" ("Route 110," IV, 16).

The very word *home* bears him back to his teenage years, shuttling
between Derry and Bellaghy. Loyalty to the originary culture asserts
itself once more in the question with which poem V begins and in the

rural images it lovingly musters. As fit subjects for poetry, neighborly pigeons can hold their own alongside classical doves, its speaker maintains; like him they are drawn toward migrancy and "homing." As he relocates himself imaginatively in the McNicholls' kitchen, his eyes alight on "a votive jampot" (*HC*, 52) positioned on the dresser, as replete a sign of piety as the Romans' Lares and Penates. Like his father's "burnished" harvest bows (*FW*, 58), Mrs. Nick's foil-wrapped oat-heads anticipate Heaney's own displays in artworks, which, though steeped in the palpable, glimmer with the possibilities of transcendence.

The occasion the ensuing sections commemorate was the first wake Heaney attended as his family's representative, a gathering mourning the loss of Michael Mulholland, a neighbor's son, drowned while swimming in the Bristol Channel. His hapless, untimely end resembles that of Palinurus, one of Aeneas's helmsmen,[13] yet Heaney avoids any specific allusion to this classical parallel in the text. Rather poems VI and VII revolve around the speaker's perspective of the wake, starting with the disorienting effects of passing successive sleepless nights grouped around an absence, as the young man's body had yet to be recovered. In another of the sequence's remarkable transformations, the grimly named "corpse house" becomes "a house of hospitalities." Metaphors drawn from music and acoustic chains ("antipho**nal** recital"; "kn**own**"/"under**toned**"/ "home"/"clothes"/"smoke"; "**ant**iphonal"/"**cl**andestine"; "**others**"/ "**un**dertoned") underscore the verifying long-term impact on the poet of what he dubs the "night school." Initiated by local elders into its known and secret history, the parish community bestows on the future poet "a right of way" (*HC*, 54).

In marked contrast to the authoritative female figure who escorts, directs, and absolves the speaker in poem VII, the woman glimpsed in VIII's early stanzas is without agency; she appears solely as a face, framed and contained in long shot. Her casting in the role of Dido can be surmised from the opening line, a rendering of *Aeneid* 6.453–54, and from her depiction as "a dim form amid shadows" with "a wound still fresh" (Virgil 1916, 565, lines 452, 450) or, as Heaney has it, "a hurt still new" (*HC*, 55).[14] That emphatically placed adverb, like its predecessor ("again"), underlines how VIII's male protagonist, like Virgil's, is conscious of the continuing suffering his abandonment causes, whereas

Aeneas is transfixed at the sight of Dido and succumbs to tears (Virgil 1916, 565, lines 455, 468, 476). Heaney's character expresses his guilt through a hurried backward glance and precipitate departure, conveyed through a swift succession of monosyllabic verbs ("switch on," "rev up," "pull out," "drive away"). In contrast to Virgil's "fierce-eyed," Phoenician queen, who diverts her eyes to "the ground" (Virgil 1916, 564, line 469) after Aeneas's failed attempt at appeasement, the figure in Heaney's poem is imagined maintaining her gaze on her lover's car and its brake lights. Appearing at a pivotal moment in the lyric, as it segues from private to collective pain, they signal that it is not just the car or the couple that are at breaking point and about to turn a corner. Late 1950s Northern Ireland emerges as the subject of VIII's closing stanzas, a culture taut with frustrations and divisions. The first signs cited are B-Special patrols, flagging down vehicles with their red lamps because of their suspicions about them.[15] For the speaker, as for his contemporaries, the import of those warning lights had yet to register, hence the portentous allusion to "pre-Troubles roads." More aggravating at the time are the sexual constraints experienced at and after dances, "holdings on" that all too often ended in "holdings back" (*HC*, 55).[16] Restraining the young was an aim all the North's religious denominations could agree on, sharing as they did St Paul's abhorrence of "fornication."[17] At the close, the speaker castigates this phase in the province's history as a "nay-saying age of impurity," the latter a term from the Catechism denoting acts of sexual misconduct.

What has been said of Czesław Miłosz, that "everyone who survives in his memory has a claim on his pen" (Carpenter and Levine 2002, ix), applies equally to Heaney. In contrast to previous lyrics, which dwell on episodes from childhood, adolescence, and early adulthood, poem IX confronts us with "what came after" (Beckett 1986, 355), crimes from the Troubles' years, injustices that persist in their wake. In contrast to Aeneas, who encounters the shades of fallen soldier-comrades (Virgil 1916, 565–69, lines 479 ff.), Heaney attends to the civilian casualties whose deaths go largely unremembered. *Their* erasure is pointedly contrasted with the fate of paramilitaries who perished in "the Struggle," beneficiaries of yearly memorialization, occupying plots separating them from the "ordinary" dead.

The two men singled out and commemorated in poem IX were personally known to Heaney and killed by paramilitaries in the early years of the conflict. Respectfully referred to as "*Mr.* Lavery" (*HC*, 56), John F. Lavery was a sixty-year-old Catholic who owned a pub in Ashley Avenue, a mere twenty yards from the Heaneys' home. He died on December 21, 1971, while trying to remove from the premises a 20lb bomb deposited in all probability by the Provisional IRA (McKittrick et al. 2007, 134). Just over a month later, during the first week of February 1972, while still reeling from the events of Bloody Sunday, Heaney learned of the death of Louis O'Neill, a fishing companion and regular "in my father-in-law's public house in Ardboe" (*SS*, 214). The forty-nine-year-old was drinking in a bar in Stewartstown, County Tyrone, when the blast from a 15lb bomb killed him instantly.[18] In "Casualty," his elegy to O'Neill in *Field Work*, the poet-persona raises questions about the degree of culpability of which his friend might stand accused. In disregarding an IRA curfew, imposed to show solidarity with the Bloody Sunday victims and their families, he is said to have broken "Our tribe's complicity" (*FW*, 23). Heaney's word choice is extremely important here, since it shifts attention from O'Neill's failure toward the notion of collective guilt within the nationalist community, which in preceding years had tolerated unjustifiable, inhuman acts carried out by the Provisionals. Revisiting O'Neill's death in *Human Chain*, Heaney portrays him as wholly victim, someone caught in "the wrong place" (*HC*, 56), an apt phrase absent from the first published version.[19] Its meaning can be extended to the whole of Northern Ireland, a place where appalling "wrong" has been and continues to be done.

Structure, sound, imagery, and diction all play a key role in containing poem IX's emotion, generating ironies, and charging the reader to write and right meaning. Its four tercets incorporate three questions, and a critical turning point on line 9, when the contrasting fates of different war casualties are broached. Mortality and finality are invoked in the shock of the opening line, where three of the four stresses fall on words semantically and aurally linked ("end," "left," and "bury"). This attunes us to the poem's play with rhythm and resonance, its deployment of alliteration and assonance, full and half rhymes ("bury"/"Lavery"; "bore"/"door"; "still"/"O'Neill"; "device"/"House"/"place";

"buried"/"Derry"; "what"/"not"/"plot"). Words are strategically placed for acoustic effect, like the "primed device" which occupies a central position in line 3, encircled by plosive "b" and "p" sounds. The repetition of the verb is very significant, since "to bear" belongs to a higher register than "to carry" or "to take" and suggests something altogether grander, heroic even. It is a verb encountered in many common phrases that have a bearing on the poem as a whole, phrases such as "bearing the brunt," "bearing arms," "bearing the consequences," "bearing responsibility," "bearing witness." That this individual, this action, this moment exist in the speaker's present is conveyed by the forward movement in tense, an idea reinforced by the choice and placing of the adverb. "Still" carries a double meaning, and serves to prolong Lavery's careful, tentative act. Ironies accrue in succeeding lines, which refer to the "*sun*-admitting door," through which less welcome visitors pass, and to "Ashley House," reduced by the bomb to dust and rubble.

The door image opens the way first to O'Neill, whose untimely death links him to the "Thirteen . . . shot in Derry" (*FW*, 22), then to countless other victims, forgotten "un-," "not," and "nor" people, consigned to invisibility over time. After death, they endure further degradation: they are deindividualized ("bodies"), treated as commodities, irretrievably damaged goods ("accounted for and bagged").[20] Meanwhile, those who bear responsibility for taking their lives are honored and celebrated by well-drilled, smartly kitted-out replacements.

A marked lightening of tone occurs in poem X, which claims, very much tongue-in-cheek, that the athletic contests Aeneas witnessed in the Elysian Fields were "Not unlike" those held on Bellaghy's yearly sports day. While Virgil's original and Heaney's "imitation" share a twilight setting, a "roseate" between-times, there close resemblances end. Rather than listening to a "live" Orpheus, the crowds in rural Derry are treated to amplified Slim Whitman, his voice "wavering" above, not weaving into, the activity on the ground. Pitched differently, Heaney's lyric delights more in the visual than in the musical, picturing "sparking dodgems, flying chair-o-planes," which, along with the mile-long line of parked cars, serve as mechanized stand-ins for book 6's "phantom" chariots (Virgil 1916, 579, line 654). Following Kavanagh's example, Heaney replaces epic heroes "who suffered wounds, fighting for their country" (Virgil 1916, 579, line 660), with humbler, down-to-earth characters. The narrator notes the footballers' passion, energy, and ruthlessness as they go "hell for leather" after the ball, inflicting "stud-scrapes on the pitch and on each other" (*HC*, 57). In the wider context of the sequence, his passing reference to the "final whistle" carries considerable resonance; it is suggestive of other endings, and, in relation to both the *Aeneid*'s religious mythology and the Christian concept of the Last Judgment, anticipates that liminal moment when the long-dead may be reborn. Again the poet through a willed regenerative act reanimates lives and times that could so easily disappear from the individual and collective memory and so bestows an afterlife in print.

"Route 110"'s penultimate offering exemplifies once more how intimations of the future are integral to Heaney's reimaginings of the past. What adds irony and poignancy to the "spot of time" poem XI replays— precious hours of unity in the Heaney father-son relationship[21]—is the writer's *and* reader's foreknowledge of imminent and recurring change. Situated "on the brink," as they "*wait* and watch," stand there "*waiting*, watching" (*HC*, 58),[22] they and we sense something uncanny afoot, "something more of the depths," as Frost has it.[23] Ahead of the particular instant that the poem records lie multiple, geographical, cultural, and imaginative relocations for the boy and man, displacements that will test their lives and work.

A wistful exclamation provides the poem's initial impetus. The speaker recalls the pleasure of fishing with his father, a rare, shared experience, transmitted in simple alliterated diction, tripping monosyllables. On one particular occasion, the habitual stillness is disturbed. At first the persona appears definite that it *was* an otter's head breaking the water surface, but then he immediately admits alternative possibilities. Magical, elusive, a creature that divides its existence between elements, the otter carries associations in Heaney's mind with both the natal terrain and his future creative life, in which Ted Hughes and his extensive bestiary would feature as seminal presences.[24]

Regardless of what caused the "gleam," whether an otter, a "ruck," or "a turnover warp," the speaker is convinced that some kind of epiphany has occurred and scores it accordingly. Plosive "k"s in "ruck," "took," "black," "Quick," "riverbank," "brink" are like snags in the flow, composed of alliterated "w," "t," "d," "s" sounds, assonantal "ɪ," "əʊ," "ɜ," "ɔ." His "No doubting / . . . Or doubting" (*HC*, 58, lines 5, 7) is designed to dismiss dissent, and even the "solid ground" is invoked for corroboration, though the uncertain light and presence of the midge-drift "ahover" seem to lessen the idea of solidity. In conveying the intensity of what he felt with and for his father, he opts for a religious image ("commingling"), one bound up with the concept of transubstantiation. With the preceding use of "as if," however, a measure of reservation is retained, qualifying his longing for the definitive ungainsayable. Diagnosing himself as "Needy and even needier for translation," the poem's speaker is referring to himself critically then and now, how he has hungered after new experiences and stepping-off points, perhaps in compensation for or as a distraction from an aching lack. Against that must be set his recognition that for any human being seeking individuation—not least a poet and critic—a constant receptivity to "translation" is an absolute necessity.

Looking back, poems XI and XII cannot but also look forward, sensing signs of "renovating virtue" (Wordsworth 1967, 577) yet to come. "Route 110" reaches its terminus alluding to an episode featured in its preamble, that moment from the *Aeneid* when Anchises relates how, following a thousand years in purgatory, some spirits receive "second bodies." Aeneas's sense of privilege at glimpsing his and his father's heirs, "glorious souls waiting to inherit our name" (Virgil 1916, 584, 586, lines 748, 758), would clearly be deeply affecting for Heaney, conscious of how he very nearly might have missed his beloved grandchildren's birth. A buoyant, look-we-have-come-through pride emanates throughout poem XII. Instantly succeeding the declarative, present-set opening, an epic simile ("As when once . . .") signals a journey back to an earlier "age of births." The speaker re-creates vividly a morning after the night before, when to "quell . . . smells of drink and smoke" following celebrations for a new arrival, one guest—clearly with a feel for the symbolic as well as the practical—gathered fresh flowers from the garden at dawn.[25] In a gesture replicating that act, and also Mrs. Nick's gift in poem V, the poet's persona arrives back in the present, beside his infant granddaughter's crib with his own "bunch of stalks and silvered heads" (*HC*, 59). In the earlier published version, he refers to this as "a morning offering"

(*RF*, 24), a phrase redolent of his Catholic childhood; in *Human Chain*, however, he opts for the somewhat awkward but more secular-sounding "thank-offering" (*HC*, 59), inserting the "morning" image at an earlier point (line 6), in order to consolidate the semantic cluster that began with "births" and "dawn" (lines 1, 2). Affirmation marks the final stanza, along with a sense of a cycle completed. Ending her "long wait on the shaded bank," "Route 110"'s dedicatee, Anna Rose, makes her first appearance, shedding "earthlight" over the assembled family. The witty depiction of the grown-ups "Talking baby talk" (*HC*, 59) manages to suggest both the way one happy event triggers memories of others, and the tendency among adults to revert to second childishness on glimpsing a baby in a cot or pram.

As *Human Chain* journeys toward its ending, it is the work of anonymous, medieval Irish authors that quickens Heaney into translation, as it did four decades previously when *Buile Suibhne* first hove into view. That early Irish verse craft was associated in his mind with sharpness and clarity is apparent from a talk he gave for RTÉ in 1978, where he endorsed Flann O'Brien's comment about its "steel pen exactness" (*P*, 181); in *Time for Verse*, a year later, he praised its "oriental fineness of line, depending on silence as much as upon speech to make its points, seeming to have been etched with a cold steel nib upon the cold air."[26] To mark the 1400th anniversary of Colum Cille's death and his own enrollment in the Royal Irish Academy in June 1997, Heaney translated "Colum Cille Cecinit" (Colum Cille sang this; Heaney 2008b, 11–23). In "Holding Patterns," an address to the Royal Irish Academy from 2008, Heaney spoke of how work on the poem heightened his awareness of similarities between the strictly disciplined, monastic world the early Irish scribes inhabited and the one he experienced at St. Columb's (2008b, 15).[27]

The first and finest of three short lyrics that make up "Colum Cille Cecinit" is voiced by a long-suffering scribe, who complains, "My hand is cramped from penwork" (*HC*, 72). Previous, rather flat renderings of this opening line read, "My hand is weary from writing" (Meyer 2010, 36) and "My hand has a pain from writing" (F. O'Brien 1974, 56). To brace his version and convey its shape and music, Heaney makes use of half rhymes (dark/ink, "streams"/"vellum," "going"/"holdings") and alliteration. As he proceeds, following the imagery in the original, Heaney delights in the intensity of the scribe's bond with nature. The tapered point of his quill is compared to a "bird-mouth," which generates "a blue-dark / Beetle-sparkle of ink" (*HC*, 72).[28] In contrast to Kuno Meyer and Flann O'Brien, who opt respectively for "draught" and "flood," Heaney depicts the text the monk transcribes as a continuously "welling" source of wisdom, a veritable "riverrun," thereby bridging the gap between an eleventh-century scribe and the Joyce of *Finnegans Wake*. The final stanza adopts a more self-reflexive direction than Meyer's, whose copyist states that his unceasing labors are carried out "for the wealth of the great" (Meyer 2010, 37), the rich and powerful who will own the manuscripts he is compiling. Whereas Meyer's pen "travels," and O'Brien's "stretches / Across the great white paper plain" (F. O'Brien 1974, 56), Heaney's "keeps going / Through books. . . . To enrich the scholars' holdings" (*HC*, 72). What we seem to be witnessing here is both identification and appropriation, as Heaney self-consciously translates himself in book after book in order to translate himself. The phrase "keeping going" has a strong Heaneyean pedigree, appearing as the title of a poem published in the *New Yorker* in 1992, as the title of a small collection published by the Bow and Arrow Press in 1993, and as the title of a poem in *The Spirit Level* (1996). In a commencement address delivered at the University of North Carolina, Chapel Hill that same year, in which the difficulty of negotiating transition was his entirely fitting theme, Heaney intimates how his own artistic journey involved repeated settings-out, phases of displacement, constant efforts to maintain momentum: "What matters at these moments of starting out is not the social and economic givens in your background, but the state of readiness of your own spirit. In fact the ability to start out upon your own impulse is fundamental to the gift of *keeping going* upon your own terms, not to mention the further and even more fulfilling gift of getting started all over again—never resting upon the oars of success or in the doldrums of disappointment, but getting renewed and revived by some further transformation" (Heaney 1997a). Continuing anxieties over his health and that of his close family, combined with excessive commitments, made the years 2008 and 2009 especially onerous for Heaney,[29] and despite his best efforts to complete *Human Chain* he fretted that it was not quite where he wanted it to be. Having determined the collection should end with a poem for his second granddaughter, he then had to settle on a suitable piece. Eventually an ideal solution presented itself,[30] when Heaney opted to work around an extract from "L'Aquilone" by Giovanni Pascoli, which he had recently translated for a *festschrift* honoring a friend of many years, the librarian and Italophile Mary Kelleher.[31] Consisting of twenty-one tercets, and modeled on the *Commedia*'s rhyme scheme (*aba*/*bcb*/*cdc*), Pascoli's poem operates in double time, re-creating contrastive scenes from childhood through the perspective of a man of advanced years. At a threshold in his life, the speaker's memories stir multiple, conflicting emotions, which are mirrored in the disturbed state of the seasons.[32] Several images—the newborn violets ("nate le viole"), the frolicking air, the green swards—suggest springtime (Pascoli 2009, 4, lines 3, 7, 8–9), yet these are interspersed with intimations of winter and mortality, in the form of "stumps of oak," "dead leaves," "hard clods" (lines 5, 6, 7); only in line 17 is it finally established that the kite flying takes place in a lingering autumn.

The very stanzas Heaney would later select to construct "A Kite for Aibhín"—4 to 12—capture beautifully the schoolboys' feverish excitement observing the kites' uncertain play, before their whole attention settles on the fate of a single kite and its suspended progress. Reliving that ecstatic moment when the kite breaks free, the poem's speaker exclaims three times in successive verses, "it rises" (s'inalza), and before long it appears merely as "a dot / Of brightness" (un punto brilla; Pascoli 2009, 6).

Then, in a blink, Pascoli's "L'Aquilone" dramatically alters direction, its subject, becoming a pale, unidentified boy, wasting away. With the poem's speaker now facing his own demise, his companion's passing seems more than ever a thing of beauty, something he regards with envy:

> I too will soon go down into the clay
> Where you sleep calmly, on your own, at rest.
> Better to arrive there breathless, like a boy
> Who has been racing up a hill,
> Flushed and hot and soft, a boy at play.
>
> (2009, 6)

In contrast to Heaney's kite-poem which ends in elation and separation, Pascoli's closes poignantly, with an image of a mother combing her child's hair tenderly, "slowly so as not to hurt you" (2009, 6). The somber turn the lyric takes from stanza 12 onwards should prompt readers to reassess preceding images and grasp their anticipatory function. Initially "breath," "air," "wind," and "breeze" seem to denote a vital force in the natural world, one that sustains the kite; by the close their remit extends to the human body. Retrospectively, attributes and associations that seemed applicable solely to the kite—paleness (line 11), whiteness (lines 12, 18), heaven (line 11), wings (line 12), flowers (lines 3, 18, 29, 30), vanishing (lines 21, 34)—can be read as portents of the child's fate, pointers to the fragility of human life in the mid-nineteenth century.

Heaney's decision to end his twelfth collection with "L'aquilone" was apposite given the prominent place Italian and Latin influences already held in the volume. The kite in the final lyric of *Human Chain* acts as an *objective correlative* for the human soul, an entity endowed with gravity and grace. The closing injunction in "A Kite for Michael and Christopher" for his sons to take the "strain," to keep faith with a family and a history "rooted" in "grief" (*SI*, 44), he extends to his new granddaughter, and in so doing he inscribes a place for her in the ancestral line, within a poetic corpus.

One of the most accomplished poems in the collection, "A Kite for Aibhín" bears witness again to Heaney's mastery of form, metaphor, rhythm, and musical effects, which does full justice to Pascoli's original. The opening lines stress air's—and by extension art's—timelessness, sacredness, ubiquity, its capacity to sustain something as delicate, yet as hardy as a kite. From the outset, alliteration ("n," "l," "t," "p," "b," "h," "s," "ŋ"), assonance ("ə," "ɪ," "i") and half rhymes ("place"/"breeze") function dynamically like an air current buoying up the contrastive signifiers that command the poet's attention:

> Air from *a*nother l*i*fe and t*i*me and **place**,
> **Pale blue heavenly** air is **supporting**
> *A* wh*i*te **wing** be*a*ting h*i*gh *a*gainst the **bree**ze
> (*HC*, 85)

That image of a "beating" wing almost certainly echoes the "great wings beating still" in Yeats's "Leda and the Swan," as Maria Johnston (2010) points out.

Stanza 2's sudden switch back to the past is signaled by a Virgilian formulation ("As when. . . .") and by the redeployment of a phrase from *North* ("All of us there"), where it similarly conveyed the idea of the family as collective entity.[33] The emphatic first-person-singular pronoun and assertive verbs at the start of stanza 3 could be regarded as marking a break from that state, though that impression is corrected by the reference to being "*back* in that field" launching "*our* long-tailed comet" (my italics). Following the same practice adopted in "A Herbal," Heaney departs from the location in the original, setting the action of *his* poem on "Anahorish" rather than "Urbino's windy hill" (Pascoli 2009, 5). With the comparison of the kite with a comet, the lyric's focus turns skyward. A dizzying array of verbs capture the kite's energetic, erratic movements, which leave the earthbound audience spellbound, jubilant. And it is with the transformative effects it inspires that the poem concludes, as its speaker calibrates the translation in body and spirit he undergoes, his hand an extension of the kite (a "spindle / Unspooling"), its ascent quickening a "longing" in his face, breast, and heart, making him a fellow "flier" (*HC*, 85). Even when the string connecting man to kite severs, rapture persists.

The kite and its disappearance, like that of Keats's nightingale, leaves the reader speculating on its multiple significations. With its frail frame, it is analogous to the human body, but also, like its predecessor, it represents the "soul at anchor" (*SI*, 44). Is it an emblem of transcendence, a reminder of the spirit's capacity to move beyond the material world? The allusions to a spindle (line 13) and broken thread (line 18), however, link it to the Fates in Greek mythology and so function as augurs of death. The kite's release in the closing line may thus reflect that "letting go" of which *Human Chain*'s title poem speaks, a willingness on the poet's part to break with the earth "once. And for all" (*HC*, 18). Like the poetic "windfall" that contains it, like the poem's dedicatee, like the whole collection, the kite is an object of remarkable and delicate beauty intimately linked to, yet "separate" and displaced from its point of origin.[34]

NOTES

The chapter's first epigraph is from Eliot ([1918] 1976); the second is from Miłosz (2001, 240).

1. The period in which Heaney began his literary career coincided with a widening of literary horizons. From the late 1950s onwards, Penguin regularly published translations and anthologies of international writing, and in the early 1960s their Modern European Poets series first appeared. Influential figures in the mid-1960s include Al Alvarez, whose *Under Pressure* (1965) introduced readers to key eastern European writers, and Ted Hughes and Daniel Weissbort, who launched *Modern Poetry in Translation* that same year. From "Learning from Eliot" (*FK*, 26–38) one discovers that this was also the time when Heaney became more fully attuned to Eliot's conception of the poet. According to Eliot's "Tradition and the Individual Talent," for poets to acquire a consciousness of their "own place in time" it was necessary to develop a "historical sense," a profound understanding of "the whole literature of Europe from Homer" onwards, its temporality and timelessness (1953, 80).

2. From the interviews of Heaney by Dennis O'Driscoll in *Stepping Stones* (*SS*, 313, 427), one learns that the Ovid extracts in *The Midnight Court* were undertaken at the request of Michael Hofmann and James Lasdun for their book *After Ovid: New Metamorphoses* (1994), while his decision to tackle *Laments* was at the urging of Clare Cavanagh and Stanislaw Barańczak in 1992.

3. Harold Bloom, in *The Anxiety of Influence* (1973), asserts that "poetic influence is gain and loss." In exemplifying the loss, he subsequently maintains that when "one poet influences another, or more precisely one poet's poems influence the poems of the other, through a generosity of spirit," this signifies weakness on the part of the writer influenced. He goes on to argue that fruitful exchanges can occur between "two strong, authentic poets" but that generally the outcome of this dialogue is a "misreading," a "distortion," and a "wilful" revision of "the prior poet" (29–30).

4. Born in Carnac in 1907, Guillevic was of peasant stock and brought up, like Heaney, in a region deemed marginal, in a community where Catholic traditions were deeply embedded. Stephen Romer (1999, 9), in his introduction to John Montague's translation of *Carnac*, stresses how the Breton poet's childhood left an "indelible print" on his writing.

5. "Its flesh was sweet / Like thickened wine: summer's blood was in it" ("Blackberry-Picking," *DN*, 20).

6. The French poet employs the impersonal pronoun *on* throughout these same sections.

7. For Guillevic, as for Heaney, nests possess a magical quality, functioning as objective correlatives for the lyric. He compares the nest's intricate structure to "treasure" and describes it as "a secret, hidden thing" (1999, 19).

8. The Loeb Classical Library translation (LCL 63) from which Heaney quotes is the work of H. R. Fairclough and dates from 1916 (Virgil [1916] 1999).

9. "To be a master of metaphor is a sign of genius, since a good metaphor implies intuitive perception of the similarity in dissimilars" (Aristotle, *Poetics* 22).

10. Heaney had opted for "under the dome of heaven" in the final line of the *Riverbank Field* version, a phrase strongly religious in resonance that had featured in his *Beowulf* translation (*B*, 15, line 414).

11. "Thick as the birds that from the seething deep flock shoreward, when the chill of the year drives them overseas and sends them into sunny lands" (Virgil [1916] 1999, 555, lines 311–12).

12. The occasion recalled in the poem is a visit to Tuscany made in 1967 to attend a sister-in-law's wedding.

13. Aeneas's exchanges with Palinurus extend from lines 337 to 384. See Virgil ([1916] 1999, 557, 559).

14. The unidentified, abandoned figure may well be the "serious girl-friend" Heaney mentions in *Stepping Stones* (*SS*, 45–46). The relationship, which occurred during his final years at Queen's, ended "in a certain amount of guilt rather than hate." In the first reference he mentions driving to dances in the girl's home place, in the later one he is specific about how "unfleshy" his earliest amorous encounters were, which fits in with this poem's ending.

15. Heaney's final year at school and entire university career coincided with the IRA's Operation Harvest campaign, which resulted in eighteen deaths and involved around six hundred separate incidents. See Parker (2007, 1–2).

16. Heaney refers in the penultimate line to "necking," a term that in Ireland referred to intimate contact while dancing, with the couple neck to neck.

17. "Every sin that a man doth is without the body; but he that committeth fornication sinneth against his own body" (1 Cor. 6:18).

18. The editors of *Lost Lives* (McKittrick et al. 2007, 150) suggest that it was probably the work of loyalist bombers. At the time, however, and in Heaney's poem "Casualty" (*FW*, 21–24), it was attributed to republican paramilitaries.

19. The *Riverbank Field* version speaks instead "of Louis O'Neill / Bomb-blasted after hours the Wednesday / The thirteen Bloody Sunday dead were buried" ("Route 110," IX, *RF*, 21).

20. More innocent bags feature earlier in "Route 110," in the opening poem's reference to a paper bag into which his copy of *Aeneid* 6 is dropped and in poem II's mention of his "bagged Virgil."

21. Extratextual evidence enables one confidently to identify the "we" on the riverbank as Heaney *père et fils*, in the time the summer before the son's departure to St. Columb's. See "Album," IV (*HC*, 7).

22. In "The Aerodrome" (*DC*, 11) Heaney had employed the same two verbs together twice to depict a moment of unity with a mother figure. Drafts of the poem in the National Library of Ireland's Seamus Heaney Literary Papers, MS 49,493/146, indicate that the woman depicted is his aunt Mary.

23. Robert Frost, "For Once, Then Something" (Frost 1978, 130–31).

24. For the impact of Ted Hughes's 1960 collection, *Lupercal*, on Heaney's poetic development, see Parker (1993, 42, 44–45, 49, 92). It could be argued that "Route 110"'s poem XI invokes the presence of *two* fathers, one biological, the other adopted.

25. This figure Heaney has identified as the artist Colin Middleton, the subject of "Loughanure" (*HC*, 61–65).

26. Seamus Heaney, transcript of *Time for Verse*, BBC Radio 4, recorded January 12, 1979, BBC Written Archives Centre, Caversham, folder WAC R19/2494/1. Among the poets featured immediately after an early Irish poem on the coming of winter are Hopkins, Keats, and Hardy.

27. He refers to how pupils "still used pen and ink" and had their days punctuated "by the ringing of bells."

28. O'Brien's rhymed translation refers to the nib's "slender beak" spewing "a beetle-dark shining draught."

29. Helen Vendler to Seamus Heaney, June 21, 2009, Helen Vendler Archive, Houghton Library, Harvard University, Cambridge, MA.

30. Seamus Heaney to Helen Vendler, November 13, 2009, Helen Vendler Archive, Houghton Library, Harvard University, Cambridge, MA.

31. Heaney (2009a, 4–6). All quotations are from Heaney's translation unless otherwise stated.

32. Cf. T. S. Eliot, "East Coker," II, in *Four Quartets*: "What is the late November doing / With the disturbance of the spring / And creatures of the summer heat, / And snowdrops writhing under feet / And hollyhocks that aim too high / . . . / Late roses filled with early snow?" (1970, 178).

33. "The Seed Cutters" (*N*, 10). Polly Devlin, Heaney's sister-in-law, subsequently employed the phrase as the title of her 1983 family memoir.

34. In "The Living Poet," an introduction to his first collection, Heaney reflects on the mysterious translations that art, like life, effects: "The subject matter is mostly autobiographical, but I should be disappointed to think that a collection of the poems would amount to no more than an autobiography in verse. I like to think of them as autobiographical the way one's sons and daughters are autobiographical: living expressions of a secret life that had been deep within one and was once mysteriously released with body and form of its own" (National Library of Ireland, Seamus Heaney Literary Papers, MS 49, 493/267, ca. 1966).

CHAPTER EIGHT

THE RELUCTANT TRANSATLANTICIST

"Like a Weeping Willow Inclined to the
Appetites of Gravity"

Elmer Kennedy-Andrews

In his early autobiographical essay "Mossbawn," Heaney lays claim to
"natural" or "original" or autochthonous identity with the land: "I would
begin with the Greek word, *omphalos*, meaning the centre of the world,
and repeat it, *omphalos, omphalos, omphalos*, until its blunt and falling
music becomes the music of somebody pumping water at the pump out-
side our back door" (*P*, 17). He emphasizes rootedness in place and com-
munity, in a sacred, feminine landscape. Yet his poetic career inscribes a
journey starting from the *omphalos* in rural Ulster and widening to in-
clude diverse cultural influences and parallels from Iron Age Jutland and
Viking Dublin, eastern Europe and Stalinist Russia, the archaic Gaelic
and classical worlds, and from America and the Caribbean. In the effort
to comprehend the inhumanity of the Troubles he had to look beyond
the immediate history of Northern Ireland for "befitting emblems of ad-
versity" (*P*, 58). In his Nobel speech he recalls as a child listening to the
radio: "I had already begun a journey into the wideness of the world.
This in turn became a journey into the wideness of language, a journey
where each point of arrival—whether in one's poetry or one's life—

turned out to be a stepping stone rather than a destination" (*CP*, 11). Language was his passport to foreign places. "I began as a poet," he says, "when my roots were crossed by my reading" (*P*, 37). Growing up on the Mossbawn farm between Protestant Castledawson and Catholic Toome, he saw himself as "symbolically placed between the marks of English influence and the lure of the native experience" (*P*, 35): "Those voices pull in two directions, back through the political and cultural traumas of Ireland, and out towards the urgencies and experience of the world beyond it. At school I studied the Gaelic literature of Ireland as well as the literature of England, and since then I have maintained a notion of myself as Irish in a province that insists that it is British" (*P*, 35). Extrapolating from this early experience of plural inheritance, he advocates both a pluralist politic (or pluralist Ireland) and a pluralist poetics: "I don't think there is one true bearer of Irishness. There are different versions . . . different narratives . . . and you start out in possession of one of these. . . . But surely you have to grow into an awareness of the others and attempt to find a way of imagining a whole thing" (Heaney 1997b, 117). Cross-cultural conversation allows one to engage imaginatively with the "other" without wishing to either efface or merge with it. Though Heaney speaks for intercultural "awareness" and "imagining," he stops short of endorsing hybridization. While cultivating larger perspectives in order to affirm a shared humanity, he nevertheless reaffirms roots and rootedness. According all members of society the right to their own beliefs and attitudes, he does not see this intercultural dialogue as part of an open-ended process of dynamic change and radical transformation at the personal or cultural level. However inclusive he wants Northern Irish politics to be, in his *Open Letter* (1983b) he bridles at being identified as British and insists on the rootedness of his cosmopolitanism:

> My *patria*, my deep design
> To be at home
> In my own place and dwell within
> The proper name.
>
> (*OL*, 10)

The linguistic hybridity inscribed by the multistranded poetic language that he so masterfully deploys is yet not "the proper name," signifying as it does loss and displacement of an original speech and identity. Unlike Joyce, who wished to fly the nets of home, Heaney, for all the ocean-straddling, culture-crossing energy of his imagination, declares for a poetry of reclamation and return: "I grew out of all this / like a weeping willow / inclined to / the appetites of gravity" (N, 43).

This is the same poet who from the beginning of his career cultivated an international persona, publishing through Faber in London, serving as professor of poetry in Oxford University (1988–89), and spending extensive periods in America as visiting lecturer at the Berkeley campus of the University of California (1970–71), visiting professor at Harvard (1982), Boylston professor of rhetoric and oratory at Harvard (1984–96), and Ralph Waldo Emerson poet-in-residence at Harvard (1996–2007). Yet in all that time, he says, he never considered moving to Cambridge, Massachusetts: "I was more like a lighthouse keeper than an emigrant. Four months on, eight ashore" (SS, 267); and asked if he always felt like a visitor in Cambridge, he replied: "How does a migrant feel? I was both home and away. I was an insider of sorts and at the same time situated at an angle to the place" (SS, 270). His perceived relationship to his American environment was not unlike the way he saw himself as both insider and outsider in relation to his Irish inheritance. From the beginning, that is, his poetry is informed by the dialectic between rootedness and openness.

In his early poetry, Heaney likes to explore the tension between the pull of "gravity" and the impulse to flight. "Gravities" acknowledges attachment to origins, the consolations of the familiar and the known:

Blinding in Paris, for his party piece
Joyce named the shops along O'Connell Street
And on Iona Columcille sought ease
By wearing Irish mould next to his feet.

(DN, 43)

The pull of gravity is associated with the sense of communal responsibility, politics, the burden of history, the sacral sense of place, and the need to be grounded in order to speak in the "indicative mood" (*SS*, 281) (by which, presumably, Heaney means to speak with confidence, authenticity, and ethical force). Countering the emphasis on "gravity" is an equivalent urge for freedom and lightening, which makes itself felt in images of flying and lightness, as in these lines from "Honeymoon Flight":

> And launched right off the earth by force of fire
> We hang, miraculous, above the water,
> Dependent on the invisible air
> To keep us airborne and bring us further.
>
> <div align="right">(<i>DN</i>, 49)</div>

The great thing is to keep the lines taut between "riding high" and being rooted: "High-riding kites appear to range quite freely / Though tied by strings, strict and invisible" (*DN*, 43). The East European poets were compelling examples of "gravity." The basis of his attraction to the East Europeans, Heaney explains, was their "resistance, defensiveness, and generally being short on the uplift factor . . . hedging the philosophic bets and so on. That attracts me very much, the sense that these are well-disposed but hard-bitten imaginations. The sense that you can't expect much from things" (Tell 2004, 42). Such a declaration contrasts with his "suspicion" of "the large gestures which are expected of American poets" (Heaney 1988b, 18). Yet by midcareer the "uplift factor" becomes an increasingly central element in Heaney's aesthetic. *Seeing Things* (1991) marks a move beyond a poetry of hard confrontation with "the real" toward a poetry of the marvelous. For Heaney, it was "Time to be dazzled and the heart to lighten" (*ST*, 50). After the objectivity of the "wire sculpture" (*GT*, 51) poetry of parable and irony that filled the pages of the previous collection, *The Haw Lantern* (1987), he wants to exchange the role of poet-as-witness for that of poet-as-prophet. In his essay "The Redress of Poetry," he speaks up for a poetry of "vision" that "disobeys the force of gravity" by quoting Vaclav Havel, whose words bear testimony to a regenerated dynamic of hope that propelled the contemporary East European independence movements even as they recall the American Transcendentalists:

Either we have hope within us or we don't; it is a dimension of the soul, and it's not essentially dependent on some particular observation of the world or estimate of the situation. . . . It is an orientation of the spirit, an orientation of the heart; it transcends the world that is immediately experienced, and is anchored somewhere beyond its horizons. I don't think you can explain it as a mere derivative of something here, of some movement, or of some favorable signs in the world. I feel that its deepest roots are in the transcendental, just as the roots of human responsibility are. (*RP*, 4–5)

The roots of Heaney's transcendent vision lie in several places—most obviously in his half-pagan, half-Christian folkloric sense of sacral landscape and his early Catholic education and religious upbringing. Magdalena Kay alerts us to the influence of the Polish poet Czesław Miłosz, whom Heaney claimed as "master" (*SI*, 110) and "hero" (Gussow 2000): "Heaney recognizes . . . that Miłosz's 'unabashed' faith in poetry drew strength from his 'impulse towards the transcendent' and certitude that 'an elsewhere' exists. . . . This is, finally, Miłosz's greatest gift, a broadly affirmative one, in which his role as secretary of invisible presences is recognized, by Heaney, as the model for an attunement to the visionary sensitive enough to recognize the transcendent in the mundane" (Kay 2012, 182). It was Miłosz, Kay opines, who helped Heaney toward identifying and achieving the "transcendent equilibrium" between gravity and grace that had preoccupied Simone Weil, the French philosopher whose thinking informs both Miłosz's and Heaney's writings. Heaney does indeed celebrate Miłosz's belief in the joy-bringing potential of art and intellect and pays tribute to the Polish poet's combination of witness and lyricism.[1] But for a sense of imaginative space and possibility, American influences, or at least contexts, are not to be discounted. Hope may be a question of anthropology rather than literary criticism, yet there are specific American views and voices that shape Heaney's creative impulse in the direction of the transcendental. Emerson, Thoreau, Whitman—their DNA signatures are inscribed on the genome of the culture in which Heaney was installed. To quote Richard Poirier (1992, 6), Emerson "helped invent that culture," or, as Harold Bloom said, "His [Emerson's] peculiar relevance now is that we seem to read him merely by living here, in this place still somehow his, and not our own" (1988, 142). It was inevitable therefore, that Heaney's contact with American culture would bring him into indirect contact with Emerson and the Transcendentalists, the early formulators of the American Dream.

Though he never explicitly references Emerson, Heaney's outlook and language (not least his aerial figures of flying, flowing, floating, and "walking on air"; *CP*, 11) can seem remarkably similar to those of his fellow Harvard man. Both had roots in the idealistic philosophy of European Romanticism, and both wrote out of a communal religious sensibility, a confidence in humanity and a faith in a fundamentally beneficent creative force. In "The Settle Bed" (*Seeing Things*) Heaney advises: "to conquer that weight / Imagine . . ." (*ST*, 28–29). And what we are asked to imagine is the surreal spectacle of a dower of settle beds tumbling from the heavens, from which "harmless barrage" we are to learn that "whatever is given / can always be reimagined, however four-square" (*ST*, 29). In these affirmations of the creative mind that ensure against undue enslavement to the past or the actual, Heaney reiterates Emerson's idea of the poet as one who "unfixes the land and the sea, makes them revolve around the axis of his primary thought, and disposes them anew. . . . The sensual man conforms thought to things . . . the poet conforms things to thought. The one esteems nature as rooted and fast; the other as fluid, and impresses his being thereon" (Emerson 1982, 65). Heaney even essays a new poetics of flux and flow, most evidently in the *Squarings* section of *Seeing Things*: "I re-enter the swim, riding or quelling // The very currents memory is composed of" (*ST*, 101). Notions of fixity and finality are dispersed: "Everything flows" (*ST*, 85); "Improvise. Make free" (*ST*, 59). He celebrates the serendipitous and random, what he calls "the music of the arbitrary" (*ST*, 59), replacing plot and logical argument with a flow of often disconnected associations, memories, ideas, and images.

Like the Transcendentalists, he sees the miraculous in the ordinary. There emerges a new relaxed and rangy style exhibiting a Whitmanesque confidence in the power of the list, and a new kind of colloquial vigor. Seeking to devise a form that will complement the arbitrary, the fluid, and the phantomatic, "the freedom and shimmer and on-the-wingness" (Heaney 1991b, 26), he experiments with a series of forty-eight twelve-liners, each of the poems arranged in four unrhymed tercets in freely handled iambic pentameter, allowing him to hold in "perfect equilibrium" the contending forces of freedom and form, movement and stasis, the ordinary and the miraculous. The sense of openness is reinforced by the use of the continuous present tense throughout the long, constellatory sequence, the handling of which he has learnt from Whitman and Pound, from Lowell's *Notebook* and John Berryman's *Dream Songs*.[2]

"Mycenae Lookout," the centerpiece of his next volume, *The Spirit Level*, is also imbued with the Emersonian spirit. Delving beneath the surface of conflict and division, Heaney penetrates to the primeval sources of nurture and power. In the final section of the poem, despair gives way to a hope that lies, not in otherworldly abstraction or mystic symbolism, but in ordinary communal effort, in the image of men working together, "puddling at the source,"

> then coming back up
> deeper in themselves for having been there,
> like discharged soldiers testing the safe ground,
>
> finders, keepers, seers of fresh water
> in the bountiful round mouths of iron pumps
> and gushing taps.
>
> (SL, 37)

Heaney's imagery testifies to faith in a transcendent power as Emerson's does in his essay "Nature": "As a plant upon the earth, so man rests upon the bosom of God: he is nourished by unfailing fountains, and draws at his need inexhaustible power" (Emerson 1982, 73). And as Emerson makes clear that salvation comes, not from without, but from realization of the God within, so the renewal that Heaney indicates lies in the hearts of the diggers themselves who in "coming back up" find they are "deeper in themselves for having been there." The diggers have penetrated to their true selves and have found the true source of their being in communal work and a renewed relationship with sacred nature. In a moment of visionary transformation, the "treadmill of assault // turned waterwheel" (*SL*, 37). "Mycenae Lookout" proclaims the audacity of hope in difficult times. It is a poem seeking to do good, to heal and to encourage, its power deriving from the poet's faith—not faith in any conventionally religious sense but faith in a transcendent, ethical order of being that is anterior to, independent of, our all-too-fallible human models of reality and meaning. Countering the contemporary distrust of the word and the poststructuralists' rejection of the possibility of truth and meaning, Heaney reworks an old-fashioned vocabulary of the sacramental and the mystical to reassert a metaphysics of presence and the transcendental belief in the oneness of all creation.

However, Heaney's engagement with America is tense and ambivalent. He reacts strongly against the American fetishization of individualism, the apparent American inability to think of collective life in terms of anything other than groups of individuals in which each member strives for personal autonomy and leaves the others to do the same for themselves. Understandably, Heaney, with his strong sense of family, tribe, and community, balked at the fierce American valorization of isolated autonomy, the prioritizing of ideals of self-sufficiency over notions of communal interdependence and responsibility. In a talk in 1979 he inveighed against "a self-regarding poetry, a poetry of the orphaned self, the enclosed psyche," a poetry that "failed to live up to E. M. Foster's imperative 'Only Connect'" (Heaney 1981, 646). Equally off-putting for Heaney was the American propensity to dream, the supposed American avoidance of reality. With John Ashbery specifically in mind, Heaney (1983c) complained of the American "hunger to be comforted" and the "bogus" language that poets used to pander to this need. He returns to the theme in his O'Driscoll interviews: "It was as if Americans had lived for years inside a geodesic dome of continental proportions—communally, sumptuously insulated from the cold blast of world poverty, not prone to anxiety about dangers in the civic and political realm. It was their pride and their luck. They lived the American dream, which is certainly 'centrally heated.' . . . Ashbery's poetry matched the uncannily insulated, materially comfortable, volubly docile condition of a middle-class population on the move between its shopping malls and its missile silos" (*SS*, 282). Ironically, for all Heaney's criticisms of the American failure to take the strain of actual experience, the Irish literary tradition may not be all that different. "Oh, the dreaming! the dreaming! the torturing, heart-scalding, never satisfying dreaming, dreaming, dreaming, dreaming!" laments Shaw's cynical Irishman Larry Doyle in *John Bull's Other Island* (1984, 81). The forward-looking American Dream seems almost a natural extension, or converse, of the backward-looking dream of "Old Ireland," both deriving from profound dissatisfaction with the present. Walt Whitman bases his poem "Old Ireland" on a shameless appeal to both the Irish and the American devotion to dream worlds. At the heart of Whitman's poem is the assumption that the dream of Old Ireland, figured in traditional Irish terms of "sorrowful mother," an "unused royal harp at her feet," mourning the death of her son who has given his life for his country, is now redundant, a thing of the past, "translated" into the American Dream of a new life in a "new country":

> Even while you wept there by your fallen harp by the grave,
> What you wept for was translated, pass'd from the grave,
> The winds favor'd and the sea sail'd it,
> And now with rosy and new blood,
> Moves to-day in a new country.
>
> (Tobin 2007, 35)

From the beginning, Heaney's is a poetry of dream. From out of the mists of time he summons ghostly presences of forgotten "mound-dwellers," "the moustached dead," "creel-fillers," and "servant boy," who lead him back into a vanished past. With the eruption of the Troubles in the late 1960s, he acknowledges in his poems and essays his own readiness to retreat from the hard truths of reality into the mythologies of the Iron Age, the Vikings, and the Norsemen as protection from the daily atrocity on the streets of Belfast, and he upbraids himself for peddling "pap for the dispossessed" (*N*, 47). Yet despite the strictures of Ciaran Carson and others, Heaney's archaeological bone dreams do not simply signify abandonment of responsibility or escape from the massacre, but rather a search for understanding and a way of coping with disaster.[3] His poetry may be more fairly described as issuing from a pervasive tension between vision and skepticism, between acknowledgment of what is and the dream of something other. *Seeing Things*—the title—encodes that tension; *The Spirit Level*—the title—foregrounds the need for balance, equilibrium, flow, redress.

Another problem with the Americans, as far as Heaney was concerned, was their readiness to cast aside the old intellectual, moral, religious, and aesthetic support systems in order to experiment with new freedoms, while running the risk of ending up orphaned, adrift, and alone. There is, says Heaney, "a certain kind of big transcendent American rhetoric which is still with us. . . . You do feel the space . . . and you feel American possibility." Wary though he may be of the American sense of "transcendence" and "possibility," he is also reinvigorated by it: "And I—as I offer these rebukes—I am rebuked in turn by their great sense of optimism. By comparison, you feel narrow, negative. In fact, I am revealed myself as a product of that physically smaller, morally tighter, politically more condensed thing in Ireland" (Heaney 1983c, 12). On reading the American poet Theodore Roethke's "In Praise of Prairies," and reflecting on the American myth of the frontier and its suggestion of ever-open possibility, Heaney felt compelled to provide an answering Irish myth. In the narrow, tight lines of "Bogland" (*DD*, 55–56) (Heaney's formalism itself an act of defiance in the face of American "open form"), he enunciates an Irish spatial poetics of boundless depth. But what is notable about Heaney's topographical language is its reliance on terms imported from the American West. Ironically adapting Whitman's New World tropes of frontiers and pioneers, Heaney imagines his Irish "pioneers" excavating "inwards" and "downwards."

The layered geology of the bog reveals an intercultural space "camped on before," and the idea of discovering some token of primordial Irishness among the detritus of the past is turned into a joke: "They've taken the skeleton / Of the great Irish Elk / Out of the peat, set it up / An astounding crate full of air" (*DD*, 55). The poem in fact deconstructs rather than consolidates ideas of stable (Irish) identity or meaning. "Eye" in line 3, which puns on the first-person-singular "I," "concedes to / Encroaching horizon." The "eye" of line 3 is repeated in line 5, where it refers metaphorically to a lake ("tarn"): that is, the eye of the bog absorbs the eye of the beholder. The first word of stanza 4 is "Butter," which is also the last word of this stanza, where "butter" is used to refer metaphorically to the bog: that is, the ground becomes what it preserves. Boundaries vanish. Fixed identities dissolve: "The bogholes might be Atlantic seepage. / The wet center is bottomless" (*DD*, 56). That last line opens up a space, an "O," which suggests several things: infinite time stretching back into the past; the limitless possibilities for poetry; the illusion of a pure identity or source. The monolithic, exclusivist "We" and "Our" so confidently posited at the beginning ("We have no prairies / To slice a big sun at evening," "Our unfenced country"; *DD*, 55) finally dissolve in the Atlanticism that invades the poem at the end.

As Jahan Ramazani remarks of "Bogland," "Poetic archaeology ironically deterritorializes the ground, which is found ever to be 'Melting and opening'" (2009, 41). Setting out to articulate a bounded national myth, Heaney ends up recognizing Ireland's inseparability from the rest of the world. Intending to counterpoint Irish and American cultural perspectives, he finds himself probing deep transatlantic flows circulating between Ireland and America. The poem in fact is generated out of a submerged transnational dynamics of ambivalent counterpoint and complicity. Not only does the illusion of a national myth paradoxically depend on foreign imports, but the dream of national origins is undermined by ironic recognition of the absurdity of national boundaries. Beyond or below the strictly circumscribed form of the imagined nation and the short-lined "artesian" poem is a supranatural wisdom that ironizes forms and boundaries of any kind. Heaney's poetic quest both recalls and parodies the nativist quest for a unitary source, ultimately discovering a past that is radically elemental, formless, incoherent, and oceanic. And yet these uncontainable mysteries that break into the poem find expression only within the confined space of the quatrain, though they point toward postnationalist, postformalist ways of thinking and feeling. The highly wrought quatrains merely heighten the irony of the poet's final recognition of the need to think in, and beyond, the boundaries of nationally imposed poetic structure. For the poem, the culture, and the individual, Heaney envisions an ending that can never be fully controlled or predicted, an ending that is a beginning, opening into new worlds. One of the reasons for placing "Bogland" at the end of *Door into the Dark* (1969), Heaney remarked, was that "it

didn't seem to stop after the last line" (*SS*, 91). Ironically, there is some-
thing more "American" than "Irish" about this valuation of openness and
process over definition and closure.

By the end of "Bogland," Heaney arrives at his own kind of "big
transcendent rhetoric" welling up from deep primeval energies with
which the poet has made contact, the "secret stations" (*DN*, 36) of his
power. But that rhetoric is troubled and uneasy. In the earlier "Lovers on
Aran," where the waves "Came glinting, sifting from the Americas // To
possess Aran" (*DN*, 47), the speaker wonders whether it is the timeless,
female sea that "possesses" the land or the hard, male arms of rock thrust
out by the land that force the sea's submission:

> Did sea define the land or land the sea?
> Each drew new meaning from the waves' collision.
> Sea broke on land to full identity.
>
> (*DN*, 47)

In "Lovers on Aran," America infiltrates the imagination to create "new
meaning," "full identity." The ending of "Bogland" is more deeply con-
sidered and felt, and exemplifies the tension between the "Northern
Irish" and "American" sides of Heaney's poetic. Placing "Bogland"
alongside Emerson's essay "Circles" highlights the essential difference
between "Old World" and "New World" perspectives. Emerson's essay
begins with the assertion that "around every circle another can be drawn.
. . . There is no end in nature, but every end is a beginning . . . and under
every deep a lower deep opens" (1982, 225). Heaney's poem features the
circular tarn, the cyclopic eye, and the ever-widening archaeological lay-
ers of history opening out into infinity, each layer of expansion arrived
at by one layer melting into the next. Contrastingly, in Emerson's trope,
there is a resistance that has to be broken down, as each circle attained
threatens to restrict and confine: "Every heaven is also a prison" (Emer-
son 1982, 278). Heaney's working of the image betrays anxiety; there is
an underlying fear of formlessness embedded in the tone of the poem, a
trepidatious wavering in his run-on lines. Emerson fears the opposite:
constriction. Heaney's hankering after the security of form contrasts
with Emerson's emphasis on free-flowing process: "But the quality of

the imagination is to flow, and not to freeze. . . . For all symbols are flux-ional; all language is vehicular and transitive, and is good, as ferries and horses are, for conveyance, not as farms and houses are, for homestead" (Emerson 1982, 279).

Heaney's ambivalent feelings about venturing into new, uncharted American terrain are apparent in other poems. In "Westering" (*WO*, 79–80), for example, written during his year at Berkeley in the early 1970s, the gravitational pull of home still exerts a powerful influence. In this poem, Heaney's California dreaming under "Rand McNally's / Official Map of the Moon" (*WO*, 79) quickly lands him back in Ireland, as he re-calls his Good Friday car journey through the Irish midlands to Shan-non airport, his point of embarkation for America. "What the California distance did," Heaney explained to O'Driscoll, "was to lead me back into the Irish memory bank" (*SS*, 142). Rather than surveying his new life on the West Coast, or commenting on the kind of New Age spirituality he had encountered at Berkeley—"all that New Age stuff, the chant and the dance, whether as a rite in the commune or a style in the poem" (*SS*, 142)—he meditates on Good Friday and the Catholicism of his child-hood. The poet's physical distancing of himself from "home" produces "a loosening gravity," this "loosening" enacted in Heaney's use of highly flexible, short-lined blank verse quatrains with their bold use of caesura and enjambment. In California, he can imagine "untroubled dust" (*WO*, 80), an ambiguous phrase that may refer to a vision of a peaceful home-land free of the Troubles, or of a people whose religious piety reduces them to a state of immobility, a living death. "What nails dropped out that hour?" the speaker asks, reflecting on both orthodox penitence and his own newfound freedom from the bonds of orthodoxy, imaged in the roads that "unreeled, unreeled" (*WO*, 80). If the poem recalls Donne's "Good Friday, 1613. Riding Westward," in which the poet prays for for-giveness for his neglect of God, symbolized by his journey westward away from the rising "sun," that is, the Risen Son / Christ, Heaney's "Westering" ends, not with spiritual renewal and reconsecration, but with the speaker's sense of an unsettling and ambiguous freedom as he gazes upon "The empty amphitheatre / Of the West" (*WO*, 80).

Structurally, the poem inscribes the characteristic Heaney dialectic of home and away that is to recur throughout his career. In "Alphabets"

(*HL*, 1–3) he traces a poetic trajectory that takes him from Anahorish to Harvard and back to childhood and "all he has sprung from." He begins with an image of himself as the prospective Boylston professor, an image that is presented with a hint of self-mockery: "The globe has spun. He stands in a wooden O. / He alludes to Shakespeare. He alludes to Graves" (*HL*, 2) (the name an ominous reminder of the loss as well as gain that comes with progress, change, travel). In charting the course of his career from Anahorish primary school to Harvard lecture hall, he also alludes to the displacement of the child embedded in a rural, natural, residually pagan first world and his reconstruction in a modern, symbolic, technological world.

> Time has bulldozed the school and school window.
> Balers drop bales like printouts where stoked sheaves
>
> Made lambdas on the stubble once at harvest
> And the delta face of each potato pit
> Was patted straight and moulded against frost.
> All gone . . .
>
> (*HL*, 2–3)

As in "Westering," Heaney shows little relocational or translocational interest in his new American environment, despite the fact that "Alphabets" was written to mark his induction into the Phi Beta Kappa American honor society. "America occasions thoughts of Ireland," Daniel Tobin astutely remarks, "rather than [being] a sustained presence in its own right" (2007, xlii). More important to Heaney than physical travel is the imaginative travel enabled by his acquisition of multiple languages—English, Latin, and Irish—which can transport him far beyond even American shores. As in "Westering," he alludes to the moon landings to suggest the distance he has traveled but also to bring the originary into relationship with the universal and eternal:

> As from his small window
> The astronaut sees all that he has sprung from,

The risen, aqueous, singular, lucent O
Like a magnified and buoyant ovum—
(*HL*, 3)

The "O" from which he and his poetry have sprung is both globe and maternal ovum. The poem enacts Heaney's inveterate homing instinct, familiar from earlier poems such as "Kinship," where he surveys the landscape of childhood from the dislocated perspectives of adulthood: "I grew out of all this / like a weeping willow / inclined to / the appetites of gravity" (*N*, 43). Identifying with the flying astronaut in "Alphabets," he assumes a free-floating view from above, an achieved detachment from, or transcendence of, all local, regional, or national bearings. Ramazani interprets the figure of the astronaut as suggesting "an older model of cosmopolitanism, a claim to universality and detachment" that differs from other globalized poetic perspectives based on "concepts of a located and embodied cosmopolitanism" and enactment of "multiple attachments rather than none" (2009, 17). Heaney's godlike, extraterrestrial self-positioning ushers in the New Critical idea of the poem as a deterritorialized "placeless heaven" (*GT*, 4), a self-contained, transcendent symbol in which the difficult conflicts of everyday life are magically resolved. Aware of his displacement from origins, from family and community, from a traditional rural folkloric ethos and magical worldview, Heaney seeks to reconstitute himself in a literary culture by poetically recuperating and re-creating the "first place" of childhood, all the time knowing that the center or point of origin is itself composite, hybrid, translocational, and coded in multiple languages (as indicated by his use of the Greek word *omphalos*) and that it may in fact be—to invoke a more sinister signification of "O"—a void. "Alphabets," looping back to childhood, completes its own circle—but does so ironically, the poet all too sadly aware of his detachment from subjective immersion in locale, burdened by a modernistic sense of alienation from a place that no longer exists in its original form.

"The Flight Path" (*SL*, 22–26) is another poem shadowed by knowledge of the toppled *omphalos*. Heaney accepts the need to rethink ideas about "home" and "identity" in relation to the experience of travel, migrancy, and diaspora, finally asserting his belief in the primacy of the mobile, autonomous imagination. Like "Alphabets," "The Flight Path" inscribes a vaguely circular pattern, beginning and ending with the "dove," one of many images in the poem associated with flight, a symbol of poetry and imagination. The poem moves through various locales (childhood farm, Glanmore County Wicklow, Manhattan, California, Harvard "Yard," New York, Belfast, Pettigo, Rocamadour in the South of France), various points in time, various levels of reality (memories of childhood, recollections of 1979, a dream of being asked to deliver a proxy bomb). Constant reference to different forms of transport—boat, jet, taxi, rocket, jumbo jet, school bus, train, car, van, Ford, moon vehicle—emphasize ideas of transit and mobility. The remembered encounter with Sinn Fein's Danny Morrison on the Enterprise Express enforces a sense of distance between the poet and his community: "When, for fuck's sake, are you going to write / Something for us?" "If I do write something, / Whatever it is, I'll be writing for myself" (*SL*, 25). Similarly, when a policeman asks him where he comes from, Heaney is again forced to acknowledge that he is "light years" away from "both where I have been living / And where I left" (*SL*, 25)—neither of which, significantly, is identified as "home."

The poet's charting of his life's "flight path" incorporates European as well as American reference points, as in the references to Horace and Dante. The secure coordinates of "home" and "belonging" are complicated, attenuated, but they are never allowed to disappear or lose their binding force. The speaker identifies with the "stay-at-homes" as well as the airborne traveler. What is distinctively "American" or "other" is assimilated into familiar Irish perspectives: "the jumbo a school bus / 'The Yard' a cross between the farm and the campus," where the Harvard "Yard" (*SL*, 24) or campus is associated in Heaney's mind with the yard on the Mossbawn farm he knew as a child. His mobility is figured in distinctively Irish terms, as "Sweeney astray" (*SL*, 24). However mobile he may be, there is no escaping the challenge of the Long Kesh hunger strikers, or the pervasive influence of a Catholic upbringing (the word *cross* or variations thereof occurring six times, and the poem finally landing at a place of Catholic pilgrimage in Rocamadour). At the heart of "The Flight Path," however, is the ideal of "writing for myself" within the context of Irish-American-European cultural influence and inter-change: the poet's experience, whether Irish or American or European, must serve that core supranational objective. "*Reculer pour sauter*" (*SL*, 23), he says in the poem, the foreign phrase invoking the story of An-taeus and Hercules but also accepting and reconciling the claims of both.

The effect of having to think of American as well as Irish audiences, of how to position his poetry in relation to each, is the subject of an ear-lier poem, "Making Strange" (*SI*, 32–33), from his *Station Island* collec-tion (1984), which describes the meeting between Heaney's Jamaican American visitor and fellow poet Louis Simpson and his County Derry father "unshorn and bewildered / in the tubs of his wellingtons" (*SI*, 32). On one hand is the parochial countryman, Antaeus, the world of custom, work, and place, the rural unlettered self; on the other, the "traveled in-telligence," the educated sophisticate, Hercules, the representative of the modern world of the car, education, ideas, and uprootedness, the ar-tistic self. His poetic voice intervenes as a third party, "a cunning middle voice" (*SI*, 32), to synthesize the polarized identities. Eventually, he finds himself "driving the stranger / through my own country, adept / at dia-lect, reciting my pride / in all that I knew, that began to make strange / at that same recitation" (*SI*, 32–33). It is through his engagement with American "otherness," his having to think of new, wider audiences, that he makes new discoveries about his ordinary assimilated Irish life.

His 2001 collection *Electric Light* ends with "The Bookcase" (*EL*, 51). Like the sofa in the forties or the settle bed, the bookcase is an ordi-nary object that serves as an entry point into memory and childhood.[4] It is redolent not only of the past but of the way personal and familial his-tory is intertwined with, and inextricable from, world history, ancient and modern. Heaney describes it in past tense; the tone is nostalgic, elegiac. He is first drawn to the craftsmanship that went into its construction. He starts by reading, not the books, but the bookcase. "Vellum-pale" re-fers not to vellum-bound books but to the shelves of the bookcase; what might be reference to text—"lines" and "measuredness"—actually de-scribes the shelves (*EL*, 51). The cabinetmaker has given the bookcase a structure that holds, protects, and supports the wisdom and knowledge that have shaped the poet's intellectual life. In its "shipshapeness," the bookcase stands as a model of the poem itself, carefully crafted, bearer of history, both personal and cultural. It is important not only for the books it holds but for the memories of a vanished world that it evokes. The color of the dust jackets brings to mind childhood memories of objects in the family kitchen. The weight of the bookcase reminds him of a farm gate. Valued memento of belonging and the past that it is, the bookcase holds the poet's word-hoard. The books that it contains signpost the directions taken by his migrant mind, the transnational nature of his reading, the disparate traditions out of which his poetic persona has been forged. "Books from everywhere" (*EL*, 51) indicates the scope of his inheritance, the cosmopolitanism of his literary influences and interests: the Celtic note of Hugh MacDiarmid and Dylan Thomas, Hardy's English voice, the Americans Frost, Stevens, and Faulkner. His bibliophile's interest in publication details ("was it Oliver & Boyd's?," "the Chatto Selected," "Murex of Macmillan's / Collected Yeats . . . their Collected Hardy," "Caedmon double album") (*EL*, 51) points to the global interconnectedness of the literary world, with London, Edinburgh, and New York featuring as the sources of material production of culture that circulates in and through Belfast. In the last section he refers first to Faulkner's novel *As I Lay Dying* and the episode where Cash makes a coffin, then to Synge's opening stage directions in *Riders to the Sea* that allude to "some boards / Standing by the wall" (*EL*, 52) in readiness to be made into a coffin. The literary references highlight the poet's preoccupation with death and loss but also with the work of craftsman or artist in reply to mutability. The poem is tensed between the stabilizing effect of carefully crafted form and intimations of shift and change: the bookcase has long since gone and exists now only in memory; the books, if they have survived, now grace other shelves; the poem is written from the point of view of the dislocated poet who, from the distance of his Dublin home, traverses a series of earlier points in time with which the bookcase is associated; the coffin metaphor drawn from an American novel, reinforced by reference to an Irish play, is finally applied to the imagined bookcase: "I imagine us bracing ourselves for the first lift, / Then staggering for balance, it has grown so light" (*EL*, 52). Here, the ambiguous final word connotes not only the dwindling of beloved objects of the past over time but also the (en)lightening effect (*pace* the volume title) of their luminous poetic re-creation through the ritual of art.

Confronted with the catastrophe of 9/11 and its aftermath, Heaney was moved to make a public statement reasserting his faith in the redress of poetry and calling for a renewed commitment to a pluralist, dialogic poetics worldwide. "Anything Can Happen," his free translation of an ode by Horace (1.34), was originally published in the *Irish Times* shortly after the attack on the World Trade Center and was republished in *Anything Can Happen: A Poem and Essay with Translations in Support of Art for Amnesty* (2004). This volume included Heaney's translation of Horace's ode followed by twenty-three translations by others of Heaney's version of Horace. Heaney and the editors presented the twenty-four translations "in pairs of what have been termed "languages of conflict" (*AH*, 19) for example, English and Irish, Hebrew and Arabic, Hindi and Urdu, Greek and Turkish, Serbian and Bosnian, in the belief that "the effort of creative individuals can promote a new order of understanding in the common mind" (*AH*, 19). "Anything Can Happen" is a powerful rewriting of an account of ancient terror to comment on the events of 9/11: "Anything can happen, the tallest towers / Be overturned, those in high places daunted, / Those overlooked regarded" (*DC*, 13). As a poet who has long mediated the experience of Irish colonial resentment, Heaney records the "daunting" of those in high places (both the ordinary workers in the Twin Towers and American government officials) while demonstrating sensitivity to the psychology of the "overlooked." The poem, Heaney explained, "is about *terra tremens*, the opposite of *terra firma*. About the tremor that runs down to the earth's foundation when thunder is heard and about the tremor of fear that shakes the very being of the individual who hears it" (*AH*, 15).

That tremor is felt again in the second poem in *District and Circle* (2006). "A Shiver" describes a man swinging a heavy metal sledge:

The way you had to heft and then half-rest
Its gathered force like a long-nursed rage
About to be let fly; does it do you good
To have known it in your bones, directable,
Withholdable at will,
A first blow that could make air of a wall,

A last one so unavoidably landed
The staked earth quailed and shivered in the handle?

(*DC*, 5)

What might at first seem another typical Heaney poem about rural work, exhibiting the typical Heaney qualities of muscular rhythm, flexible syntax, and vivid, precise diction, becomes, in the context of 9/11, an emblem of George W. Bush's imperialist policy of "shock and awe" that initiated the war in Iraq. The military context is made explicit in the reference to the *testudo* (the tortoise formation adopted by Roman legions in ancient warfare), which is the word Heaney uses to describe the sledge-man's stance: "lower back shock-fast / As shields in a *testudo*" (*DC*, 5). Questions are raised about the actions of the American government in the aftermath of 9/11 ("does it do you good"), especially since they were "Withholdable at will." The hand that wields the sledge is also the hand that made the earth quail and tremble when America attacked Baghdad in 2003.

Frequently in this volume, the claims of the public world break in upon private consciousness and scenes of rural Irish quiet. Another sonnet, "Anahorish, 1944," returns to "my place of clear water," now shadowed by war—the arrival of American GIs "hosting for Normandy" (*DC*, 7). The poem is a refraction of contemporary images of American military imperialism, for behind the poem, Heaney explains, was the American invasion of Afghanistan and newspaper reports "of these opium farmers by the roadside watching the American troops go up and down" (Campbell 2006). The situation in the poem recalls "The Toome Road," where the speaker, meeting a convoy of British soldiers coming down the road, adopts the proprietary voice of the resentful native staking his claim to originary ground: "O charioteers, above your dormant guns, / It stands here still, stands vibrant as you pass, / The invisible, untoppled omphalos" (*FW*, 15). However, in "Anahorish, 1944," Heaney, through strategies of irony, imitation, and subversion, breaks down the binary of colonizer and colonized that structures "The Toome Road." "We were killing pigs when the Americans arrived" (*DC*, 7), "Anahorish, 1944" begins. The whole poem is placed in speech marks, suggesting that it is Heaney's recollection of the precise words of another witness—a neighbor, Heaney tells us, who worked in the local slaughterhouse. Casting the poem as reported speech indicates that what the neighbor had to say—that neighbors and outsiders alike have blood on their hands—represented a crucial insight in the life of the young Heaney when the safe and predictable world of childhood suddenly came under threat. References to "gutter-blood" and the "squealing" of butchered pigs are ironically juxtaposed with the announcement of the newly arrived American troops, many of whom, once they reached the Normandy beaches, would meet a similar fate to that of the pigs. "Not that we knew then," the speaker continues, "Where they were headed, standing there like youngsters / As they tossed us gum and tubes of coloured sweets" (*DC*, 7). "Youngsters" could refer to either the American GIs or the slaughterhouse workers, pinpointing the unusual affinities and identifications that produce the "liminal spaces" and "contact zones" of a transnational, transcultural poetics.

The militarization of modern life resulting from American foreign policy and the general atmosphere of geopolitical upheaval are evoked in the title of another poem, "Helmet." Reprising the commemorative aesthetic of earlier work in which contemplation of a cherished object confirms his link with the past, the poet, displaced from "first world" to New World, establishes an alternative lineage, drawn from the gift of a fireman's helmet presented to him over twenty years before by an Irish American Boston firefighter, Bobby Breen. Contrasting with his Irish ancestry of silent rural diggers and farmers, Heaney's diasporic heritage is more explicitly heroic and "poetic":

> "the headgear
> Of the tribe," as O'Grady called it
>
> . . . .
>
> In right heroic mood that afternoon
> When the fireman-poet presented it to me
> As "the visiting fireman"
>
> (*DC*, 14)

Fire Chief O'Grady's reference to the "tribe" is ambiguous, as he could be thinking atavistically of his (and Heaney's) Irish tribal origins, or diasporically of the "tribe" of largely Irish American firefighters who make up the Boston fire department (which had a controversial record of racial discrimination), or globally of the "tribe" of firemen-poets. The poem, however, goes on to clarify the poet's own understanding of "tribe" as ineluctably intercultural, an understanding enacted in the poem's hybridization of different vocabularies, figures, mythologies, and inheritances. Heaney draws attention to "the crown— // Or better say the crest" (*DC*, 14), preferring the classical, heraldic notions of military prowess associated with "crest" to the civilian connotations of "crown," and then proceeds to reroute heroism, wresting it from imperial Greco-Anglo-Saxon types such as Perseus and Beowulf and transferring it to Irish American firemen like Bobby Breen. Irish American heroes, names, and myths are grafted onto colonial paradigms. Crossing national and temporal boundaries, "Helmet" links the Boston firemen analeptically with the warrior-heroes of the past and proleptically with the New York firefighters who distinguished themselves by their bravery and self-sacrifice in the aftermath of 9/11: "And rubble-bolts out of a burning roof / Hailed down on every hatchet man and hose man there / Till the hard-reared shield-wall broke" (*DC*, 14). The hyphenated Anglo-Saxon usages such as "fire-thane's shield" and "shield-wall" remind us of the foundational hybridity of British culture, the always already hybridized, layered, "camped on before" nature of any cultural space. In a poem like "Helmet," the empire writes back to claim a place in the roll call of heroes for a nation that has been devastated by colonialism, stripped of its indigenous culture, and dispersed across the globe.

The shadow of 9/11 falls over even innocent-seeming poems about rural Ireland such as the first poem in the book, "The Turnip-Snedder" (*DC*, 3). This poem may at first seem like a straightforward revisiting of old material, in this case a piece of farm machinery, which Heaney describes with the robust energy and rugged diction of his characteristic farmyard realism. Extending the inventory of farming armory in earlier poems such as "Digging" (*DN*, 13), "The Barn" (*DN*, 17), "The Wife's Tale" (*DD*, 27), and "The Pitchfork" (*ST*, 23), "The Turnip-Snedder" is weighed down with arms and armor: "body armour," "breast plate," "four braced greaves." Like an ancient warrior the turnip-snedder is "standing guard" (*DC*, 3). The poem ends with a protracted image of horrifically mechanized slaughter:

> as the handle turned
> and turnip-heads were let fall and fed
>
> to the juiced-up inner blades
> "This is the turnip-cycle,"
>
> as it dropped its raw sliced mess
> bucketful by glistering bucketful.
> (DC, 3–4)

The cover of the American Farrar, Straus and Giroux edition of *District and Circle* is a photograph of a young man in his Sunday best looking out at the reader.[5] Like a gunner with his cannon, he stands beside a squat, cast-iron contraption—a turnip-snedder—upon which his hand rests proprietorially and reassuringly. As Heaney interprets the image, there lies behind the facade of agrarian innocence a deeper, disturbing ethos of violence. Written from the very heart of the American academy during the post-9/11 reign of terror, "The Turnip-Snedder" invokes the pastoral simplicities of Mossbawn in the midst of the catastrophic human consequences of American foreign policy on a global scale. As such, this poem and others in this volume recalling the poet's rural childhood function as a kind of counterdiscourse unsettling the dominant discourse from inside. The turnip-snedder trope is produced from within the American imperium but still contests it. It represents not apolitical memory or unqualified subversion, but a kind of complicitous critique: the violence that America unleashed after 9/11 is latent in the ordinary farmyard activities that Heaney recalls from childhood. The poem, that is, is wryly ironic, setting two worldviews not merely side by side but in a relation of dynamic tension, producing a reverberation between realities, between meanings, that is an affront to both the myth of rural Ireland and the propaganda of imperial America. Postcolonial doubleness—the seeing of cultures in terms of one another—finds its literary equivalent in the perceptual split or stereoscopic vision of the poem's ironic mode. America makes strange—horribly strange—the old world of the childhood farm, even as childhood memory disrupts and devours the big world of American geopolitics.

The result is a defamiliarization of the cultures of both the native and the imperial power. This newly hybridized discourse reorients perception because its constituent parts—the native and the foreign, the "Irish" and the "American"—rebound from each other to shocking and deeply disturbing effect. In earlier poems, such exchanges between the resurrected past and the emergent present, between one culture and another, are transformative. The recapitulation of an idyllic past enables self-consolidation and self-projection. Here the past offers no such reassurance. Rather, past and present interpenetrate one another, producing shifting, ambiguous relations of dominance.

Likewise, it would be impossible not to read the title poem without thinking of the fallout from the American "war on terror" as visited upon London by the 7/7 bombers who killed fifty people and injured more than seven hundred in the Underground's District and Circle line in 2005. However, Heaney transcends the topical and the political, preferring to take his bearings from Eliot's *The Waste Land*, Dante's descent into hell in the *Inferno*, and the symbolic figure of an Orpheus-like busker who forces him to review his conflicted sense of artistic responsibility:

> Had I betrayed or not, myself or him?
> Always new to me, always familiar,
> This unrepentant, now repentant turn
> As I stood waiting.
>
> (*DC*, 18)

Set in the London Underground, the poem elaborates an image that is the antithesis of rooted existence and stable identity. The poet, situated in the flashing, noisy world of the Underground, conscious of international crisis and haunted by the anxieties of contemporary life, looks to the world of his youth for ground and footing:

And so by night and day to be transported
Through galleried earth with them, the only relict
Of all that I belonged to, hurtled forward,
Reflecting in a window mirror-backed
By blasted weeping rock-walls.
Flicker-lit.

(*DC*, 19)

Frequently, especially in the poems of the second half of the book, memories of the childhood home are invoked as antidote to the sense of dread and insecurity that attended 9/11 and its aftermath. Thus a series of poems on family life—"The Lift" (*DC*, 42–43), "A Hagging Match" (*DC*, 62), "Chairing Mary" (*DC*, 67), "Quitting Time" (*DC*, 69), and "The Blackbird of Glanmore" (*DC*, 75–76)—affirm the values of love and stoic endurance that Heaney sets against the contemporary climate of global nihilism and despair. In "The Tollund Man in Springtime," the ancient figure is once more resurrected to proclaim a message of springtime renewal and hope: "Late as it was, / The early bird still sang, the meadow hay / Still buttercupped and daisied, sky was new" (*DC*, 56). In addition, in the face of atrocity, Heaney joins hands with a chain of rescuers, predecessors, and fellow artistic spirits from round the world— Miłosz, Neruda, Seferis, Auden, Wordsworth—who affirmed commitment to the saving power of poetry. "Canopy," in *Human Chain* (2010), pays tribute to British artist David Ward's 1994 public art installation *Canopy*, in which taped recordings of speakers reading in different languages on the theme of place were hung in the branches of trees in Harvard Yard. The sounds

made sibilant ebb and flow,
Speech-gutterings, desultory

Hush and backwash and echo.
It was like a recording of antiphonal responses
In the congregation of leaves.

Or a wood that talked in its sleep.
Reeds on a riverbank. . . .

                    (*HC*, 44)

The poem transports us back to the whispering landscapes of
Heaney's childhood, back to "the soft voices of the dead" and the sounds
of the "tawny guttural" Moyola "breathing its mists through vowels and
history" ("Gifts of Rain"; *WO*, 25), back to the old settle bed with "its
old sombre tide awash in the headboard: / Unpathetic *och ochs* and *och
hohs*, the long bedtime / Anthems of Ulster" ("The Settle Bed"; *ST*, 28),
back to childhood memories of the "litany" of the "rosary . . . dragging /
mournfully on" ("The Other Side"; *WO*, 35). The means of techno-
logical modernity, recruited to the service of art, not only transmit the
babel of voices speaking out of multiple cultural inheritances but also
transform difference and division into the comforting sounds of an old
nature magic, a lost primordial dreamtime.

NOTES

1. See Heaney's (2004c) obituary tribute "In Gratitude for all the Gifts";
his article on Czesław Miłosz's centenary (Heaney 2011); and his elegy for
Miłosz, "Out of This World" (*DC*).

2. See Heaney's review of M. L. Rosenthal and Sally Gall's *The Modern
Poetic Sequence* (Heaney 1983a).

3. See Ciaran Carson's (1975) critique of Heaney's mythologizing pro-
cedures.

4. Heaney's poetry is full of such objects: ancestral photograph, civic print,
harvest bow, granite chip, smoothing iron, pewter plate, iron spike, snowshoe,
pitchfork, biretta, settle bed, school bag, and swing.

5. Heaney dedicates the poem to the painter Hughie O'Donoghue, who
discovered the photograph in a car boot sale and used it as the inspiration for a
series of paintings entitled *Parable of the Prodigal Son.*

CHAPTER NINE

CREDITING MARVELS OR TAKING RESPONSIBILITY

Vocation and Declarations of Intent by
Seamus Heaney after *Seeing Things*

Bernard O'Donoghue

When the Nobel Prize for literature was conferred on Seamus Heaney in 1995, the citation described with remarkable concision what his pre-eminent virtues have been agreed to be, and it has been frequently quoted: the prize was awarded in recognition of his poetry's "combination of lyrical beauty and ethical depth, which exalt everyday miracles and the living past." This summary is impressively comprehensive, not least in emphasizing the "combination" of the lyricism and the ethics. The two cannot easily be untangled in Heaney's work; what I want to argue here is that this inextricability has been a feature of the poetry from start to finish of his career, and especially up to his book *Electric Light* in 2001. When he has been misrepresented or misunderstood, it has often been by proposing too stark a duality between the two positions and by accusing the poet accordingly of either keeping to—or failing to keep to—one pole or the other.

To emphasize this duality throughout Heaney's career is not entirely in keeping with what might be called the standard narrative of his writing lifetime, especially in its first half, up to *Seeing Things* in 1990. This narrative begins by noting that the talented young writer of the first collections in the 1960s showed an extraordinary capacity for exact expression and evocation—the "lyricism" of the Nobel citation—but goes on to say that these qualities were overtaken by public events. Although the poet himself said, "Up to *North*, that was one book" (Haffenden 1981, 64), it seemed that there was already a divide between the early country poems (even if there was a marked antipastoral element in the young naturalist who already seemed troubled by violence and threat) and the poems that were written in response to "the Troubles," the Irish political poems. *North*, Heaney's most insistently and controversially public volume, was a powerful response to the "neighbourly murder" (*N*, 16) of the era in Northern Ireland. That was an era in which, as several of the Northern Irish writers observed, to comment on the political situation invited accusations of exploitation, while to ignore it made one open to the accusation of an ivory tower indifference to public trauma. In addressing public issues in the era of "the Troubles," particularly in the "Bog Poems," Heaney adopted an archaeological conceit, figuring those "thin small quatrain poems" (Heaney 1979b, 16) as drills or augurs that penetrated the surface of Northern terrain to find a root of violence underneath it.

With the publication of *Field Work* in 1979, Heaney—responding perhaps to the accusation of determinism in suggesting that violence somehow "came with the territory"—said he was trying to "lengthen the line again," claiming that the shortness of a line was constricting and that he now aspired to "an opener voice and to a more—I don't want to say public—but a more social voice" (1979b, 21). But we recognize in this aspiration for a freer, "opener" voice one that Heaney had already expressed before when he said of the place-name poems in *Wintering Out*—"Broagh" (*WO*, 27), "Anahorish" (*WO*, 16), and others—that he wrote them with "a great sense of relief," "a joy and devil-may-careness" (Heaney 1982, 70). It is clear, it seems, that Heaney wished from the first for a poetic and linguistic freedom rather than, or in conjunction with, public answerability. The opposition itself, rather than either of its poles, seems to be genetic—something that is central to his poetic. And, sure enough, after the failed attempt to escape to an unvaryingly "more social

voice" (Heaney 1979b, 21) with *Field Work*, the pressure of public cir-
cumstance at the end of the 1970s and into the era of the hunger strikers
in the early 1980s seemed to lead to the appearance of *Station Island*, a
book partly dominated by public issues again, with its more personal,
lyrical poems parceled away in an admired third section called "Sweeney
Redivivus" (*SI*, 97–121). *The Haw Lantern* in 1987 offers a relaxing of
this public predominance, as a personal book shadowed by wonderful
poems on the deaths of parents; but even this book also contained the
"From" poems, which attempted to incorporate a different political per-
spective through the samizdat poets of eastern Europe. Writers like
Zbigniew Herbert and Czesław Miłosz stood for political responsibility
and artistic freedom at once. But the occurrence of both of those kinds
of poems—the "Clearances" (*HL*, 24–32) sonnets on the death of the
poet's mother, side by side with poems like "From the Frontier of Writ-
ing" (*HL*, 6)—still brings together the personally lyrical and the morally
responsible.

Here I want to look at the developments in Heaney's conflicting
sense of responsibility and artistic freedom in the second half of his ca-
reer, from *Seeing Things* onwards, arguing that the inextricable combina-
tion of these impulses was already well established both in the poetry
and in the prose discussion of it in writings like *The Government of the
Tongue* (published in 1987, the same year as *The Haw Lantern*). First,
though, it is interesting to ponder where this inescapable sense of re-
sponsibility originated. In an insightful review of *The Haw Lantern* Ian
Hamilton perceptively linked this feature to the expectation of Catholic
boys of virtue and talent that they should "go for the church": become
priests. Hamilton says, "What is attractive about Heaney's response to
his vocation is that he is never entirely happy that it is *he* who has been
chosen: a childhood spent wondering how to avoid the priesthood had
perhaps ill-prepared him for such singularity" (1987, 10–11). It does not
reduce the shrewdness of Hamilton's insight to say that that childhood
development of strategies of avoidance also *well* prepared him for the
problems raised by this singularity of vocation. After all, few things are
described as a vocation: perhaps only the religious life and a writer's life.
In any case, that inculcated sense of election remained an important idea
for Heaney.

That sense of vocation, or election, is not merely a passive matter—waiting for a "call." It also carries responsibilities. In taking on the role of the poet, Heaney was assuming these responsibilities as well as rights and freedoms. It could be argued that it was an inarticulate sense that nobody in Ireland was equipped to take on those responsibilities after his death that made the loss of Heaney in 2013 feel not only grievous but critical. From the start of his career there was a conflict between duty—religious, social, familial, political—and freedom from responsibility, the things he called "devil-may-careness" or "an opener voice," long before the Nobel citation recognized the amalgam of the ethical and the lyrical in his work.

The conflict had already become explicit at several points: notably at the publication of *Wintering Out* and *Field Work*, as I have said. But, again according to the standard narrative of Heaney's development, the place where it is declared most signally is in *Seeing Things* in 1991, especially in the celebrated poem "Fosterling," where he introduces this notion of artistic freedom as if it was something entirely new: "Me waiting until I was nearly fifty / To credit marvels," such as "the tree-clock of tin cans / The tinkers made." The poem concludes that it has taken "so long for air to brighten / Time to be dazzled and the heart to lighten" (*ST*, 50), exercising the same trope of frustrated artistic freedom, but now apparently setting out with a new determination to indulge such freedom.

So does this really represent the change of direction that it was greeted as? Have the volumes of Heaney's remaining twenty-three years taken a different position in this argument between lyrical freedom—the marvelous—and public responsibility, as the end of "Fosterling" suggests? To begin to answer this, we must go back to an earlier *ars poetica* poem to which "Fosterling" is a clear reference, "Fosterage" (*N*, 71), the second-to-last section of the sequence "Singing School" (followed finally by "Exposure"; *N*, 72–73) that ends *North*. Although "Exposure" has received more attention, with its declaration of the poet's "responsible *tristia*" and its concluding somewhat cryptic (if expressive) regret at missing "The once-in-a-lifetime portent, / The comet's pulsing rose" (*N*, 73), "Fosterage" could be seen as a more crucial poem in the development of Heaney's poetics. It opens with a quotation from the great apologist for imaginative freedom Wallace Stevens, "Description is revelation" (*N*, 71)—an apt summary of what the early Heaney's gift had been agreed to be. The poem goes on to quote Michael McLaverty, an admired short-story writer and headmaster of the school where Heaney taught, who, "in 1962," according to the poem, gives the young poet the same injunction toward literary freedom that will be given by James Joyce at the end of the "Station Island" sequence in 1984. McLaverty is quoted at some length in the poem:

> "Listen. Go your own way.
> Do your own work. Remember
> Katherine Mansfield—*I will tell*
> *How the laundry-basket squeaked* . . . that note of exile."
>
>   (*N*, 71)

But Heaney—or the voice of the poem—says impatiently, "But to hell with overstating it," before quoting McLaverty again: "Don't have the veins bulging in your Biro" (*N*, 71). (I will return to the curious, and characteristic, use of a demotic phrase—like "to hell with overstating it" here—by which the poet seems momentarily to lose patience with what the poem is expressing, just as in "Weighing In" in *The Spirit Level* he will underline what is being said in the poem with the exclamation "for Jesus' sake" [*SL*, 18]. These phrases serve as a further undermining of the overliteral, unambiguous acceptance of the imperatives of argument—a tactic that is central to Heaney's rhetoric.)

So, one way and another, the new resolve in *Seeing Things* turns out after all not to be a *new* resolve.[1] What is more, Heaney makes it clear that this is the case by stating it in a poem that, even in its title, takes us back to a poem that says something very similar (as of course the Joyce of *Station Island* does):

> You lose more of yourself than you redeem
> doing the decent thing. Keep at a tangent
> When they make the circle wide, it's time to swim
> Out on your own and fill the element
> with signatures on your own frequency.
>
>   (*SI*, 93–94)

But what varies in these repeated declarations of intent is not the bids for freedom, which are always couched in much the same terms, centering on the adjectival phrase "your own" ("Do your own work," "on your own frequency"), but the versions of responsibility, guilt, or duty they are opposed to. McLaverty says not to overstate "that note of exile"; Joyce warns against being in thrall to "the decent thing" and against taking too seriously the "peasant pilgrimage" (*SI*, 93) of *Station Island*; "The Flight Path" in *The Spirit Level* addresses the temptation to dedicate a poem to the Dirty Protests of the late 1970s. So in looking at the books from *Seeing Things* on, I want to explore what things exactly artistic freedom is *now* opposed to. What I want to argue in conclusion is that, although Heaney always sets up the opposition between duty and artistic freedom, and on different occasions seems to tip the scales toward one or the other (from this point on the notions of redress and balance become increasingly dominant in his criticism too), his own position is always twofold. His "temper is not Brechtian" (Heaney 1991a), he told Melvyn Bragg in the course of an interview on the occasion of the publication of *Seeing Things*: that is, he is not an agitprop, political writer; but he is far from being an ivory tower aesthete either. The challenge for the poet is to find a "middle way" that expresses duty and freedom: what he called "a cunning middle voice" in the poem "Making Strange" in *Station Island* (*SI*, 32–33).

To attain such a medial, balanced position was not easy in the Ireland of the last third of the twentieth century when Heaney's star was in the ascendant. However, it remained a crucial imperative, for a perfectly clear and familiar reason, one that is not confined to the circumstances of Northern Ireland. People may write on political issues without having the skills to write well; others may write well without taking responsibility for what they write about. The difficulty is to join the two positives together. It was put gloomily toward the end of Auden's iconic poem on the death of Yeats: time, which in practice for the writer means literary reputation, "worships language and forgives / Everyone by whom it lives" (1979, 82). All other considerations—beauty, bravery, innocence—are transient. Most disturbingly, Time forgives ethical shortcomings, moved only by stylistic qualities:

Time that with this strange excuse
Pardons Kipling for his views,
And will pardon Paul Claudel,
Pardons him for writing well.

(1979, 82)

This is the crux of the matter for the single-minded argument for an aesthetic rather than an ethically aware view of writing. There is no doubt that Heaney—any more than Auden—would not "pardon" Claudel for his authoritarian and reactionary views, however well he wrote. But there is, nevertheless, an attempt in works such as *The Government of the Tongue* to consider whether writing has "its own jurisdiction" (*GT*, 92), beyond ethical imperatives.

It is indisputable that in *Seeing Things* itself, where the commitment toward "the marvellous" is made, political poems are much less frequent. When the book appeared in 1991, readers who had admired Heaney's unflinching representation of public realities sometimes expressed disappointment with this turn toward the visionary or ethereal. The volume is bookended by two crossing-over, revenant passages; it begins with the Golden Bough lines from *Aeneid* 6 (*ST*, 1–3)—the passage that confers on Aeneas the right to pass through the underworld, and in particular to meet his dead father who will prophesy historical greatness for Rome; and it ends with the encounter with Charon from *Inferno* 3 in which the ferryman—again following *Aeneid* 6 (*ST*, 111–13)—grudgingly concedes passage to Dante because entitlement to travel has been granted by a higher authority. Between these two passages of vocational entitlement, the first half of the book is taken up with a highly effective series of personal poems, and the second half consists of the celebrated forty-eight poems of twelve-line triads, which are also almost invariably personal or literary in their subjects. There is one very powerful exception to this nonpolitical rule in the second half, one that echoes the Virgilian opening and the Dantesque closing of the book. The last poem in the group of twelve headed "Crossings" (number xxxvi in the whole sequence) describes a "scene from Dante" in which a group of civil rights marchers "like herded shades" are ushered in fear back to their parked car by "policemen's torches" and find that the car "gave when we got in / Like Charon's boat under the faring poets" (*ST*, 94). In this case, the personal experience is itself political, and the poet does not flinch from evoking the full emotion of the political encounter. And this passing reminder also brings to mind a resonant observation from *Electric Light* that I will return to because it is central to Heaney's ethical-poetic complex: in "Known World," the poet who seems to be airily indulging his freedom among his fellow poets in the Balkans reminds us that

> That old sense of a tragedy going on
> Uncomprehended, at the very edge
> Of the usual, it never left me once.
>> (*EL*, 21)

To put it another way, the poet is still inclined to feel "lost, unhappy and at home"; escape into the refuge of the free world of letters, ignoring the tragedy of political realities whether in Ireland or the Balkans, is not so easy.

But that is to anticipate. *Seeing Things* in general bears out the dedication to the marvelous and personal. And then in 1994 the series of cease-fires that greatly reduced the political temperature in Northern Ireland began to take effect. It seemed that the turn away from a concern with public events that *Seeing Things* declared was a kind of literary cease-fire of its own. The crucial question was: Would this tendency be borne out by Heaney's next book? As well as the cease-fires, before the appearance of that book (though not of course before the writing of the poems it contained) Heaney was awarded the Nobel Prize. But when *The Spirit Level* appeared in 1996, it contained some of the most searingly outspoken poems of public statement Heaney had written since the Bog Poems, particularly in the sometimes savage central sequence "Mycenae Lookout" (*SL*, 29–37). The surprising temper of this book returned to matters of responsibility and entitlement, especially entitlement to opinionated declaration. The genial and evocative poems that the book starts with are suddenly displaced by two poems of sectarian atrocities: the blown-up lorry in the remarkable sestina (not a form associated with public declaration), "Two Lorries" (*SL*, 13–14), and the murder of the "Part-time reservist," witnessed by Heaney's brother Hugh, to whom the volume's "Keeping Going" (*SL*, 10–12)—one of Heaney's greatest poems—is dedicated.[2] The quiet, precise description of this killing is described with the same unforgiving anger as the killing of William Strathearn in "Station Island VII" (*SI*, 77–80). So the rediscovered sense of the "marvelous" of "Fosterling" has by no means dismissed the outrage with which Heaney always responded to sectarian violence.

Equally remarkable in the catalog of poems of opinionated declaration is "Weighing In," a poem in which Heaney refuses to turn the other cheek, opting instead "to cast the stone." While acknowledging that there are "Two sides to every question," this poem too falls back—as I have said already in reference to "Fosterage"—on a jagged argot to declare the right to speak up in an opinionated, self-righteous way:

> Still, for Jesus' sake,
> Do me a favor, would you, just this once?
> Prophesy, give scandal, cast the stone.
>   (*SL*, 18)

Though this seems a rather different matter than whether to choose political declaration or artistic freedom, in the context of Heaney's poetry we can't fail to be reminded by the last phrase here of the admission of guilt in "Punishment," where the poetic voice is identified as "the artful voyeur" who "would have cast . . . the stones of silence" (*N*, 38). *The Spirit Level* is not a continuation of the liberated, marvel-crediting spirit of *Seeing Things*, but neither is it a full-scale return to the world of atrocity. The balance is wonderfully held in the beautiful poem "Damson" (admirably analyzed by Helen Vendler [1998, 105–7] in her book on Heaney), where "the damson stain" seeping through the plasterer's "packed lunch" is reflected by the bleeding of his grazed knuckles but is also an image of "the wine-dark taste of home": "The smell of damsons simmering in a pot, / Jam ladled thick and steaming down the sunlight" (*SL*, 16). The implication, as often in this book, is that it may not be so easy to separate the violent and the injurious from the domestic after all—something that was true even in *Death of a Naturalist*.

Two altogether more disturbing poems occupy and dominate the center of *The Spirit Level*, "The Flight Path" (*SL*, 22–26) and "Mycenae Lookout" (*SL*, 29–37). The textual history of "The Flight Path" is particularly interesting: it was first published in *PN Review 88* (November–December 1992) as "For Donald Davie The Flight Path" before being included in *The Spirit Level* simply as "The Flight Path," with merely a note under "Notes and Acknowledgments" at the back saying, "'The Flight Path' originally appeared in *PN Review 88*, a special issue celebrating Donald Davie's seventieth birthday. It is published here in memory of Donald Davie, who died in 1995."[3]

There are considerable changes in this version in *The Spirit Level* from the text published in *PN Review*; I am dwelling on them at some length here because they are an interesting case of a change in the imperatives to which Heaney's aspiration toward artistic freedom is opposed. First of all, the eighteen-line section 3 in *The Spirit Level*, describing Heaney's commuting life between Wicklow and the United States and ending with "Sweeney astray in home truths out of Horace / *Skies change, not cares, for those who cross the seas*" (*SL*, 24), replaces (and, it might be claimed, improves on) the very brief and cryptic section 3 in the earlier version: "Horace was right: there is no alibi. / Sunk in the home truths is the way to fly" (Heaney 1992, 31). Perhaps this, more briefly, amounts to the same thing; and perhaps the idea that truths, even after the flight to see them, remain rooted in the home is a first hint of an idea that will become central in the volume *District and Circle*.

"The Flight Path" primarily deals with air travel, but it crosses into ideas of travel from place to place and life to life—from Manhattan to California to "Glanmore. Glanmore. Glanmore. Glanmore" (*SL*, 23). But the change in the section describing an encounter on a train, at the end of an air flight, is much more dramatic. That section—the best-known section and the only substantial part that is included in *Opened Ground* (side by side with the new section 5, an eight-line addition)—begins: "The following for the record in the light / Of everything before and since" (*SL*, 24), introducing the encounter with someone who joins the poet in his railway carriage to ask him the famous question: "'When, for fuck's sake, are you going to write / Something for us?'" (*SL*, 24). In

Stepping Stones Heaney recalls this encounter, revealing that the inter-locutor was "the Sinn Féin spokesman Danny Morrison, whom I didn't particularly know at the time" (*SS*, 257). Heaney's much-quoted remark is that in this period of the Dirty Protests, he "had toyed with the idea of dedicating the Ugolino translation to the prisoners. But our friend's intervention put paid to any such gesture. After that I wouldn't give and wasn't so much free to refuse as unfree to accept" (*SS*, 258)—alluding to Yeats's accolade in "The Tower" to the Anglo-Irish "people of Burke and Grattan / Who gave though free to refuse" (Yeats 1965, 198).

The differences here from the earlier version published in *PN Review* cast some light, I think, on the changes in Heaney's views of responsibility and political declaration. In that version the opening two lines lead to a very different anecdote. I am quoting it here at some length because of the decidedly different slant it gives to the poem, in-troducing a whole new "Other Side" from Heaney's Protestant neighbor described sympathetically with that term in *Wintering Out* (*WO*, 34–36), as well as a different take on "art and politics":

> Not long after the Birmingham bombings
> A couple of us flew from Belfast, drunk
> As lords, miming into sick-bags, doing
> Photo-cartoons on the in-flight magazines—
> Rent-a-Paddy Inc., in full production!
> In which state, IN BLOCK CAPITALS, one filled out
> (As instructed) an Embarcation card.
> Previous address. Address in Britain.
> Duration of Visit. Purpose of. . . . We were
> Headed for a seminar (what else)
> On art and politics. At any rate,
> Under Purpose of Visit, this bard wrote
> TO EDUCATE (IF POSS.) SOME ENGLISH PEOPLE
> And thought no more about it.
>
>   The plainclothes man
> Who checked us through Arrivals took his time.
> "What's this then, sir?"

> "What's what?"
> "This here, sir."
> "That?
> Oh, that's what I'm across here for. You see
> The address? It's the university."
> "All the same, it's a bit sarcastic, sir."
> "It's what we call in Ireland an English joke."
> And all jokes stopped. Anti-terrorism,
> Special powers and acts, arrests, detentions—
> At least our story held when they phoned out.
> We sobered up and a second form was brought.
> (Heaney 1992, 31–32)

Such aggressive or passive-aggressive challenges by authority are an established motif in Heaney ever since "The Ministry of Fear" in *North*: "What's your name, driver?" "Seamus. . . ." "*Seamus?*" (*N*, 64). Other examples are "the quiver in the self" in "The Frontier of Writing" in *The Haw Lantern* (*HL*, 6) or "the scene from Dante" in *Squarings* xxxvi in *Seeing Things* (*ST*, 94). In *The Spirit Level*, this rather scary story is dropped entirely. Now, after the opening two lines "for the record," we go straight into what was section 5 in *PN Review*, the train encounter in 1979 that is the most quoted section of the poem.

The poet's answer to the question "When, for fuck's sake, are you going to write / Something for us?" is "'If I do write something, / Whatever it is, I'll be writing for myself.' / And that was that. Or words to that effect" (*SL*, 25). The section ends with a gloomy recall (in the 1990s) of how in that period of the "Dirty Protests" the "gaol walls all those months were smeared with shite," concluding with a quotation of Heaney's own translation in *Field Work* of the Ugolino passage from *Inferno* 33 where Ugolino gnaws on the head of Archbishop Ruggieri. He has then, after all, linked the Dirty Protest prisoners to Ugolino.

What we might conclude from this shift of emphasis between 1992 and 1995 (the year after the first cease-fires) is that of these two recalled events—the Birmingham Pub Bombings were November 1974, and the Dirty Protests and hunger strikes started in the late 1970s—the threat of officialdom is coming to seem not the most vital. However we interpret this change, there is no doubt that *The Spirit Level* is an assertively political book where it chooses to be. It is not the book that we might have expected to follow the move toward "crediting marvels" (*ST*, 50) in *Seeing Things*. No poem of Heaney's is more jagged in diction and more grim in its view of the impact of the public on the personal than "Mycenae Lookout," especially section 2, "Cassandra," which, in the voice of the Watchman observing Agamemnon's return from Troy, declares that there is "No such thing / as innocent / bystanding" (*SL*, 30). Of course there is: both Cassandra, with her "Little rent / cunt of their guilt" (*SL*, 32) (*their* guilt: not hers) and the "little adulteress" of "Punishment" (*N*, 38) are innocent bystanders. But the question in this poem is whether "A wipe / of the sponge" (*SL*, 33) cleans the slate; "Weighing In" concludes fiercely, "At this stage only foul play cleans the slate" (*SL*, 19).

It is important to understand that neither position—vengeance or bystanding—is a conclusive stance taken by the poet. The significance of these poems, particularly when taken with humane masterpieces like "Keeping Going" (*SL*, 10–12), "Damsons" (*SL*, 15–16), and "A Call" (*SL*, 53), is as a reminder that, even as things relax historically, it is never possible to find a single solution. The writer's responsibility—the vocation to which he or she has been called or has chosen—is to remain vigilant and unaligned. Heaney's next two books bear out this sense of being on guard. *Beowulf*, of which he published his celebrated translation in 1999, is a poem that is increasingly shadowed by familial and political violence and tragedy as it approaches its end. This dark shadow carries over into Heaney's next volume of poems, *Electric Light* in 2001. It suits that book because of the many elegies for friends, family, and colleagues of Heaney that the second of the book's two parts comprises: elegies for Ted Hughes, Zbigniew Herbert, Joseph Brodsky, Norman MacCaig, Rory Kavanagh. The memorial quality of this second part is summed up in the beautiful title of the poem about the deer park in Magdalen College where Heaney stayed while he was Oxford professor of poetry from 1989 to 1994, "Would They Had Stay'd" (*EL*, 68–69) (from *Macbeth*).

The division of *Electric Light* into its two parts is in keeping with a practice that Heaney has followed since *North*; it is strikingly true of *Station Island* and *Seeing Things*, for example. But just as the intimidating "Scene from Dante" infiltrated the personal theme of the twelve-line "Squarings" in *Seeing Things*, we find in *Electric Light* that the borders between the book's two sections are permeable. In general, Part I features the pastoral and the personal, and Part II is elegies. "Part I" begins with a series of brilliantly evocative poems of description—the form that Heaney has been a master of since *Death of a Naturalist*—and returns to the Lowellian ambition to describe things as they are by their "Real Names." ("The Real Names" [*EL*, 44–50] is the title of the poem for Brian Friel that, we learn from Rand Brandes [2009, 32], Heaney had considered using as the title for the whole book.) There are three Virgilian eclogues (*EL*, 11–12, 31–34, 35–37), and "Known World" (*EL*, 19–23), a poem apparently of poetic license—the poet or artist's right to his own jurisdiction, in the argument between "Art and Politics" that was the topic ("what else!") of the seminar in the earlier version of "The Flight Path."

In fact "Known World" takes us back to the two recalled periods of the versions of "The Flight Path," in remembering the Struga Poetry Festival of 1978 "When we hardly ever sobered" (*EL*, 19). It might be suggested that this poem—another on the drunken theme—replaces the encounter with the challenging customs officer in the *PN Review* that was left out of "The Flight Path" in *The Spirit Level* (and of course in *Opened Ground*). They are companion poems, of the same genre of loosely linked and loosely written sequences—though there is not yet a name for that genre. "Known World" begins with '*Nema problema!*'" (*EL*, 19), a clichéd and careless phrase that is undermined by its repetition in the last line, with the addition of a further cliché: "*Nema problema. Ja.* All systems go" (*EL*, 23). Of all the self-accusations and admissions of guilt throughout Heaney's writing this is the most telling because of its place in this somber book of elegies.

Within the poem itself we are given a corrective to lightheartedness: the question is "How to read sorrow rightly, or at all?" (*EL*, 21), at the end of a section that begins with the crucial lines already quoted here:

> That old sense of a tragedy going on
> Uncomprehended, at the very edge
> Of the usual, it never left me once.
>
> (*EL*, 21)

This sense of the inescapability of tragedy is most eloquently expressed in the course of the most eloquently lyrical sequence, the "Sonnets from Hellas" (*EL*, 38–43). "The Augean Stables" begins by identifying the poet's "favorite bas-relief" (*EL*, 41) of Athene and ends with one of the most shocking of the sectarian killings in Heaney's poetry:

> And it was there in Olympia, down among the green willows,
> The lustral wash and run of river shallows,
> That we heard of Sean Brown's murder in the grounds
> Of Bellaghy GAA Club. And imagined
> Hose-water smashing hard back off the asphalt
> In the car park where his athlete's blood ran cold.
>
> (*EL*, 41)

Electric Light is full of flowing water, often in its attempts to wash clean (like the sponge in "Mycenae Lookout") various defilements: "the deep-dung strata / Of King Augeas' reeking yard and stables" (*EL*, 41). This cleansing can be an innocent, domestic activity, as at the end of "Bann Valley Eclogue": "Cows are let out. They're sluicing the milk-house floor" (*EL*, 12). But mostly this "sluicing" is a matter of purgation. It is noticeable that the exercise in Heaney's purgatory volume, *Station Island*, is hardly concerned with purging at all, but with the encounters with the dead (which Dante's *Purgatorio* of course also foregrounds). In *Electric Light*, the idea of cleansing and catharsis is relentless, to a significant extent suggested by *Beowulf*, where the evil world of the monsters is cleansed (*gefaelsod*; *B*, 82) by the hero's triumphant intervention.[4]

It is clear that by this time a simple model of Heaney as opting for public responsibility or artistic freedom is altogether too crude. The two imperatives are inextricably linked: indeed, the word *imperative* is itself reductive. Whether in Northern Ireland or beyond it, for the serious writer there is no question of ignoring the political world or of confining comment to political commentary. The world's marvels have to be credited too. And in the same way that the sense of tragedy at the edge of the usual can never be ignored, so must the everyday experience that the public and the social are made up of be put into the reckoning. From *North* onwards Seamus Heaney's vocation was to represent this intricate complex. Central to that complexity was the fact that, even after the cease-fires and the reconstruction of civil society, cleansing and reparation were necessary.

District and Circle in 2006 contains a masterly sonnet, "Quitting Time," on the subject of cleansing in its domestic, agricultural sense, beginning with "the hosed-down chamfered concrete" (*DC*, 69) that pleases the poet's brother Hugh at the end of the farming day. As a whole, the book was interpreted in the light of its title, again with the London Underground in the title poem and the chthonic underworld in the following poem "To George Seferis in the Underworld" (*DC*, 20–21). The implication of the title also was the idea of circling back to the originary district. But rather as the darkness of *Beowulf* shadowed *Electric Light*, the events of 9/11 are dominant in the early part of *District and Circle*, most famously in the Horace translation "Anything Can Happen" (*DC*, 13) but also in a more personal way with Bobby Breen's Boston fireman's "Helmet" (*DC*, 14), which takes on an enhanced significance with the fate of the New York firefighters in 2001. What this shows clearly is that Heaney's motivation to address public trauma in Northern Ireland was not only a matter of the local district; the serious writer must deal with the world as it presents itself. The writer will know his or her own locality best: the strangers find the "*gh*" in "Broagh" difficult to manage (*WO*, 27). But "Nihil humanum me alienum puto": the dilemmas of humanity are everyone's concern everywhere.

District and Circle ends with "The Blackbird of Glanmore" (*DC*, 75–76), a poem that brings together many of Heaney's concerns: the blackbird; the lines translated in his version of Sophocles' *Philoctetes*, "I went away to the house of death, to my father," which gathers up the poet's fixation on the events of *Aeneid* 6 (*CT*, 64); the four-year-old brother whose death was commemorated in "Mid-Term Break" (*DN*, 28); and—an addition to the details of that poem—the neighbor who saw "at the time" (*DC*, 75) that the blackbird was an ill omen. It is remarkable how these poems, confirmed by the subjects of *Human Chain*, prepare the way for the poet's death, as in the affecting final poem of that last volume, "A Kite for Aibhín," the kite that "takes off, itself alone, a windfall" (*HC*, 85).

It is too soon to say quite what shape Heaney's corpus as a whole will take: what kind of relationship his "Last Poems," like Yeats's, will bear to what went before. What I am suggesting here is that the major themes are sustained right through to *Electric Light*, which seems to me to have been underappreciated as yet: a candidate for the equivalent to Yeats's *The Tower* perhaps. Heaney's last two volumes are—if not quite revenants from the afterlife like Yeats's poems after "Under Ben Bulben"—almost afterwords, wonderfully judged and liberated personal poems that stand outside the life's work to which Heaney's vocation drew him. I have been arguing that, although Heaney always sets up the opposition between duty and artistic freedom, and on different occasions seems to tip the scales toward one or the other, his own position is always twofold. He quoted more than once Yeats's triumphant declaration "The contrary of this is also true." It is tempting to say that after *Electric Light* the demands of Heaney's vocation were satisfied and he was at last free to dwell exclusively on the personal and the elegiac. The spirit of the poetry was at liberty to be entirely personal, entirely "non-Brechtian." But it is the greatness of Heaney's achievement that, until that near-terminal point, he never allowed himself the license to be only a personal poet. And, to repeat something I have said already, it may be that it is the maintenance of this dual principle that has made the world of poetry in English feel so rudderless without him.

NOTES

1. John Wilson Foster (2009, 206 ff.) sees the turn toward the marvelous as a recognition of what was already there, calling it an "accrediting" of poetry, as in the title of Heaney's Nobel lecture.

2. Lines like those on the victim here make accusations like those advanced by James Simmons, Adrian Frazier, and John Wilson Foster (in the *Cambridge Companion to Seamus Heaney*) that—in Foster's terms—"Ulster Protestants rarely figure and when they do are rarely sympathetic or if so, then marginal or merely glimpsed" (2009, 219) simply puzzling. Few figures of pathos in Heaney are more devastatingly sympathetic than this "Part-time reservist, toting his lunch-box."

3. I am greatly indebted to Michael Schmidt for the textual history of the poem set out here.

4. This verb, meaning to "cleanse" or "purge," occurs five times in the poem.

PART FOUR

Luminous Things and Gifts

When he writes about places now, they are luminous
spaces within his mind. They have been evacuated of
their status as background, as documentary geography,
and exist instead as transfigured images, sites where the
mind projects its own force.

—Seamus Heaney, "The Placeless Heaven:
Another Look at Kavanagh"

CHAPTER TEN

SEAMUS HEANEY'S GIFTS

Henry Hart

Seamus Heaney was not only one of the most gifted modern poets; he was also one of the most generous with his gifts. Shortly after his death on August 30, 2013, the Irish writer Theo Dorgan (2013) spoke for many when he said about Heaney: "He understood that the poetry was a gift. And he respected the gift. He knew that the gift came from elsewhere. And he understood that his duty was to immerse himself in the craft so as to do justice to the gift."

Heaney's preoccupation with gifts and gift giving began during his Catholic boyhood in Northern Ireland and continued, as did his preoccupation with Catholicism, throughout his life. In interviews and poems, he traced his vocation as a writer back to the gift of a fountain pen that he received from his parents when he left his family farm at the age of twelve to attend St. Columb's College, a private Catholic secondary school in Derry (or Londonderry, as Protestants call it). Before dropping him off at his dormitory on August 9, 1951, the Heaneys drove the short distance across the Ulster border to Buncrana in the Republic of Ireland to procure the pen. More than a half century later, Heaney commemorated the gift in "The Conway Stewart," a poem that associated the deluxe pen with his "gift" as a writer. With its impressive English name, "14-carat nib," and "Three gold bands in the clip-on screw-top" (*HC*, 9) the pen was what Lewis Hyde in *The Gift: Creativity and the Artist in the Modern World* calls a "gift of passage" or "threshold gift" (2007, 52). It celebrated Heaney's crossing of numerous borders and his initiation into a rigorous academic culture very different from the culture he left behind at Mossbawn, his family farm.

Recalling his trip to boarding school in a friend's car (his family was too poor at the time to own a car), Heaney once remarked: "I crossed some kind of psychic shadow line when I was driven [to St. Columb's College]" (quoted in Madden and Bradley 2004, 72). If his first twelve years at Mossbawn had been a "pre-reflective," "pre-literate," "pre-historical" "doze of hibernation" in a womblike "den-life" (*CP*, 9–10), as he said in his Nobel Prize speech, he experienced a painful second birth at St. Columb's. Having severed his umbilical connection with family and farm, he grew so depressed during his first weeks and months that he could barely eat. "I had no appetite for anything except grief" (Madden and Bradley 2004, 73), he confessed. Rather than counsel and console, the priests made matters worse by lining up the new boys in a big study hall and unleashing "the terror of the strap." Decades later, the trauma of that initiation and the punishments that followed it were still vivid in Heaney's memory. "That first day there was a definite sense of scare," he said. "You had come from a home and suddenly you were in an institution. I was homesick for weeks, and very vulnerable" (Fitzpatrick 2010, 60). Along with the feeling of being incarcerated in a heartless institution, Heaney for the first time had to contend with an urban culture where sectarian conflicts simmered or violently erupted. In the rural community around Mossbawn, which was thirty miles northwest of Belfast, Protestant and Catholic neighbors had been friendly or at least had maintained a facade of civility.

Heaney quickly realized that survival and success in this hostile environment depended on using his gift of a pen and his gift for writing as weapons. In "The Conway Stewart," he compared his pen rather melodramatically to a shotgun with a "mottled barrel" and a "Pump-action lever" (*HC*, 9) to underscore his embattled state. At the beginning of "Digging," another self-portrait of Heaney as a conflicted young man, he also struck a militant pose, gripping his "squat pen . . . snug as a gun" (*DN*, 13). While some of his Nationalist peers chose to wield actual guns for the IRA, Heaney decided he would take arms against his troubles—both his personal troubles and Ulster's political Troubles—with his fountain pen. He also used his pen as a tool to forge links in a "human chain," as he would later call it, connecting him with home. His "long-hand / 'Dear'" (*HC*, 9) alluded to at the end of "The Conway Stewart" was the first word—the first link—of a chain of letters home.

From his first major poem, "Digging," to one of his last published poems, "On the Gift of a Fountain Pen," Heaney conceived of writing as a struggle to affirm an independent self, but also as a religious act in the root sense of the word *religious—re-ligare*—to "bind back" or "bind again." Writing allowed Heaney to establish bonds with sources of sustenance in the past. Again and again he would "bond" with Moss-bawn, returning to his first home as a source of inspiration and subjects for poems. As his career progressed, he came to think of his bond with Mossbawn as one governed by the principles of gift exchange; he had received great gifts from his parents and farm at Mossbawn, so it was incumbent upon him to reciprocate by returning gifts to his original community and to others as well. His pastoral home was a gift that kept giving, but as Heaney morphed into "Famous Seamus" and demands on his time multiplied, the obligation to reciprocate became an exhausting burden. "On the Gift of a Fountain Pen" casts an older man's cold eye on "the years / Of every . . . obligation / Imposed and undertaken" that threatened to sap his original gift for writing. Suffering Keatsean "fears / That poems may cease to be," Heaney worries that he has squandered his gift in the dutiful fulfillment of obligations, those bonds (the Latin root of *obligation, ob-ligare*, means a "binding toward") that he also felt a religious compulsion to ratify. Was it a "mistake" or a "virtue" to honor "every . . . obligation?" he asks, no doubt thinking of the many social functions (honorary degree ceremonies, book launches, exhibition open-ings, lecture series, poetry readings, summer schools, charity events) that distracted him from poetry. Heaney never resolves his ethical dilemma. Instead, in a show of Keatsean "negative capability," he remains boister-ously creative despite his uncertainties. He takes up his pen and writes a poem about continuing to write poetry. "I dip and fill. And start again," he says, "doubts / Or no doubts. Heigh-ho" (Heaney 2013c, cover). He ignores his anxieties, at least for the moment, to celebrate his gift.

Throughout his career, Heaney used his pen in a self-reflexive way—to write about how best to use his pen. To whom or to what should he devote his gift, and how should he reciprocate for the many gifts bestowed on him? he obsessively asked. His enrollment at St. Columb's, which was made possible by the gift of a scholarship, spurred his early sense of obligation to benefactors. Although he was deeply grateful for the financial gift and later for the title of head prefect, an honor bestowed on him by St. Columb's president, as he accrued prestigious titles and awards over the subsequent years he grew increasingly anxious about his willingness to reciprocate and increasingly frustrated by the number of obligations imposed on him. Many of the quarrels in his poems revolve around the moral imperative to reciprocate. Sometimes he berated himself for neglecting poetry to honor his obligations to others; sometimes he berated himself for neglecting others to honor his obligations to poetry. His vacillations, as for Yeats, spurred quests for resolutions in an ongoing dialectic that kept him creative.

The title poem in *Human Chain* illustrates his vacillating attitudes toward the obligations of gift exchange. After paying homage to aid workers who offer gifts of food to those in need, he extols the sense of freedom the workers feel after they have unburdened themselves of gifts. Recalling similar labors as a farmboy at Mossbawn—specifically his job of swinging bags of grain onto a trailer—he declares: "Nothing surpassed // That quick unburdening, backbreak's truest payback, / A letting go which will not come again. Or it will, once. And for all" (*HC*, 18). Wearied by a lifetime of constant giving, Heaney implies that the obligations of gift exchange can bind the giver to a kind of backbreaking "human chain" gang. Only when he unbinds his shackles and shuffles off his "mortal coil"—another kind of human chain—will he experience an ultimate "letting go" and be absolutely free. Death, in other words, can also be regarded as a kind of gift or "payback."

In his pioneering study *The Gift*, first published in 1924 as *Essai sur le don: Forme et raison de l'échange dans les sociétés archaiques*, the French sociologist Marcel Mauss explained the benefits and burdens of gift exchange that Heaney gives lyrical expression to in his poems. Mauss concluded that "the obligation . . . to give presents," "[the obligation] to receive them," and "the obligation to reciprocate" established a network of bonds that brought people together but also threatened to entrap and burden them. If obligations were not fulfilled properly, antagonism ensued. Productive communication and commerce, especially in precapitalist societies, depended on strict adherence to the rules of gift exchange. "To refuse to give, to fail to invite, just as to refuse to accept [gifts]," Mauss wrote, was "to reject the bond of alliance and commonality" (1990, 13) and to court social breakdown. Gift exchange with the gods was equally important and equally prone to trouble. Worshippers sacrificially offered gifts to the gods with the hope that the gods would reciprocate. The gods, of course, did not always provide the gifts requested by the worshippers.

Heaney's preoccupations with charitable and sacrificial gift giving intensified under the tutelage of St. Columb's priests. At the heart of the Catholic faith that Heaney practiced and studied at boarding school was the Eucharist, commemorating the gift of Christ's flesh and blood for the redemption of humanity. The word *Eucharist*, from the Greek *eu-kharistia*, originally meant "giving blessed gifts" or "giving grateful thanks" (the Greek *kharis* was sometimes translated as "gift"). During the Rite of Blessing and Sprinkling Holy Water near the beginning of the Catholic celebration of the Eucharist, the priest announced that he was about to supervise a gift exchange: "God our Father, your gift of water brings life and freshness to the earth; it washes away our sins and brings us eternal life. . . . Renew the living spring of your life within us and protect us in spirit and body, that we may be free from sin and come into your presence to receive your gift of salvation" ("Orders of Mass"). In the "sacred mysteries" of the ritual that followed, the priest symbolically presented Christ's gifts—the bread and wine of his flesh and blood—to communicants, who reciprocated by giving thanks and vowing to serve Christ faithfully. The purpose of the sacred gift exchange, the priest reminded his congregation at the end of the ceremony, was to restore a peaceful, loving bond between God and his people.

Heaney found a detailed explanation of the church's view of gifts in Charles Hart's *The Student's Catholic Doctrine*, which his teachers used as a textbook. In addition to the main gifts of Christ's flesh and blood, according to Hart, "The seven gifts particularly attributed to the Holy Ghost are *wisdom, understanding, counsel, fortitude, knowledge, piety*, and *the fear of the Lord*" (1931, 277). Another "supernatural gift of God" (1931, 165) was the urge to be charitable. In the intricate logic of the church, God gave the soul gifts that made the soul want to give gifts back to God and to others; by making sacrifices and giving charitably, a person "approach[ed] nearest to God" (1931, 165), the supreme gift giver.

Heaney never abandoned many of the values inculcated by his early Catholic teachers. Throughout his life, as his friends observed, he could be charitable to a fault. A book could be written about all the gifts he gave to hospitals, libraries, literary journals, environmental groups, non-sectarian schools, peace organizations, literary societies, human rights groups, family members, friends, and various people in need. Although his Catholicism altered as he matured, he remained committed to the church's fundamental ethos of gift giving. He also remained sympathetic to the Catholic notion of the Creator as a gift giver, the creation (the "given") as a miraculous gift, and Christ as a God who exemplified gift giving. Like Stephen Dedalus, who proposed in *A Portrait of the Artist as a Young Man* that the artist resembled "the God of the creation" as well as "a priest of eternal imagination, transmuting the daily bread of experience into the radiant body of everliving life" (Joyce 1992, 215, 221), Heaney came to think of his poetry writing as a Eucharistic transmutation of the "given" into a redemptive gift. Aware that he had been blessed with numerous gifts, he felt obligated to give thanks to the gift givers and share his gifts with as many people as possible.

At Queen's University from 1957 to 1961, in between attending Mass, serving as a Catholic Student Union official, and taking pilgrimages to Lourdes and St. Patrick's Purgatory, Heaney began to develop an archetypal understanding of Catholicism's "sacred mysteries." Although he acknowledged that "all of the great spiritual writers were constantly being applied, in digested, pre-packaged form, by preachers at retreats, and were generally in the Catholic air I breathed at boarding school," it was Thomas Merton's *Seeds of Contemplation*, which he said he read at Queen's in "a pious spirit," and Evelyn Underhill's writings on Christian mysticism that pointed Heaney toward the universal underpinnings of his Catholicism.[1] Underhill in her encyclopedic study *Mysticism* showed how the mystic's "intangible quest" (1999, 3) for union with the Creator resembled the mythical quests of classical heroes that began with a departure from the status quo, an initiation into the trials and "Mysteries" (1999, 4) of an otherworld, and a return to society with boons to distribute. For Underhill, Dante's *Divine Comedy* exemplified the universal pattern of "the Mystic Way" (1999, 129).

Heaney came to regard *The Divine Comedy* similarly, borrowing Joseph Campbell's formula for the universal "monomyth" to describe Dante's quest for union with God. About "the standard path of the mythological adventure," Campbell wrote in *The Hero with a Thousand Faces*, "A hero ventures forth from the world of common day into a region of supernatural wonder: fabulous forces are there encountered and a decisive victory is won: the hero comes back from this mysterious adventure with the power to bestow boons on his fellow man" (1949, 30). In an article on the *Divine Comedy*, Heaney said, "Its big shape is the archetypal one"; it begins with a "faring forth into the ordeal," proceeds "to a nadir," and concludes with Dante "returning to a world that is renewed by the boon won in that other place" (1980b, 14). Heaney focused on the first stage of the journey that culminated in the transcendental realm "greater than our speech" and "above mortal conceiving" (Dante 1939, 481), where Dante experienced a mystical union with the source of creation, "the Love that moves the sun and the other stars" (Dante 1939, 485), as he called it at the end of the *Paradiso*. For Heaney, Dante's greatest boon was the epic map of the *via mystica* that he gave to the world when he published *The Divine Comedy*. Even after Heaney repudiated the Catholic orthodoxy of his youth, this map continued to guide his thought and conduct until the end of his life.

Published in 1961, *Seeds of Contemplation* provided Heaney with a more up-to-date map of the mystic's journey. For Merton (1961, 1), the mystic embarked on a contemplative journey "beyond reason" and "beyond discourse" toward union with an "invisible, transcendent and infinitely abundant Source." Contemplation of this mysterious "Source" depended on the "gift of awareness . . . of infinite Being" that allowed the mind to view "contingent reality as . . . a present from God, as a free gift of love" (1961, 2). Throughout *Seeds of Contemplation* Merton repeated his conviction that the mystic's contemplation of the "Source" and the "mysterious work of creation" depended on a "gift of God" (1961, 4) and that the creation was the most sublime gift of all. Heaney would pay homage to this sort of mystical perspective most directly in his translation of a poem by St. John of the Cross, which he incorporated in "Station Island" (section XI). Heaney introduces his translation with an anecdote about the childhood "gift [of a kaleidoscope] / mistakenly abased," and then offers St. John of the Cross's ruminations on the Creator as a mysterious gift giver whose "eternal fountain" appears transmogrified in the "living bread" (*SI*, 89–90) of the Eucharist.

Merton, who acknowledged St. John of the Cross as one of the primary influences on *Seeds of Contemplation*, viewed the Creator in the same way: as an archetypal "Source" that defied categorization but who appeared in the gift of the creation and in Christ, the "mysterious ineffable Divine Person" who represented the Creator on earth. At the end of *Seeds of Contemplation*, Merton, like Underhill, mapped the mystical journey toward the divine "Source" as if it were a reiteration of the "monomyth." The journey began with a departure from "the old world of our senses" (Merton 1961, 174), proceeded to an initiation into a "dark night of the soul" that appeared "strange, remote and unbelievable" (1961, 174), culminated in a triumphant moment during which the hero received "a pure gift of God . . . with thanksgiving, happiness and joy" (1961, 178), and ended with the contemplative returning to society with the power to bestow a boon—"the gift of God's love" (1961, 208)—on others.

During the year following his graduation from Queen's, Heaney received inspiration for his contemplative pursuits from another source—the gift (which he had to return) of Patrick Kavanagh's *A Soul for Sale* from the writer Michael McLaverty. The poems about the harsh realities of poor Irish farmers convinced Heaney to look for examples of godly and poetic gifts in his own farming experience. In a retrospective article about Kavanagh in a 1979 issue of *The Listener*, Heaney emphasized his contemporary's preoccupation with gifts:

> When Patrick Kavanagh looked for an image to express his sense of the origins of poetic gift, he returned again and again to the image of mist and fog [on his family farm]. It is an image of creation that

lies perhaps at the bottom of all our minds. A picture conjured up perhaps out of the Book of Genesis where God the Father breathes and incubates the world out of the steam and swirl of chaos. But Kavanagh connected creativity with the natural mother as well as with the Divine Father, and he also knew himself to be the son of a place as well as the son of a woman. In his imagination, the nurturing fog hung forever above his birthplace. (Heaney 1979c, 577)

Kavanagh became one of several poets who prompted Heaney to trace the origins of his own literary gifts back to a paternal artist-god, a maternal fertility goddess, and a mysterious muse hovering over his birthplace—his family farm at Mossbawn. Kavanagh also helped reconcile Heaney to the sad fact that being divinely—or at least humanly—gifted was both a boon and a burden. As Heaney remarked, "Kavanagh escaped [the farming life] through his gift of imagination," used his redemptive "gift for recreating that Eden time" of his childhood on the farm, and expressed "gratitude for the simple gift of life" (Heaney 1979c, 578) in his poems but also suffered estrangement from the pastoral community he eulogized. Literary success elevated him to a social class that was alien to the farming class of his family and friends. Heaney felt the pangs of estrangement from his home community just as sharply as Kavanagh: "All he's ever wanted to do is go back [to Mossbawn] . . . his paradise . . . his Eden," Heaney's wife once told a reporter (McCrum 2009). But Heaney could not go back in any meaningful way after his parents sold Mossbawn in 1954 and moved to a different farm. This loss, which was motivated by the death of Heaney's younger brother Christopher in a road accident near the farm, fueled Heaney's efforts to recapture his Eden time in poems. Once again, Heaney could be talking about his own origins and his own creative gift when he said of Kavanagh: "From beginning to end, he was entranced with his own creativity and grateful for it; yet it left him in an uneasy relationship with his own place and his own people" (Heaney 1979c, 577). Following the parameters of gift exchange, Heaney kept reciprocating for the gifts bestowed on him at Mossbawn by writing tributes to what he had been given there. His comment that "underlying almost everything Kavanagh wrote, there is an astonishment at the fact that he is writing at all" applies equally to

Heaney's feeling of astonishment at the gifts he received from his humble parents and their humble farm.

Heaney's devotion to his home territory and interest in gift exchange drew him to P. V. Glob's archaeological accounts of ancient fertility sacrifices in *The Bog People*, a book Heaney bought as a Christmas present for himself in 1969. He wrote his first poem based on the Bog People, "The Tollund Man," on Easter Sunday 1970. As he explained to a journalist, the so-called "Tollund Man"—the corpse offered as a gift to a fertility goddess and preserved for two millennia in the peat near Tollund, Denmark—"is a kind of Christ figure: sacrificed so that life will be brought back. . . . He is a symbol to me of [a fertility] sacrifice to the goddess of territory, and in many ways the political upheavals of Ireland, especially in the 20th century, have been a renewal of that kind of religion" (Garland 1973, 629). For Heaney, the Tollund Man and his sacrificial cohorts discussed by Glob were prototypes of Christ, Irish political martyrs, and poets like himself. In his bog poems, he agonized over the violent ways martyrs gave—or were forced to give—the gift of life to ensure that the gods of the land gave gifts back to the community, in the form of either abundant crops or social justice. One of the reasons he chose poetic artifice over political sacrifice was that it was a nonviolent form of gift giving. Still, he worried about the ethics and efficacy of his gifts.

Heaney got another opportunity to scrutinize the ethics of gift exchange when he translated *Beowulf*. In his introduction, he could have been referring to the Troubles in Northern Ireland when he said of Beowulf's Scandinavian culture: "All conceive of themselves as hooped within the great wheel of necessity, in thrall to a code of loyalty and bravery, bound to seek glory in the eye of the warrior world" in which "the greater nations spoil for war and menace the little ones [and] . . . bloodshed begets further bloodshed, the wheel turns, the generations tread and tread and tread" (*B*, xiv). Echoing Gerard Manley Hopkins's lament in "God's Grandeur" that "generations have trod, have trod, have trod" on God's earth, Heaney looked back at Beowulf's fusion of pagan and Christian values with ambivalence. On the one hand, he admired Beowulf's "superb gifts as a warrior" (*B*, xviii) and his charitable way of distributing gold "in bent bars as hall gifts." There was something noble and "religious" about the ethos of "defending one's lord and bearing heroic witness to the integrity of the bond between him and his hall-companions—a bond sealed in . . . peace-time feasting and ring-giving" (*B*, xv–xvi). Like Heaney's Catholic culture, Beowulf's Nordic culture revolved around bonds established by gift exchange. Beowulf, in fact, enjoyed something close to divine status among his men. He had the power to destroy "the hell-brute" (*B*, 89) Grendel because of "the wondrous gifts God had showered on him" (*B*, 89), and as "the lord of men / who showered you with gifts" (*B*, 193) he imitated God's gift giving. The dragon, by contrast, hoarded gifts.

In Beowulf's warrior culture, rulers hailed gift exchange as the fundamental principle of good governance, but they also knew that their gift-giving ceremonies were simply pauses in an ongoing cycle of combat. According to Hrothgar, king of the Danes, civil relations with Beowulf's Geats in southern Sweden depended on perpetual gift giving and reciprocity. "For as long as I rule this far-flung land," he proclaimed, "treasures will change hands and each side will treat / the other with gifts" (*B*, 127). To stress the importance of these gifts, Heaney, following the *Beowulf* poet, lavished attention on neck rings, arm rings, helmets, swords, horses, and even women given as presents to pacify belligerent or potentially belligerent warriors. Gifts were also given to gods to assure peace. The Geats burned gifts of "helmets, heavy war-shields and shining armour" (*B*, 211) on Beowulf's pyre to persuade the "Lord of All," who "swallowed the smoke," to preserve tranquillity. As Mauss observed: "Gifts to humans and to the gods . . . serve the purpose of buying peace between them both" (1990, 17). Beowulf's sacrificial pyre, however, may not have pacified the "Lord of All." The poem concludes with ominous signs of future violence.

According to Mauss: "It is they [the gods] who are the true owners of the things and possessions of this world. With them it was most necessary to exchange [gifts], and with them it was most dangerous not to exchange [gifts]. . . . The purpose of destruction by sacrifice is precisely that it is an act of giving that is necessarily reciprocated" (1990, 16). Heaney highlighted this view of divine ownership and reciprocity at the beginning of *Seeing Things*, a volume published a decade after he began translating *Beowulf*. The crucial gift-giving scene occurs in his translation of a passage from book 6 of *The Aeneid*. At a churchlike "altar"

(*ST*, 2), the Sibyl of Cumae, whom Heaney calls a "priestess" of "mysteries" (*ST*, 1), tells Aeneas that if he wants to commune with his dead father in the underworld he must first break "the golden bough" from a sacred tree and give it "to fair Proserpina, to whom it belongs / By decree, her own special gift." Aeneas, following orders, breaks off the "special gift" from the tree and gives it to the goddess who created it, who owns it, and who will re-create it. When the Golden Bough "is plucked," Heaney points out, "a second one always grows in its place" (*ST*, 3). In the ending of Heaney's translation "The Golden Bough," unlike the ending of *Beowulf*, there is every indication that the divinity who receives the sacrificial offering will reciprocate in a satisfactory way.

Having lost his father in 1986, Heaney sought solace by retracing Aeneas's journey to the underworld, where a goddess healed wounds and allowed a bereft son to commune with his dead father. Heaney's translation, which brought a section of Virgil's epic back to life, was an act of mourning that also brought his father's spirit back to life. The poem that followed "The Golden Bough" drew on Virgil again, but this time to mourn and resurrect another person who had recently died—the poet Philip Larkin. In "The Journey Back," Heaney alludes to Virgil's appearance at the beginning of *The Divine Comedy* where he converses with Dante about descending into the underworld of the *Inferno*, although now it is Larkin who girds himself for the journey rather than Virgil, Aeneas, or Dante. In canto II of the *Inferno*, from which Heaney borrows several lines for his poem, Dante betrays his anxieties about the arduous journey into the abyss when he declares: "I am not Aeneas; I am not Paul. Neither I nor any man thinks me fit for this" (Dante 1939, 37). Dante, of course, overcomes his fears and fulfills his mission. Larkin, in Heaney's view, lacked the courage, intellect, and messianic ambition of a Dante. In "The Journey Back," Heaney changes the Dantean context from the end to the beginning of Christ's life and has Larkin ruefully concede: "I might have been a wise king setting out / Under the Christmas lights" (*ST*, 7). The implication is that Larkin was too anti-Christian, narrow-minded, and Scrooge-like to fare forth like the gift-bearing Magi on a journey toward a divine epiphany. Heaney made a similar criticism in "Englands of the Mind" when he faulted Larkin for his "refusal" to explore "race memory," the "myth-kitty," and the philological depths of language. Larkin possessed a great gift but refused to deliver it; he "deliberately curtailed his gift for evocation, for resonance, for symbolist *frissons*" (*P*, 164), by relying too heavily on his narrow-minded secular humanism.

If Heaney shackled Larkin to the "the heartland of the ordinary" (*ST*, 7) as his whipping boy in "The Journey Back," it was because Heaney was struggling to leave the ordinary behind and focus more on the extraordinary. Many of Heaney's poems in *Seeing Things* and subsequent volumes track journeys away from the "Heaviness of being" (*ST*, 50), as he calls it in "Fosterling," toward a visionary imagination that "credit[s] marvels" (*ST*, 50). Like Blake, he no longer wants merely to see mundane things with the outward eye; he wants to see miraculous things with the inner eye. He explains his new literary goals, however, the way he explained his former goals—in terms of gift exchange. In "The Settle Bed," which serves as a poetic manifesto in *Seeing Things*, he explains his new direction with a fable about how the imagination receives the "given"—the gift of quotidian reality—and transfigures it into something marvelously rich and strange. The cumbersome, "cart-heavy" (*ST*, 28) settle bed (a kind of primitive sofa-bed) represents the "given" for Heaney in part because it was a piece of furniture at Mossbawn that became an actual gift "willed down" (*ST*, 28) to him and transported to Glanmore Cottage, his country residence south of Dublin. "Imagine a dower of settle beds tumbled from heaven," he declares. "Learn from that harmless barrage that whatever is given // Can always be reimagined" (*ST*, 29). The "dower" or gift of the heavy bed, like the "heaviness of being," can and must be transformed by the visionary imagination.

Like Shield Sheafson weighed down with weapons on his funeral ship or the crewman who appears in a heavenly boat to "the Monks of Clonmacnoise / . . . at prayers inside the oratory" (*ST*, 62) in "Lightenings," the visionary poet in "The Settle Bed" experiences a feeling of liberation and "lightness of being" once the "given" has metamorphosed into the marvelous. He is "free as the lookout" who returns from his crow's nest above the fog to the ship's deck and finds "The actual ship had been stolen away from beneath him" (*ST*, 29). Rather than resent the loss of his old ship, he revels in the way it has magically vanished. "Who ever saw / The limit in the given anyhow?" (*ST*, 46), Heaney asks in a related poem, "Wheels within Wheels," in *Seeing Things*. Those who accept limits, who see things as they are and accept them for what they appear to be, according to Heaney, will miss out on the "access of free power" (*ST*, 46) that comes from seeing things as they might be or as they should be in a better world.

Actual gifts turn into emblems of the poet's visionary gifts with remarkable frequency in Heaney's later poetry. In *The Spirit Level* (1996), he again inaugurates a book by paying tribute to an actual gift—in this case a Native American rain stick that his friend and bibliographer Rand Brandes gave him during a conference in Lenoir-Rhyne, North Carolina, in the spring of 1992. The cactus stalk, which Brandes had purchased in San Francisco, was supposed to bring rain when it was turned upside down and its inner grit fell, making a sound like rain. For Heaney, the falling grit imitates not only the "gifts of rain" (*WO*, 23), as he called them in a poem with that title in *Wintering Out*, but also the voice of the gifted poet. "Upend the rain stick and what happens next / Is a music that you never would have known / To listen for" (*SL*, 1) he says, drawing attention to the mysteries of both the rain stick and the poet's voice. Like his Conway Stewart fountain pen, the rain stick has a renewable potency; it can work its sympathetic magic again and again. Its power remains "undiminished for having happened once, / Twice, ten, a thousand times" (*SL*, 1). At the poem's conclusion, revising the biblical aphorism about the wealthy man having as much chance of entering the kingdom of God as a camel passing through the eye of a needle, Heaney observes that the music of poetry, no matter how many times he hears it or creates it, makes him feel "like a rich man entering heaven / Through the ear of a raindrop" (*SL*, 1). The artist-god's gift, like the Creator's gift, appears to be eternal.

Later in *The Spirit Level*, Heaney celebrates the first known English poet, Caedmon, for possessing the same magical gift embodied in the rain stick. Caedmon's gritty, down-to-earth, alliterative music is as "undiminished" over time as the Creator's gift Caedmon praised in his famous, seventh-century Anglo-Saxon "Hymn." Heaney feels a special bond with this ancient poet because, like Heaney, he spent his pre-literary days herding cows and absorbing the lessons of the Catholic Church. As the story goes, while working as a farmer at the Whitby

Abbey in Northumbria, Caedmon received the gift of poetic song in a dream. Heaney identifies so closely with this pastoral gift-giving scene that he treats Caedmon as if he were a neighbor farming on the banks of the Moyola River near Mossbawn. "Caedmon too I was lucky to have known," he writes in "Whitby-sur-Moyola." Caedmon's gift, like Heaney's and Kavanagh's, liberated him from the hardships of the agricultural life by giving him access to what he called "the Creator's might and His mind-plans, / the work of the Glory-Father" (Caedmon 1979, 20). Caedmon's hymn to God the Father reminds Heaney of the creative gifts of more worldly fathers. The "human chain" implicit in "Whitby-sur-Moyola" links Heaney the Mossbawn farmboy to his cattle-raising father, his father's relatives (the Scullions), his poetic father Hopkins, and his other poetic father the *Beowulf* poet. When Heaney remarks of Caedmon's voice, "His real gift was the big ignorant roar / He could still let out of him, just bogging in / As if the sacred subjects were a herd / That had broken out and needed rounding up" (*SL*, 50), Heaney sketches the genealogy of his own poetic gift. As he said in his introduction to *Beowulf*, it was the alliterative clangor and weighty sonority of his father's relatives, "the big-voiced Scullions" (*B*, xxvii) who farmed close to Mossbawn, that shaped his poetic voice in "Digging," his *Beowulf* translation, and many of his other poems as well. In "Whitby-sur-Moyola" he traces that "big voice" back to Caedmon's "gift."

At the beginning of *Electric Light* Heaney eulogizes another patriarchal gift giver. In "Out of the Bag," he uses the Latin word *miraculum* (*EL*, 8) to give biblical *gravitas* to what was a familiar occurrence at Mossbawn—the appearance of Dr. Kerlin to deliver babies (Heaney was the first of nine). The special sheets put on Mrs. Heaney's bed "again and again" for childbirth were "wedding presents," and to her eldest child Seamus the babies were presents as well. Less tutored in the facts of life than in the doctrines of the Catholic Church at the time, Heaney presumed that his mother was a kind of Virgin Mary and that the doctor was a kind of magus—or magician—delivering gifts of babies to her in his black bag. "All of us came in Doctor Kerlin's bag," Heaney recounts. "He'd arrive with it, disappear to the room / And by the time he'd reappear . . . / . . . its lined insides . . . / Were empty for all to see" (*EL*, 6). To the innocent Heaney, Dr. Kerlin also resembled Father Christmas with

"Hyperborean, beyond-the-north-wind blue" eyes (*EL*, 7), except he showed up at all times of the year rather than only on Christmas Eve and he delivered just one gift from his bag. "And what do you think / Of the new wee baby the doctor brought for us all / When I was asleep?" (*EL*, 10), Heaney's mother would ask him after she gave birth. To underscore the awe that he felt as a boy at the mysteriousness of these births, he refrains from answering the question at the end of the poem. He merely implies that he witnessed each birth at Mossbawn as if it were a miraculous gift like the birth of the Christ child in the manger.

In *District and Circle* Heaney continues to commemorate actual gifts that transported him into the miraculous "precinct of vision" (*EL*, 10), as he calls it in "Out of the Bag." But he also suggests that he is not worthy of some gifts, that the obligations of gift exchange have exhausted him, and that—like Larkin in "The Journey Back"—he resents being forced, either by his conscience or by others, to play the role of a gift-giving magus. When he examines Bobby Breen's "Boston fireman's gift" of a helmet, which he received at a Cambridge poetry reading, he confesses in "Helmet" that the "scarlet letters on its spread / Fantailing brim" (*DC*, 14) sting him with shame. Unlike Hester Prynne's scarlet letter for adultery in Hawthorne's tale, these scarlet letters remind Heaney of his failure to actively save people. Referring to the helmet and to the life of sacrificial engagement it represents, he concedes that he is not "up to it"; he has never "served time under" any sort of helmet, and in general he refrains from "heroic," hands-on involvement in crises (*DC*, 14). Pondering the New York firemen's battles against the World Trade Center's fires ignited by terrorists as well as Beowulf's battles against terrorizing monsters and fire-breathing dragons, Heaney chastises himself for remaining safely ensconced on the sidelines. He feels obligated to prevent and redress disasters but confesses that he is no Beowulf and no Bobby Breen. Rather than plunge into the fray, he typically retreats to write poems about those heroes who do the saving.

The sonnet sequence "District and Circle" recapitulates the idea dramatized in "The Golden Bough" that in order to make heroic journeys into menacing infernos one must make sacrifices. In this case, however, Heaney refuses to offer a sacrificial gift to the god who presides over the underworld. When he meets a musician playing a tin whistle in the London Underground, he "trigger[s] and untrigger[s] a hot coin" (*HC*, 17) in his pocket, just as he once fingered his pen as if it were a gun. The tin-whistler, a mythical archetype resembling both Orpheus and Charon, offers his gift to Heaney in the form of music, but Heaney passes by without reciprocating by giving him a coin. When he joins the "human chain" on the subway car, he asks rather awkwardly: "Had I betrayed or not, myself or him?" (*DC*, 18). The circling car reminds him of the "familiar / . . . unrepentant" and then "repentant turn" (*DC*, 18) of his obsessive conscience. Consternation and guilt fester as he rides the London Underground. He broods on his sin of omission like a shade chained in a circle of Dante's *Inferno*, albeit a poetic shade who ultimately transforms his penitential brooding on his failure to give into the gift of a poem.

What makes Heaney's gift exchanges problematic in "District and Circle" is his vestigial sense of alienation from urban, technologically sophisticated environments. As if remembering London's historical role in oppressing Irish-Catholic nationalists like himself, he continues to identify with his rural roots at Mossbawn where his family had no electricity, running water, telephone, or car. Among all the tech-savvy city-dwellers in modern-day London, he feels like a prehistoric outsider. In another sonnet sequence, "The Tollund Man in Springtime," he adopts the persona of the Iron Age man who reminds him of his own "archaic," "ahistorical," down-to-earth "den life" that he enjoyed at Mossbawn. The Tollund Man passes "unregistered by scans, screens, hidden eyes" (*DC*, 55) through the modern "virtual city" because he is the ghost of a man who died during the fourth century BCE, but also because he symbolizes Heaney's invisible, primordial self beneath his mask of an up-to-date, smiling, public man. More at home in the Iron Age than in the Computer Age, Heaney merges with the "disembodied" Tollund Man to form a compound ghost who is antagonistic toward his technological surroundings. He expresses his "Newfound contrariness / In check-out lines, at cash-points, in those queues / Of wired, far-faced smilers" (*DC*, 57) by flaunting "A bunch of Tollund rushes—roots and all— / Bagged in their own bog-damp" (*DC*, 57). Worried that he has given up too much of his original identity to modern culture, Heaney and his ghostly alter ego clutch tokens of their primeval roots to remind themselves and everyone else that those roots are a continuing source of vitality.

"The soul exceeds its circumstances" (*DC*, 56), Heaney proclaims in his poem about the revenant Tollund Man. Ever since his departure from Mossbawn in 1952, the date that marked the death of his naturalist-self, Heaney had agonized over the proper relationship between the soul and its circumstances. The quotation about the soul's excess comes from an obituary essay by Leon Wieseltier about Heaney's friend, the Polish writer Czesław Miłosz, who died in 2004. According to Wieseltier, Miłosz during his long life "discharged his obligations to his age and his obligations to his soul" (2004, 1) out of a conviction that he had been endowed with competing gifts for political activism, mystical contemplation, and poetry. Like Merton, with whom he carried on a long correspondence, the Catholic Miłosz conceived of the Creator as a mysterious gift giver and the creation as a sacred gift that carried with it obligations to reciprocate. "There are nothing but gifts on this . . . Earth" (Miłosz 1981, 186), he wrote in "A Separate Notebook." As he made clear in *The Captive Mind*, he considered the main boon he received from the Creator to be the "gift" (Miłosz 1953, 240) of his poetic imagination. Wieseltier pointed out that Miłosz also possessed a "rare gift of knowing how to be at once troubled and unperturbed" (2004, 1) during historical crises—a gift nurtured by his study of Catholic contemplation and mysticism. "We cemented our friendship," Wieseltier said, "with the discovery that we shared an envy of mystics" who regarded "the things of this earth" as a "miraculous" and "incomprehensible . . . mystery" (2004, 2). In the poem "Thankfulness," a paean to Eucharistic gift exchange quoted by Wieseltier at the end of his eulogy, Miłosz wrote: "You gave me gifts, God-Enchanter. / I give you thanks for good and ill" (1953, 3). These lines on gifts received and given back could have served as an appropriate epitaph for Heaney as well as for Miłosz.

In fact, when pressed by an RTÉ journalist near the end of his life about an epitaph, Heaney offered words referring to gifts and gratitude that came from a passage in Sophocles's *Oedipus at Colonnus* that he translated when Miłosz died. At the end of the play, a messenger who has witnessed the king's mysterious descent into the underworld says: "Wherever that man went, he went gratefully" (Corcoran 2013). Although Miłosz once admitted that he felt "stretched," as if on a rack, "between contemplation of a still point and the demands of history" (*SS*, 260), according to Heaney his Polish friend never lost his sense of gratitude for the Creator's gifts. When Miłosz died on August 14, 2004, Heaney said he was reminded of Miłosz's poem "Gift" that expressed gratitude for nature's splendor around his California house. Heaney felt a similar "thanksgiving and admiration" for Miłosz himself. "I could easily have repeated to myself the remark he once made to an interviewer, commenting upon his epigram, 'He was thankful, so he couldn't not believe in God.' Ultimately, Miłosz declared, 'one can believe in God out of gratitude for all the gifts'" (Heaney 2004c, 4). Like Merton, Miłosz awakened Heaney's contemplative and mystical impulses to express gratitude for the Creator's gifts.

In addition to writing a eulogy, Heaney paid his respects to Miłosz by attending his funeral, which involved a High Mass in Krakow's Mariacki Church, and by writing an elegy based on the Mass. Heaney's poem, "Out of This World" in *District and Circle*, recounts the Eucharist at the funeral as if it were Miłosz's thanksgiving for the "God-Enchanter's" gifts. Although God had become a mythical archetype for Heaney, he concedes in his elegy that he bowed "during the consecration of the bread and wine," received "the mystery" of God on his tongue, and could not "disavow words like 'thanksgiving' or 'host' / or 'communion bread'" (*DC*, 47). No doubt, thinking of Miłosz's own religious evolution, Heaney looks back at his youthful Catholic convictions from the point of view of an ecumenical older man. He tells the story of his pilgrimage as a teenager to Lourdes, in France, where in 1958 he carried the sick to the healing shrine and attended the "underground basilica" memorializing Bernadette Soubirous's visions of the Virgin Mary. He now calls the famous subterranean church built with thick walls of cement "The concrete reinforcement of the Mystic- // al Body, the Eleusis of its age" (*DC*, 49). To his mythical perspective, Catholic and pagan rituals appear to enact similar communions with a mysterious divine gift giver. The descent into the underground church at Lourdes is "catholic" in the original sense of the Greek word *katholikos*; it is "universal." It recapitulates the Tollund Man's descent into the fecund peat bog, Virgil's descent into the underworld to pluck the Golden Bough and commune with his father, Christ's descent into hell after the Crucifixion, Dante's epic descent into the Inferno, and Persephone's descent into Hades' underworld in the Eleusinian mystery cult. As Lewis Hyde explained in *The Gift*, poets such as Ezra Pound esteemed the Eleusinian mystery cult in ancient Greece because it was devoted to the idea that ongoing gift exchange produced fertility, natural abundance, artistic creativity, and social prosperity. Pagan initiates at Eleusis took a vow of silence to protect the mystique of the rites that reenacted Persephone's wintry descent to Hades and her joyous, springtime ascent to her mother Demeter, the goddess of grain. Like their mystical heirs in Christian tradition, the Greek worshippers also kept silent out of awe before the gifts of creation and re-creation. The words *mystery* and *mystic*, as Hyde and other scholars have noted, derive from the Greek word *muein*, which meant to close the mouth, to remain mute or silent. Reverential silence was the natural response to the mystery of the Creator's gift.

Heaney followed Pound and other modernists in viewing gift exchanges in pagan fertility cults as precursors to Christian rituals of gift giving and thanksgiving such as the Eucharist. As a Catholic youth on a retreat or pilgrimage, a university student reading about the contemplative's *via mystica*, an ecumenical adult participating in Mass, or a poet writing mythological poems, Heaney paid homage to the gift givers, whether they were parents, artist-gods, religious avatars of the Creator, or the original Creator. His later books made a concerted effort to "credit marvels"—both natural and supernatural—as well as the visionary imagination that transformed "given" realities into marvelous poetic gifts. Like his early hero Kavanagh and later hero Miłosz, Heaney registered his astonishment at being blessed with a great gift. He was grateful for it and so were his readers. As his friend Bill Clinton said in a moving tribute: "Your poetry has been a gift to the people of Ireland and to the world and a gift to me" (McGreevy 2013). When Heaney died in 2013, eulogy after eulogy praised his willingness, despite his occasional gripes about obligations to reciprocate, to share his gifts.

NOTE

1. Seamus Heaney to author, pers. comm., June 4, 1987.

CHAPTER ELEVEN

"Deep Down Things"

The Inner Lives of Things in Later Heaney

Richard Rankin Russell

> Generally speaking, my poems come from things remembered, quite often from away back, or things I see that remind me of something else. Sometimes the thing has an aura and an invitation and some kind of blocked significance hanging around it.
>
> —Seamus Heaney, *Stepping Stones*

> Heaney's is a world defined as much by objects, and by the relations of objects to people, as by the relations of people to one another.
>
> —Hugh Bredin, "A Language of Courage and Love of Objects"

> The status which the Catholic church enjoyed, and which drew the young to it, was based upon a mindset which recognized the value in making this thing, here and now, other.
>
> —Robert Welch, "Sacrament and Significance"

Chris Arthur has compellingly pointed out, "For whatever reason, it seems we are afraid to acknowledge the voices speaking in the things around us" (2012, 117), yet Seamus Heaney has always made such an acknowledgment, to the betterment of both his poetry and his readers' lives. Blake Morrison's (2013) moving essay written after Heaney's death muses that "for Heaney, there were marvels enough in this world, and never mind the next. Ordinary objects and places—a sofa, a wireless, a satchel, a gust of wind, the sound of rain—were sanctified." And Paul Muldoon (2013) memorably remarked at that time about Heaney's poetry, "rarely had we seen such a high quotidian quota." No poet since Gerard Manley Hopkins (and before him, Wordsworth) has investigated the life of things the way in which the late Heaney did. Hence, the title of this essay with its reference to Hopkins's Petrarchan sonnet, "God's Grandeur," part of which Heaney has used for the title of his own, uncollected poem.[1] From the opening poem, "Digging," in his first full volume, *Death of a Naturalist* (1966), to the final poem in his last major volume, *Human Chain* (2010), "A Kite for Aibhín," Heaney probes the things inhabiting and coloring our lives, from potatoes and peat in the former poem to the kite in the latter one. He has done what Norman Wirzba argues we should all do: "respect the integrity of things by giving them the space to be themselves" (2003, 88–89). Moreover, the material arc Heaney traces from the "cool hardness" of the potatoes and the "soggy peat" to that ineffably soaring kite constitutes one of the great explorations of physical things in poetry (*DN*, 1, 2). He has cited approvingly several times the closing lines of Czesław Miłosz's "Blacksmith Shop": "It seems I was called for this: / To glorify things just because they are" (*SS*, 303), and he shares this desire to glorify things, to celebrate their existence, with Miłosz and Hopkins.

While Hopkins, however, inspired by Duns Scotus, largely confines himself to articulating the *quidditas* or "thingness" he finds in nature, such as the lives of stones, dragonflies, and kingfishers that he limns in the poem "As kingfishers catch fire," Heaney explores not only natural, living things but also, perhaps even more persistently, what Heidegger, in his essay "The Origin of the Work of Art," terms "equipment."[2] Heidegger believed that "as a rule it is the use-objects around us that are the nearest and authentic things. Thus the piece of equipment is half-thing, because characterized by thingliness, and yet it is something more; at the same time it is half art-work and yet something less, because lacking the self-sufficiency of the art work. Equipment has a peculiar position intermediate between thing and work" (1971, 29).[3] My analysis of the

things in the poems that follow treats them as Heideggerian "equip-
ment" and shows how Heaney establishes their authenticity as "half-
thing" and "half art-work." As part of his apprehension of their inner
"lives," he perceives their energies and apprehends how these things
connect us to the earth and to the beyond, much like Heidegger's ex-
ample of the jug in his essay "The Thing." In this way, Heaney reverses
the Orkney poet Edwin Muir's argument that "the vast dissemination of
secondary objects isolates us from the natural world in a way which is
new to mankind, and . . . this cannot help affecting our sensibilities and
our imagination" (1962, 8). Instead, Heaney transforms such objects into
things with their own radiant life. His poetry suggests the truth of what
Barbara Johnson has claimed: "Where but in art do we really encounter
the materiality of daily life? . . . Perhaps, after all, it takes art to bring out
the thingliness of things" (2008, 61). Finally, Heaney's sense of things
blends with his sense of words as material in the poems from the last two
decades of his life. Therefore, his "thing poems" attempt to suture the
long-held Western divide between *res* (thing) and *verbum* (word) that
crept in after the Renaissance, when it was previously generally agreed
that everything had its own distinctive name. Heaney's later poems col-
lapse the recent distinction between *res* and *verbum*: poems *are* things.
Therefore, these intricately wrought poems about made things them-
selves reflect the ornate structures of the objects they portray, a double
act of thingness, self-contained yet grounded in the traffic of the real
world and reaching toward infinity.

The title of Heaney's *Seeing Things* (1991) has often been taken
to signify his turn toward what he termed in his Nobel Prize address,
Crediting Poetry, the "marvelous,"[4] yet to apprehend the marvelous, I
argue, we must reexamine, *see* anew, the quotidian, material things in his
later volumes, beginning with *Seeing Things*, that speak their identities
and yet gesture beyond that identity toward the transcendent. I want not
only to draw our attention to the perduring physical objects in Heaney's
later poetry as worthy of examination in their own right but also to
highlight the way in which these objects are transformed into things and
extend beyond the realm of the physical into the poetic and the spiritual
by virtue of his imagining of them. When Heaney asks at the beginning
of lyric "xxii," from "Squarings," "Where does spirit live? Inside or

outside / *Things* remembered, made *things*, *things* unmade?" (my italics), one gets the sense he may be willing to grant that all three sets of things could have some sort of spirit life (*ST*, 76).

Bill Brown, the pioneer of thing theory, has argued that literature transforms things and enables them to escape one strand of modernity's attempt to render objects as having no value except "use or exchange, secularizing the object's animation by restricting it to *commodity* fetishism alone" (2004, 185).[5] Although Heaney does not make such a distinction between *object* and *thing*, I do throughout this essay, using *thing* consistently to connote an object that has not been reduced to mere commodity and that has been elevated to the status of thing through his powerful imagination.[6] I examine the emotional content and context of these things by recourse to the phenomenological theories articulated by Heidegger in the essays "The Origin of the Work of Art" and "The Thing"; by Gaston Bachelard in *The Poetics of Space*; and later by Edward Casey in *Remembering* and elsewhere. Citing one of Heaney's best-known poems, "The Harvest Bow," Ben Howard has even identified what he calls the "thing-poem": "Like many of Heaney's strongest poems, 'The Harvest Bow' is a 'thing-poem,' a sub-genre in which a concrete object—Rilke's panther, Bishop's fish—comes under intense contemplative scrutiny" (2014, 167). I explore Heaney's most considered assessment of the life of things—his essay "Place, Pastness, Poems: A Triptych" (1985–86)—along with his later "thing-poems" such as "The Pitchfork," "Wheels within Wheels," lyrics from "Squarings" (*Seeing Things*); "Wordsworth's Skates" and "To George Seferis in the Underworld" (*District and Circle*, 2006); "Pangur Bán" (uncollected, 2006), and "A Kite for Aibhín" (*Human Chain*, 2010).[7]

Interested from the beginning of his career in the emotional aspect of things, Heaney began working out a theory of objects and their emotive power in "Place, Pastness, Poems: A Triptych." There, Heaney suggests that Thomas Hardy's poem "The Garden Seat" implies how a "ghost-life . . . hovers over some of the furniture of our lives . . . the way objects can become temples of the spirit" (*PPP*, 30). Casey claims that "even mute material things, inanimate as well as animate, can be thoroughly memorial in status: they, too, can embody memories and are not limited to evoking them. . . . *Any thing* . . . can become memorial: can become a bearer of memories with as much right as a monument built to stand forever" (1987, 310). Heaney certainly evinces a similar belief and has located the source of many of the things he found auratic in "the top of the dresser in the kitchen of the house where I lived for the first twelve years of my life" (*PPP*, 32). Rather than merely discovering an assemblage of often broken or disused objects, Heaney, upon opening this drawer, felt "all that dust and rust and stillness suggested that these objects were living some kind of afterlife. Something previous was vestigially alive in them. They were not just inert rubbish but dormant energies, meanings that could not be quite deciphered" (*PPP*, 32). In the act of attending closely to these things, Heaney began the dynamic process of recognizing them and retrieving them from the category of inert objects. Jon Erickson emphasizes that "the *process of objectification* itself . . . is never completed. It is in fact an aspect of ongoing *consciousness* that it needs to objectify things to re-cognize them in the first place; this is a function of memory. An 'art object,' a 'literary object,' even a 'theoretical object,' is not something static; rather, it is something that is always being objectified as long as attention is paid to it" (1995, 4–5). Always a careful observer of his surroundings, as his career progressed Heaney paid even more attention to things, especially things from childhood that held powerful, attractive forces. He also realized that previous owners had caressed these things and thus imbued them with affections, even rendering them literary—what he has praised elsewhere as Pablo Neruda's concept of "impure poetry": "the used surfaces of things, the wear that hands give to things, the air, tragic at times, pathetic at others, of such things."[8]

Heaney's language in "Summoning Lazarus" and in "Place, Pastness, Poems" anticipates what Sara Ahmed has argued about "objects of emotion" that "become sticky, or saturated with affect, as sites of personal and social tension."[9] While understandably, more critical attention has been paid to his poems about the "Troubles" in Northern Ireland and that conflict's aftermath, many of his poems from the last twenty years of his career attempt to recover those "dormant energies" and reveal them to us. Crucially, the form of Heaney's poetry enables a recovery of such energies because, as Denis Donoghue has argued, "Form is the achieved, purposed deployment of energy, energy available on need and not there till looked for" (2003, 123). Form leads us into intimate relations with things, helping us to draw nearer to them through the act of perception. Ortega y Gasset lamented that the trajectory of European painting gradually moved from "proximate to distant vision," and he valorizes instead proximate vision, which allows us to perceive things "with the indefinable corporeality and solidity of filled volume. We see it 'in bulk,' convexly. . . . Proximate vision has a tactile quality. What mysterious resonance of touch is preserved by sight when it converges on a nearby object?" (1968, 111, 113).[10] Or by art, we might add. Heaney's singular poems, by the work of their form, invite us into the proximate vision he cast upon particular things, communicating a tactile sense of the perceived to us and something of the wonder evoked in that perception. He privileges poetry as capable of seeing deeply into the life of things and becoming a conduit of their power.

In my following analysis of the poems, I hold that as Heaney's poems turn more toward spiritual matters beginning in *Seeing Things*, the language becomes more pared-down, emphasized in some poems by his privileging of the tercet as his primary form, but also by its paradoxically becoming more concentrated, more material, to express the weighty quality of his objects that sometimes literally lift off and glide away, as in the case of the title implement from "The Pitchfork."

In some instances, the poem itself seems to become, or tries to become, at one with the thing it portrays, a conflation of *res* and *verba*. Bernard O'Donoghue has commented upon Heaney's interest in such a meeting of things and words in his insightful reading of the passage in "The Loaning," from *Station Island*, where the lost words fly out from their hiding places: "What it does ostensibly is to close the gap between word and thing. Its [the poem's] production is not only a physiological process; it is a physical one" (1994, 97). By so doing, Heaney follows an ancient theory going back to Plato in the *Cratylus* that "only one name exists to convey the special thingness of objects," a theory that English Renaissance poets, especially Spenser, also held.[11] He affirmed this viewpoint by using an epigraph citing Miroslav Holub's "On the Necessity of Truth" in an early draft of his 1983 pamphlet poem for the Field Day Theatre Company, *An Open Letter*: "The right name is the first step toward the truth which makes things things and us us."[12]

Heaney's interest in things, their inner lives, and the emotional pressures they exert upon us likely arises in part from his deep interest in the Romantic poets, especially Wordsworth, who argued in his and Coleridge's preface to *The Lyrical Ballads* that poetry should make the ordinary extraordinary.[13] Heaney actually cites this passage from that preface in his introduction to the selection of Wordsworth's poems he edited: "A common incident is viewed under a certain 'colouring of imagination'; ordinary things are presented to the mind in an unusual way and made interesting by the poet's capacity to trace in them, 'truly though not ostentatiously, the primary laws of our nature.'"[14] His approval of this poetic strategy in Wordsworth suggests he has similarly traced "the primary laws of our nature" through seeing into the life of things. In "Wordsworth's Skates," which he collected in *District and Circle*, he hears "the whet and scud of steel on placid ice," and sees something imperishable about the Romantic poet's skates, "Not the bootless runners lying toppled / In dust . . . / Their bindings perished, // But the reel of them on frozen Windermere / As he flashed from the clutch of earth along its curve / And left it scored" (*DC*, 22). Such lines recall the lovely language of book I of *The Prelude* when Wordsworth recalls himself and his boyhood companions, "shod with steel," hissing "along the polished ice in games / Confederate" (1994, 319). More important, Heaney celebrates the perduring, memory-evoking qualities of the steel in Wordsworth's skates that enabled him to score the surface of frozen Lake Windermere. These things have a literal cutting edge, implying the continuing importance of words that are sharp, that can slice into a subject and get a grip on it.

The "curt cuts of an edge" in "Digging" also come to mind in this regard (*DN*, 1), but much more recently, in the poem preceding "Wordsworth's Skates" from *District and Circle*, "To George Seferis in the Underworld," Heaney concludes by praising the particular keen edge of dialect words such as the Irish for rushes, *seggans*. He muses that he wants "a chance to test the edge / of *seggans*, dialect blade / hoar and harder and more hand-to-hand / than what is common usage nowadays: / sedge—marshmallow, rubber-dagger stuff" (*DC*, 21). Such a recovery of *seggans* and its signifying power becomes a crucial maneuver in this volume, since it suggests that Heaney believes that words have gradually lost their rhetorical power to evoke a particular thing or even person. Instead, he privileges *verba* as *res* in many instances from his later poetry; words have a heft and power to them as they always have had in his work, but now the things themselves, which often are used to pierce or cut, are coincident with the word that signifies them. Moreover, the poems that feature these objects themselves become instances of *res*; Heaney even has stated that a poem is "the *made* thing" (2009b). He has suggested, moreover, that art is sufficient unto itself and thus is healthy and sound, noting that "the virtue of poetry and art in general resides in the fact that it is first and foremost a whole thing, a hale thing, a thing formally and feelingly sound, right within itself, a thing to which the ultimate response—if not always the immediate response—is 'yes'" (2002c, 8). Elsewhere, he affirms this stance, arguing that the word *poetry* is "a noun aspiring . . . to the condition of verb—a noun because *as a work of art it must retain a definite thinginess*, but verb-like nevertheless, because it represents an act of mind and an act of making" (Heaney 2001b, 20; italics mine). Hopkins's insistence that his poems about natural objects "instress" or capture the "inscape," or distinctive individual identity of the thing or person, exemplifies this sense of the poem as *res* and *verba* for Heaney.[15]

Additionally, Heaney's theory of things and poetry was shaped indelibly by his upbringing in the Irish Catholic Church, an institution that valued everyday things and viewed them sacramentally. Robert Welch has offered the fullest and most valuable discussion of this mindset, which takes as a touchstone the anonymous ninth-century ancient Irish lyric sometimes called "The Scholar and His Cat," which Heaney himself has translated as "Pangur Bán" (Heaney 2006b). Quoting Séan Ó Riordáin's contention that "a poem is not a feeling, it's a being," Welch suggests that "The Scholar and the Cat" creates a "situation in which the two separate beings of the scholar and his cat are involved severally yet conjoined in a new 'at-one-ment.'" Furthermore, and crucially for understanding Heaney's view of things, Welch identifies "this capacity, this measured yet intense allowing of a thing or being its own life, while holding back from it, maintaining a reserve, a decorum, an awe—this is the central element in the mind-set reflected in the poem" (1996, 105–6). He argues that "it is this element, this cool finesse holding in reserve vast charges of the energy hurtling through all things that is one of the distinguishing marks in the way the Irish view the world" (1996, 106). Certainly, in our current globalized and globalizing world, this outlook has been greatly diminished, along with the institution that promoted it for a long time, the Irish Catholic Church, but Heaney seems to fully share this perception. As Welch contends, such a perception is not unique to the Irish, but at least until some point in the twentieth century "this characteristic," which Welch sees at bottom as spiritual, "holds good more consistently and more steadfastly than is often the case in other cultures" (1996, 106).[16]

Fascinatingly, this deliberate setting aside and singularizing of everyday things, a propensity that Welch argues is part of the Irish Catholic "sacramental" outlook, may be thought of as inherently modernist. Indeed, Welch cites the lines from Hopkins's "As kingfishers catch fire"—"Each mortal thing does one thing and the same: / . . . / Selves—goes itself"—to suggest that the turn in Catholicism at the time toward devotion and veneration, what Emmet Larkin termed the "Devotional Revolution," was entirely in accord with the drift of modernist psychology, philosophy, and literature to seek out, explore, and expose "the intrinsic traits of people and things."[17] Certainly, there were key differences between modernism and the newly modern iteration of Irish Catholicism that tried to jettison its underpinnings as a folk religion, but their shared attention to a concentrated gazing upon a particular thing suggests how a significant strand of both movements generally valorized and aestheticized the singularity of the everyday thing. Aspects of the medieval mind, too, prized this deep contemplation of the thing, and in Heaney's translation "Pangur Bán" he points out how the titular cat's pursuit of a mouse and the medieval monk's of words result from "Concentration, stealthy art." While "his round bright eye / Fixes on the wall," the scribe "Exercise[s] my weaker gaze / On the sharply argued page" (Heaney 2006b).[18] Such an artistic pursuit for Heaney strengthened as he aged into a complex poetry that itself sometimes became one with the object it portrayed.

Consider, as an example of this later poetry, the language and the form of "The Pitchfork" from *Seeing Things*: the solid quatrains give the object depicted a weight, but after two stanzas, each consisting of one sentence, the language of the third quatrain is reduced to its essence, a series of adjectives that shade into verbs by third line of the stanza:

> Riveted steels, turned timber, burnish, grain,
> Smoothness, straightness, roundness, length and sheen.
> Sweat-cured, sharpened, balanced, tested, fitted.
> The springiness, the clip and dart of it.
>
> (*ST*, 25)

We have seen such a succession of adjectives before in Heaney's poetry; for instance, the victim portrayed in "Strange Fruit" is described as "Murdered, forgotten, nameless, terrible / Beheaded girl" (*N*, 39). But the adjectives here gradually acquire a burnished quality themselves as they process in front of us, and by the third line of the stanza the pitchfork is characterized by verbs only. In the last line of the stanza, the pitchfork stands revealed in the near sentence of definite article, noun, another definite article, two verbs, and prepositional phrase. It is as if the implement gathers itself syntactically, grammatically, and by the fourth line stands poised to be thrown, as it is indeed imagined to be in the next stanza.

That third quatrain is the exact center of the poem, framed by two quatrains that precede and come after it. They effectively frame the pitchfork portrayed in the shorn language of the middle stanza. The pitchfork is sufficient unto itself, complete in itself, earthed and grounded, yet seemingly yearning to leave the earth. Heidegger's example of the jug as the thing par excellence comes to mind here. As he somewhat cryptically but insightfully muses, "The jug is a thing insofar as it things. The presence of something present such as the jug comes into its own, appropriatively [*sic*] manifests and determines itself, only from the thinging of the thing" (1971, 177). To return to Hopkins, we might paraphrase this by saying that the jug or the pitchfork or indeed the poem itself "Selves—goes itself." And yet none of these draw away from us—rather they draw us into their presence ineluctably but delightfully. Heidegger argues that "in thinging, it stays earth and sky, divinities and mortals. Staying, the thing brings the four, in their remoteness, near to one another" (1971, 177). The dynamic process of the energies of a thing or a poem cannot be stopped or frozen once we are in proximity to them. As Heidegger insists, "The thing is not 'in' nearness, 'in' proximity, as if nearness were a container. Nearness is at work in bringing near, as the thinging of the thing" (1971, 178). Heaney's pitchfork constantly is brought near to us as we perceive it in its essence, its flight, and its reception at the end of its flight.

By stanza 4, the pitchfork that was readied to throw in the first stanza—"When he tightened his raised hand and aimed with it, / It felt like a javelin, accurate and light"—takes off into space. Then, "when he thought of probes that reached the farthest, / He would see the shaft of a pitchfork sailing past / Evenly, imperturbably through space." The tool seems to hang in the air for an eternal present, silent, rushing by but still visible, "Its prongs starlit and absolutely soundless—" (*ST*, 25).

In stanza 5, the last stanza, the pitchfork has acquired agency and displaced the speaker of the poem as it escapes even the procession of adjectives and verbs used to describe it in stanza 3. Following the dash at the end of the fourth stanza, we are simply told, "But has learned at last to follow that simple lead / Past its own aim, out to an other side / Where perfection—or nearness to it—is imagined / Not in the aiming but the opening hand" (*ST*, 25). Now the pitchfork travels through some sort of barrier "out to an other side," and whereas it was originally described as, "Of all implements," coming "near to an imagined perfection" by being "aimed" in stanza 1, now we get a sense of another person, perhaps, standing ready to catch it on the other side. That person imagines being, not a "warrior" or "athlete" like the thrower, but a receiver characterized by his "opening hand" (*ST*, 25). In between the throwing and the receiving hands on each side, the pitchfork sails, on its own, leading itself on.

Although the analogy might seem strained at first, the pitchfork and its being wielded and thrown, then received, may stand for a poem, which is lovingly constructed, seasoned, as it were, in the mind of the poet, tested, and then thrown out into the world, taking on its own life, to be received by readers and listeners.[19] In apprehending how this later Heaneyean thing and its arc can resemble poetic creation, publication, and reception, we see how his conception of things—and their relationship to poetry—has changed from some of his earliest poems. The objects examined in poems from the 1960s such as "Digging" and "The Forge" certainly are bound up in analogous relationships to poems, their inspiration and creation, but the "reception" of these objects is not considered. The objects are simply there for us to inspect them and stay literally in place—the potatoes, the turf, the anvil, and the horseshoe—whereas the pitchfork and other things in *Seeing Things* and after move, shimmer, even try to disappear. Heaney's things in the later poetry take on, sometimes literally, a life of their own and a movement and rhythm of their own even as they become coterminous with the poem itself. They invite us to take part in their inner life and to experience something like the creative process. Being "equipment," to use Heidegger's specific term, they are half created objects, half things, in a space between. And yet that space they occupy seems both intimate and vast.

A related principle to understanding the life of things as Heideggerian equipment that is related to poetry in such works as "The Pitchfork" and others in Heaney's last volumes involves this intimate immensity, a space whose existence Gaston Bachelard illuminates in *The Poetics of Space*. Bachelard argues that "to give an object poetic space is to give it more space than it has objectivity; or, better still, it is following the expansion of its intimate space" (1994, 202). Recall that Heaney's pitchfork "has learned at last to follow that simple lead / Past its own aim, out to an other side." Extrapolating from Bachelard, we might then say that if we give the poem as found thing its own space, it overspills its brim, its formal limits, and moves into intimate space where we can receive it and wander in it. Poems—good poems—are very difficult to properly and fully explain because of their intimate immensity that we must live in to experience them. In experiencing them, we become caught up in them (and are often unable to articulate what they "mean"), gazing at such intimate objects as the pitchfork, yet finding ourselves in a space so vast it scarcely seemed imaginable before we entered the room of the poem. When Heaney asks in lyric "xxii" of *Squarings*, "How habitable is perfected form?" he is thus likely describing the experience of moving into a poem through the act of reading (*ST*, 76). Moving objects increase this sense of vastness, since, as Bachelard points out in his analysis of Baudelaire, "Movement itself has, so to speak, a favorable volume, and because of its harmony, Baudelaire included it in the esthetic category of vastness" (1994, 193). We might say, then, in light of Bachelard's apprehension of movement and inclusion of it, via Baudelaire, as a "category of vastness," that "The Pitchfork" and other such poems have a limited "volume" or depth on the page that is quickly increased by the movement of the objects portrayed within.

Nowhere is this volume so expansive as in the moving bicycle wheel of "Wheels within Wheels," a poem whose series of circles that the poet recalls inhabiting as a boy suggests the continuing validity of Daniel Tobin's contention in *Passage to the Center: Imagination and the Sacred in the Poetry of Seamus Heaney* (1998) that a search for the center lies at the heart of Heaney's work. This neglected poem courts a gritty, Larkinesque reality in its opening but by its conclusion acquires an intimate immensity that indicates just how Heaney's ordinary objects become not simply radiant but limitless, opening worlds beyond our ken. The first quatrain of "Wheels" offers in its straightforward rhetoric a promise that Larkin made in his early poetry—that we will be less deceived than we previously were: "The first real grip I ever got on things / Was when I learned the art of pedaling / (By hand) a bike turned upside down, and drove / Its back wheel preternaturally fast" (*ST*, 48). But "things" is ambiguous: does it suggest something like "life" or "reality" or literal objects? We struggle for our own grip on the first line after concluding our reading of this stanza. Actually, "things" may denote the "back wheel" of the "upside down" bicycle, but as that wheel spins, Heaney's speaker seems to "see into the life of things," to quote Wordsworth, and the wheel's revolutions in their intimate immensity beckon us into the world of the poem and into something like the ethereal realm.[20] Thus as the bike wheel and the poem spin they are made strange to us, yet familiar.

Formally, we leave the familiar comfort of the opening couplet and are plunged into a series of unrhymed lines, exposed to the poem's revolutions, much as the speaker recalls being transported by the turning bicycle wheel. If this process works properly, we enjoy submitting to the movement of the poem and vanishing into its life, just as the speaker recalls loving "the disappearance of the spokes, / The way the space between the hub and rim / Hummed with transparency" (*ST*, 48). Given that Heaney has often written movingly about what happens almost magically in the space between things, he endorses this liminal location in which transparency hums and catches us up into the life of this long-vanished thing. The air itself within this space becomes shaped by the wheel's revolutions even as the poem continues through most of this first stanza with no rhymes. The invisible air is thus "hooped" and can in turn render formed objects formless, inchoate. For instance, a potato thrown into this space becomes "mush and drizzle," while a "straw frittered" (*ST*, 48). The spinning wheel's spokes slice and shred quotidian objects, much as the turnip-snedder, in the later poem of that name, does. In so doing, it becomes something other than its functional self that normally causes locomotion; instead, it generates considerable energies that transport us literally and figuratively out of reality into the marvelous, where we ourselves are shaped and forwarded into a glimpsed future.

As the young boy worked those "pedal treads," they gradually "began to sweep your hand ahead / Into a new momentum—that all entered me / Like an access of free power . . ." (*ST*, 48). While the pitchfork in the earlier poem forwards itself, free from the hand that releases it, the wheel here finally transforms not only the potato and the straw but also the perceiving subject, whose hand takes on a "new momentum" as it becomes part of the wheel's velocity. This "access of free power" that the speaker attains is something like an *omphalos*, a resonant word both for Joyce's Stephen Dedalus in the first episode of *Ulysses* at the Martello Tower and for Heaney, who has consistently been drawn to such imagined and real locations and who uses the word *omphalos* specifically in "The Toome Road."[21] Crucially, unlike the well in the second part of the poem, which is a given, natural *omphalos* where water oozes out, this *omphalos* is a mechanical one that must be created by the boy's hand. Yet it nonetheless enables him to enter into a space whereby "belief / Caught up and spun the objects of belief / In an orbit coterminous with longing" (*ST*, 48). This complicated phrase suggests that belief is analogous to that childhood wheel—it is necessary to believe in order to transform everyday reality into the orbit we desire.

Not content with this "manufactured" *omphalos*, the speaker decides to place it into the natural conduit of the well because "enough was not enough. Who ever saw / The limit in the given anyhow?" (*ST*, 48). Presumably, placing one *omphalos* into another would generate even more power and transformative visions. And indeed, for a while, this maneuver does. When the speaker touches "the tyres / To the water's surface, then turned the pedals," wheels of infinity seem to rotate and remake the world: "The world-refreshing and immersed back wheel / Spun lace and dirt-suds before my eyes / And showered me in my own regenerate clays" (*ST*, 49). We are seemingly back in an Eden of sorts where the world is washed afresh and represented to us, just as the speaker's body is covered with "regenerate clays" that hint at his origins. Covered, clothed in clay, he returns to the earth through the "muddy, dungy ooze" (*ST*, 48), yet gazes up at the "Spun lace and dirt-suds" as they are launched skywards. Again, he enters the space between—this time between earth and sky. He manages to combine the power of these two *omphaloi* and catch himself up as a transported object "For weeks," during which time "I made a nimbus of old glit, / Then the hub jammed, rims rusted, the chain snapped" (*ST*, 49). A "nimbus" can signify a rain cloud, but the usage here likely connotes something like a radiant halo around a saint or divine figure. Heaney the young boy thus figuratively transformed himself into a saintly figure through spinning mud and clay upon himself, a wheel within a wheel, a nimbus generated by a bicycle wheel. Yet material reality intrudes and it is as if the very elements conspire against him to jam the process and stop it. Once the wheel can spin no more, the nimbus dissipates and the child can never recapture that feeling of radiance until he attends a circus.

There, he sits within a wheel or "circus ring, drumrolled and spotlit," while "Cowgirls [are] wheeled in, each one immaculate / At the still centre of a lariat" (*ST*, 49). Wheels within wheels within wheels within wheels, a triple image, whirl him up into another *omphalos*. The cowgirls are caught up within their spinning lariats, standing within a circle of light inside the circus ring. The last two lines of the poem, another couplet with "pirouette" chiming with "*Stet!*", return us sonically to the opening couplet where things are pedaled, yet for a poem that features a series of enjambed lines to echo the onrushing, transformational power of the bicycle wheel, then the wheel's immersion in the well (and semantically, "well" is contained within "wheel"), the series of full stops that conclude the poem jar at first: "*Perpetuum mobile*. Sheer pirouette. / Tumblers, Jongleurs. Ring-a-rosies. *Stet!*" (*ST*, 49). Rather than show us the seemingly continuous power of the other *omphaloi* through enjamb-ment, here Heaney attempts to freeze through a series of verbal snap-shots the various dynamic circles he saw as a child at that long-ago circus. Even if those revolving rings of tumblers, jongleurs, and lariat-twirling cowgirls have long stopped spinning, Heaney recovers them through the power of his pen, finally inserting himself into the poem as a writer who uses his creative power by recourse to the proofreader's notation to "keep the same," "*Stet!*," here rendered as an exclamatory imperative. He renders these snapshots forever revolving in these stripped-down lines bereft of traditional sentence structure, reduced to their essences of adjectives, nouns, and verbs. In his equation of the turning objects of his past and the bodies in motion that adorn that cir-cus ring, the speaker suggests a continuity of life between seemingly in-animate objects and humans.

Bachelard believes that "a poet . . . . knows that when a thing be-comes isolated, it becomes round, assumes a figure of being that is con-centrated upon itself" (1994, 239). Such a statement holds true for any object that is perceived and thus transformed into a thing; but it must especially hold true for things that are round or create roundness, such as the childhood Heaney's wheels. And in perceiving the roundedness of these many images of circles, Heaney must have been confirmed in him-self: as Bachelard claims, "Images of full roundness help us to collect ourselves, permit us to confer an initial constitution on ourselves, and to confirm our being intimately, inside" (1994, 234). Caught up in wheels within wheels, the young Heaney must have felt his bounded being soar outside its limits yet also be affirmed in its existence.

"Wheels within Wheels" may give the fullest sense in later Heaney of his belief that people and things, properly and lovingly contemplated, interpenetrate each other, a traditional view because the "conceptual polarity of individualized persons and commoditized things is recent and, culturally speaking, exceptional," as Igor Kopytoff has pointed out (1986, 64).[22] Heaney's connection between people and things is affirmed by many of our best thinkers. For instance, Bruno Latour holds that "things do not exist without being full of people" and that any consid-eration of humans must involve an apprehension of things.[23] Conversely, in a certain sense, people are things through our embodiment: "Visible and mobile, my body is a thing among things; it is one of them. It is caught in the fabric of the world, and its cohesion is that of a thing. But because it moves itself and sees, it holds things in a circle around itself," as Maurice Merleau-Ponty puts it (1964, 163).[24] The young Heaney's explicit attraction to wheels and circles recalled in "Wheels within Wheels" thus may suggest how he sensed that they imaged the way in which his body moved among things and encircled them.

Heaney's lyric xl from *Squarings* suggests he found himself at one with everything around him as a child of four who "turned four hundred maybe, / Encountering the ancient dampish feel / Of a clay floor. Maybe four thousand even" (*ST*, 94). Recall the "regenerate clays" the young Heaney sprayed upon himself in "Wheels within Wheels" once he set the bicycle wheels in the well. He has spoken often of how he grew up in a nearly prehistoric era before electric light, a time he describes in his Nobel Prize address as "ahistorical, pre-sexual, in suspension between the archaic and the modern" (*CP*, 9). To register his at-oneness with such basic elements of the world as the clay floor, he mentions the "terracotta water-crock" and simply states "Ground of being" with a full stop afterwards to begin the third tercet. Playing on the Anglo-Saxon kenning of "earth-house" to convey a grave, he uses that phrase for his childhood home at Mossbawn to show how such a primal relationship to the earth and the quotidian objects and implements around him prepared him for a life of writing about such things: "Out of that earth house I inherited / A stack of singular, cold memory-weights / To load me, hand and foot, in the scale of things" (*ST*, 94). Here memory becomes weighted like a stack of cold iron, and the poet perceives himself as embodied thing weighing in the balance of "the scale of things"—the world around him and its actual objects. In returning to dwell upon the things of that childhood world that seemed to have a life of their own (often examples of Heideggerian "equipment"), Heaney reenters his own earlier life as a "thing among things" and explores remnants of his memory freighted with the emotion of childhood.

In the hinge poem of *Seeing Things*, "Fosterling," Heaney rehearses the "heavy greenness" and "in-placeness" of a picture, likely of a Dutch landscape that reminds him of his childhood terrain, and its "immanent hydraulics" that make up "My silting hope. My lowlands of the mind."

The weighty matter of Northern Ireland, even the mantle of the poet who must write of such "things" in a time of violence that seemed to last forever is signified by the opening of the sestet: "Heaviness of being. And poetry / Sluggish in the doldrums of what happens." This Shakespearean sonnet itself begins to lift off, as it were, by lines 11 and 12, when the poet ruefully recalls that it took him until he was nearly fifty to "credit marvels," much "Like the tree-clock of tin cans / The tinkers made." This functional thing becomes a sign of things-that-could be, no longer simply telling time but outstripping time itself, gleaming a future beyond us where we might reimagine ourselves and our relationships to others and things. Heaney has rehearsed this newfound ability to credit marvels in *Crediting Poetry*, but the role of things in this transformation has never been fully elucidated. The concluding couplet sonically suggests the harmony he felt around this time in his career: "So long for air to brighten, / Time to be dazzled and the heart to lighten" (*ST*, 52). Intriguingly, things remain part of this headier, higher atmosphere, but they are flicker-lit with an effulgence, signified by the color gold that runs through *Seeing Things* and beyond and freighted with a new ethereality.

Words now are transposed and they become lighter, as does Heaney's turn from the quatrain form to the tercet form. Such a movement is signaled in "The Birthplace," originally published in 1978 but not collected until the publication of *Station Island* in 1984. This tripartite, tercet-driven poem concludes with a section that anticipates the language of lyric xl from *Squarings*, featuring "the words of coming to rest: // birthplace, roofbeam, whitewash, / flagstone, hearth, / like unstacked iron weights // afloat among galaxies" (*SI*, 35). The charged aura and airiness around Heaneyean things is signified too by the tercets that drive the entire *Squarings* sequence, a form poised between the finality of the couplet and the heaviness of the quatrain and whose formal qualities I cannot explore sufficiently in the space remaining.[25]

I would conclude with a brief consideration of Heaney's translation of Giovanni Pascoli's poem "L'aquilone" as "A Kite for Aibhín," collected in *Human Chain*. This kite "takes off, itself alone, a windfall," a fitting tribute to and summa of Heaney's long exploration of things, perhaps the apotheosis in his canon of "things thinging," in Heidegger's phrase

(*HC*, 85). Transformed from mere object by virtue of its flight and Heaney's imagination, the kite soars above us, suggesting both the intimacy we can have with things and their ultimate beyondness. It also suggests the animated quality of poetry as it hovers near us, yet then eludes us sometimes. Finally, it achieves what Heaney speaks of in "Place, Pastness, and Poems" as "a kind of moral force" because the kite is yet another thing "seasoned by human contact." Such things "insist upon human solidarity and suggest obligations to the generations who have been silenced, drawing us into some covenant with them" (*PPP*, 31). Heaney's poem looks back to his earlier "A Kite for Michael and Christopher" and the suggestion there that their holding of the kite string will equip them for the strain of suffering in their own lives (*SI*, 44), and forward to the joy he hopes his granddaughter Aibhín will have in her own life that will be lived mostly without him. The tail end of the poem, that last dangling line of modified Dantesque terza rima, becomes identified with the kite's tail, and the poem seems to pull off a magic trick, nearly slipping the bounds of the page and floating away. Nothing will replace the nearness of Heaney to us when he walked in the world or the way he could enact "things thinging" in his memorable poetry recitations. But we should take considerable comfort that his poems about things will continue to be carried by us, seasoned by human contact, caressed by our own teaching and writing about them, passed on to succeeding generations. Things (and poems) can live forever. World without end.

NOTES

The chapter's three epigraphs are from Heaney (2008c, 255), Bredin (1984, 18), and Welch (1996, 109).

1. The phrase occurs in the tenth line of Hopkins's Petrarchan sonnet "God's Grandeur": "There lives the dearest freshness deep down things" (Hopkins 1985, 27). See Heaney's "The Dearest Freshness" (2000a, 7).

2. For an extended comparison between Hopkins and Heaney that occasionally contrasts their view of things, including flora and fauna, see Liu (2010). I clearly depart from Liu when he argues that particularly in *Seeing Things*, "the poet, though willing to 'be dazzled' and 'see things,' becomes instead a mere observer of still life objects—literally, *la nature morte*—and misses the vivifying principle" (2010, 275–76). Liu believes that "compared with Heaney, while

facing the created world, Hopkins is more like a reader of dynamic narratives than an observer of static objects" (2010, 289). Although I believe Liu is correct about the active Catholic underpinning of Hopkins's poetry and its relative absence as a "vivifying principle" in Heaney's, Heaney nonetheless uses his Catholic imagination to read the "dynamic narratives" of things that he sets apart because of his sacramental upbringing and renders extraordinary, perceiving that they have continuing lives of their own.

3. For the best discussion of this essay of Heidegger and also his concept of "the Thing" in relationship to poetry, see Barbara Johnson (2008, 61–82).

4. Heaney, in *Crediting Poetry*, observes, "I began a few years ago to try to make space in my reckoning and imagining for the marvelous as well as for the murderous" (*CP*, 20).

5. Bill Brown, *A Sense of Things* (2001, 185). See Ian Hodder, however, for a much more negative assessment of the relationship between people and things. For instance, Hodder points out that "things have lives of their own that we get drawn into, and society depends on our ability to manage this vibrancy of things effectively, to produce the effect of stability. . . . We are . . . deeply entangled in the vitality of things and the assemblages of their relations" (2014, 21). Later, he argues, "We seem caught; humans and things are stuck to each other. Rather than focusing on the web [of "meshworks or networks of interconnections" between humans and things] as a network, we can see it as a sticky entrapment" (2014, 25).

6. For an alternative approach focusing on the changing perceptions of the "object" in art and literature, see Erickson (1995).

7. There are many more such poems whose consideration lies beyond the scope of this essay. I provide a discussion of the thingly lives of the turnip-snedder and the harrow-pin in the poems bearing those titles from *District and Circle* in Russell (2014, 350–51).

8. Heaney's "Summoning Lazarus" (1974, 741). Elsewhere, in "The Pathos of Things" (2007a, 21), he has written of how the Japanese concept of *mono no aware* entered English language poetry through the Imagist poets such as Ezra Pound, approvingly defining the concept: "Literally meaning 'pathos of things,' it usually refers to sadness or melancholy arising from a deep empathic appreciation of the ephemeral beauty manifested in nature, human life or a work of art."

9. See Ahmed (2004, 11). She argues that such stickiness is "*an effect of the histories of contact between bodies, objects, and signs,*" noting further that "what sticks 'shows us' where the object has travelled through what it has gathered onto its surface, gatherings that become a part of the object" (2004, 90–91).

10. See also Stewart (2002, 157–58) for a brief but discerning discussion of the connections between nearness and aesthetic perception in Heidegger's essay

"The Thing," in Ortega's "On Point of View in the Arts," and in Heinrich Wölf-flin's theory of empathy in "Prologomena zu einer Psychologie der Architektur."

11. See Hunt (2012–13, 250–51). Ferry argues that "this assumption of the bond between name and thing was so widely held that it was shared and cited even by [Renaissance] writers whose opinions differed profoundly on many other matters" (1988, 72).

12. Seamus Heaney, "An Open Letter," typescript, n.d., Seamus Deane Papers, Manuscript, Archives, Rare Book Library, Emory University.

13. But see Paul Muldoon (2013) for an argument that Heaney's "engagement with the things of the world was so unadorned as to invite comparison with John Clare—yes, except a clearer John Clare."

14. See Wordsworth and Coleridge's preface to *Lyrical Ballads* (Wordsworth 1994, 433) and Heaney's introduction to his selection of Wordsworth's poems (Heaney 2001c, viii).

15. See Gardner (1985, xx–xxiii) for a short but incisive discussion of inscape and instress. Heaney argues in his essay "The Convert" that in Hopkins's poetry thingness and words merge: "World becomes word: the volume and density of the actual has been transformed into a high linguistic voltage. To read these poems is to go through the hoops of the palpable" (1989b, 15). For a thoughtfully argued review of Hopkins's influence on Heaney in the poems of *District and Circle*, see Bleakney (2006, 29), who argues that "few [poets] remain as unashamedly in thrall [to Hopkins] as Seamus Heaney; as enchanted with the physicality of language; as attuned to the natural order."

16. In the only previous article-length treatment of Heaney and things, Stephen Regan points out "the extent to which the poems risk suggesting that a metaphysical or spiritual quality adheres to objects of memory. Although Heaney is cautious in using the term 'relic,' and therefore any overt indication of Catholic worship, the poems nevertheless yearn for some transcendental significance. Out of this tension between the palpable physicality of the object and its potential spirituality emerge many of Heaney's most memorable poems" (2014, 320).

17. Welch (1996, 12). For the full text of "As kingfishers catch fire," see Hopkins (1985, 51).

18. Hugh Bredin cannily observes this medieval aspect of Heaney in relation to things when he points out in his review of *Station Island*, "There is something of the medieval in Heaney; few people nowadays realize that objects have any character. But here he compels us into their alien and patient world, where they await the touch of a mind, the touch of a word, then spring into the vivid life of the inanimate" (1984, 18).

19. Such a reading has been anticipated to some degree by Tobin, who thoughtfully claims that "what Heaney affirms here is a view of poetry as parable that bears witness to the advent of an unintended, unexpected, but nevertheless

palpable grace manifesting itself through the ordinary, what he calls in 'A Basket of Chestnuts' 'a giddy strange assistance'" (1998, 257). Heaney himself has likened using a pitchfork in hay to artistic work in *Stepping Stones*: "Angling the shaft and the tines so that the hay turned over like a woven fabric—that was an intrinsically artistic challenge. . . . Using the pitchfork was like playing an instrument. So much so that when you clipped and trimmed the head of a ruck, the strike of the fork on the hay made it a kind of tuning fork" (*SS*, 336).

20. The passage occurs in line 49 of Wordsworth's "Lines Composed a Few Miles above Tintern Abbey" (Wordsworth 1994, 67).

21. See line 17 of Heaney's "The Toome Road" (*FW*, 15): "The invisible, untoppled omphalos."

22. Kopytoff argues that perceiving the separation of things and people is unique to the Western mind, "intellectually rooted in classical antiquity and Christianity," but "becom[ing] culturally salient with the onset of European modernity" (1986, 84).

23. Latour (2000, 10), cited in Bill Brown's "Thing Theory" (2001, 12).

24. Bill Brown, "Thing Theory" (2001, 4) cites the crucial phrase from Merleau-Ponty: "Body is a thing among things."

25. See Russell (2014, 240–78, 356–92) on Heaney's tercet form for a full and considered exploration of that form.

CHAPTER TWELVE

"Door into the Light"

The Later Poems of Seamus Heaney

Stephen Regan

After the harrowing intensities of *North* (1975), with its unforgettable
display of bog bodies and its incessant funeral rites, *Field Work* (1979)
seemed to mark for Seamus Heaney a necessary phase of personal re-
covery and artistic redirection in the rural domain of Glanmore. The
title of the later book, *Field Work*, implies some continuity with the out-
door, farming preoccupations of Heaney's first full-length collection of
poems, *Death of a Naturalist* (1966), while also hinting at a subtle explo-
ration of new possibilities. It carries suggestions of sustained labor, a de-
termined reopening of familiar ground, as well as a return to the trusted
pastoral mode. In that difficult interim between *North* and *Field Work*,
Seamus Heaney (1979b, 20) wrote to Brian Friel that he "no longer
wanted a door into the dark" but "a door into the light . . . to be able to
use the first person singular to mean *me* and my lifetime." The emphasis
here is on light as the enablement of unfettered subjectivity, a way of
writing in which the self can be clearly expressed and apprehended. At
the same time, the implied process of moving *into* the light also has pow-
erful political and philosophical implications that resonate throughout
Heaney's career.

North had ended with the declining "last light" of "December in Wicklow" and with a self-lacerating meditation on missed opportunities, magnificently captured in the image of a lost comet, with its "million tons of light" reduced to a "glimmer of haws and rose-hips" (*N*, 72). Perpetuating this anguished quarrel with the self, *Field Work* opened with "Oysters," initially celebrating a revived appetite for the purely sensuous delight of poetry—"My palate hung with starlight"—but turning once again to self-recrimination and unease, with the speaker "angry that my trust could not repose / In the clear light, like poetry or freedom / Leaning in from sea." Stung by the "Glut of privilege," the poem confesses its agitation as traces of imperial history and thoughts of violence cluster around the image of oysters. Even so, the poem powerfully registers that "clear light" as a longed-for ideal, and it firmly and appropriately aligns the unhindered lyric impulse with "freedom," as the closing stanza turns toward the open expanse of the sea (*FW*, 11).

Light has multiple and diverse functions in Heaney's poetry. At a fundamental level, it serves as a principle of poetic composition, an integral component of the cognitive and imaginative processes of poetry, from seeing and perceiving objects in the world to reflecting upon them and re-creating them in the mind. Increasingly, the light that streams into the poems comes to be equated with political hope and the possibility of change, tentative at first but gaining in assurance from volume to volume. The equation of a more relaxed and hopeful self with the processes of peace and reconciliation is repeatedly acknowledged in the symbolic play of light and lightening. In the later poems, especially those in *Seeing Things* (1991) and *Electric Light* (2001), light provides a host of theological and eschatological possibilities, a powerful metaphorical medium for dwelling on final things.

Heaney's longing for a door into the light returns us immediately, of course, to the publication of *Door into the Dark* in 1969. "The Forge," an accomplished sonnet in that early collection, opens with a declaration of "negative capability" (Keats 1990, 370) and a determination to encounter the dark places of artistic creation, even while being in the grip of uncertainties, mysteries, and doubts: "All I know is a door into the dark." The blacksmith's anvil is imaginatively transformed into "an altar" as the sonnet slips from octave to sestet, confirming the role of the forge as a dark cave of making where craft and labor combine with inspiration and dedication. The aspiring poet finds an exemplary music in "the hammered anvil's short-pitched ring" and a startling image of inspiration in the "unpredictable fantail of sparks" (*DD*, 19). Looking back on these early ideas of poetic composition in the interviews in *Stepping Stones*, Heaney is drawn to the theories of Carl Jung by way of explanation, and especially to the function of symbolic archetypes in poetry: "You learned that, from the human beginnings, poetic imagination had proffered a world of light and a world of dark, a shadow region" (*SS*, 472). Indeed, much of Heaney's early poetry corresponds to Jung's (1967, 265–66) fundamental concern with acknowledging and exploring personal darkness: "Filling the conscious mind with ideal conceptions is a characteristic of Western theosophy, but not the confrontation with the shadow and the world of darkness. One does not become enlightened by imagining figures of light, but by making the darkness conscious." That willed enlightenment, a stage of personal development beyond the child's narcissistic staring into water, is memorably evoked in "Personal Helicon," the manifesto poem with which Heaney closes *Death of a Naturalist*: "I rhyme / To see myself, to set the darkness echoing" (*DN*, 57).

It is clear, too, that Heaney's early ideas of poetic conception and gestation are influenced by a modern poetics that had begun to absorb the findings of psychology while simultaneously moving away from a long tradition of Romantic idealism. The fertile darkness of Heaney's first two volumes, in particular, recalls T. S. Eliot's (1933, xiii) idea of "the dark embryo" that appears in the poet's consciousness and gradually takes on the form and speech of a poem. Even so, the creative impulse that continues to motivate and inform much of Heaney's writing, right through to *Electric Light* at the beginning of the next century, is the familiar Romantic belief in the illuminating power of the imagination, an idea well known to Heaney's generation of undergraduate students in English through the massive popularity of *The Mirror and the Lamp* (1953) by M. H. Abrams. The Keatsean imperative of going forth with lamp in hand takes on a new urgency in *Wintering Out* (1972) and *North* (1975) as Ulster enters a traumatic phase of political darkness.

Across the broad spectrum of poetic theory, then, Heaney's apprehension of light draws on the legacy of the Romantic poets, especially

Wordsworth, Blake, and Keats, while acknowledging the experimental play of light and the new art of epiphany in the work of modernist writers, including Eliot, Joyce, and Yeats. At the same time, the light that spills into Heaney's poetry emanates from his own local origins and experiences. By his own admission, his way of seeing the world places him in the company of Patrick Kavanagh rather than Yeats, with a "fundamentally Catholic mysticism" being grounded in everyday domestic realities: "My starlight came in over the half-door of a house with a clay floor, not over the dome of a Byzantine palace; and, in a hollowed-out part of the floor, there was a cat licking up the starlit milk" (*SS*, 318).

The function of "Sunlight," the first of the two dedicatory "Mossbawn" (*N*, 8–9) poems with which Heaney opens *North*, is to provide a bright and sustaining image of beneficence in which the love and security associated with home act as a stay against the darkness that follows. There is a reassuring certitude in the simple declarative past tense of the opening line: "There was a sunlit absence" (*N*, 8). The abstract "absence" has a strangely liberating effect here, allowing a momentary contemplation of nothing but the light itself. The play of light turns absence into a positive, creating space for tranquillity and stillness. The poem contrives to do what other poets have failed to do, making the sun stand still, but its most potent achievement is in its revelatory figuring of love "like a tinsmith's scoop / sunk past its gleam / in the meal-bin" (*N*, 9). There is a nurturing plenitude in "scoop" that makes it an apt image of love, but the persistence of light in the buried "gleam" lifts the poem from its modest kitchen setting into a numinous present, where hope and inspiration might still be found.

"Gleam" has a venerable place in poetic tradition, registering both a lost potential, as with Wordsworth's "visionary gleam" (1984, 298) and an elusive future, as in Tennyson's "Ulysses": "Yet all experience is an arch where thro' / Gleams that untravell'd world whose margin fades / For ever and forever when I move" (1969, 563). In Heaney's *North* it reappears in the title poem, in which the imagined tongue of a Viking longship bids the poet, "Lie down / in the word-hoard, burrow / the coil and gleam / of your furrowed brain." The instruction here is to "Compose in darkness," but darkness now signifies not so much the fertile place of making in *Door into the Dark* as a necessary withdrawal, perhaps even self-protection. At one level, what Heaney proposes in "North" (*N*, 19–20) is a tempered modernist poetics of occasional epiphanies rather than a Romantic ideal of sustained visionary power: "Expect aurora borealis / in the long foray / but no cascade of light" (*N*, 20). At another level, though, "the long foray" carries obvious suggestions of conflict and warfare, as well as aptly describing the poet's self-imposed intellectual endeavors. The image of "aurora borealis," better known as "the northern lights," brilliantly conveys the northern geography of the book while also fixing the image of the poet as a watcher of the skies intent on discovering beauty in the shifting, uncertain lights drifting through winter darkness.

Throughout the 1970s, then, Heaney's imagination moves furtively through a poetry of "night and light and the half-light" (Yeats 1965, 67). In his prose writings in the early 1980s, there are signs of a deeply felt need to open the door into the light even further and embrace an art of brilliant luminosity. "The Main of Light" was written for the *festschrift* volume *Larkin at Sixty* (1982) and reprinted in *The Government of the Tongue* (1988) and *Finders Keepers* (2002). It retains its freshness and appeal as a positive reappraisal of the poetry of Philip Larkin. The essay begins, however, not with Larkin, but with Shakespeare, and with the startling way in which "the mind's eye gets dazzled by 'the main of light'" as we progress from "nativity" to "maturity" in sonnet 60 (*FK*, 145). Heaney's enthusiastic appreciation of a poetry of intense vision and revelation draws him to a previously unacknowledged brightness and brilliance in Larkin's poetry, but it also signals the direction in which his own poetry would tend from this time onwards.

Challenging the familiar critical assessment of Larkin's downbeat, empirical way of seeing the world, Heaney claims that "there survives in him a repining for a more crystalline reality" and an appetite for "the sensation of revelation." He traces "a stream of light" that flows through Larkin's poetry, noting how it generates a "hymn to the sun" in "Solar," and how a "light-filled dilation" at the center of "Deceptions" transposes that poem from "lament to comprehension" (*FK*, 146–48). He claims that the concluding lines of "Here," with their magnificent vision of "unfenced existence / Facing the sun," constitute an "epiphany," and he goes on to reveal the many and various effects of light in "Water," "'The

Whitsun Weddings," "An Arundel Tomb," and "High Windows": "The minute light makes its presence felt in Larkin's poetry he cannot resist the romantic poet in himself who must respond with pleasure and alacrity" (*FK*, 149–50). The final, generous assessment of the work is that "Larkin also had it in him to write his own version of the *Paradiso*" (*FK*, 152). We know, in retrospect, that Heaney had it in him, too.

The challenge to the poet going forth, lamp in hand, in the bitter political climate of the 1980s is well illustrated in the title poem of *The Haw Lantern* (1987). Here, it seems that the poet is still "wintering out" and that the emblematic red berry of the hawthorn is a votive light for his beleaguered art: "The wintry haw is burning out of season, / crab of the thorn, a small light for small people." That small light modestly instills in the people a measure of self-respect, "not having to blind them with illumination." In the turn of what looks like an inverted sonnet, the tree comes to resemble the cynic Diogenes roaming through daylight Athens with his lamp, in search of "one just man." Now the light of poetry, it seems, takes on a more active civic role, but one as much given to self-scrutiny as to the judgment of others. The image of the red berry as a "blood-prick" suggests a pricking of the conscience, and one in which the poet is as implicated as his readers (*HL*, 7).

It is not until *Seeing Things* (1991) that Heaney allows the main of light to flood into his work with the transforming power that he had commended in the essay on Larkin. The impulse is candidly announced in "Fosterling," with its rueful acknowledgment of "Me waiting until I was nearly fifty / To credit marvels" (*ST*, 50). The title and the epigraph acknowledge the "heavy greenness" of nationalist politics, as well as the burden of the poet as "water carrier" in John Montague's early poem of that title. "Fosterling" also brings to mind the growth of a poet's mind "Fostered alike by beauty and by fear," prompting us to look back to *North* and the quotation of those lines from Wordsworth's *Prelude* in the epigraph to "Singing School" (*N*, 62). As in the earlier poem, Yeats is also a shaping presence, with "The Song of Wandering Aengus" providing the stirring image of "brightening air" (Yeats 1965, 54) and "Easter 1916" reminding us that "too long a sacrifice / Can make a stone of the heart" (Yeats 1965, 180): "So long for air to brighten, / Time to be dazzled and the heart to lighten" (*ST*, 50).

A further instance of "tremendous change" (*SS*, 326) in Heaney's life and work, "again something to do with getting near fifty," is recorded in "The Skylight," the seventh sonnet in "Glanmore Revisited" (*ST*, 37). As Heaney acknowledges in the *Stepping Stones* interviews, Glanmore Cottage had become for him not only a workspace and a retreat but a physical embodiment of what Wallace Stevens describes as "the imagination pressing back against the pressures of reality." Having initially opposed the idea of introducing a skylight to the roof of the cottage, Heaney returned from Harvard and found light flooding through the low ceiling: "I lifted up my eyes to the heavens" (*SS*, 325–26). The resistance and the release are skillfully manipulated in the octave and sestet of the sonnet, with the turn amply registering a shift of mood and outlook: "But when the slates came off, extravagant / Sky entered and held surprise wide open" (*ST*, 37). Unexpectedly, but assuredly, the poetry acquires its own "light-filled dilation," admitting that "crystalline reality" so admired in "The Main of Light." The experience brings with it, for Heaney, the sought-for healing and forgiveness that had seemed so difficult to obtain in "The Haw Lantern." The cynic Diogenes makes way for the man sick of palsy, lowered through the roof in St. Mark's Gospel (2:4) to be physically and spiritually restored. Along with this newfound spiritual valency comes a newfound conception of unroofed poetry, a preoccupation with unroofed dwelling places, and a visionary apprehension of an unroofed world.

Complementing the new Glanmore sonnets in *Seeing Things*, and displaying a "tongue-and-groove" (*ST*, 37) poetic craft, is a sequence of "Squarings," consisting of four sections, each with twelve poems (*ST*, 51–108, 325). Each poem has twelve lines, arranged in four stanzas. The four-square architectural solidity of the sequence nevertheless allows for freedom of poetic composition. Heaney's method of working was to establish a firm structure but also invite a content that was "wide open to whim" and sensitive to speed and chance: "I felt free as a kid skimming stones" (*SS*, 319). *Squarings* has various meanings, ranging from the child's adoption of a position in playground games with marbles to a more serious, adult "squaring up" to the world. The sequence is sensitive, too, to the play of light. As Neil Corcoran observantly notes: "'Squarings' is opulent in its lexicon of luminosity: its individual poems have, among other such usages, their brilliancies, radiance, blazing, dawning, brightness, illumination, flaring, sealight, glitter, shine, gleam, burnish, phosphorescence, beaming, shimmer, flashing, fireflies, starlight." He helpfully acknowledges, as well, the "Dantean inheritance" in the sequence, recalling T. S. Eliot's appreciation of Dante's "masterly use of that imagery of *light* which is the form of certain types of mystical experience" (Corcoran 1998, 174). Heaney's "Squarings" are, among other things, reflections on the afterlife, on judgment, and on the final journey of the soul, but they are also elegiac evocations of absence, including the absence of belief.

The opening section of the sequence, "Lightenings," gives notice of "Shifting brilliancies" that are both aesthetic, in terms of the luminous visual images embedded in the poems, and spiritual, in terms of the fluctuating longing for knowledge and revelation that the poems convey. Light aids meditation and brings to mind unforgettable anticipatory images of "the particular judgment," the moment of final spiritual reckoning in Catholic theology. These images are brilliantly ushered in by "winter light / In a doorway" and "A beggar shivering in silhouette." The scene is spectacularly desolate and unroofed, with the abandoned house or "wallstead" anticipating Heaney's translation of *Beowulf* a few years later: "Bare wallstead and a cold hearth rained into— / Bright puddle where the soul-free cloud-life roams." The ambivalence here (souls free among clouds, but also clouds free of souls) percolates through "Lightenings," prompting a poetry that provides no great revelation or clarification, just "old truth dawning" (*ST*, 55). Even so, it is "still susceptible to the numinous" (*SS*, 319). For all his later disparagement of Larkin as a poet of "last things," especially when compared with Yeats (*FK*, 316), it is Larkin who provides the "gazing out" and sanctions the impulse behind the repeated qualification of "nothing" in "Nothing magnificent, nothing unknown." As with Larkin's "deep blue air," there is both intense exhilaration and infinite emptiness in Heaney's "unroofed scope" (Larkin 2012, 80).

"Lightenings" involves a prolonged meditation on the meaning of "lightening," without any arch or affected postmodern self-reflexiveness. In fact, the self-scrutiny is conducted with a striking combination of colloquial ease and theological scholasticism, one leading us gently into the other, from "that" to "this":

And lightening? One meaning of that
Beyond the usual sense of alleviation,
Illumination and so on, is this.

(*ST*, 66)

The meaning in question, couched in the brittle terms of a dictionary definition, has to do with what Heaney elsewhere defines as "a flaring of the spirit at the moment before death." This is "lightening" in the special sense of "being unburdened and illuminated" (*SS*, 321). It is, of course, just "one" meaning, and it doesn't displace the more obvious and immediate sense of "lightening up" alluded to in "Fosterling" (*ST*, 50). Even so, light in *Seeing Things* guides us unswervingly into the realm of eschatology. It also guides us, just as surely, into the realm of the political. Poem xxxvi of *Squarings*, part of the "Crossings" section of the sequence, recalls the civil rights marches that Heaney took part in, but it does so "in the light" of a later life. The danger of the march and the confrontation with the police is now defused and seen in the broader aspect of the poet's expansive imaginative life. The poem opens with the Old Testament valley of darkness (Psalm 23:4) and closes with the classical myth of Charon, the ferryman of the dead, but it is Dante who prompts the comparison between fireflies and the "unpredictable, attractive light" of the policemen's torches (*ST*, 94). There are multiple crossings here, and the crossing to a new, and later, imaginative conception of the event does not displace the powerful memory of that initial crossing to safety in a time of panic and uncertainty.

There is no doubt that a further letting in of the light was occasioned by the IRA cease-fire at the end of August 1994, and that much of the "lightening up" in Heaney's work at this time had to do with changing political relations that permitted a new, if somewhat guarded, optimism. There is confirmation of this in a short article, "Light Finally Enters the Black Hole," written by Heaney for the Dublin *Sunday Tribune*, just a few days after the announcement was made, and later reprinted as "Cessation": "I went outside to try to re-collect myself and suddenly a blind seemed to rise somewhere at the back of my mind and the light came flooding in. I felt twenty-five years younger. I remembered what things had felt like in those early days of political ferment in the late sixties" (*FK*, 45). A hope that new possibilities might quell the political conflict of the previous twenty-five years flows through the Nobel Prize acceptance speech, "Crediting Poetry," in 1995, and it manifests itself in the forward-looking poems of *The Spirit Level* in 1996. The changing political circumstances of the early 1990s encourage Heaney to look again at the familiar places associated with his earlier work and to see them in a new light. "Tollund" (*SL*, 69) is an especially important instance of this act of reappraisal, since it inevitably calls to mind the ritual violence of "The Tollund Man" and the poet's pained condition of feeling "lost, / Unhappy and at home" (*WO*, 48). Dated "September 1994," "Tollund" candidly announces a post-cease-fire perception of having "traveled far." A new sense of being "at home" infuses the closing lines of the poem, in which the poet appears as revenant, "Unfazed by light, to make a new beginning" (*SL*, 69). The revisiting of old haunts in a new light is evident, too, in the later poem, "At Toomebridge," in *Electric Light* (2001). This time, Heaney returns to a place that has strong associations with both historical memory and more recent political events—"Where the checkpoint used to be. / Where the rebel boy was hanged in '98"—both now receding in the electrically charged atmosphere in which the poet senses the possibility of the marvelous in the "shining" water of the River Bann. The slippage from "slime" to "silver" (not "slither") in "the slime and silver of the fattened eel" releases a sudden sense of promise and well-being, subtly triggering a subliminal connection between electric eels and electric light (*EL*, 3).

The title poem of *Electric Light* alludes to the electrification of rural areas, including County Derry, in the 1930s and 1940s, but it also clearly signals the emergence of a new and bright conception of poetry and poetic vocation. It is as if the poet's memories are given a powerful new charge. A switch is pressed and a light shines searchingly over the long perspective of the past sixty years. "Electric Light" gives symbolic resonance to the light switch and the wireless knob, granting the mature writer a new way of seeing his own poetic calling and of tuning in to the voices of his education, including those of T. S. Eliot, James Joyce, and Philip Larkin. In a Poetry Book Society Bulletin, later reprinted in the *Guardian*, Heaney gives a candid account of how the poems in *Electric Light* were composed and how perspective brings significance. His lucid explanation has a particular bearing on the title poem: "Incidents from childhood and adolescence and the recent past swim up into memory: moments that were radiant or distressful at the time come back in the light of a more distanced and more informed consciousness" (Heaney 2001d).

"Electric Light" opens with a pre-electric image of candle wax, but also with the possibility of epiphany. The grandmother's mangled thumbnail, likened to the congealed "Candle-grease . . . dark-streaked with soot," is transformed by the light of imagination into a thing of beauty, "puckered pearl." As we slip from tercet to tercet, new shapes and patterns of memory are brought into play. The "ancient" mangled thumb is now likened to "Rucked quartz" and leads us down the rock-strewn footpath to the Sybil's cave in Virgil's *Aeneid*. The grandmother, a modern Sybil in her unzipped "fur-lined felt slippers," would not be out of place in *The Waste Land*, except that Heaney's attitude is one of familial warmth and attachment rather than comic condescension or ironic disdain. We are reminded here of the Sybil as she appears in the epigraph to *The Waste Land*, from the *Satyricon* of Petronius: "Nam Sibyllam quidem Cumis ego ipse oculis meis" (Eliot 1967, 37; With my own eyes I saw the Sibyl at Cumae). The child's vision of the grandmother has the force of revelation, occurring "in the first house where I saw electric light." The electric light is left "turned on" to appease the homesick child, but what might have been a "waste of light" is seen retrospectively to have had a productive power in shaping the growth of the poet's mind (*EL*, 80).

Like the Sibyl, the grandmother speaks in whispers, and her "Urgent, sibilant" implorings—"'What ails you, child, / What ails you, for God's sake?'"—awaken a poetic intuition of linguistic strangeness, as well as registering the child's troubled awareness of being "unhomed." The adult poet's fascination with *ails*—"*Ails*, far off and old"—recalls the similar fascination of Stephen Dedalus with the word *tundish* in *A Portrait of the Artist as a Young Man* (Joyce 1992, 204). Recovering the word *ails* from memories of childhood, Heaney recalls being struck by its "difference and oddity," by its quality of "*echt*-Englishness" (*SS*, 403). The phonetic equation of the grandmother's sibilant, sibylline English with the lapping of water transports us to England. The second part of the poem recalls the young poet's journeys from Belfast to London by ferry and train, in the process echoing and re-echoing the "brow-to-glass transport" of journeys made by Philip Larkin and Louis MacNeice. The image of "fleeting England" seen from a railway carriage emulates the vision of "The Whitsun Weddings" with its "backs of houses," and Heaney, like Larkin, imaginatively aligns the rural and the urban, the contemporary and the historical (Larkin 2012, 56). His "Fields of grain" (recalling Larkin's "squares of wheat") are brilliantly transformed into "the Field of the Cloth of Gold," a reference to the famed meeting place of Henry VIII and Francis I in 1520 (*EL*, 81).

The guiding spirit in part two of "Electric Light," however, is T. S. Eliot, and the echoes of Eliot further develop the association of poetic calling with the play of light. The artistic arrivals conjured up by "Splashes between a ship and dock" bring to mind Eliot's "Animula" (1929) with its startling opening quotation from Dante: "'Issues from the hand of God, the simple soul,' / To a flat world of changing lights and noise." Eliot's brilliant exploration of the innocent soul that comes alive to "Pleasure in the wind, the sunlight and the sea" before studying "the sunlit pattern on the floor" is, for Heaney, an exemplary instance of the young artist's coming to consciousness (Eliot 1967, 70–71). It perfectly adumbrates his own steady emergence into the light—his entry into England, into English, and into poetry itself. That process is aptly conveyed, as well, in the memorable London image of emerging "From tube-mouth into sunlight" (*EL*, 81). The compound "tube-mouth" cleverly catches a number of mouths: the mouth of a baby being bottle-fed, the mouth of a river (linking his own native River Moyola to the Thames), and the mouth of the London Underground providing an exit from darkness into light. It recalls, as well, W. H. Auden's famous pronouncement on the persistence of poetry in his elegy for Yeats: "It survives, / A way of happening, a mouth" (1945, 50). Southwark summons the aspiring poet with its traces of Chaucer's Canterbury pilgrims and Shakespeare's Globe, but the light of inspiration in literary London is undeniably Eliot's, with Heaney re-echoing the words of St. Augustine already echoed in *The Waste Land*: "To Southwark too I came" (*EL*, 81).

The child's reaching for the light switch and the wireless knob points to sources of illumination and inspiration, both of them associated with technological change, that complement and extend the other symbolic objects and places of inspiration in the early poems of *Death of a Naturalist* and *Door into the Dark*: the bog, the well, the forge. The repeated admission, "They let me and they watched me," works as a mantra, giving concentration and emphasis to the rhythmic interplay of volition, assent, and guidance by which the child acquires the light of knowledge in the adult world. The memory of the child who "roamed at will the stations of the world" substitutes the stations of the cross with the glowing radio stations of the wireless set, without cancelling the intimations of pain and suffering that come with the passage from innocence to experience (*EL*, 81). At the same time, the phrase cunningly echoes "the stations of the breath" in Dylan Thomas's wartime elegy, "A Refusal to Mourn the Death by Fire of a Child in London" (1966, 94).

Heaney's own wartime experience in rural Derry is recalled in "All quiet behind the blackout," a line that both echoes the title of a well-known antiwar novel (*All Quiet on the Western Front*) and looks back to Heaney's "Stations" (that title once again pointing to rites of passage) in which "behind the blackout, Germany called to lamplit kitchens through fretted baize" (the wireless set). In that same prose poem or "station," titled "England's Difficulty," Heaney remembers the bombing of Belfast: "I was on somebody's shoulder, conveyed through the starlit yard to see the sky glowing over Anahorish" (*OG*, 83). Here, and in "Electric Light," the fluctuation of light and darkness sensitively records the anxieties and hopes of a child "fostered alike by beauty and by fear." Like the tick of the two clocks in "Sunlight," the "ticking" of knitting needles induces a counterintuitive sense of time stilled while time is actually passing, but like the ticking of the bicycle in a later poem in *North*, "A Constable Calls" (*N*, 67), it also prompts uneasiness. The child's fear is projected onto the grandmother's gashed thumbnail, but there is beauty, too, in the "plectrum-hard, glit-glittery" nail, which becomes an art object, redolent of light and music ("glittery" nicely qualifying the slimy "glit" of the earlier "Fosterling" while keeping contact with it). More than a keepsake, "it must still keep / Among beads and vertebrae in the Derry ground." "Keep" here is finely chosen, as well as deftly placed at the end of the penultimate line: keep as "remain" but keep as "due observance of some ritual," as with "keeping the faith." There is an afterlife here, an afterlife predicated on the preservation of objects, that takes us back to "Bogland." There is also continuity and trust in the image of the "dirt-tracked flint and fissure" of the nail, a keeping of faith with Heaney's own earlier work embedded in the darkness of the earth (*EL*, 81).

"Electric light shone over us," the poem recalls (*EL*, 81). The plural pronoun suggests inclusiveness and togetherness in those wartime years of change and uncertainty. There is a whimsical hint of prayer, as well, as Heaney remembers a prominent line from the Catholic liturgy for the dead: "And let perpetual light shine upon them," a line that he cites approvingly many times in his prose writings, interviews, and other poems. The brief article in which he explains the title of his new book in 2001 carries the heading "Lux Perpetua":

> Once *Electric Light* got written, I had no doubt about it as the title poem. Apart from anything else, the brightness of my grandmother's house is associated in my mind with a beautiful line from the Mass for the Dead—"*Et lux perpetua luceat eis*," "And let perpetual light shine upon them"—a line which is also echoed in one of the sections of "The Real Names." Then, once I settled on the title, I began to see what I hadn't seen before, that there was light all over the place, from the shine on the weir in the very first poem to the "reprieving light" of my father's smile in the penultimate line of the penultimate poem in the book. And as well as this, there is an almost equally pervasive note of elegy. (Heaney 2001d)

The father's smile appears, memorably and movingly, in "Seeing the Sick," which recalls the old farmer's shrinking stature not long before he died. The "reprieving light" implies an easing of pain, but the happy associations of summer are dimmed by the harsh truth of a morphine-induced oblivion: "His smile a summer half-door opening out / And opening in. A reprieving light. / For which the tendered morphine had our thanks" (*EL*, 79).

That reprieving light shines on Heaney's meditations on his own mortality, on poems that might be described as self-elegies, and there are times when his later poetry recalls (and resembles) the elegiac writings of the metaphysical poets, especially Herbert, Donne, and Vaughan. Among the many obituaries, tributes, and commentaries published after the poet's death at the end of August 2013 was a short memoir by Andrew O'Hagan, recalling a journey that he took with Heaney and Karl Miller to visit the grave of that great elegist and poet of light, Henry Vaughan, overlooking the River Usk, near Powys, in Wales (O'Hagan 2013). Echoes of Vaughan permeate Heaney's musings on the afterlife in *Seeing Things*, though a question mark punctuates an illustrious line from the work of the seventeenth-century poet: "*All gone into the world of light?*" (*ST*, 104). "Perhaps," the poem continues, "As we read the line sheer forms do crowd / The starry vestibule." Heaney's appreciation of the lyrical beauty of Vaughan's elegiac poetry is tempered by a meditative circumspection. The alternative to Vaughan's starry vision of the dead congregating in heaven is bluntly stated and reinforced by the division between stanzas: "Otherwise // They do not." The contrary image of "lucency" in blanched worms seems too stark an image to set against Vaughan's starry canopy, but what redeems it is Heaney's more elaborate metaphor of nighttime fishing, which lifts us from the homely to the metaphysical. In its contemplation of emptiness, however, Heaney's angling in the dark approaches the chastened universe of Wallace Stevens, as he imagines lifting a line "For the nothing there—which was only what had been there," but the poem swiftly restores the enduring mystery of life and death in the archetypal image of a dead leaf swirling in the stream, "Swifter (it seems) than the water's passage" (*ST*, 104).

Light shines perpetually in Seamus Heaney's poetry. It has its first glimmerings in poems conceived in darkness and brought into luminous being. Images and ideas are recovered from the dark earth of memory and subjected to the light of creation. Sparks fly as forms are beaten out like metal in the dark forge of poetry. The interplay of darkness and light becomes the prevailing metaphor in a poetry self-consciously preoccupied with memory and perception, especially in the books published in the 1960s. In the 1970s and 1980s, however, writing in a subdued light becomes a necessary condition in a tense and sometimes turbulent political climate, and the image that then prevails is that of the servant boy "swinging a hurricane-lamp / through some outhouse" in *Wintering Out* (*WO*, 17). The directive to "Compose in darkness" takes on enormous historical and political significance in *North* (*N*, 20), a poetic ideal demanding patience and fortitude in the midst of violence. If the lightening up that characterizes the later Heaney of *Seeing Things* and *Electric Light* is attendant on the poet's own mortality ("Me waiting until I was nearly fifty"), it is also surely a consequence of a political optimism that lifts the blinds at the back of the head. A more equable light shines in the work composed in the 1990s and later, enabling a poetry of meditation and spiritual scrutiny, of quiet celebration and elegy. This might seem too neat and simple a pattern to impose on a poetic career of such range and diversity, but the idea of imagining the world in terms of archetypal patterns was one to which Heaney readily gave his assent, even while gently mocking his own coming to consciousness as a writer: "You had your puny south Derry being within the great echoing acoustic of a universe of light and dark, death and everlasting life, divine praise and prayers for the dead: as in 'Grant them eternal rest, O Lord, and let perpetual light shine upon them'" (*SS*, 471). Of the many Latin tags that Seamus Heaney cherished, *Lux Perpetua* seems particularly apt, both as a description of those later poems that fearlessly open a door into the light and as an epithet for a poetic career and destiny of undimmed greatness.

PART FIVE

USUAL AND UNUSUAL SPACES

I loved the disappearance of the spokes,
The way the space between the hub and rim
Hummed with transparency.
                              —Seamus Heaney, "Wheels within Wheels"

CHAPTER THIRTEEN

"Scatter-Eyed / And Daunted"

The "Matrixial Gaze" in *Seeing Things*

Moynagh Sullivan

> The Thing is the psychoanalytic analogue of Merleau-Ponty's "flesh [chair] of the world." Presubjective and preobjective, it precedes the separation into subject and object, and the differentiation between self and world. It embodies human incorporations of the outside in the inside and of the inside in the outside.
> —Bracha L. Ettinger, *The Matrixial Borderspace*

> The Matrixial (object/*objet a* of the) gaze is between shared thing and lost object, belonging to a plural-partial subjectivity.
> —Bracha L. Ettinger, *The Matrixial Gaze*

> But when he came back, I was inside the house
> And saw him out the window, scatter-eyed
> And daunted, strange
> without his hat.
> —Seamus Heaney, "Seeing Things"

Seamus Heaney's work explores a feminine aspect of experience in very powerful ways, and indeed his great popularity may in large part be due to the manner in which his work can be said to be implicated in the creative and physic process of what philosopher, psychoanalyst, and artist Bracha L. Ettinger calls the matrixial realm. Ettinger's work proposes a parallel psychic dimension, the matrixial borderspace, which is closely tied to but not reducible to late prenatal experience, and which provides the means for artistic connection along the borderspaces of ourselves. For a poet who has so powerfully connected with so many readers, the visual remains a critical element in his work. Henry Hart, in a 1994 essay, "What Does Heaney See in *Seeing Things?*," seeks to understand the poet's vision in this collection, centering its curiosity on Heaney's line of in-sight (1994, 33–42). Using the things that can be seen, and drawing on the work of Ettinger on the matrixial stratum, in this essay I want to explore how *Seeing Things*, a collection primarily about the loss of Heaney's father, invites us to see the condition of that loss beyond the considerable personal grief involved, to see in the matrixial field.

Matrixial theory was originally primarily a theory of psychoanalysis and artwork, a means of theorizing the gaze that coevolved with Ettinger's own artistic practice and clinical experience, but it has been used in a range of interpretative practices. It has many applications for poetry given that it is a form of writing so powerfully dependent on the condensation and figural qualities of the image, an observation especially true of a collection called *Seeing Things*. In her 1995 essay "The Matrixial Gaze," Ettinger, working through the history of psychoanalysis as well as philosophical thinking in the areas of desire, ethics, and aesthetics, makes the persuasive case for what she calls a matrixial stratum of subjectivization as preceding the phallic stratum and existing on a complementary and subadjacent plane to phallic ordering and the construction of meaning.[1]

The "phallic" realm is so-called because, in classical psychoanalysis from Freud to Lacan, becoming a subject means becoming subject to the Law of the Father under the threat of castration. A symbolic order is thus produced that is governed by what Lacan called the "transcendental signifier of the phallus" (Cornell 1999, 68) because, as Lacan argued, gender difference is the first distinction that infants experience, and thus this acknowledgment is what brings them into subjectivity—that is, experiencing the self against an Other. All subsequent elaboration of increasingly complex linguistic and social relations is then predicated upon this foundational difference, so that differences and oppositions (I/not-I, nature/culture, presence/absence, body/spirit) in this symbolic order with which we are so familiar are all located in the context of the primary spectacle of sexual difference that keeps them all in their place.

We are familiar with such narratives of emergence and becoming that accompany the subject on the phallic plane. We are used to the quest narrative, the epic, the battles, the foundational laws, the matricide and parricide that accompany the allegories of psychic differentiation, which are also the archetypes of most national and foundational literatures. At one very obvious level, starting as it does with a classical foundational quest-text and unfolding into its own journey, *Seeing Things* operates within these structures. It also, I want to contend in this essay, operates on the matrixial stratum, in which the matrixial I and non-I co-emerge alongside the *agon* and struggle of the I and not-I of the subject on the phallic plane (Ettinger 1995, 47). In other words, there is a dimension of our being, called to by artistic experience, that is aware of a shared habitus, and of an ongoing process of transforming alongside and within another transforming body—that of the mother—that is co-present alongside our differentiated phallic self and that relies, not on difference, but on connection.

To date, readings of gender in Heaney's work (including my own), whether proceeding from the view that gendered polarities are natural and desirable, or alternatively from a feminist awareness of the cultural and political constructedness of hierarchical gender differences, depends to a greater or lesser extent on mapping oppositions between absence and presence, degrees of activity and passivity. Patricia Coughlan's powerful essay "Bog Queens" (1991, 88–111) reads Heaney's poetry on this plane of oppositions and difference, which has been largely been the register in which politics, history, and subjectivity meet. As such, each of these studies of Heaney's work operates on "the phallic stratum" of meaning: a realm identified by Ettinger (1995) as defined by markers of oppositionality such as absence and presence, or activity and passivity. Arguably, these readings were at some level about women in a patriarchal culture and about how, even in the work of the kindest and most enabling of artists and writers, as Heaney was, the feminine can be reinscribed in a culture that does violence to women as subject and bodies.

Critics who have responded to how femininity is deployed in his work have often been read as contentious, and their explorations of questions of gender have been seen as somehow in "bad form" or against the spirit of his work. This touchiness is in itself interesting; it suggests that his work may derive much power from aspects that are intertwined with, or connected to, something feminine, and that to name this connection can somehow undo the mystery or the magic that attaches to its affect. Matrixial theory provides us with a mode of reading a feminine dimension in Heaney's work that does not re-essentialize "the Feminine," as aspects of Jungian archetypal thinking have been prone to do. Ettinger reminds us that the matrix is not about replacing or displacing Oedipus and does not advance an archetype of womanhood. Instead, it asserts a plane in which the "co-emerging I and non-I join the emerging self" (2006, 47), which is also matrixially unique. She writes that the matrix is not "about women, but about a feminine dimension of plurality and difference of the several in joint subjectivity" (1996, 152).

This I and non-I participate in "transmission, co-affectivity, co-acting, co-making" that occurs "in the archaic relations between each becoming-subject and the m/Other" (Ettinger 2006, 166). Ettinger's proposal that the matrixial is a psychic structure with every bit as much resonance as the Oedipus Complex is a serious proposition, and it suggests that although over an average life span we spend only a very small part of our lives in the womb, the matrixial forms a template that supports our psychic life on earth just as our physical skeleton supports our flesh. This is an experience of being that will never leave us but will continue to resonate throughout our life. One of the ways in which the matrixial is experienced postnatally is through encounters with artwork, in a process Ettinger calls *metramorphosis* where the traces of unconscious trauma "can be transmitted from one subject to another." In metramorphosis, a subject's boundaries are tuned "into thresholds, and co-affectivity turns the borderlines between subjects in distance-in-proximity and between subject and object, into a shareable borderspace" (Ettinger 2006, 166).

Critics have noted how much thresholds feature in *Seeing Things*, but they are largely thought of as lines to be crossed or exceeded. Hart notes that *Seeing Things* "continually draw[s] attention to gates, thresholds, borders, limits, lines, doors, ceilings, roofs, circles, and squares," and he reads the attention paid to both sides of these thresholds as evidence of Heaney's "dialectical mind," where "limits provoke sublimation and sublimity-journeys or visions below or beyond the threshold (as the etymology of sublime—"*sub-limen*" and "*sublimis*"—paradoxically indicates)" (1994, 36). In a similar vein, Elmer Kennedy-Andrews writes that "images of thresholds, doorways and latches are prominent in the book, indicating [Heaney's] Janus-like attitude, facing back into the ordinary, yet 'waiting to credit marvels.' In the sonnet 'The Skylight,' the octave is devoted to emphasising the speaker's satisfaction with the claustrophobic security of a stuffy, womb-like attic sealed off from the world outside" (1991, 27). Here, in the description of the "stuffy, womb-like attic," the opposition between a containing, too-small space and a boundless sky is emphasized, as the threshold leads to freedom and escape. This is certainly one of the antimonies that support Heaney's craft, a dialecticism also referred to by Hart when he writes that these limits are mastered, "breached," "through a perception of limits and their overthrow" (1994, 39), and in terms of reading this as occurring on the phallic stratum, there is nothing here to surprise longtime readers of Heaney for whom such oppositions and symbolic "marriages" are a well-worn groove. Fran Brearton notes that Heaney's aesthetic is predicated on same/other thinking, and that, especially in terms of his critical writings from the 1970s, the "following 'binaries' may be either directly extrapolated or inferred: Masculine/Feminine; England/Ireland; Active/Passive; (Protestant/Catholic); History/Mystery; Craft/Instinct; Sense/Sensibility; Structure/Sound; Consonants/Vowels; (Male poet/Female poet)" (2008, 78). Fittingly remarking that "his 'binaries' are deeply embedded in his aesthetic practice," this reading accounts for the structuring of the symbolic order on which his by now considerably complex and layered symbology depends. In relation to *Seeing Things*, Hart notes that "Heaney's poems are testaments to the necessity of these oppositions. In 'Casting and Gathering' he says 'I trust contrariness' and exemplifies the idea with two fishermen on opposite banks of a river. One is severe and repressive; the other is laid-back and expressive. Heaney's point at the end, however, is that they are interchangeable: 'I see that when one man casts, the other gathers / And then vice versa, without changing sides'" (1994, 38). Such repetitions would appear to continually foreclose the possibility of access to the feminine, but in Heaney's work there has always been a countercurrent, a disturbance, that has meant that each of these neat oppositions promises to becomes its own opposite, to unfold into its own difference, but in an asymmetrical manner, which cannot be accounted for by invocation of an *objet a* alone in his work. Douglas Dunn testifies to this when he writes that "sensations from the borderline between the literal and what might be recur frequently in the collection. They are partly explained by Heaney's relish in those moments when what he sees, touches, smells, hears or tastes are inseparable from the beautiful. Five very highly developed senses can lead their exponent to believe in the possibility of a sixth" (2001, 212). If we read along the phallic plane, which is dialectically, thresholds are doors or windows that divide contrasting spaces, whereas in met*ra*morphosis they become the "shareable borderspace" of coaffectivity, which is what we see in "Field of Vision." In "Field of Vision," a woman is constructed as both the gazer, "looking straight ahead / Out the window," and the window (she is "steadfast as the big window itself"), as well as the iron gate and whitewashed pillars (*ST*, 22) that frame the poet's education in *Seeing Things*:

> Face to face with her was an education
> Of the sort you got across a well-braced gate—
> One of those lean, clean, iron roadside ones
> Between two whitewashed pillars, where you could see
>
> Deeper into the country than you expected
> And discovered that the field behind the hedge
> Grew more distinctly strange as you kept standing
> Focused and drawn in by what barred the way.
>
> (*ST*, 22)

As the structures that represent the edges of things, the lines of the gate, the hedge, the "chrome bits of the chair," "drawing him in" and simultaneously "barring the way," she is the borderspace that coaffects (with) him, and precipitates his transformation qua empathy and strangeness, through recognition and reserve, and also through proximity and distance. Through this artwork, we see how the poet sees, and we also see the repressed pain of this woman, "braced" for fortitude and forbearance by a culture that disables its differences. As window gate, she is looked through and at, and she herself gazes through the window and gate to the "same acre of ragwort, the same mountain" (*ST*, 22). In other words, instead of the woman as the border that marks antipathetic values and registers, a plane of relating is affected by the threshold that allows seepage from the subsymbolic of the matrixial into the phallic symbolic order, where the unconscious affects of antecedents, the traumas of the ancestors, are received and brought in some way into representation, or into the field of desire that shapes the artwork and its reception. We are constructed as seers as well as readers, invited to see as well as to read— to see a great many things, and to see the markings on the page and the lines as material objects as much as to see through them to ourselves. So what can we see that we may usually see through?

SCATTER-EYED

In this collection the loss of the father is symbolized by the scattering of the gaze so that the "thing" can be seen. *Scatter-eyed* is a local term in Northern Ireland, used to refer to someone who has been scared half to death or "shook," perhaps into temporary madness, in shock. Outside of its idiolectic use, it also cues us into a deteriorating of eyesight, usually as a result of advancing years, whereby light is scattered by colliding with the particles of a medium, such as those of air or water, recalling the final lines of part ii of "Seeing Things":

> All afternoon, heat wavered on the steps
> And the air we stood up to our eyes in wavered
> Like the zig-zag hieroglyph for life itself.
>
> (*ST*, 17)

According to Ettinger (1995, 57), "If the thing is, as Merleau-Ponty writes, the 'flesh [*chair*] of the world' and as French psychoanalyst,

Jacques Lacan, argues, the *objet a* which stands in for the loss of the archaic mother, and the breast, then there is no shortage of things which embody human incorporations of the outside in the inside and of the inside in the outside." The *objet a* comes into existence only through the symbolic castration involved in the Oedipal scene, and it is only after this has been successfully completed that it can assume its function as an imaginary recompense for the loss of the mother, often through figuring the phallus as the marker of her loss. Thus a symbolic order is assembled upon the Name of the Father. According to Lacan, it is often figural, and it occurs or appears at borders and edges, the lines of which it also appears to be, simultaneously representing presence and lack, here and beyond. The *objet a* serves as a symbol of the lack, and is a Thing, and given that it stands in for the Name of the Father, it is usually (but not always) phallic and is often imbued with ritual or ceremonial power. The "figure of the father" himself is one such cultural symbol. The various rods, pens, and plows all functioning as the *object a* in Heaney's work need little rehearsing and connect not only generations of the men-folk in Heaney's family but also a nexus of paragenerational fellow poets.

In *Seeing Things* Heaney has rehearsed them himself, and Guinn Batten notes how in this collection his own work becomes the subject of his poetry itself (2008, 178–92). *Seeing Things* is self-consciously full of things that perform the function of the *objet a*. In fact, it is almost as if we are initiated to a code, a "code of images" (*ST*, 75), in which Heaney literally creates his own images as a form of language for us, embodying the *objet a* that functions both as a figure and as the linguistic symbolic system he has "gathered" over his writing life. The Sybil of Cumae whose chanting opened the collection (*ST*, 1–3) was granted eternal life from Apollo, the god of poetry, until all that was left of her was her voice. Heaney, the aging poet, is here identified with the visionary woman, the prophetess, as well as with Aeneas, the founder of Rome, both of whom are linked to the Roman alphabet, which was said to have come to Rome from Cumae. In *Seeing Things*, we are invited to see the different means of expressing number, as the poems are titled and numbered both in a mixture of the decimal Hindu-Arabic numeral system and in Roman numerals, which are of course letters. Much as the *Aeneid* provides the material for the poetic quest in *Seeing Things*, so the Roman alphabet provides the material to make words into language and numbers into codes. Two poems, "1.1.87" (*ST*, 20) and "1973" (*ST*, 34), represent dates in numeral terms, and not in text, as is more usually the convention. The "Glanmore Revisited" (*ST*, 31–37) section is subdivided Indo-Arabic numerals, and in Part II, *Squarings*, the four long poems, numbers 1 through 4 in Indo-Arabic numerals, are then subdivided into sestets by Roman numerals, the counting system drawn from the Roman alphabet, where number and word drew on the same root. The Indo-Arabic numeral system represents the structure of another order, a "shareable borderspace" of a transpositional system, to the common root of letter and number in the Roman system. Heaney's use of plurals is especially interesting in the context of seeing a matrixial dimension to this work. From "Markings" to "Crossings," in this collection the plurality of experience is shown to the reader time and again in the word "things" that we encounter.

Other examples of *objet a* are either overfetishized or not fit for purpose. The Name of the Father and the Law of the Father are seen to be undone and to unravel in this collection—which is notable for its high number of words beginning with "un-" prefixes. "Markings" draws self-conscious attention to this, as the "field of grazing" is "to be ploughed open / From the rod stuck in one headrig to the rod / Stuck in the other" (*ST*, 9). This evocation of the "rod," the forked hazel stick from "The Diviner" (*DN*, 36), disrupts the function of the seemingly obvious phallic plow, the *objet a*. The diviner can "see" water via the rod, "under the bumpy ground." Ettinger argues that "in art, repetitions in amnesiac working-through do not re-establish the lost object. Rather, they make present the unpresentable Thing, crypted in the artwork's unconscious, that keeps returning because its debt can never be liquidated" (2006, 158). Thus the poem's invocation of another of Heaney's powerful and heavily gendered images, the "door into the dark" (*DD*, 19), directly calls the *objet a* into the field of vision:

> All these things entered you
> As if they were both the door and what came through it.
> They marked the spot, marked time and held it open.
>
> (*ST*, 9)

The father's missing hat has left him looking strange to the boy, and as a result, his father is "daunted." This is in contrast to the hatted priest in "The Biretta" (*ST*, 26–27): "his reverence wears a hat. / Undaunting, half-domestic, loved in crises." The authority of the hat is borrowed from its being an inversion of the matrix. In the poem, a mediation on Mathew Lawless's painting *The Sick Call*, the priest's hat and symbol of his authority is imagined otherwise and turned upside down, to become a paper matrix, a structure for poetry: "A paper boat / or the one that wafts into / The first lines of the Purgatorio / As poetry lifts its eyes and clears its throat" (*ST*, 27). It is also turned inside out, and "its insides were crimped satin" that "left a dark red line on the priest's brow" (*ST*, 26). The following prayer is italicized and embedded in the poem:

In the name of the Father and of the Son AND

Of the Holy Ghost . . .

(*ST*, 26)

The stanzaic enjambment on "*AND*," as well as the capitalization, suggests the loss of the archaic mother, whose blood and body are being passed around in communion, for which the Name of the Father stands. The communion Mass is here revealed as the *objet a*, but this collection needs us to see even more.

As readers, we usually "see through" the structure of the Oedipal frame to the tragedy of loss, of death, the joy of (re-)birth, mystery, the ambivalence, the great unknowability of life. The phallic stratum is governed by submission to the law via the Oedipal scene, the very Oedipal scene that Heaney here revisits and restages as a failure and an undoing of the law, of the father, and of the past in *Seeing Things*. The affect of this "undoing" of the passage to the symbolic is perhaps one of the things that has led critics to seeing the collection as a sort of middle stage, or as neither one thing nor another. *Seeing Things* is thought, not to strictly exemplify Heaney's later work, but rather to reflect a transitional stage, bringing together his two strands of earlier, more concrete, earthy, and air-filled, sky-filled work before full movement into his later, more classically inflected poetry. Hart wrote that *Seeing Things* "harmonizes the heavy, earthbound 'plop and slap' sound effects of his first books and the more subliminal, philosophical style of *Station Island* and *The Haw Lantern*, creating what might be called a 'middle style'" (1994, 42). Long before *The Spirit Level*, *Electric Light*, *District and Circle*, and *Human Chain*, to critics, *Seeing Things* appeared to testify to the possibility of what can now be retrospectively classified as a distinct Heaney late oeuvre.

This observation suggests that this work feels like a rest on the way to somewhere else, a passage between stages, that it is an emerging but "not quite realized" collection, an impression created in part because of the use of the gerunds in poem titles such as "Crossings," "Markings," "Three Drawings," and "Casting and Gathering," and in the title poem "Seeing Things." Additionally, the titles of the poems in this collection move between singular and plural things and times. The seven sonnets entitled "Glanmore Revisited" (*ST*, 31–37) are about "things" or time, with the exception of "Bedside Reading" (*ST*, 36), and Part I finishes with "Fosterling" (*ST*, 50). Part II / *Squarings* (*ST*, 53–110) moves back to gerunds with "Lightenings," "Settings," "Crossings," and "Squarings," and the epigraph is a translation of lines 82 through 129 of Dante's *Inferno*, which returns once more to the singular and the definite article, "The Crossing" (*ST*, 111–13). "Glanmore Revisited" announces a return to the past and signals moving into the "intransitive": "So 'scrabble' let it be. Intransitive" (*ST*, 31). This middle passage of a collection, which now appears to reach both backwards and forwards, represents a process of undoing of the certainties of history that coincided with the loss of Heaney's father, and the subsequent resurrection of loss of his mother, his grief for whom is powerfully revisited here too.

The scatter-eyed father recalls the scattered oak leaves of the Sybil, who cannot reassemble her prophecy into its original form if the leaves have been dispersed. Intertextually this recalls the epigraph from the Sibyl of Cumae in T. S. Eliot's *The Wasteland*, and Tiresias's lines, borrowing from Aeneas, on having "foresuffered all" (Eliot 1963, 62), as well as the motif of fishing and of the underworld, combining in a postmodern derangement of the Fisher King. Stylistically, *Seeing Things* has been structurally compared to other modernist poems, departing from Heaney's usual lyric arrangements. Hart notes that in the "long poetic sequence (48 sections of 4 tercets) called 'Squarings' . . . as in many modernist sequences, the events and objects dwelled upon are arranged with apparent randomness" (1994, 42), and this collection begins with strong gestures toward Eliot, the managing editor of Heaney's publisher, Faber and Faber, from 1925 to the 1960s. In this post, Eliot not only established Faber and Faber as a gold standard in poetry but also became something of a poetic foster father to succeeding generations of (largely) male poets, from W. H. Auden, Stephen Spender, and Cecil Day-Lewis to such poets as Philip Larkin and Ted Hughes. In *Seeing Things*, Heaney writes for Larkin and Hughes, and poems for his father are interspersed with poems about and for these poetic predecessors, who had both been published by Faber before Heaney. Part I begins with "The Journey Back," in which "Larkin's shade surprised me" (*ST*, 7). Larkin was finally published by Faber and Faber in 1964 and died some five years before the publication of *Seeing Things*.

This poem is followed by "Markings" (*ST*, 8–9) and by "Three Drawings" (*ST*, 9–12), for his father, and then by "Casting and Gathering" (*ST*, 13), for Hughes. Hughes was only nine years older than Heaney and was more like an older brother than some sort of poetic forebear; he was first published by Faber in 1957, nine years before Heaney was published by Faber himself. In this way, Heaney sustains and foregrounds connections between all of these poets and Faber, a type of poetic coemerging that evokes matrixial distance and closeness, castings and gatherings. Other dedications are found in "The Sounds of Rain" (in memoriam Richard Ellmann) (*ST*, 48); "The Schoolbag" (in memoriam John Hewitt) (*ST*, 30); and "Glanmore Revisited" (in memoriam Tom Delaney, archaeologist) (*ST*, 31). The whole collection is dedicated to Derek Mahon, who, Dunn remarks, is the youngest of them, and thus matrixial connection "undoes" the usual order of father and son. The shades of Dante and Virgil are implied in "The Golden Bough." Asking that the Sybil teach him the way to "the King of the Underworld's gateway," Aeneas prays for "one look, one face-to-face meeting with my / dear father," and beseeches her to "take pity / On a son and a father," reversing the familiar logical rhythm of the father and the son (*ST*, 1) of Christian liturgy and replacing the definite article with an indefinite one, moving all the time into a son-father relationship made increasingly ambiguous as the more familiar patrilineal order of authority is rearranged within a matrixial language.

The following poem, "The Ash Plant," the "golden bough" in this collection, begins with these lines:

> He will never rise again but he is ready.
> Entered like a mirror by the morning,
> He stares out the big window, wondering,
> Not caring if the day is bright or cloudy.
>
> (*ST*, 19)

A series of movements between generations and perspectives yet again problematizes the forward imperative of the Oedipus; Part I begins with a sonnet called "The Journey Back" (*ST*, 7). Many of the titles of poems feature numbers—or figures if you like, inviting us to see the figural dimension to this work. Poems such as "Man and Boy" (*ST*, 14), "The Ash Plant" (*ST*, 19), "1.1.87" (*ST*, 20), and "The Pitchfork" (*ST*, 23) show the figure of the father, but in many of these poems the father is not sure-footed or the carrier of order, but rather the agent of disorder. He is infirm, unable to control a "rusted" horse, not watchful or law-bringing but "Scatter-eyed and daunted" (*ST*, 18). Instead of instilling the fear necessary for submission to the law under the threat of castration, Heaney's father is himself fearful, unable to tame the horse, and indeed he is himself tamed, as *daunted* comes from the Latin *domare*, meaning "to tame" or "to break in."

He does not enforce the law, and in this way Oedipus is undone. He is scared of blinding his son ("Burn me in the eyes"; *ST*, 18). As his father shows fear, he is returned to boyhood, his range of sight reduced to that of his juvenile height, as he carries the news of his own father's death:

> My father is a barefoot boy with news,
> Running at eye level with weeds and stooks
> On the afternoon of his own father's death.
>
> (*ST*, 15)

This reversal of order is continued in "Man and Boy" where the speaker's father indicates the proper order of things in his "old, and heavy / And predictable" joke, when he advises him to "Catch the old one first," for "then the young ones / Will follow, and Bob's your uncle" (*ST*, 14), but the poem, as Dunn obverses, "conjures up a triple haunting" (2001, 212). After this first stanza, however, the presumed naturalness of imperative is questioned in the image of the salmon jumping, "Back through its own unheard concentric soundwaves" (*ST*, 14), leading to an image of a mower, recalling the reaper leaning "forever on his scythe" (*ST*, 14), whose telegraph of death is sent through "the final perfect ring" between father and son: "'Go and tell your father,' the mower says / (he said it to my father who told me)" (*ST*, 14). While the salmon jumps through "concentric sound waves" to spawn, here the poem brings the news of death. We are once more cued to see sound, the "concentric sound waves," and the word *mower* becomes "mother" when pronounced in "Anahorish" idiolect with its "soft gradient / of consonant, vowel-meadow" (*WO*, 16), where the "o" is sounded out as a diphthong and the "w" echoes the aspirant "th" dip in the middle of "mother." Here, in this word, which looks one way and which sounds out another order, life and death meet, and the poem once more returns us to origin myths, founding stories, and starting points; through the "things" that are seen and heard, the things that are seen to be heard, and a story of father and son, such myths find their mother form. Aeneas, the founding father of Rome, carried his father Anchises "on these shoulders through flames" (*ST*, 1), but in "Man and Boy" the father "piggybacks" the son, "At a great height, light-headed and thin-boned, / Like a witless elder rescued from the fire" (*ST*, 15).

Seeing Things opens with Aeneas's plea to Sibyl to meet his father's spirit, and the translation goes as far as the Golden Bough, but not as far as the warning told by the Sibyl of the unburied and drowned Misenus, who was drowned for impudently challenging the gods to a contest in making music on a conch shell. It is as if the "concentric sound waves" of the conch shell can be heard resonating through the collection, directing us to see and hear the "undrowned father" (*ST*, 18) denoted in part iii of the next, and title, poem, "Seeing Things" (*ST*, 16–17). In the final lines of this poem, the speaker says:

I saw him face to face, he came to me
With his damp footprints out of the river,
And there was nothing between us there
That might not still be happily ever after.

(*ST*, 18)

The undrowned father exists before the Oedipal in the matrixial, and he is returned to this psychic structure in this collection through the seeing encounters of the matrixial gaze.

THE FIELD OF THE GAZE

In a collection about loss and objects, *Seeing Things* desires our gaze, needs us to see its things. It brings us into what Lacan calls a "dialectic of desire" (2006, 679) where it wants to be the "object" of our desire; like the child seeking to be what the mother desires, it seeks to be the reader's *objet a*. By positioning itself in the visual field, the collection marks out for us an invocatory world of sounds and rhythms that slip from our grasp as easily as they have from the poet's. But there is something else going on besides the loss of the archaic mother through the story of castration, through "presence-absence relation" (Ettinger 1995, 47), an aesthetic powerfully called up in Heaney's sequence "Clearances," as Batten has so persuasively argued. Heaney's meditation on his father's passing has recalled the archaic absence that his father's presence shored up. Equally, however, the collection also invites us to consider that dialectic of desire in a wider field of vision and directs us as well to the "triangulation" represented by the matrixial gaze.[2]

The third angle in the "triangle" of the matrixial gaze is the field of desire itself, where what Ettinger identifies as the "*link a*" creates a shared borderspace of coaffect, which is pre-*objet a* but palpable. In other words, the field of the gaze itself, in which a connection is created between artist, artwork, and viewer, is brought into the picture. The matrixial gaze is predicated on such a triangular set of relations, in which the artwork/text, the reader/viewer, and the writer/artist create primary meanings as borderlinks, "as becoming with, as shareability and differentiation in co-emergence, and not as absence related to an in-visible figure of difference, not even as an in/out nor as an on/off (or any variation of the presence/absence) scansion that is always linked to the subject as One versus the Other or the world, and to transforma-tion as castration" (Ettinger 1995, 47). In our seeing Things, the Field is marked for us early on, and it is foregrounded above subjective experi-ence or consideration of the collection's multiple objects.

"Markings" (*ST*, 8) queers the pitch of the phallic economy, where drawing, seeing, and crossings take the reader into another scopic field. After "The Journey Back" (*ST*, 7), "Markings" starts with setting out the terms for play. The game of football becomes quite other, though, as the matrixial is brought into place under the auspices of another register coming to the fore. Play is the vehicle here, transporting the poet and reader into this encounter with difference. In Seminar XI, *The Four Fun-damental Concepts of Psychology*, Lacan elaborates the gaze as the "field" of desire where the visual field is at once a geometrical, ocular field and a somatic, sexual field of gazes (1963, 256). "Markings," recalling the poet's childhood, and addressed to his younger self at play in parts II and III, begins geometrically, presaging the "Squarings" that order the visual field in *Seeing Things*:

> We marked the pitch: four jackets for four goal posts,
> That was all. The corners and the squares
> Were there like longitude and latitude
> Under the bumpy ground, to be
> Agreed or disagreed about
> When the time came.
>
> (*ST*, 8)

Here in this field, lines are highlighted: "the line our called names drew" that the players "cross," the "loved lines pegged out in the garden" (*ST*, 8), and "the outline of a house foundation" (*ST*, 8) mark out actions like games, house building, plowing, and digging. Each line that goes into the building of this material order recalls more generally the con-struction of a symbolic order based on the Law of the Father, and spe-cifically in Heaney's own set of symbolic coordinates, the spade in his

originary act of poetic "Digging": "The spade nicking the first straight
edge / along the tight white string" (*ST*, 8). The lines that lead "back-
wards and forwards" (*ST*, 9) are also crossed, and in this "Some limit
had been passed," because for all of the corners and squares, the "right
angles" and "straight edges," there is also the *objet a*, which moves the
gazer and the players from the football pitch into another order of play-
ing in this field of vision: "As the light died and they kept on playing /
because by then they were playing in their heads" (*ST*, 8). This other di-
mension, where time "was extra, unforeseen and free," where "the actual
kicked ball came to them / Like a dream heaviness," and where sound
cues the reader to otherness ("Breathing in the dark and skids on the
grass / Sounded like effort in another world"; *ST*, 8), does not require
material sight.

Sound also cues us to this otherness in the field, when the gaze is in-
voked by the sibilant skidding of gaze in graze: "or the imaginary line
straight down / A field of grazing" (*ST*, 9). The imaginary line, a line of
poetry, exists in both fields, like the *objet a*, an edge between each terrain,
one of which is concerned with elaborating symbolic systems and the
other of which invites us into the triangular field of the matrixial en-
counter, the touch and coemerging with the artwork. As Kinsella elabo-
rates on Ettinger's work, "The matrixial link *a* resists the Phallus and
weaves a becoming threshold into culture so that new concepts of the
primal scene—which Freud and Lacan considered as repressed and in-
cluded within the castration paradigm—can be laced into and enlarge
the Symbolic" (2013, 92). In the first sections, as many scholars have al-
ready noted, activity and passivity, nature and craft, hardness and soft-
ness are dialectically opposed, and "Markings" self-consciously brings
this into visibility:

> Pale timber battens set at right angles
> For every corner, each freshly sawn new board
> Spick and span in the oddly passive grass.
>   (*ST*, 8–9)

But the patterns sounded out in "battens" are part of the fresh extension
of the poem's "span" to mark another field, playing with the title of

Heaney's earlier collection, also written in Glanmore, *Field Work*. This different field is vividly evoked by triangulation in "The Schoolbag" (in memoriam John Hewitt) (*ST*, 30), which creates a triangle between Hewitt, poetry, and Heaney. The schoolbag, described as "light," "supple and unemptiable," is declined, not along the lines of empty or full, but as a "conjurer's hat," a "word-hoard," and a "handsel" shared between him and Hewitt across lines and times. The final couplet, "As you step out trig and look back all at once / Like a child on his first morning leaving parents" (*ST*, 30), addresses himself and Hewitt both, looking back and stepping out, going forwards as well as backwards. *Trig* is a term for smart and trim, as well as a schoolboy abbreviation for trigonometry, the science of measuring triangles. Further, the field of the matrixial gaze, instead of alternating between absence and presence, enacts a process of "continual attuning and re-adjustments of distance in proximity" (Ettinger 1995, 47). In *Preoccupations*, Heaney writes that Hewitt's "vision is bifocal" (*P*, 147), able to look both close and far away with equal attentiveness.

This bifocality is startlingly shown in the distance-in-proximity of Glanmore, the Wicklow Cottage originally owned by Heaney family friend Anne Saddelmeyer, in which Heaney's key early works *North* and *Field Work* were written. *Seeing Things* was also written in Glanmore, by which point the Heaneys owned the cottage. The Heaneys moved there in the early seventies when there was civil unrest and violence in Northern Ireland, and the movement between those two collections and *Seeing Things* is evident in the ways in which the poet revisits questions of loss and death, birth and regeneration. Retuning to this cottage to write a collection in which he "undoes" the overdetermination of some of his earlier symbolism, especially in the context of gender, calls up a matrixial field of desire very powerfully. The particular birth of a child that is reinvoked in the beautiful and delicate "A Pillowed Head" in the revisited section of the Glanmore sonnets is the birth of his daughter, an interruption of the patrilineal line, the undoing of the imperative of Oedipal inheritance, and an undoing of any need for (fore)closure. This represents an opening. The lines "Matutinal. Mother-of-pearl" (*ST*, 38) recall dawn of life, the early morning gathering of matter that will pollinate and reproduce, as well as the iridescent and beautiful inner lining of some shells, the visual equivalent of conch music perhaps. The layers of luminescent beauty and scattered prismatic light replace the "diamond absolutes" and "prismatic counselling" heard by the "inner émigré" of "Exposure" (*N*, 73), this time without the heaviness of accusation, or guilt for having chosen and battened down around those he loved; now, back in Glanmore, the poet recalls the scattering of light with gratitude and celebrates the bringing of life to that home.

Here the trauma of that stage in history is figured in his wife's conscious choosing of life and the trauma of bringing forth life. It is as if this was swelling under the *objet a* in his earlier work and is now being brought into the field, showing how, as Kinsella describes it, "this matrixial gaze, inflamed with the affect of the corpo-Real, occasions the possibility for *borderlinking with the dimension beyond appearance*: a transconnection to the matrixial stratum that surfs beside and beneath the phallic level of identity" (2013, 262). This borderlinking with the dimension beyond appearance involves going through both the birth canal and the eye. The introduction of the "trauma" of birth (*ST*, 38), as more archaic trauma before the trauma of castration, presages the transgressive rebirth into the matrixial announced at the start of "Crossings":

> Let rebirth come through water, through desire,
> Through crawling backwards across clinic floors:
> I have to cross back through that startled iris.
>
> (*ST*, 79)

The imagery of the scattered light and eye continues in the "startled iris," recalling the goddess of the rainbow, the phenomenon created when light is both refracted and reflected in water. Rainbows are made up of full circles, but we see only the semicircle of the belly; the underside of the rainbow is not visible. We see only the upper part of the full circle where light meets water—much like the outside of the pregnant belly. We live in the underworld and the amniotic sea when in the womb, and Iris was also humankind's companion down into the sea. Thus this journey to the underworld, via undoing the foreclosures of castration, and through the "Iris," a flower that in the work of Georgia O Keefe represents the female genitalia, is indicated when the collection begins with a translation of lines 98 through 148 from book 6 of the *Aeneid*, called "The Golden Bough," in which Aeneas asserts that "already I have foreseen and foresuffered all" before he asks the Sibyl of Cumae to "open the holy doors wide" (*ST*, 1), suggestively recalling the door that is closed on the underworld of the maternal belly, the way back to which is governed by the father-king. The iris is also the part of the eye that gives the eye its color and controls the muscles that dilate the pupil, affecting the amount of light entering the eye—the "zigzag" scattering of the "hieroglyph of life" itself.

Seeing Things appears to articulate a desire to get before and beyond the foreclosure of the Oedipal scene in its self-consciousness about its "things," a point noted by Hart when he writes that "while Heaney respects his father's ideal of limits, in this poem [*Squarings*, xxxiii] and in many others he also announces his freedom from all such patriarchal strictures" (1994, 42). *Seeing Things* initiates an encounter with a field in which we are asked to startle our "Irises" into other lights in the field of Heaney's objects, scattering our certainties and absolutes, and trusting in an encounter with the things he re-declines for us:

> They gazed beyond themselves until he eased
> The brake off and they freewheeled quickly
> Before going into gear, with all their usual old
> High-pitched strain and gradual declension.
>
> (*ST*, 44)

As Kinsella points out, "Ettinger theorises the matrixial gaze as a touching gaze because before we were ever looked at, or touched by the gaze, we were being aesthetically affected and aroused into life by being affected by an unknown other whom we could not see, who could not see us but whose affect touched us beyond the domain of tactile touch" (2013, 254), and this is the seeing gaze that affects us, and through which we are finally called into seeing.

NOTES

The chapter epigraphs are from Ettinger (2006, 113–14), Ettinger (1995, 47), and *ST* (18).

1. See Kinsella for an excellent elaboration of Ettinger's theory and practice: "Thus Matrixial theory is an intervention in psychoanalytic thought as it elucidates a stratum of subjectivity that does not collapse into the binary and phallic conceptualizations of subject/object, self-other, that frame psychoanalytic thought" (2013, 25).

2. "Ettinger's articulation of the triangulated relation between artist, artwork, and viewer is closely related to her elucidation of the matrixial gaze, which she offers a supplement to Lacan's conceptualization of the gaze. She suggests that three types of gaze should be identified:

I. The phallic post-Oedipal mastering gaze.
II. The gaze of the phallic *objet a* that traces loss or archaic lack through castration.
III. The matrixial gaze of the matrixial object/*objet*/link *a*.

Theorizing a matrixial gaze, Ettinger seeks to distinguish between a "post-Oedipal active gaze with 'armed eyes' that is linked to gender identification, a phallic gaze that is tracing the *objet a*, and a pre-Oedipal passive gaze as a matrixial *objet*/link *a* linked to lost archaic part-objects" (Kinsella 2013, 89).

CHAPTER FOURTEEN

"Beyond Maps and Atlases"

Transfiguration and Immanence in the
Later Poems of Seamus Heaney

Daniel Tobin

At the end of *Stepping Stones*, Seamus Heaney gives a moving meditation
on what was surely the welcome experience of freedom and release when
he departed the busy professional life of Dublin for the haven of Glan-
more. "Often when I'm on my own in the car," he reflects, "driving down
from Dublin to Wicklow in spring or early summer—or indeed any time
of the year—I get this sudden joy from the sheer fact of the mountains
to my right and the sea to my left, the flow of the farmland, the sweep
of the road, the lift of the sky. There's a double sensation of here-and-
nowness in the familiar place and far-and-awayness in something im-
mense" (*SS*, 475). Beyond the immediacy and elegance of Heaney's way
with language, his description of this familiar trip toward what had been
for more than thirty years a vitally creative space at once central to his
writing life and eccentric from the business of writing quietly and in-
delibly situates the poet in a state of dynamic equilibrium. The poet's
passage out and away is equally a passage into the now and here. He is
surprised by joy in the perception of his passing through, typically in be-
tween and almost at the threshold between orders of being, his percep-

tion balanced in the scales across scales, his consciousness riding happily in the gulf between familiarity and immensity. Given the poet's expansive range of vision, it feels apt to venture substituting the words *immanent* and *transcendent* for *familiar* and *immense*, since these religiously charged terms underscore how profoundly animating both impulses have been for Heaney's imagination. The essentially religious aspect of his work is all the more necessary to contemplate now that he has gone into both—into the utter immanence of his home ground and the utter transcendence of what he called that "bright nowhere" (*HL*, 32).

The double sensation Heaney speaks of in *Stepping Stones*, his double vision of immanence and transcendence, surfaces in a plenitude of guises and contexts throughout his essays and in his poetry, and emphatically so in the late poetry. In "The Redress of Poetry," he invokes Simone Weil's *Gravity and Grace* in order to highlight art's ability to tilt "the scales of reality toward some transcendent equilibrium" (*RP*, 3). Here, *transcendence* refers to poetry's capacity to resolve potentially intolerable realities by transporting poet and reader to "a higher level of consciousness" through some "symbolic resolution" of the threat presented by history (*PW*, 6). Heaney's perception carries significance beyond the historical context of the Troubles. The impact of poetry on consciousness exemplifies an adaptation of Jungian thought into Heaney's poetics, and as late as *Stepping Stones* he acknowledges the importance of Jung for his understanding of religion (*SS*, 471). One hears the same understanding of poetry's transformative force in an early statement from *Preoccupations* where he affirms that poets develop their art through trust "in certain moments of satisfaction which you know intuitively to be moments of extension" (*P*, 54). In short, the principle of self-transcendence resides at the core of Heaney's poetics even as his poetry keeps ties to the known world. This interplay of immanence and transcendence, of familiarity and immensity, finds one of its richest articulations in "Something to Write Home About," where a remembrance of venturing into the Moyola River as a child segues to a meditation on Hermes, the god of boundaries:

> The Romans kept an image of Terminus in the Temple of Jupiter on Capitol Hill and the interesting thing is that the roof above the

place where the image sat was open to the sky, as if to say that a god of the boundaries and borders of the earth needed to have access to the boundless, the whole unlimited height and width and depth of the heavens themselves. As if to say all boundaries are necessary evils and that the truly desirable condition is the feeling of being unbounded, of being king of infinite space. And it is that double capacity that we possess as human beings—the capacity to be attracted at one and the same time to the security of what is intimately known and the challenges and entrancements of what is beyond us—it is this double capacity that poetry springs from and addresses. (*FK*, 51–52)

The point to be made in light of this meditation is that Heaney envisions the intimately known and the beyond, the immanent and the transcendent, as a reality of consciousness that is ineluctable and constituent of what it means to be human. The goal for the poet who would be "most the poet," then, "is "to attempt an act of writing that outstrips the conditions even as it observes them" (*RP*, 159). Such a master of the art must interpose "his or her perception and expression" in the action of making the poem with such intensity that the poem "will transfigure" the conditions out of which it is made (*RP*, 159). One should say that transfiguration constitutes the ultimate aim and essential technique of Heaney's poetry, a technique that is itself an expression of the double human capacity to be drawn simultaneously into the world and into history and what exceeds our apprehension. For Heaney this dual capacity so informs poetic practice that it makes poetry "a ratification of the impulse toward transcendence" (*SS*, 470). This impulse finds dramatic expression in Heaney's late poetry, where many of his leitmotifs and figures find new embodiments and reinventions, and the poet reconsiders his journey in the art from the chastened standpoint of death's inevitability.

As I have written earlier, starting with the sound of water gushing from the pump in the Heaney yard when he was a boy, and the reiteration of that sound in the word *omphalos*, meaning "the navel," the stone that figuratively marks the center of the world, the key to the sense of place in Heaney's early poetry is "the sacred center" (Tobin 1998, 1ff.; *SS*, 8). Around this center the reality of the poet's world assembles, and he is drawn to dig into its space—the first world of the yard, the bottomless bog, and still deeper into the locus and process of reciprocal violence in *North*. The poetry reorients with "the door into the light" that is *Field Work*, after which the figure of the center transfigures into the "empty source" of *Station Island* and the "vacant center" of *The Haw Lantern*. In *Seeing Things*, Heaney's orientation shifts strongly from centripetal to centrifugal (*SS*, 178), though ultimately Heaney's work embodies a dynamic equilibrium between the two movements. "Poetic form is both the ship and the anchor," as Heaney reflected in *Crediting Poetry*. "It is at once buoyancy and a holding, allowing for . . . whatever is centrifugal and centripetal in mind and body" (*CP*, 29).

Beginning with *Seeing Things* and *The Spirit Level*, everything figured in Heaney's later poetry assumes an almost numinous presence. Things become at once apparent and transparent, and within this double state of visionary intensity the elusive center might be said to represent "the point at which the being of things is constituted in union with emptiness, the point at which things establish themselves, affirm themselves and assume a position" (Nishitani 1982, 130; Tobin 1998, 273). In the late poems, the center as the key figure in Heaney's poetry assumes an ontological locus more than a geographical one. As he told Dennis O'Driscoll, "The ideal preoccupation for a poet is the word *is*" (*SS*, 304). The wayward motion from the center takes the fore, at least outwardly, though both orientations—the wayward and the homeward—are bound inextricably to the poet's being and the historical, mythological, and ontological preoccupations of his art. Heaney's poetry never turns its back on memory and place, even as his work forays into new territory. Since so many of Heaney's poems in the last three books are rooted in memory, the entire evolution of his oeuvre might best be described as parabolic—an arc pitched outward that nonetheless pitches back to its origin, only to pitch itself out again—the spiral movement doubling back with a new expansiveness of vision. That movement also evinces the pattern of an enwound journey where consciousness functions as a self-reflecting mirror intensifying and transfiguring whatever it comes to know. Poetry for Heaney ideally composes an order "where we can at last grow up to that which we stored up as we grew" (*CP*, 11). The phrase articulates a parabolic movement, a double movement around a central axis, the mirroring of symmetry as well as a forward motion that leaves nothing behind but gathers identity forward. We see this parabolic movement in the late poem "At Toomebridge," where Heaney declares that "negative ions in the open air / Are poetry to me as once before / The slime and silver of the fatted eel" (*EL*, 3). Those negative ions are a bit of the immensity, an emptiness clarifying home through the poet's transfiguring vantage at once home and away. The imagination at its widest arc undergoes a "reformation," as he reflects, but does so by being "drawn in and drawn out through the point of origin" (*CP*, 28).

The presence of the parabolic in Heaney's work underscores an observation Richard Kearney made about his poetry—that the poems "are in fact not primarily about place at all; they are about transit, that is, about transitions from one place to another" (2006, 217). Important early poems like "The Peninsula," "The Tollund Man," "On the Road," and "Station Island" epitomize Heaney's liminal orientation to his subjects. Poetry itself, he claimed, is more a threshold than a path (*GT*, 108), and this judgment finds ample structural evidence in the late poems. "Known World" is an especially strong example, though one can also reference "The Little Canticles of Asturias," "Sonnets from Hellas," "District and Circle," and "Route 110," to name only a few. In each of these poems, the looser "weave" of Heaney's orchestration allows for sections to pass through thresholds into next and next, often with a simple asterisk separating them—the poems moving from threshold to threshold associatively rather than pursuing linear or numerical progression. It is as if the poems harbored wormholes carrying the poet imaginatively from place to place, from present to past, and poising him for the next arc outward toward some new signature. Early in "Known World," Heaney portrays himself in his privileged position as poet among other poets where he is outwardly as much a smiling public man as he is an artist. In the poem's third section, however, the poet flashes back to the place of origin:

> At the still center of the cardinal points
> The flypaper hung from our kitchen ceiling,
> Honey-strip and death-trap, a barley-sugar twist
> Of glut and loathing . . .
>
>   (*EL*, 23)

From his far-flung vantage beyond his known first world Heaney's center appears anything but sacred; rather, the figure exudes the glutted insularity and unspoken danger of pre-Troubles Northern Ireland. The intensely communal premodern world into which Heaney was born reveals itself as a death trap where cultural and religious assumptions that positively define the sense of place might easily devolve to tribalism: "congregations blackening the length / And breadth of summer roads" (*EL*, 24). Home in this incarnation is a version of hell where a honey strip transfigures into "a syrup of Styx," and "an old gold world-chain the world keeps falling from / Into the cloud-boil of a camera lens" (*EL*, 24). This rapid-fire metamorphosis of figures embodies Heaney's technique of transfiguration achieved at astonishing speed, the strip transforming itself into Stygian syrup, then into the world-chain that is deconstructed by the camera lens. We have moved in the span of three short lines from a 1950s Northern Irish farmhouse back into the mythic past and forward again to the postmodern present. The span of that transfigurative movement traces the span of the poet's consciousness, as well as its "fall" from premodernity into postmodernity over the course of Heaney's lifetime. Now a countervailing perception manifests: "Were we not made for summer, shade and coolness," Heaney reflects, "and gazing through an open door at sunlight?" The poet answers his own question with a resounding *Yes* (*SS*, 475). The question is essential both to the "Known World" and to the impetus behind Heaney's work, for it functions as a kind of prism through which the human place becomes clarified. Heaney's question subtends the poet's artistic concerns—like the scoop in "Mossbawn: Sunlight," one of his great early poems, where love sinks "past its gleam / in the meal bin." Here, again, is the center in its loving aspect embedded almost beyond representation, past its gleam in the immanent body of the world.

In the penultimate section of "Known World," Heaney takes us through yet another imaginative portal to an observance of the Greek Orthodox Madonna's Day: "Icons being carried, candles lit, flowers / And sweet basil in abundance, some kind of mass / Being celebrated behind the iconostasis" (*EL*, 26). "I had been there, I knew this," he reflects, "but was still / Haunted by it as by an unread dream." In effect, the distance Heaney travels enables him now to intensify his consciousness—

to extend his imaginative reach. The encounter's haunting nature is what furthers the poet, for the unread dream requires that it be read, and the reading of the dream becomes nothing less than an enlargement of consciousness and available reality. Not surprisingly, in the poem's last section, on the plane back all systems are "go" imaginatively as well as literally. We encounter this same parabolic pattern in section 2 of "The Little Canticles of Asturias," where again on the road the poet sees "men cutting aftergrass with scythes / Beehives in clover, a windlass and a shrine" and becomes immediately "a pilgrim new upon the scene / Yet entering it as if it were home ground" (*EL*, 29). Similarly, in "The Augean Stables," a bas-relief of Herakles altering the course of the River Alpheus to wash the king's stables triggers Heaney's memory of a murder at the GAA Club in Bellaghy. He imagines "hose-water smashing hard back off the asphalt / In the car park where his athlete's blood ran cold" (*EL*, 48). Here, a scene from Greek myth transfigures into an event from the poet's own lifetime. The trajectory appears retrospective, and it is, but Heaney's use of myth assumes imaginative commerce between present and past, almost a currency to the past beyond any deep cultural inheritance. It is as if the poem were evidence of the transfiguring action of the poet's consciousness, sustained as it is by the underlying similitudes of tradition, and that creative action makes the poem's transfigurative method prospective as well as retrospective. "Poetry," Heaney once observed, "has to be a working model of inclusive consciousness" (*RP*, 8).

Heaney's underworld journeys exemplify particularly well the transfigurative commerce between past and present in the late poems as well as such conscious inclusivity. The sonnet sequence "District and Circle" is at once a prospective passage through the London Underground and a retrospective encounter with the poet's past:

So deeper into it, crowd-swept, strap-hanging,
My lofted arm a-swivel like a flail,
My father's glazed face in my own waning
And craning . . .

(*DC*, 21)

Here transfiguration involves the superposition of the poet's father's face on his own, so that the father's face and the poet's face wane and crane together. What we have is the figural inverse of an eclipse, a mutual illumination of coembodiment, a split second in which the poet and his father are copresent and coterminous, as though the poet were himself now a shade among shades: "And so by night and day to be transported / Through galleried earth with them, the only relict / Of all that I belonged to . . ." (*DC*, 21). It is as if, having crossed over like Virgil in book 6 of *The Aeneid*, the poet had lost the Golden Bough that enabled him to emerge again into the light of day. Heaney first uses the motif in *Seeing Things* with his translation, "The Golden Bough," one of his many afterlife poems. He advances the motif again in "Route 110," where eleven memory-driven sections employ book 6 in the manner of a figural palimpsest, a kind of background archetypal passage for the poet's life and art, only to see the poet arrive in the twelfth section at "the age of births," with his granddaughter emerging from the "underground" of the womb.

Finally, in "Chanson d'Aventure," Heaney's near-death experience as the victim of a stroke takes its figural impetus from Donne rather than Virgil—though Dante also haunts in the poem's tercets in which the bell that could toll the poet's death rhymes tellingly with "Bellaghy," the place of birth: in the poet's end is his beginning, the parabolic figure inscribed in a single, subtle rhyme. Here, again, the past rises vitally into the present now in the person of the adolescent poet as college bellman, a figure that deftly shape-shifts into the charioteer at Delphi, "his left hand lopped / From a wrist protruding like an open spout" (*HC*, 14). Heaney's abbreviated line, itself lopped, eventually evokes the charioteer's gaze, which is another figure for the utter transcendence of death, "empty as the space where the team should be." The scene transfigures again when the charioteer's posture becomes the posture of the poet "doing physio in the corridor" (*HC*, 14), slowly emerging from this real-life near descent into the underworld. What links the poem's figures through the rush of transfigurations is the presiding activity of love—the "ecstatic gaze" of the poet and his wife across the bisected and bisecting gulf that would rend body and soul apart and them apart from each other.

In "Chanson d'Aventure," the empty space into which Heaney's figural proxy gazes is death, the "utter emptiness forever," as Larkin names it in "Aubade." In "Joy or Night," Heaney argues on principle against Larkin's claim that "death is no different whined at than withstood" (*RP*, 155). On the contrary, Heaney affirms that when "human consciousness is up against the cliff-face of mystery, confronted with the limitations of human existence itself," that is exactly the time when poetry needs to offer "a vision of reality" that is "transformative" so that the mind can "conceive of a new plane of regard for itself, a new scope for its own activity" (*RP*, 159–60). Larkin's "Aubade" falls short for Heaney because, to borrow from Czesław Miłosz, it "endows death with a supreme authority" (*RP*, 158). Heaney objects to Larkin's vision (not the artistry of the poem) because it "indulges" in a mood that refuses to be "transfigured." "Death withstood is indeed very different from death whined at" (*FK*, 354), Heaney counters. So while Heaney does not "decry" the emotion, nor deny the poem's greatness, the still greater directive of poetry as transfiguration drives his critical judgment (*SS*, 474).

Undergirding Heaney's critical acumen and his poetic of transfiguration is his stated belief that "the order of art becomes an achievement intimating a possible order beyond itself," which means "art is not an inferior reflection of some ordained heavenly system but a rehearsal of it in earthly terms" (*GT*, 94). Heaney's conviction would appear now to resonate powerfully with Miłosz's protest against Larkin's very great and brutally unflinching poem: "Poetry has always been on the side of life. Faith in life everlasting has accompanied man on his wanderings through time, and it has always been larger and deeper than religious or philosophical creeds which expressed only one of its forms" (quoted in *RP*, 158). In *Stepping Stones* and elsewhere Heaney openly confesses his lapse from his childhood faith, as "pre-modern" and indigenous as Miłosz's. Yet despite this lapse, Heaney's sensibility remains bound to a fundamentally religious awareness that infuses his work from beginning to end. "The following of art is little different from the following of religion in the intense preoccupation it demands," Yeats wrote, and Yeats's conviction stands as epigraph to *Preoccupations*. In "The Sense of Place," the root of the Latin word *religare*, to bind fast, shapes Heaney's discussion of the sacramental aspect of place (*P*, 134). Heaney also quotes appreciatively Ted Hughes's observation that "poetic imagination is determined finally by the state of negotiation—in a person or a people—between man and his idea of the Creator" (*P*, 91; *SS*, 390). In an interview with June Beisch, Heaney (1986a, 169) further observed that "it is difficult for poetry to survive in a society that loses its religious dimension," which makes poetry, in turn, "a religious act in itself and not a parallel." He reaffirms that view in *Stepping Stones* when he speaks of poetry as "an ancient and sacred art," maintaining that the poet's charge is essentially "a sacred charge" and that his early Catholicism "provided a totally structured reading of the mortal condition which I have never quite deconstructed" (*SS*, 457, 471). The claim underscores Heaney's view that "far from being deprived of religion in my youth I was oversupplied" (*SS*, 318). Despite owning that "we have lost the overall, ordering Christian myth of 'down there, up there, us in between'" and that he has embraced "a general, generational assent to the proposition that God is dead" in place of the previously "living myth" (*SS*, 295, 472), Heaney remains in what he calls "the Stephen Daedalus frame of mind" (*SS*, 318). Part and parcel of that frame of mind is the impact religious thinkers like Mircea Eliade have had on Heaney's work, as have fundamentally religious poets like Hopkins, Eliot, Dante, and R. S. Thomas. All of Heaney's reflections on God, religion, and their relation to poetry merely elaborate a point he made to Rand Brandes: "I believe the condition into which I was born and into which my generation in Ireland was born involved the moment of transition from sacred to profane . . . the transition from a condition where your space, the space of the world, had a determined meaning and a sacred possibility, to a condition where space was a neuter geometrical disposition without any emotional or inherited meaning" (Heaney 1988b, 6). The emptiness into which Heaney's Delphic charioteer gazes in "Chanson d'Adventure," and into which Heaney gazes, is precisely this desacralized space, a space that, worse than death, is death neutered of any emotional and inherited meaning. At stake in Heaney's poetic of transfiguration is nothing less than what he deems to be poetry's sacred charge to answer death's ultimate negation. To press the point home, having left the inherited system, Heaney regards poetry at its most vital as "a coherent system or order of understanding" (*SS*, 458) even before the most psychically and ontologically exposed of conditions.

The poet's awareness of death's surrounding and negating emptiness in the late poems reverberates with his observation in "Squarings" of "old truth dawning," that "there is no next-time-round" (*ST*, 55). Despite Heaney's confirmation that the sequence is rife with his "fardle" of Catholic beliefs, Dennis O'Driscoll seizes on the poet's apparent conviction in "Squarings" "that there is no afterlife" (*SS*, 319). Heaney does not deny it but qualifies the reading when he affirms that the poem "is still susceptible to the numinous." Such qualifications suggest that the presiding awareness of death's negation is being contested by the poet in light of his undisputed belief in poetry's native impulse—its impulse toward transcendence. As Heaney said in *Crediting Poetry*, "Without needing to be theoretically instructed, consciousness quickly realizes that it is the site of variously contending discourses" (*CP*, 13). The impulse toward transcendence appears most firmly sustainable only in light of the world's valuation in an order of being that transcends the powers of human representation—a reality toward which human representation nonetheless points. There resides the essential problem, the core of the contention embodied in the late poems. How can poetry be a rehearsal of a heavenly order, or any system of order, when such orders are themselves no longer believable? As Heaney observed of his early faith, "If you desert the system, you're deserting the best there is, and there's no point in exchanging one great coherence for some other ad hoc arrangement" (*SS*, 318). He may have deserted the system, but his work does not and cannot desert it in the sense that it is "supersaturated" with what Yeats might have labeled a "phantasmagoria" of figures and motifs drawn from Heaney's early Catholic faith—not to mention other systems, Jungian and otherwise. From this most essential and most pressing standpoint, Heaney's poetry is at odds with itself, fruitfully at odds, for the quandary of his poetics and his reliance on the figural defines the parameters of his fundamental argument with self—the double vision that defines his work.

We find the argument explicitly shaping such late poems as "Loughanure," where Heaney speculates that the only afterlife may be one that can be found in art, which makes art a substitute for religion. "So this is what an afterlife can come to?" he reflects in this elegy for the painter Colin Middleton, "A cloud-boil of grey weather on the wall / . . . a remembered stare" (*HC*, 59). It is a cloud-boil also into which the gold chain of the vertically organized cosmos drops in "Known World." Here the painting frames and contains the storm. Still, countering his own argument, Heaney questions whether such a vision is

> an answer for Alighieri
> And Plato's Er? Who watched immortal souls
> Choose lives to come according as they were
>
> Fulfilled or repelled by existences they'd known
> Or suffered first time round.
>
> <div style="text-align:right">(<i>HC</i>, 60)</div>

"And did I seek the Kingdom? Will the Kingdom / Come?" Heaney reflects later in the poem before he drives "homesick," "unbelieving" with Mount Errigal on the skyline, seeing it rather than some heavenly order as "the one constant thing" while he attempts "To remember the Greek word signifying / A world restored completely" (*HC*, 62). The word the poet does not remember, the absent theological principle, is *apokatastasis*, which was the center point of Gregory of Nyssa's mystical theology more than 1,500 years ago. The desire to remember in the context of this poem of unbelief is as significant as the poet's lack of belief, and without that desire Heaney's poetry would lack dramatic necessity as well as most of its imaginative resources.

So while Heaney affirms something of a faithless embrace of "the numinous" in his connection to "earthlife" (*DC*, 66), his embrace of the immanent finds a necessary counterforce in the "impulse toward transcendence." More significantly still, if, as Heaney observes, the poet's "impulse to raise historical circumstance to a symbolic power" is necessarily linked to "the need to move personal force through an aesthetic distance" (*PW*, 55), then the collective personal force of Heaney's poetry originates in the historical loss of a presiding religious myth. What he sees as the ambitious poet's need to interweave "imaginative constants from different parts of the *oeuvre*" (*GT*, 162) begins to resonate with something very like a comprehensive vision of reality. The loss fueling that ambition is not only cultural and historical; it is also ontological. The preponderance of Heaney's own imaginative constants derives from a vision of cosmic comprehension the dilution of which exemplifies yet another principle he garners from Jung: "that the trauma of the individual consciousness is likely to be an aspect of the forces at work in collective life" (*PD*, 3). In his case the trauma exemplifies the "generational" recognition that God is dead. Or, as T. S. Eliot observed: "This I think is the great distress of the modern world, that it is neither Christian nor definitely something else" (2013, 64). So while a poem like "To Mick Joyce in Heaven" envisions "a house with no upstairs" as "heaven enough to be going on with," and "Out of This World" can declare that the loss of faith "occurred off stage," Heaney confesses he still cannot "disavow words like 'thanksgiving' or 'host' / or 'communion bread'" (*DC*, 45). They have, he affirms, "an undying / tremor and draw, like well water far down"—the well water of Heaney's original *omphalos*. Such poems reiterate the trauma and distress of his loss of faith while simultaneously seeking to align the poet's imagination with a core ontology that makes poetry, like faith, possible. No wonder Heaney envisions "spirit" breaking over "to raise a dust / in the font of exhaustion" (*SI*, 121). Heaney's poetry persists in that double vision where the irreducible immanence of the world leads to an awareness of death no less urgent than Larkin's— emptiness understood as empty. At the same time, the immanence of the world, groundless as it appears to be, suggests a contrary vision of emptiness as the vehicle for transcendence—the *via negativa* born out of the trauma of consciousness that proves the being of things in their fragile relationship to each other. "Nothingness," as Heaney quoted approvingly, citing Richard Ellmann, "could be pregnant as well as empty" (*PW*, 60).

It is important to recognize that Heaney's declaration that "poetry is a ratification of the impulse toward transcendence" is itself a kind of faith statement arising out of his contested nexus of belief and unbelief. The last section of "Out of This World" bears this out. Heaney envisions his exemplar, Czesław Miłosz, "as out of this world now / As the untranscendent music of the saw / He might have heard in Vilius or Warsaw / And would not have renounced, however paltry" (*DC*, 49). Why would poetry understood as a ratification of the impulse toward transcendence bring us to a vision of the untranscendent? For one thing, the immanent music of the saw, the music of what happens, as much as the severing cut of death, requires the qualifying negative—the "un-"

that clarifies "transcendent," the negative that renders transcendence visible. The word embodies the contested nature of Heaney's vision. Immanence and transcendence, like dual aspects of one reality, hinge together in Heaney's neologism. Their essential codependency is perhaps no more evident than when one compares "Postscript" to "Ballynahinch Lake." Here is the end of "Postscript":

> You are neither here nor there,
> A hurry through which known and strange things pass
> As big soft buffetings come at the car sideways
> And catch the heart off guard and blow it open.
>
> (*SL*, 70)

"Postscript" ends with what is nothing less than one of Heaney's most ecstatic visions of transcendence revealing itself, paradoxically, within the condition of immanence—as though each were the completion of the other. The heart opens ecstatically outward in every sense and unaccountably, like a moment of sheer grace. By contrast, the poet's stopped car at Ballynahinch Lake in "the spring-cleaning light / Of Connemara on a Sunday morning" leads only to the banal recognition that "it had indeed been useful to stop" (*EL*, 31). The swans that appear in "Postscript" among the other workings of light on the Flaggy Shore trigger an experience of the uncanny—of the heart's *kenosis*, its self-emptying into immensity. Transcendence becomes realized as an immanent momentary awareness of self-completion, really a self-extension, a stretching outward from the self. This is more than Frost's momentary stay against confusion. We are left in a space close to the mystical threshold where "the open" points to what lies beyond representation, beyond "created" consciousness: the "more" that David Bentley Hart affiliates with "the realm of the immanent" when it shows itself to be a "distinct mode" within a wider transcendence (2003, 13), so that the two are bound together "analogically" rather than "dialectically" (2003, 136), that is, as manifested by their fundamental coinherence.

By contrast, the water birds and play of light at Ballynahinch Lake merely "unhouse" something indeterminate before the poet and his companion continue their drive. We are left in a wholly horizontal

reality, a faring forward through time and space, where immensity de-
volves to opacity. Of "Ballynahinch Lake" Heaney reflects, "I suppose
the poem is saying 'find the mortal world enough'—something 'Post-
script' would find difficult to agree with" (*SS*, 366). In "Postscript"
something happens that charges the human heart to exceed its purely
immanent capacities, and consequently the heart is charged beyond
itself; in "Ballynahinch Lake" the heart is discharged of anything but its
own worldly control—the steering wheel's round "keeping going" to
borrow a phrase from Heaney's poem of that title (*SL*, 10–12). Where
"Postscript" projects the poetics of transfiguration toward its onto-
logical fulfillment in what exceeds representation, "Ballynahinch Lake"
deflects consciousness and writing back into the "untranscendent"
world, the world of the figural without appeal to what underwrites the
writing itself beyond the conscious will to write.

The word *consciousness* appears often in Heaney's prose, specifically
when he wants to underscore the action of poetry bringing conscious-
ness to a new level of insight and regard. As he observes in "Learning
from Eliot," "In the realm of poetry as in the realm of consciousness
there is no end to the possible learnings that might take place" (*FK*, 41).
Poetry, like any art, is nothing if not a product of the individual con-
sciousness embedded in experience and tradition, the extended "horizon
of consciousness" (*SS*, 407), and Heaney's indebtedness to what has been
called the figural imagination is profound (Scott 1971, 3 ff.). His con-
viction that poetry "transfigures" reality depends on that cultural sub-
stratum of thought. His use of figures and the transfiguration of those
figures likewise rely on this substratum. As William Lynch knew, the
whole nexus of the figural tradition itself redounds to the question of
consciousness: "What is this separateness and division in man of self
as subject and self as object which differentiates his self-consciousness
from that of God? It is precisely consciousness. It is the one original,
unifying form that steps in now as the *differentiating* factor" (2004, 204).
In Western tradition, figural interpretation evolved as the connective
tissue that linked the differentiated consciousness to a "higher" unity
presumably transcending it. "Figural interpretation," as Erich Auerbach
recounts, "establishes a connection between two events or persons, the
first of which signifies not only itself but also the second, while the
second encompasses or fulfills the first" (1984, 53). Both are historical

events, yet we recognize the connection between them through "a spiritual act." This premodern way of seeing reality turns on the idea that "earthlife" is "thoroughly real, with the reality of the flesh into which the Logos entered, but its reality is only the *umbra* or *figura* of . . . the ultimate truth, the great reality that will unveil and preserve the *figura*" (1984, 72). Dante's *The Divine Comedy* is the crowning poetic achievement of this vision of reality. It is telling that in "Envies and Identifications: Dante and the Modern Poet" Heaney acknowledges "this hankering for a purely delineated realm of wisdom and beauty sometimes asks literature to climb the stair of transcendence and give us images free from the rag-and-bone shop reek of time and space" (*FK*, 186). Heaney is on that stair belatedly in "Postscript," or minimally on its threshold, and he is there in other later poems as well.

Key to the figural imagination and key to Heaney's transfigurative poetic is the idea that, in fact, the poet does not need to leave the rag-and-bone shop world to ascend the stair of transcendence. As William Lynch again observes, within the figural vision "the temporal flow of human life" may be seen as "a *formed* thing, a significant form. It is a progressive and planned movement into and within the infinite" (2004, 58). From this vantage, the *transit* of Heaney's poems both individually and collectively exemplifies how poetry is a formed thing made through time, a weave of imaginative constants. Despite the poet's lapse of faith, Heaney's poetry may be read most profitably as a latter-day example of the figural imagination decentered from the tripartite cosmos of heaven-earth-hell in which the poet grew up and recentered along its own axis. If the decline of the figural imagination still constitutes "the fundamental dilemma of modernity" (Scott 1071, 25), and if postmodernism involves "an impasse where the very rapport between imagination and reality seems not only inverted but subverted altogether" (Kearney 1988, 3), then Heaney's poetic of transfiguration either is merely vestigial or inhabits the transit from premodern to postmodern world in a way that is critically and genuinely exemplary for our time. And if, as Heaney believed, the "shock waves of the consciousness reflect the upheavals of the surrounding world," then the poet who would be "most the poet" must allow that condition—the condition of increasing ontological as well as religious doubt—pervasively into the work without losing the thread of meaning that holds the entire weave together. To lose that thread would be to write the kind of "dematerializing" poetry that is anathema to Heaney's whole sensibility (*SS*, 274).

Heaney's poetry accords remarkably with the directive to reflect the shock waves of consciousness precisely *because* of its contested nature. Yet it faces extreme doubt in a manner that refuses "the process of dematerializing" (*SS*, 449). For all the attentiveness in his poetry and prose to the spiritual conditions of his time and to the historical conditions that have led us here, Heaney affirms that he "can't conceive of a poetry that hasn't a subject to deal with" (*SS*, 449). This conviction goes to the heart of his vision of reality, however lapsed his religious views, as well as to the heart of his poetry. These lines from "A Herbal" make that clear:

> If you know a bit
> About the universe
>
> It's because you've taken it in
> Like that,
>
> Looked as hard
> As you looked into yourself,
>
> Into the rat hole,
> Through the vetch and dock
> That mantled it.
>
> (*HC*, 43)

For Heaney there is nothing immaterial about the world, and there is consequently nothing immaterial or dematerializing about language. The world as it *is*, is alive with transfiguration: you take in the world, the world takes in you. The operation is at once mimetic, "like that," and transfigurative because boundary breaking. Though Derry and Derrida contended with each other in the poems of *The Haw Lantern* (*SS*, 287), Heaney's engagement with the ontologically subversive conditions of postmodernism is testimony to just how perspicaciously he allows the contemporary climate into his consciousness without losing connection to "our veritable human being" and, consequently, to poetry's power "to persuade that vulnerable part of our consciousness of its rightness in spite of the evidence of wrongness all around us, the power to remind us that we are hunters and gathers of values" (*CP*, 29). Such proclamations bear urgently on Heaney's figural imagination and its appeal to truth, to the idea that in poetry "truthfulness becomes recognizable as a ring of truth within the medium itself" (*CP*, 28). The lines "Because you have taken it in / Like that" embody what is essential to the figural imagination: the world is real and we know it is so because of the grounding of consciousness in a broader similitude on which language depends. The disruptive effect of Nietzsche's declaration "God is dead" and Heaney's tacit "generational assent" to that condition stands at odds with Heaney's stated poetics and his practice of the art. In the figural vision of reality, consciousness and the world are linked in similitude, or, as Heaney declares, "I had my existence. I was there. / Me in place and the place in me" (*HC*, 44). Such a vision of intimate communion need not appeal to doctrine to be regarded veritable. On the other hand, "A Herbal" ends with lines that speak movingly to the spiritual longing that implicitly undergirds both Heaney's work and its broader significance:

> Where can it be found again,
> An elsewhere world, beyond
>
> Maps and atlases,
> Where all is woven into
>
> And of itself, like a nest
> Of crosshatched grass blades?
> (*HC*, 44)

The end of "A Herbal" juxtaposes the centripetal and centrifugal poles of Heaney's imagination, its parabolic dynamic now pitched into the utterly transcendent where it doubly performs the transfiguration of self into world and world into self ("Me in place, the place in me"), and then of the transcendent into the immanent, the immanent into the transcendent. Heaney's figure of crosshatched grass blades is the humble equivalent of Dante's figure at the end of the *Divine Comedy*, a knot where all is in-woven into one. The figure of Dante's Cosmic Rose admits a Reality beyond representation. It represents the point at which the figural transcends itself in a mystical singularity of One in Many, Many in One, and All in All. Heaney's late woven nest and his earlier harvest bow are both "knowable coronas," artistic "love knots" that envision the end of art as a peace passing our understanding. Each brings the longing for transcendence-within-immanence home in the homeliest of figures.

That figure is itself nested in a question in Heaney's poem. It is an advent desired that speaks equally to the poet's ontological doubt and his enduring faith in language. Heaney's doubt is not inconsiderable, and his evocation of a converse cosmic state of things likewise shapes the late poems. One encounters a contrary figure of reality's self-enwoven nature in "A Stove Lid for W. H. Auden," where "the mass and majesty of the world" distill into a cast-iron lid that transfigures in turn into a "hell-mouth stopper, flat earth-disc." What it stops us from seeing fully is "dark matter in the starlit coalhouse"—a cosmos sustained by its own self-consumption (*DC*, 73). What is the point of transfiguration in such a cosmos, absent an afterlife, particularly since the technique of figuration itself rests on the fundament of a worldview that has given way for the poet? Here we find the demonic aspect of Heaney's self-enwoven reality. In "Slack" he revisits the coal house motif, where the coal and the sound of coal, like the sound of water, convey figural as well as literal weight. The poet, "remembering it," hears it tip and slush from the bag with the word *catharsis*. The literal sound resounds in the figural word, which means "purgation" and which in its Greek root (*katharos*) means "to clean." The coal house transfigures from a version of hell to a version of purgatory. Likewise, in "The Turnip-Snedder" the cast-iron machine declares its figural reality out of the literal: "'This is the way God sees life,'" / it said, 'from seedling braid to snedder'" (*DC*, 3). We are placed through the language of the thing now given language into a God's-eye view of our passing reality. We are shifted from a place into the placeless, into the unconditional realm of the *deus absconditus*. Irrespective of his lapse of faith, all of Heaney's thing poems retain the assumption that poetry bears "an ark of the covenant between language and sensation" (*CP*, 12). That covenant is the basis for Heaney's continued faith in the figural and the transfigurative. It is not surprising, given such statements, that Heaney saw the arrival of poetry in his life as a "redemptive grace" (SS, 96).

Heaney viewed the world in which he grew up as "medieval" in its vision, and the continuance of the figural imagination in his work bears witness to those sources. If art is ideally "an order where we can at last grow up to that which we stored up as we grew" (CP, 11), then the whole body of a poet's work should leave nothing truly formative behind. In Heaney's case this means drawing liberally from the latter-day "medieval" world into which he was born. "Vitruviana" exemplifies well how Heaney transports the medieval into the contemporary and forces one of its principal figures to take the strain of what he called "the very extremity of our late twentieth century knowledge" (CP, 19). The medieval philosopher and theologian Vitruvius advanced a theory of proportion that manifested the communion of microcosm and macrocosm, the harmonic link between the immanent and the transcendent in the work of art. The key figure of Vitruvius's conception was the *Homo Quadratus*, the four cornered human figure that was mathematically expressive of a more comprehensive reality—from the four cardinal points to the four winds to the four seasons, and so on (Eco 1986, 35). The first section of "Vitruviana" depicts Heaney as a young boy standing "in the deep pool at Portstewart" up to his chest with his arms out and his legs wide apart like "Vitruvian man" (EL, 63). The poem then places us on the football pitch where the boys performing calisthenics are spreading themselves "on the wind's cross" so that they mimic a Giotto mural of St. Francis receiving the stigmata. The figure of the young poet as Vitruvian man transfigures into the figure of Christ on the cross, or rather a football field full of Christs with the figure of St. Francis adding greater visual cohesiveness to the pattern of connection across time. By the end of the poem, echoing Eliot's *The Waste Land*, the poet confesses he can connect only "some bits and pieces" (EL, 64). Now, on Sandymount instead of Margate Strand the poet engages in a "seaside whirligig"—*Homo Quadratus* again marking out "the cardinal points," ecstatically outstretched. In that moment the "down to earth" light begins "to fan out and open up." The Vitruvian figure retains imaginative force to bring the immanent world, "the grey matter of sand and sky" (EL, 64), to the brink of a transcendent amplitude within and not above the world.

Heaney's reanimation of the figural, the transfiguring intensity of his innovation within the tradition at this late, lapsed cultural moment, is even more richly realized in "St Kevin and the Blackbird." The poet portrays the saint at prayer, kneeling in his cell, arms out, palms turned up, "stiff as a crossbeam," when the blackbird lands, at which point the saint finds himself "linked / Into the network of eternal life." According to the legend, the saint is "moved to pity" and so has to stay in that position "Until the young are hatched and fledged and flown" (*SL*, 20). The second half of the poem shifts to a self-reflexive meditation that forces the reader to "imagine being Kevin," since the whole thing is "imagined anyhow." The poem reorients from a legend reimagined to a self-reflexive fable about the imagination itself, and as such an inquiring performance into the nature of the figural. The poem even requires the reader to enter the mind of St. Kevin, his tribulation and his self-transcendence—requires readers/listeners to transfigure themselves consciously into the one who prays in the poem, as in the legend, in utter, self-emptying compassion:

> Alone and mirrored clear in love's deep river,
> "To labour and not to seek reward," he prays,
>
> A prayer his body makes entirely
> For he has forgotten self, forgotten bird
> And on the riverbank forgotten the river's name.
>   (*SL*, 20–21)

Helen Vendler offers an evocative reading of "St Kevin and the Blackbird" "in which stoicism turns into something almost indistinguishable from lyric death" (1998, 163). I want to pursue a different tack. St. Kevin's prayer links him to "the network of eternal life," and not only natural life, which brings the saint's apparent resignation expressly into the broader context of the eternal. Resignation before one's natural fate is one thing; the profoundest connection to an order of being that transcends immanent nature is another. Stoicism makes no such claim; St. Kevin's faith does, and it may well be argued that it is his concentrated contemplation that enables this transfiguration even of nature itself. Heaney has given us scenes where people have had to *thole*, sto-ically, to suffer and endure through experience. There is something more suggested in St. Kevin's act. By the poem's end he is "mirrored clear in love's deep river." This is the opposite of the Stoic's *apatheia*, the subjugation of emotion. This is, on the contrary, a vision of abounding compassion. The picture we are given is that of the most intense kind of contemplation, indeed mystical concentration, that enables the saint to enter a condition mirrored that runs deeper and is more real than the mundane reality we perceive as immanent life. St. Kevin enters this condition at the threshold of conditions by remaining "stiff as a cross-beam." He embodies in his gesture the figure of Christ on the cross. The saint's bodily configuration is not unlike that of Vitruvian man, a living axis, outstretched. He is thus both himself and a figure of Christ, just as Christ anticipates the figure of Vitruvian man—*Homo Quadratus* and *imitatio Christi* in one.

This linking together of figures reflects the underlying core pattern of the figural vision of reality—all are mirrored together *through and not despite* their individual natures. St. Kevin's all-encompassing forgetting of the self, the bird, even the name of the literal river he prays beside, is a measure of his presence reflected in love's deep river where the saint is mirrored, where he is transfigured. Both the saint and the reader—by proxy of the poem's invitation to "imagine being him"—step beyond the threshold condition where the mirror, the figure, becomes reality, the really real. The poet, regardless of his own attitude toward the faith of his upbringing, has brought us to the brink of mystical union. The *via negativa* arrives at this self-transcending outcome, an encounter with superabundant being, and it does so without denying immanent reality, for both are nothing other than part and parcel of each other. By de-constructing its own transfiguring operations, the poem effectively re-constructs the figural method and, as its ontological requirement, the subtending linkages of possible meaning that language embodies, albeit imperfectly. The poem's new level of consciousness might look like lyric death but its more salient countermeasure is the fulfillment of lyric life—the fulfillment of self in superabundance. Representation has be-come something close to real presence. In "St Kevin and the Blackbird" Heaney has given us an incomparable example of the poem as post-modern icon.

Rivers, from the Moyola through "love's deep river," flow through Heaney's poetry. While in "St Kevin and the Blackbird" love transfigures saint and (potentially) reader, by the poem's end we can appropriately ask, "Where are we?" Are we over the mirrored brim into the transcendent or still on the mirrored bank of the immanent? The poem brings us to the point of recognition where the dichotomy nearly falls away. Without direct appeal to doctrine, but with a sure link to the figural tradition, Heaney's parabolic double sensation, his double capacity, his double vision, wants it and has it both ways imaginatively. We find this same paradoxical coinherence, or communion of immanence and transcendence, again in Heaney's translation of a sonnet by Joachim Du Bellay (1522–60), "Du Bellay in Rome." The poem, currently uncollected, was completed shortly before Heaney's death:

> You who arrive to look for Rome in Rome
> And can in Rome no Rome you know discover:
> These palaces and arches ivied over
> And ancient walls are Rome, now Rome's a name.
>
> Here see Rome's overbearing overcome—
> Rome, who brought the world beneath her power
> And held sway, robbed of sway: see and consider
> Rome the prey of all-consuming time.
>
> And yet this Rome is Rome's one monument.
> Rome alone could conquer Rome. And the one element
> Of constancy in Rome is the ongoing
>
> Seaward rush of Tiber. O world of flux
> Where time destroys what's steady as the rocks
> And what resists time is what's ever flowing.
>
> (Heaney 2013a, 6)

Where "St Kevin and the Blackbird" foregrounds microcosm, one life's transfiguring entry into the flow of eternal life, "Du Bellay in Rome" foregrounds macrocosm, a vision of civilization—and by inference all civilizations—as "the prey of all-consuming time." One could not, apparently, find a more countermeasuring vision to "St Kevin." On the other hand, while "the one element / Of constancy in Rome is the ongoing / Seaward rush of Tiber," "Du Bellay in Rome" concludes with a similar paradox of self-enwoven doubleness: "O world of flux / Where time destroys what's steady as the rocks / And what resists time is what is ever-flowing." One can read these lines as, indeed, stoic—or Heracleitian. Civilizations resist time despite time—they *thole*. Life comes to nobility in the face of inevitable consumption within a self-consuming cosmos. But that is not exactly what the last line says. The last line inscribes a kind of equivalence: what resists time equals what is ever flowing. One can alter the equation to say exactly the same thing through the elision of one of the terms: what resists time equals what resists time; what is ever flowing *is* what is ever flowing. Both are obviously tautological. The line Heaney wrote, however, performs a coincidence of opposites. Resistance to time and the flow of time appear to be different but are actually the same. The same may be said of immanence and transcendence. Both "St Kevin and the Blackbird" and "DuBellay in Rome" ride on a vision of the ultimate reality as flow. It is as though transcendence in Heaney's figurations were not at all a matter of otherworldliness, nor a matter of "*tholing*" against the inevitable whether withstood or whined at; rather they are a depth below being itself, at once underlying and flowing through the immanent, as if in the late poems the "eternal fountain" Heaney translated in "Station Island" from St. John of the Cross—"all source's source and origin"—were prevailingly present timelessly through time: "eternal life" equals "what's ever flowing."

"What resists time is what's ever flowing," another example of Heaney's self-inwoven locutions, also can be read as the first half of a syntactical chiasmus, not unlike Donne's "for I / except you enthrall me, never shall be free, / Nor ever chaste, except you ravish me" (1971, 315). Were one to complete the chiasmus it would read: "What resists time is what's ever flowing. What is ever flowing is what resists time," so that the trope's structure, its cross, reveals the implied tautology. What I hope to draw out by making this implication plain is the thread that ties these kinds of self-enwoven observations in Heaney's work to the parabolic nature of his figural imagination that envisions transcendence sustaining meaning in the immanent world. Traditionally, the figural imagination aligns the horizontal axis of human experience with the vertical axis of the heavenly, as do parables, the word *parable* originating from the same root as "parabola." Heaney has lapsed from belief in the second, "otherworldly" orientation toward transcendence, but he retains "the impulse toward transcendence," and hence the idea of transcendence in its true analogical configuration, along the immanent axis as a necessary condition for poetry.

In view of Heaney's affirmation of "the impulse of transcendence," it is interesting to see how the figure of Christ assumes a small but vitally important place in the late poetry in spite of his loss of faith. The figure of Christ appears early in Heaney's work in "Limbo," where an illegitimate infant is netted by fisherman: "Even Christ's palms, unhealed / Smart and cannot fish there" (*WO*, 70) the poet declares, effectively subverting the spiritual largesse of Christ's divine healing by ironically taking the doctrine of limbo as a neither-damned-nor-saved-zone in the afterlife to its logical conclusion. In "Seeing Things," by contrast, Heaney envisions Christ's baptism carved in stone as an emblem of *claritas* where the thin, hard lines represent at once the river's flow and the stone, making the stone "alive with what's invisible" (*ST*, 17). Poetry's power to transfigure, rendered brilliantly in "Seeing Things," gains explicit credence in "The Government of the Tongue," where Heaney claims that while poetry's power in the face of history appears nil, its power is also potentially "unlimited." Heaney's figure for poetry's potentially transcendent power is Jesus's own writing pictured in the eighth chapter of John's Gospel. Like Jesus's letters written in sand, poetry "holds attention for a space" and as such "functions not as distraction but as pure concentration, a focus where our power to concentrate is concentrated back on ourselves" (*GT*, 108; *SS*, 383). In short, poetry's power rests in its ability to mirror consciousness back upon itself in a self-transcending, parabolic loop. The moment when concentration concentrates back on itself recalls, again, St. Kevin, "the self-entranced" or "self-enraptured man," one linked through the concentration of contemplative practice into the network of eternal life. Poetry would appear to have its teleology in that vision of self-transcendence.

Yet all of these examples underscore Jesus's *immanence*, the "untranscendent" side of the Incarnation equation of human and divine. There is nothing inherently antiorthodox about this, nor is there anything antiorthodox in Heaney's view that Jesus must have died "a howling, animal death" (*PW*, 51). The Socinian heresy held that Jesus's humanity was a mere phantomlike appearance disguising his divinity. This view is neither traditionally Christian nor, apparently, the lapsed poet's. Rather, as William Lynch recognized, the "man in the street" often understands what the intellectual does not: "that true reality is contained within the dramatic, temporal life of the body" (2004, 59). Nowhere do we see this reality more dramatically portrayed in Heaney's work than in another uncollected poem, "The Latecomers":

> He saw them come, then halt behind the crowd
> That wailed and plucked and ringed him, and was glad
> They kept their distance. Hedged on every side,
>
> Harried and responsive to their need,
> Each hand that stretched, each brief hysteric squeal—
> However he assisted and paid heed,
>
> A sudden blank letdown was what he'd feel
> Unmanning him when he met the pain of loss
> In the eyes of those his reach had failed to bless.
>
> And so he was relieved the newcomers
> Had now discovered they'd arrived too late
> And gone away. Until he heard them, climbers
>
> On the roof, a sound of tiles being shifted,
> The treble scrape of terra cotta lifted
> And a paralytic on his pallet
>
> Lowered like a corpse into a grave.
> Exhaustion and the imperatives of love
> Vied in him. To judge, instruct, reprove,

And ease them body and soul.
Not to abandon but to lay on hands.
Make time. Make whole. Forgive.

                    (Heaney 2014)

In its off-rhymed tercets, Heaney's brilliant poem envisions a harried Jesus, a figure of ultimate celebrity, God-made, "plucked and ringed" by those who want his healing touch, a touch that sometimes fails. This Jesus, besieged by admirers and those asking for his presence like a rock star or world-renowned poet, must overcome the natural human inclination to feel that the gift concentrated in him is being drawn out of him by too many would-be links. He would appear to be the antithesis of the utterly concentrated St. Kevin. Those tercets, vaguely Dantean, "hedge" us in within Jesus's own dark wood: "Exhaustion and the imperatives of love / Vied in him." Could there be a more human identification with Jesus's predicament? Yet it is precisely the humanity of Jesus in Heaney's poem, the immanent human being, that catalyzes the poem's vision of transfiguration in the daily groundwork of salvation in not absconding from that work. Time, the flow of time, all-consuming time, is made in every sense in the last line. Time through the figure therefore becomes a matter of making whole—a way of forgiveness. In "The Latecomers," Heaney's Jesus performs an act of transfiguration upon the figural imagination itself to reveal its ethical aspect. Poetry as a form of concentration must turn outward, not only back toward the self, so Heaney's Jesus dramatizes the struggle between one's subjectivity and the other as ethical subject: the world that stands before one, also hedged in by individuals linked by need with little awareness of any broader line to eternal life, much less each other. Implied here is another aspect of Heaney's continued reliance on the figural: the truth that the figural itself needs to be "fully aware that meaning does not originate within the narrow chambers of its own subjectivity but emerges as a response to the *other*, as radical interdependence" (Kearney 1988, 387). The figural imagination as such is predicated on that interdependence, as it is on an analogical vision of reality. Such a vision of interdependence requires an axis of value, the always exceeding surplus that likewise requires difference, and thereby posits a vision of reality with all of its often debilitating and brutal pressures as, ultimately, symphony rather than cacophony. With "The Latecomers" Heaney's double take of immanence and transcendence, as well as his contested views of inherited belief and generational lapse, would appear to resolve in ethical alignment, an unforeseen *claritas*. The end of the figural imagination rebounds to its source and center: in the kinship of things that do not look akin.

"Death is the *side of life* that is turned away from us," Rilke wrote, but he qualifies that conclusion when he reflects, "The true figure of life extends through both domains, the blood of the mightiest circulation drives through *both: there is neither a here nor a beyond, but a great unity*" (quoted in *RP*, 140). Despite what appears at the end to be a merely "ceremonial" assent to the religious practice of his youth (*SS*, 472), Heaney's work never abandons the impulse, the need, to pursue what Rilke called "the true figure of life." It is not surprising that Heaney quotes appreciatively Rilke's profound reflection in *The Redress of Poetry*. His sensation of doubleness on the road to Glanmore, his unstinting faith in the double human capacity to embrace the immanent and the transcendent, the transcendent *through* the immanent and vice versa, and hence his belief in the power of poetry to transfigure, depends on the reality of some great unity, despite the loss of an overarching system of belief. As he envisions in "A Kite for Aibhín," the final poem of *Human Chain*, "Air from another life and time and place, / Pale blue heavenly air is supporting / A white wing beating high against the breeze, / And, yes, it is a kite!" (*HC*, 85). The at once ordinary and miraculous support of the invisible is what allows Heaney to affirm the "windfall" the kite will come to after it breaks loose from the poet's hands, "separate, elate . . . itself alone," so that the kite becomes wholly transparent to the figure of a soul. As Fred Marchant observed, this "windfall" reminds one "of Whitman's line that death might just be luckier than we supposed" (2011, 4). Heaney's "windfall" is a self-emptying and a fulfillment—the amplitude beyond the known, the possibility of which can only be realized after the kite's, the soul's, release. And the word echoes its use in "Kinship" from *North*, where the center is figured as "a windfall / composing the floor it rots into" (*N*, 43)—a figure of life's endurance out of death.

At the same time, "A Kite for Aibhín" echoes still further back to origins—the air is from "another life and time," so the poet's release embodies all the reflexivity of his entire body of work—the double motion of a backward look that discovers new signatures far afield. "And there I was in the middle of a field" (Heaney 2013b, 1), Heaney reflects in another of his last poems, "In a Field." It is the same field into which he strayed, he recounts in "Mossbawn," the "sunlit lair" of a first memory amid the pea drills, and voices calling his name. Now, as it turns out, at the end of his life he reimagines the scene again that he imagined "so long and often." And now it is his sister's husband Mick Joyce stumbling "from the windings' magic ring" to take the child Heaney by a hand, he says, "to lead me back / Through the same old gate into the yard / Where everyone has suddenly appeared. / All standing waiting" (*DC*, 12). In the end, Heaney envisions that farthest possible reach in the most intimate setting, what he once called the "indigenous afterlife" (*GT*, 9)—everyone, all, standing waiting: all in all. So Heaney's parabolic arc, his art's journey of transfiguration, ends where it began, the end the beginning, the beginning in the end, in the final windfall of *all*, the full manifestation of the pattern, as if the whole long arcing centrifugal movement had suddenly zeroed centripetally to the stillness of a single point, what Augustine saw as the most perfect figure, the true center that is "the beginning and end of itself" (Eco 1986, 43). It is appropriate to the completed pattern of Heaney's work that a Joyce figure takes him by the hand to forward his return, just as that other less homely Joyce figure fortified him to "fill the element / with signatures on your own frequency" (*SI*, 94). "Tell the truth. Do not be afraid," as Heaney glossed James Joyce's meaning at the end of "Station Island" to Dennis O'Driscoll (*SS*, 250). "Do not be afraid," *Noli Tamere*: Heaney's final text to his wife moments before he died. These patterns of repetition and relation, strangely enwoven retrospectively now in the work and in the life, threads of figures really, suggest, almost, that Heaney's faith in poetry has always had an awareness of "something luckier" behind it, something to keep the figures going and keep them true despite the reality of death and the inevitable dark glass of our seeing—something almost, but not quite, beyond belief.

CHAPTER FIFTEEN

THE POETICS OF REVERIE AND REVELATION IN THE LAST POEMS

Rand Brandes

Children are abandoned and abused, badgered and bullied. They are conscripted and killed, molested and murdered. They die quickly in birth or slowly after long illnesses. They struggle with disabilities and dependencies. Accidents take them or maim them. Poverty and starvation ravage their lives. They are trafficked across international lines. Their worlds are small and stay small, without horizons. For these children childhood is a nightmare from which many do not wake, and if they do, their traumas wait for them with their fingers on future triggers.

These undeniable realities have become the stuff of much postmodern poetry, including the poetry of Seamus Heaney. These childhoods, French phenomenologist Gaston Bachelard would argue, are the childhoods of the Jungian animus: of history, of psychoanalysis, of biography and autobiography.[1] Bachelard writes: "It is the task of the *animus'* memory to tell the facts well in the objectivity of a life's history" (1969, 105). The animus childhood for Heaney, in both the poetry and the prose, is definitively documented for the moment in *Stepping Stones*. The interview establishes the "who," "what," "where," "when," and "why" of the poet's journey. This is the known life, the life that the poet is conscious and willing to share. The interview format emphasizes the process of self-discovery while bringing with it the objectivity of the critical conversation. Of course, the self-analysis stops short of being fully confessional, maintaining an appropriately dignified distance.

Bachelard, however, is not interested in the childhood found in the prose of *Stepping Stones* or the information it brings to the poems. He argues that there is a place in the theoretical world and in the conversations of critics for an engagement with the past through poetry that does not require a "historical context," since the poetic images taken from childhood are timeless when experienced in reverie, a reverie animated by the archetypes of the collective unconscious. This critical approach does not deny the significance, even centrality, of interpretations informed by history and other fields of aesthetic discourse; it simply offers an alternative to the "reality function." Bachelard muses: "But doesn't reverie, by its very essence, liberate us from the reality function? From the moment it is considered in all of its simplicity, it is perfectly evident that reverie bears witness to a normal, useful *irreality function* which keeps the human psyche on the fringe of all the brutality of a hostile and foreign non-self" (1969, 13).[2] Heaney made the same argument from the moment he began to dream through his poems and to feel into the otherworld of words.

In contrast to the animus childhoods, according to Bachelard, there are the Other childhoods of the anima, of metaphysics of the poet in exaltation. These childhoods, lived and relived under the sign of the anima, are the childhoods that revive us and reconnect us to the human chain and the creative cosmos. It is the difference between a childhood "kite" that reminds the poet of a "flitter of blown chaff" or a "small black lark" and whose string is "a wet rope," and a kite that is "A white wing beating high against the breeze," whose string is like the stem of a "thin-stemmed flower" (*HC*, 85).[3]

Seamus Heaney, in moments of deep reverie and revelation, privileges the bright-eyed child and robust childhood as both creative subjects and poetic objects despite his keen sense of the problematic nature of the childhood of the animus in relation to postmodern precepts. Heaney argues in *Crediting Poetry* that poetry cannot limit itself to the "murderous" in the world or be limited by it—that poetry, as a creative construct and source of essential human values, must accommodate and promote the "marvelous" (*CP*, passim). As an expression of the anima, the marvelous is ahistorical, perhaps antihistorical. Heaney has put his faith in the marvelous ever since in one of his earliest poems he dared to "stare, big-eyed Narcissus, into some spring," going against "all adult dignity" (*DN*, 57).[4] From a more general literary perspective refracted through Bachelard's idea of reverie, the animus can be seen as "Heaney-the-writer-of-prose and giver-of-interviews," while the anima can be seen as "Heaney-the-poet and keeper-of-the-mysteries." As Bachelard says: "The reverie which wants to express itself becomes poetic reverie" (1969, 186), and "Poetic reverie revives the world of original words" (1969, 188).[5] This is the language landscape of the anima.

Heaney continues to write the world under the sign of the anima with even more enthusiasm and intentionality in his last two collections, *District and Circle* and *Human Chain*. As Heaney ages and begins to feel the world and words begin to slip away, the dream child, like wise old Virgil, guides and renews his spirit for what would become his final journey. All of Heaney's fears and hopes fill the space between the opening poem of *District and Circle*, "The Turnip Snedder," and the closing poem of *Human Chain*, "A Kite for Aibhín." In addition, the final poems of these two volumes, "The Blackbird of Glanmore" and "A Kite for Aibhín," are not tombstones/headstones but curbstones, like those at Newgrange, which serve as portals into the next phase of existence. Through the restorative powers of reverie Heaney moves from the hopelessness manifest in the turnip snedder to the hope of the kite, from the prison of history to the freedom of flight into, not away from, self-revelation and a higher order of responsibilities.

The child reconstructed in reverie opens the doors of perception for the aging poet, often through archetypal images. While childhood memories and the child as character/performer/acting agent have been central to Heaney throughout all of his works, they become even more significant in his later poems. Common wisdom says, and science now confirms, that the older we get the more vivid our memories from the past become, sometimes diminishing the clarity of the present. Heaney was not immune to this natural process, nor did he ignore it in his later poems. The older he became the more important the child and child-hood became as images of original inspiration, knowledge, and human values. After a lifetime of writing, Heaney's faith in poetry and belief that it can still make a difference in the world are rooted in his childhood memories retrieved in moments of reverie. These reveries open up the present so dramatically that the poems enter the realm of revelation. Through reverie the poet not only relives the past as he imagines it but also lives the future as he knows it. This poetic engagement of the anima through reverie is not some New Age, feel-good, find-the-child-inside-yourself therapeutic method that encourages in adults an infantile self-indulgence and instant gratification. For Heaney, the childhood of the anima is the source of his creative being itself; this is the mysterious (universal and timeless) place that the poet returns to and from during the act of creation in moments of reverie: "On the grass when I arrive / . . . / In the ivy when I leave" (*DC*, 76).

The Jungian animus and anima are hypothetical constructs. They are emblems that emerged out of Jung's encounter with the symbolism of alchemy and that now reside in his theories regarding the collective unconscious and archetypes. Considering them as gender specific, with animus being the masculine principle and anima being the feminine principle, gives rise to all types of problems in relation to privilege, stereotypes, essentializing, and identity politics. Still, these constructs provide a potent lexicon with which to explore and express our sense of the personal and impersonal contents of the self. When seen as a means, a shorthand, for exploring some fundamental dualities in our lives and in our ways of knowing the world, the animus and anima can be very helpful, as they were to Bachelard when he codified the poetics of rev-erie in relationship to the collective unconscious and the archetypes of the child and childhood.

The child archetype according to Bachelard is the primum mobile, setting the entire creative cosmos in motion: "And when one has made the archetypal power of childhood come back through dreams, all the great archetypes of the paternal forces, maternal forces take on their ac-tion again. . . . Both escape time. Both live with us in another time" (1969, 125). Heaney returns to where the archetype is "immutable, im-mobile beneath memory," where the poetic potential of the child may be most fully actualized (Bachelard 1969, 125). Heaney does not remember or recall the anima childhood as much as he relives it with an interiority, immediacy, and intensity that have come to signify his poetic genius. It becomes the measure and redress of all things adult: "We were small and thought we knew nothing / Worth knowing" (*SI*, 45). In "The Blackbird of Glanmore" and "A Kite for Aibhín," Heaney brings to life a child and an original childhood that we can freely breathe *in*: "Thus poems come to our aid in finding the breathing of the great gusts again, the original breathing of the child who breathes the world. . . . What a magnification of breath there is when the lungs speak, sing, make poems! Poetry helps one breathe well" (Bachelard 1969, 182).

Gaston Bachelard, in his last significant work, *The Poetics of Reverie: Childhood, Language, and the Cosmos*, helps us understand the significance of the child as a source of pure personal and impersonal poetic inspiration in Heaney's final poems. Bachelard argues that the child sits tensely under the sign of "happiness" and "well-being"—the anima—and that childhood is most fully engaged in moments of non-nostalgic poetic reverie. However, Bachelard does not direct us through the land of the lotus eaters. He writes: "But our goal is not to study dreamers. We would die of boredom if we had to make inquiries among the companions in relaxation. We wish to study not the reverie that puts one to sleep, but the *working reverie* [*rêverie oeuvrante*], the reverie which prepares works. Books, and no longer men, are then our documents, and our entire effort in reliving the poet's reverie is to feel its working [*oeuvrant*] character" (1969, 182). These are W. B. Yeats's dreams that bring with them cultural responsibilities.

Bachelard's *The Poetics of Reverie* is a celebration of the power of the poetic image to bring health and happiness to those open to its creative potential: "Reverie helps us inhabit the world, inhabit the happiness of the world" (1969, 22); "To designate a dreamed world well, it is necessary to mark it with a happiness. . . . So we are always coming back upon our thesis that we must affirm in general and in detail that *reverie is a consciousness of well-being*" (1969, 177–78, italics mine). To be open to reverie is to be willing to dream with and ultimately through the poet and his word-images in order to return to an original self that is whole and one with the world: "In their cosmic reverie, poets speak of the world in original words, in original images. They speak of the world in the language of the world" (Bachelard 1969, 188). The original self and world are manifest in the solitude of the child and in a "*childhood* [that] *lasts all through life*" (1969, 20). This daytime dreaming, signified by "reverie," is done while awake and conscious, when there is a "cogito"—"The dreamer of reverie remains conscious enough to say: it is I who dream the reverie" (1969, 22). Reverie is made possible by a dynamic combination of memory and imagination, the soul and the mind. It is an existential experience shared by the dreaming writer and the dreaming reader and is most fully realized in the poetic image under the influence of the child archetype.

Furthermore, Bachelard notes a "redoubling of reverie late in life," which is not surprising (1969, 102). He says: "These [childhood] memories which live by the image and in virtue of the image become, at certain times of our lives and particularly during the quiet age, the origin and matter of a complex reverie: the memory dreams and the reverie remembers" (1969, 20). In old age the sagacious poet will not long for the virility and society of youth, but for the original world of "firsts" that retune, recenter, and reconnect the creative Self to the world.[6] Bachelard's *Poetics of Reverie* helps to explain how and why the child and childhood memories, even in the context of the "terror of history" (Eliade 1971, 150), become more potent as Heaney ages. The increased presence comes from Heaney's elemental alchemical mythopoetics and his ongoing affinity for the transcendental aspects of Jungian psychology. Bachelard, writing in old age and worn out by the claims of history and prohibitions and phobias of political artists and thinkers, embraces Jung as well.

The lyrical and late Heaney writes under the sign of the "anima" as understood by Jung via Bachelard.[7] This is true despite the fact that Heaney lived through the stridently antitranscendent rise of Marxist theory and poststructuralist attacks on the mythic, the organic, the original. Jung was in the air when Heaney began to write, and critics noted the shared worldviews almost immediately. There is much about Jungian psychology for which Heaney has a natural and cultivated affinity, and which he continued to find of use throughout his writing life and into his later works. Of particular use was Jung's theory of the collective unconscious and archetypes, which the poet encountered in the works of his touchstone, mostly mythic, poets. Like W. B. Yeats, Robert Graves, and Ted Hughes, who engaged the occult and the mystical as if reliable realities because they (in)formed and energized their poetic imaginations, Heaney assumes a Jungian disposition to decode the self and history. When the Jungian collective unconscious or archetypes (or the Great Memory or the White Goddess or shamanistic flights) are used as an enabling imaginative force, it does not matter at the end of the day whether they "are real"; what matters, as with a belief in God or immortality, is what is done with that belief. While some theorists will consider this approach to living with and engaging in the unknown Other as delusional at best and dangerous at worst—especially in a post-colonial and economically polarized Irish context—Heaney's poetry always encourages us to follow a certain path because it is right for us; it brings us pleasure and greater self-understanding.

When the ghost of Joyce instructs the poet to fill the world "with signatures on your own frequency" (SI, 94), the poet is instructing the reader to do the same. Jung says in an interview, "One should not be deterred by the rather silly objection that nobody knows whether these old universal ideas—God, immortality, freedom of the will, and so on—are 'true' or not. Truth is the wrong criterion here. One can only ask whether they are helpful or not, whether man is better off and feels his life more complete, more meaningful and more satisfactory with or without them" (1977, 449). There are obvious moments in Heaney's work where Jung helps the poet make the most of his psychic impulses (impulses of his psyche), as in the bog poems and in the many journeys into the darkness of the self and the international underworlds of ancient mythologies. Heaney's deep sympathy for and openness to Jung's worldview was also the result, in part, of the poet's growing up in the Derry countryside in an almost prelapsarian, preindustrial world alert to the seasons and the rhythms of farm life, a world where time feels circular, even round under the dome of the sky.

The central concepts of Jungian theory are those of the collective unconscious and its archetypes. There is much misunderstanding regarding these concepts, which contemporary therapist/thinkers like Barbara Stevens Sullivan have attempted to address. In *The Mystery of*

Analytical Work: Weavings from Jung and Bion, Sullivan comments, quoting Jung: "Jung defines archetypes (the contents of the collective unconscious) as pre-existing inherited forms, but he goes on to say, they are '*forms without content*, representing merely the possibility of a certain type of perception and action.' . . . They are 'the unconscious images of the instincts themselves . . . *patterns of instinctual behavior*'" (2010, 45). It is important to note that the collective unconscious is universal in the way that instincts are and that these "possibilities" are made manifest in poetic images.

Thus, Sullivan continues, "The archetypes are not fixed entities. We cannot say how many archetypes there are. . . . Jung named certain common archetypes (or archetypal images) like the Mother, the Child, the Wise Old Man, but for our purposes here, rather than thinking of archetypes as discrete entities, it is more helpful to think about the inborn archetypal world as a fluid universe where archetypes that may or may not be named merge into each other and constellate our fundamental reactions to human life" (2010, 45). Still, Bachelard makes a similar, though much more passionate, point: "The archetypes are reserves of enthusiasm which help us believe in the world, love the world, create our world. . . . Each archetype is an opening on the world, an invitation to the world. . . . And the archetypes will always remain origins of powerful images" (1969, 124–25). Bachelard's "reserves of enthusiasm" literally bring shape and substance to the "forms without content." So the challenge is to focus on the potentiality of the archetype as both presence and absence, past and future. Furthermore, it is equally challenging not to think of the collective unconscious as something "out there," in space above us, or "in there," in our minds/brains/DNA somewhere hidden like the unconscious itself.

Sullivan quotes Jung again: "We call the unconscious 'nothing,' and yet it is a reality *in potentia*. The thought we shall think, the deed we shall do, even the fate we shall lament tomorrow, all lie unconscious in our today. . . . The unconscious has a Janus-face: on one side its contents point back to a preconscious, prehistoric world of instinct, while on the other side it potentially anticipates the future—precisely because of the instinctive readiness for action of the factors that determine man's fate"

(2010, 45–46). Heaney was constantly in touch with these forces and knew what treasures lay buried in the unconscious—images, etymologies, entire mythologies—all existing outside of time and space in pure potentiality. Bachelard considers the collective unconscious from the perspective of cosmicity and "pure memory." Furthermore, he imagines a realm of "pure" personal memories that exist "beyond memories told and retold." This pure memory, like the collective unconscious, is timeless. "When reverie goes so far, one is astonished by his own past, astonished to have been that child. There are moments in childhood when every child is the astonishing being, the being who realizes *the astonishment of being.* We thus discover within ourselves an *immobile childhood, a childhood without becoming,* liberated from the gearwheels of the calendar" (1969, 116). This is the timeless realm of the poetic image, the spoken image, which one sees not only with one's eyes but also with one's entire being, one's "astonished being."

The menacing music of the slicing blades in *District and Circle*'s opening poem, "The Turnip Snedder," sets the tone for one worldview in the volume—that we live in a heartless and mechanical world and universe devoid of meaning, mercy, and hope. No one and no thing shall be spared—animal, vegetable, or mineral. More metonymy than metaphor, the machine is, like pain, a mutilator of language—shredder and beheader—the original metaphysical multinational military complex. There is no end in sight, no revelation, no resurrection or rebirth, just meaninglessness filling the vacuum of space. Even the innocent participate (without irony) in their own demise. From this perspective, the youth pictured in the cover image of the Farrar, Straus and Giroux edition of *District and Circle*, the image that initiated the poem, stands in for Jehovah, turning the handle of hell on earth.[8] As harbinger, he enters the Shakespearean echo chamber of laments: "As flies to wanton boys, are we to the gods. They kill us for their sport" (Shakespeare 1972, 140). Towers fall, subways collapse, suicide bombers ride the bus to work, and the sledgehammer comes down hard. Ruthlessness and revenge rule the endless darkness of the animus. This is the poetry of witness, the poetry of the murderous, the poetry of the perfect memory Heaney described long ago in the "Grabaulle Man":

I first saw his twisted face

.   .   .   .

in a photograph,

bruised like a forceps baby,
but now he lies
perfected in my memory,
down to the red horn
of his nails,

hung in the scales
with beauty and atrocity.

(*N*, 36)

Like the photographic memory, the snedder says it all; the poet has nothing else to add. Hope and history clang cacophonously. Heaney has thrown down the gauntlet in the opening poem of *District and Circle* and dared the reader to pick it up. This is an adult poem, like Ted Hughes's "Crow," but even more terrifying because what was imagined has come to be.

A folio edition facsimile of the plays of Shakespeare, opened to *Measure for Measure* 3.1, rested on the bookstand in Ted Hughes's writing room upon his death: "Be absolute for death" (Shakespeare 1965, 66). Seamus Heaney definitely knew secondhand and perhaps firsthand this fact about how Hughes left this world.[9] While initially appearing to harmonize with the absolute closure of the slicing snedder, Heaney reappropriates the famous passage from *Measure for Measure* in *District and Circle*'s final poem, "The Blackbird of Glanmore"—a poem of revelation and rebirth through reverie. Like Thomas Hardy, who, standing at the threshold of a new century, found hope and peace in "The Darkling Thrush," Heaney stands at the threshold of a new millennium and finds the same in the blackbird's "ready talkback." Heaney experiences in "The Blackbird of Glanmore" nothing less than a radical readjustment and transformative reevaluation of life before and after death.

"The Blackbird of Glanmore" begins in reverie, in an original stillness, in ancient solitude. All that is about to happen has already happened inside the poet and outside of time, thus the present tense: "Breathe. Just breathe and sit" (*DC*, 75). The blackbird, as an image of the Otherness of nature and the life force itself, is there before the poet arrives and after the poet leaves—in nature, in the (Irish) literary tradition. The bird's actual size is in direct opposition to its cosmic significance and anticipates a similar ratio of the child to the adult world. The bird is small; the child is small. As Bachelard argues: "In every dreamer there lives a child, a child whom reverie magnifies and stabilizes. Reverie tears it away from history, sets it outside of time, makes it foreign to time" (1969, 133). This process of magnification triggers a dramatic shift of values, spiritual values, as one experiences the world through a timeless childhood:

> The pure memory has no date. It has a *season*. The season is the fundamental mark of memories. What sun or what wind was there that memorable day? That is the question which gives the right tension of reminiscence. Then the memories become great images, magnified, magnifying images. They are associated with the universe of a season, a season which does not deceive and which can well be called the *total season*, reposing in the immobility of perfection. Total season because all its images speak the same values. . . . The seasons of childhood are the seasons of the poet. . . . And the seasons, armed with their original dynamism, are the seasons of Childhood. (1969, 116–17)

The child brought back to life in the poem is both the autobiographical child, Christopher, and the child in the poet. The poet does not dream or imagine the child of his reverie, he "think[s] of one gone" (*DC*, 75). Bachelard's *cogito*, the "I" that is dreaming, is present as the disheartened self is revitalized and reborn. Christopher has not aged in the poet's mind, nor has the archetypal child. The poet's wonder is doubled in the reader who has never known the dancing child, just "the corpse" of "Mid-Term Break" (*DN*, 28). Both exist outside of time in a total season of love.

One would have to dig deep into Heaney's oeuvre to find the phrase "I love" as it is used in the poem: "It's you, blackbird, I love" (*DC*, 75). Some of Heaney's most famous poems rely on "love" for their emotional

impact and metaphoric power, as in "Poem" from *Death of a Naturalist*—
"Love, I shall perfect for you the child" (*DN*, 48) —or "And here is
love / like a tinsmith's scoop / sunk past its gleam / in the meal-bin" from
North's "Mossbawn: Two Poems in Dedication" (*N*, 8). This "love" ele-
vates the "bird" to what Bachelard would call a "cosmic image," which
"gives us the whole before the parts. In its exuberance, it believes it is
telling the whole of the Whole. It holds the universe with one of its
signs. A single image invades the whole universe" (1969, 175). This "cos-
mic image" outshines the "bird on the shed" that the neighbor "never
liked." The bird of darkness, death, and doubt followed the child out of
the past, unwelcomed and yet unforgettable in the world of time. The
Glanmore blackbird, as cosmic image, creates the conditions necessary
for the reunification of man and child. The image "diffuses throughout
the universe the happiness we have at inhabiting the very world of that
image. In his reverie without limit or reserve, the dreamer gives himself
over, body and soul, to the cosmic image which has just charmed him"
(Bachelard 1969, 175).

The resurrection in "The Blackbird of Glanmore" of Heaney's
brother, Christopher, whose funeral is the subject of one of Heaney's
most famous early poems, "Mid-Term Break," is certainly one of the
most revelatory moments of his later poems. Though never alive in
Heaney's verse, Christopher is probably one of the best-known children
in all of modern poetry. "The Blackbird of Glanmore" documents the
rebirth of the poet and the child through reverie. However, from the
perspective of Bachelard, the biographical child may be the emotional
and psychological center of the poem, but the archetypal child is the
one that reunites the poet with generative self and creative cosmos.
Who resurrects whom here—is Heaney the midwife to the birth: "And
I think of one gone to him / A little stillness dancer— / Haunter-son, lost
brother—" (*DC*, 75), or is it the unnamed child and blackbird of the col-
lective unconscious that bring about the (re)birth of the poet: "Hedge-
hop, I am absolute / For you" (*DC*, 76)?

Heaney could have resurrected Christopher at any time over the
past forty years, placing him among the ghosts of *Station Island* or in the
Virgilian underworld. From the psychological/biographical perspective
one could argue that the grief was so great that the poet needed time to

heal. From the phenomenological perspective of reverie the poet needed to reach the point in his life when he could get outside of time, when the powers of reverie were most intense and most needed: "The being of reverie crosses all ages of man from childhood to old age without growing old. And that is why one feels a sort of redoubling of reverie late in life when he tries to bring the reveries of childhood back to life" (Bachelard 1969, 102).

The poet is always "arriving" when entering the mythic consciousness through reverie and "leaving," not though as first thought: "In dreaming on the universe, one is always *departing*; one lives in the *elsewhere*—in an elsewhere that is always *comfortable*. To designate a dreamed world well, it is necessary to mark it with happiness" (Bachelard 1969, 177). Despite the blackbird's Sweeney-like edginess and the ominous archaic tone of the shadowy neighbor's "yon bird," the happiness of the child "cavorting through the yard" of both Mossbawn and Glanmore collapses time and expands the poet's capacity for hope and peace. The poet's out-of-body experience, as in "Seeing Things" and "Alphabets," could not be more transcendent. What is going on in the poem, in the poet, when "for a second / I've a bird's eye view of myself" (*DC*, 76)? The poet is breaking away from the gravitational pull of the autobiographical self, the animus self. He leaves behind the material world, the political world of "automatic locks," those socially constructed barriers to illumination, revelation, transformation.

The spiritual dimension of the reverie is foregrounded when the shadow cast by the mortal self appears on the raked gravel of a Zen garden "In front of my house of life" (*DC*, 76). This house counterbalances if not cancels the "house of death" appearing earlier in the poem. Again Bachelard: "Through the cosmicity of an image then, we receive an experience of the world; cosmic reverie causes us to inhabit a world. It gives the dreamer the impression of a *home* [*chez soi*] in the imagined universe. The imagined world gives us an *expanding home*" (1969, 177). The poet in flight is looking down and back in time to a moment of wholeness and harmony. If he "is" the bird for just a second, he is also the world becoming conscious, conscious of itself, of reuniting the world and self as in a moment of wonder. "The world wishes to see itself," "Everything I look at looks at me," and the "world dreamer does not regard the world as an object. . . . He is the contemplating subject" (Bachelard 1969, 185). Poet as waking dreamer, as bird man, as visionary is what turns the speaker into the intrepid adventurer.

There are premonitions of this cosmic rebirth throughout *District and Circle*, most notably in "The Tollund Man in Springtime" (*DC*, 55–57). This moment of renewal and recommitment to a future life makes it possible or is made possible by rejecting the passage from Shakespeare that closed the book of Ted Hughes's life and served as the epitaph for T. S. Eliot's "Gerontian." The poet had to liberate himself from the nihilism of his literary ancestors and those he admired. The childhood reverie created the space in which the aging and ailing poet could reclaim life. It is the child who frees the poet through the power of the original experience, the living child.

The primordial energy of the child as archetype in "The Blackbird of Glanmore" is captured in the word *cavorting* (*DC*, 75). The strangeness of this word, coming as it does etymologically out of the American Wild West and originally referring to horses, foregrounds the instinctual energy of the collective unconscious and the power of the animated archetype. The instinctual energy, the mercurial force, of the child archetype is carried over to *Human Chain*, where it sets the entire volume in motion. The wind in "Had I not been awake" (*HC*, 3) that blows open the book and then carries it away is one of the great archetypes of the life force itself and the creative imagination on high alert. The wind is the pure potentiality of the child of the unconscious and a manifestation of the "instinctive readiness for action" that wakens the somnambulist poet to reverie and that will determine his fate. The child is the *spiritus mundi*, Hermes the trusted courier and herald, getting the poet up and going for the many poems of reverie that fill the book and serve as links between the past, present, and future. The poet, like Buddha, becomes "he who is awake"—the forces at work bring a cosmic clarity and an everyday revelation/exuberance. The childhoods of the animus, of history, are certainly to be found throughout *Human Chain*, but it is the childhood of the anima, of reverie, that leaves all possibilities open in "A Kite for Aibhín" (*HC*, 85).

Heaney has always acknowledged how lucky he was, both in his life and in the writing of those poems, which he perceived as gifts. "*You are steeped in luck*," say the "eaves" in "The Sounds of Rain" (*ST*, 49).[10] Thus it is not that surprising, and is actually comforting, that the last poem in his last volume of poems speaks to a bright future made possible through the power of reverie and the child outside of time. Bachelard observes: "An excess of childhood is the germ of a poem" (1969, 100). Childhood wonder brings with it words and images out of the impersonal past of the self that testify to the endless potential for self-renewal and a crossing over into a happiness through poetry. Again Bachelard: "Thus, childhood images, images which a child could make, images which a poet tells us that a child has made are, for us, manifestations of the permanent childhood. Those are the images of solitude. They tell of the continuity of the great childhood reveries with the reveries of the poet" (1969, 100). Heaney uses in an interview an expression that is particularly poignant here: "I'm what Tom Paulin once called a binge writer. My typical surge would last three or four months. Not every day necessarily but in a coherent self-sustaining action, when you have that happy sense of being confirmed. When you're high as a kite, really, on a high that only poetry can give" (1997b, 132).

The wind of "A Kite for Aibhín" is older than the wind, of "Postscript," another volume-closing poem of happiness and health—of wellbeing and harmony. It is the poet capturing the uplift of the midlife moment, the "big soft buffetings" that blow the heart wide open in "Postscript" (*SL*, 70). The wind of "Postscript" is the wind of time, of the maturing poet. Textually, the wind in "A Kite for Aibhín" comes to the poet from another country and another time, and it speaks another language. However, through reverie, that is, through reliving an imagined childhood experience under the sign of the anima, Heaney makes Giovanni Pascoli's "L'aquilone" his own. Heaney first published "A Kite for Aibhín" as "The Kite" in *Italian Poetry: An Anthology* (Brock 2012). Heaney (2012) says that he "translated this poem for Mary Kelleher because of her love of Italy, Italian people and Italian culture" and he quotes a phrase from Yeats to acknowledge other "Italian-Irish connections." "The Kite" translation was composed of twenty-one tercets and a closing single line (sixty-four lines). The wind that blows through the nineteen lines of "A Kite for Aibhín" has acquired a significance following the death of the poet that perhaps only Heaney himself knew that it would have. The fact that the poem has a linguistic antecedent does not diminish the power of the poem. Bachelard (1969, 122–23) suggests by quoting Henri Bosco that reverie itself is a carrying over, like translation: "From an imaginary memory, I retained a whole childhood which I did not yet know to be mine and yet which I did recognize." In hindsight, the poem is filled with prescience and foreknowledge free of foreboding. The child is present at the end of life and has never left the poet: "*Childhood lasts all through life.* It returns to animate broad sections of adult life. . . . But in waking life itself, when reverie works on our history, the childhood which is within us brings us its benefits. One needs, and sometimes it is very good, to live with the child he has been. From such living he achieves a consciousness of roots, and the entire tree of his being takes comfort from it. Poets will help us find this living childhood within us, this permanent, durable immobile world" (Bachelard 1969, 20). It is the child that has "planted feet" facing "Anahorish Hill." Heaney the poet has come again with and through the child to the center and source of his being. The words have carried him here like the wind carries the kite. The entire landscape becomes animated. The poem's images radiate through the eyes of the childhood relived in reverie. The child energizes the poem, which puts the poet in a state of exaltation, of exuberance. The wind, as a "poetically privileged" image, according to Bachelard (1969, 176), is what brings the poet's past and future to life: "Thus poems come to our aid in finding the breathing of the great gusts again, the original breathing of the child who breathes the world" (Bachelard 1969, 182). The "Breathe. Just breathe" of "The Blackbird of Glanmore" has paid off. The translation, suspended in reverie, has made it possible for the poet to enter a past that is and is not his. The return to Anahorish Hill makes this a personal one, but as an aging poet he needs a more powerful and ancient source if he is to carry on: "Reverie teaches us that the essence of being is well-being, a well-being rooted in an archaic being" (Bachelard 1969, 193). It is not only the memory reimagined of a sunny spring day that brings the poem and the poet to life but also the dynamism generated by the play of archaic and archetypal energies and images.

The opening line of "A Kite for Aibhín" establishes the "irreality" of what is to follow and the otherness from where the wind came: "Air from another life and time and place" (*HC*, 85). "Air" sounds especially technical here and self-contained as if it had substance. An elemental alchemy transforms the "air" into the grandeur of "heavenly air." Bachelard notes: "A particular cosmos forms around a particular image as soon as the poet gives the image a destiny of grandeur" (1969, 176). Another transformation takes place when the poem and poet become centered by the evocation of "Anahorish Hill." This late in the poet's life, the hill has taken its place among the great mythological literary landscapes. Just saying "Anahorish" and seeing it start to glow on the spellchecking screen has the effect of an incantation, of exaltation. Past, present, and future can be found in the cosmicity of the reverie. Initially the poet "trooped out" with other children and is referred to in the first person: "I take my stand again" (*HC*, 85). However, the poem shifts from the "I" of the poet as child to the older non-I "kite flier" who has a "longing in the breast." The "longing" is clearly connected to the joy of the moment as it is reimagined in the flight of the kite. This longing is dependent upon the power of the poet to relive his childhood through reverie. He remembers as if his life and all of its happiness depended upon it. This is not a nostalgic desire to live in the past but a desire to use the past to live even more fully in the future. The breaking of the string is the necessary separation of the historical memory and biological body from the memory that lives under the sign of the animus and the imagined self. "A Kite for Aibhín" does not convey the sense of disappointment in the closing line that one finds in "Blackberry Picking" (*DN*, 20) or even the sense of resignation as one accepts one's place in the Human Chain. The poem ends on a high note with the promise of freedom, and perhaps even peace, that can be found only outside history.

One of the great pleasures of Heaney's poetry is its invitation to dream, to join the great dreamers of the ages—not to escape "reality" but to come into contact with its most essential joys through language and images with deep imaginative and etymological roots that satisfy and sustain us. Seamus Heaney has counted the links in the Human Chain like prayer beads through the centuries. His final revelation comes when the chain turns to string turns to stem turns to song. The child whom he has protected his entire life, who foreshadowed him and follows him, and who called to him now calls to us: "The writer wants to convince the reader of the reality of cosmic forces in action in images of flight. He has a faith which, still greater than that which moves mountains, makes them fly. Aren't the summits wings? In his call to a sympathy of imagination, the writer harries the reader, he dogs him. It seems to me that I hear the poet saying: 'Won't you ever fly away, reader! Are you going to stay seated, inert, while a whole universe is stretched toward the destiny of flying?'" (Bachelard 1969, 207).

NOTES

1. Bachelard has little time for Freudian psychoanalysis in the *Poetics of Reverie* and says that he will "leave aside the animus projects" (1969, 21). Later he declares: "One analyzes a childhood better with poems than with memories, better with reveries than with facts. It is meaningful, we believe, to speak of a poetic analysis. The psychologists do not know everything. Poets have other insights into man" (1969, 124–25).

2. Fredric Jameson argues that the epistemological approach taken by Bachelard and by this essay is dangerous: "To imagine that, sheltered by the omnipresence of history and the implacable influence of the social, there already exists a realm of freedom—whether it be that of the microscopic experience of words in a text or the ecstasies and intensities of various private religions—is only to strengthen the grip of Necessity over all such blind zones in which the individual subject seeks refuge, in pursuit of a purely individual, merely psychological, project of salvation. The only effective liberation from such constraint begins with the recognition that there is nothing that is not social and historical—indeed, that everything is 'in the last analysis' political" (1981, 20).

3. Several of the poems collected in *Open Ground* have been revised, including "A Kite for Michael and Christopher." In the first edition of *Station Island* the quoted passage reads: "an armful of blown chaff" (*SI*, 44).

4. Bachelard writes: "The well is an archetype, one of the gravest images of the human soul. That black and distant water can mark a childhood. It has reflected an astonished face. Its mirror is not that of a fountain. A narcissus can take no pleasure there. Already in his image living beneath the earth, the child does not recognize himself. A mist is on the water; plants which are too green frame the mirror. A cold blast breathes in the depths. The face which comes back in this night of the earth is a face from another world. Now, if a memory of such reflections comes into a memory, isn't it the memory of a before-world?" (1969, 114).

5. Roland Barthes, in *The Pleasure of the Text*, contrasts his concept of jouissance/bliss, which resists, transcends, and undercuts articulated expression, with

Bachelard's reverie on poetic reverie: "For Bachelard, it seems that writers have never written: by a strange lacuna, they are only read. Thus, he has been able to establish a pure critique of reading, and he has grounded it in pleasure: we are engaged in a homogenous (sliding, euphoric, voluptuous, unitary, jubilant) practice, and this practice overwhelms us: *dream-reading*. With Bachelard, it is all poetry (as the simple right to discontinue literature, combat) that is credited to Pleasure. But once the work is perceived in terms of a *writing*, pleasure balks, bliss appears and Bachelard withdraws" (1975, 37). For Bachelard, Pleasure resides in the poetic image and speaks the language of the anima.

6. "[Shum] argued that the reminiscence effect, the relative ease with which older people remember events from about their twentieth year, is a consequence of the fact that a greater number of time markers is available for that period. If time markers do indeed order networks of associations, as research seems to indicate, then the same time markers will also be able to call up memories, so that there is a positive correlation between the number of time markers and the density of memories. Typically, time markers are "my first meeting with . . . the first time I . . . when I first began to . . ."—all of them memories that contribute so much to the reminiscence effect. Time markers, in short, do not merely mark periods and dates, *they also give rise to reveries in old age*" (Draaisma 2006, 218; italics mine).

7. Heaney was familiar with Bachelard's *Poetics of Space* and uses a passage from the book as an epigraph for the Field Day limited edition of *An Open Letter*. One would assume that Heaney would not miss the Jungian dimensions of Bachelard's work.

8. Heaney has stated that the poem grew out of his encounter with the image of the snedder that he found in a catalog of works by Hughie O'Donohue, to whom the poem is dedicated.

9. This information was supplied by the Stephen Enniss, who had access to Hughes's writing room when evaluating Hughes's archive for Emory University. Enniss states that he surely would have mentioned such a poignant and profound discovery to Heaney during conversations about Hughes's death and Heaney's own dealings with Emory. There is also the chance that Heaney saw the room and text himself when visiting Carol Hughes.

10. Heaney says in the *Paris Review* interview when asked about luck: "No, I still think that I have been inordinately lucky. I regard first of all the discovery of a path into the writing of poems as luck" (1997b, 129–30).

CHAPTER SIXTEEN

"The Door Stands Open"

Liminal Spaces in the Later Heaney

Eugene O'Brien

In August 2004, Seamus Heaney was in Dublin, awaiting the news of the death of a poetic mentor, someone whom he held in very high regard, namely, Czesław Miłosz. His admiration for Miłosz is complex, as he speaks of valuing his ability to "to glorify things just because they are" and notes approvingly Miłosz's dictum that "the ideal life for a poet" is to contemplate the word *is* (Heaney 2004c, 4). However, despite this location of Miłosz in the actual, it is to the aesthetic, and the world of visual art, that Heaney turns when he wishes to find images of the man and his work. In an ekphrastic dyad, he suggests that the life of his friend can best be encapsulated in two mimetic works of art, which have "a typically Miłoszian combination of solidity and spiritual force" (2004c, 4). The first is Jacques Louis David's "The Death of Socrates," which has the philosopher on his bed, expounding on the doctrine of the immortality of the soul. The second is an Etruscan sarcophagus in the Louvre, "a mighty terracotta sculpture of a married couple, reclining on their elbows." The woman is positioned on the man's left side, "couched close and parallel, both of them at their ease and gazing intently ahead at something which by all the rules of perspective should be visible in the man's outstretched right hand." However, nothing can be seen, even though the couple's gaze seems to be "full of realization" (2004c, 4). For Heaney, the attempt to express the invisible, the attempt to locate one's gaze on the real world, while at the same time attempting to access the numinous and the transcendental that can be tangentially accessed from that world, is what makes Miłosz such an important force in his life, because Heaney too shares these concerns, and in this chapter those concerns will be traced across his later work.

The key image in the Etruscan sculpture is the empty space at which the couple are gazing, as this symbolizes the sense that poetry can allow for access to dimensions of knowledge and experience that are not immediately accessible to the language of prose. In an interview with Dennis O'Driscoll, Heaney is asked the telling question: "What has poetry taught you?" and he answers that it has taught him that "there's such a thing as truth and it can be told—slant" (SS, 467). This term is borrowed from Emily Dickinson's poem "Tell All the Truth but Tell It Slant" (1924, 506–7), and the fact that this term originates in such an oblique poet as Dickinson is interesting in itself, as the many dashes and ellipses in her writing can be seen as opening a space for the unconscious dimension of her thinking. It is as if she knows there are aspects of her thought and feeling that cannot be written, but the dashes provide a space, a Derridean non-lieu, which allows that space to become a site of signification and a place of entry into the poem by the other, be that the unconscious or the interaction of the reader. Speaking to Richard Kearney about philosophy, Derrida (1995, 159) says that his "central question is from what site or non-site [non-lieu] can philosophy as such appear to itself as other than itself, so that it can interrogate and reflect upon itself in an original manner." In a parallel manner, poetry can create a similar space from which to access a different realm of experience from the norm: it, too, can become a nonsite of access, which allows space for that gaze of which Heaney spoke concerning the Etruscan sarcophagus. Heaney speaks of how his own study in Strand Road has remained quite Spartan, and he explains that he wants it to be "a dis-place, if you like. Like most places of writing" (SS, 231). One could see poetry as a similar "dis-place," or "non-site," a discourse where images and worlds oscillate and where meanings are only glimpsed. In an essay on Dante, Giorgio

Agamben notes that the poetic stanza "constitutes a threshold of passage between the metrical unity of *ars* and the higher semantic unity of *sententia*" (Agamben and Heller-Roazen 1999, 36; italics in original), and Heaney's idea of a "dis-place" reinforces this view of poetry as a discourse that allows for a different kind of thinking.

Hannah Arendt (1968, 50), in her introduction to Walter Benjamin's *Illuminations*, makes the point that in the work of Benjamin we are dealing "with something which may not be unique but is certainly extremely rare: the gift of thinking poetically"; I would contend that in the work of Seamus Heaney we are dealing with a similar phenomenon. In his writing, as I will demonstrate, we see a nuanced attention to language and to how it achieves its aims both consciously and unconsciously. Heaney, like Martin Heidegger, forces us to recognize the "complicity between the matter and the manner of thinking as the presence of figurality itself, as the folding or thickening of the limits of language" (Allen 2007, 95). Language, while it can be logical, must also be necessarily more than logical as it enunciates, albeit in slanted form, the unconscious; for Heaney as well as Heidegger, "Buried in all language is the rift between world and earth. Poetry reveals that rift. Revealing that rift poetry lets words speak" (Harries 2009, 116). What Heaney admires about the work of Miłosz is that he is able to grant the authenticity of both modes, and this complexity mirrors what Heaney has always seen as the epistemological force of poetry, which is that it should be "a working model of inclusive consciousness. It should not simplify" (*RP*, 8). Telling the truth slant, or seeing the world from a different perspective, as well as valuing that difference, is at the core of Heaney's aesthetic imperative. He has invoked Osip Mandelstam to criticize "the purveyors of ready-made meaning" (*GT*, 91), as for him, poetic truth constantly strives to reach beyond such ready-made meanings: like the Etruscan couple, it looks to the space. Heaney sees the literary as "one of the methods human beings have devised for getting at reality" (2003, 3), and in a manner that recalls his idea of telling the truth slant he adds that literature's diversions are not to be taken as "deceptions but as roads less traveled by where the country we thought we knew is seen again in a new and revealing light" (2003, 3).

His ways of getting at the reality of his dis-place of writing illustrate this, as they are full of the "revealing light" of the image, the symbol and the oneiric. He speaks of a welcoming dream that he had in the early stages of living in his new home in Strand Road and that he took as a "good omen." In the dream, he opened a doorway to the attic and "down the stairwell there came this immense flood of crystal clear water full of green roses, washing over me but not in any way panicking or threatening to drown me" (SS, 31). Here there is a dual perspective as the real move into the new home is unconsciously sanctioned and valorized by the oneiric flow of water. That the opening of a door is the catalyst for this fusion of the conscious and unconscious is noteworthy. In "Clonmany to Ahascragh" in *Electric Light*, he speaks of this dream, and again it is framed by two doors:

> Be at the door
> I opened in the sleepwall when a green
> Hurl of flood overwhelmed me and poured out
> Lithe seaweed and a tumult of immense
> Green cabbage roses into the downstairs.
> No feeling of drowning panicked me, no let-up
> In the attic downpour happened, no
> Fullness could ever equal it, so flown
> And sealed I feared it would be lost
>
> If I put it into words.
> But with you there at the door
> I can tell it and can weep.
>
> (EL, 75–76)

The sense of putting the experience of this other world, this sensation of fullness, into words is validated and enabled by the two doors in the poem. The new place is important because Heaney had been very happy in his former home, the "hedge school of Glanmore" (FW, 34), where he had been for "four years" (FW, 43), from 1972 to 1976. This was his first attempt at being a professional writer, and he found Glanmore to be "absolutely the right place for writing." He again explains this sense of finding a new world and a change of pace by using the resonant metaphor of the door: "Every time I lifted the latch on the door into our little scullery, the sound and slack fall of it passed through me like gratitude. Or certitude. Theseus had his thread, I had my latch and it opened for me. Or rather, it opened *me*" (*SS*, 227). The doors, in the case of both homes, both places of writing, were transformative of the person himself, and it was while he is in the garden of his home in Strand Road that he learned of the death of Miłosz.

He recalls that he was in at home when the call came, and it was a summer's day where the weather was "Californian": "Thanksgiving and admiration were in the air, and I could easily have repeated to myself the remark he once made to an interviewer, commenting upon his epigram, 'He was thankful, so he couldn't not believe in God.' Ultimately, Miłosz declared, 'one can believe in God out of gratitude for all the gifts'" (Heaney 2004c, 4). Thus, when Heaney heard from Jerzy Jarniewicz about the death of Miłosz, he "wasn't knocked askew. Instead, there was an expanding of grief into the everlasting reach of poetry," as in the Dublin sunlight the remembered figure of Miłosz in his hillside garden in San Francisco merged with the mythical image of "Oedipus toiling up the wooded slope at Colonus, only to disappear in the blink of an eye." Heaney develops this point by noting that when he looked, Miłosz was there "in all his human bulk and devotion, when I looked again he was not to be seen—and yet he was not entirely absent" (Heaney 2004c, 4). The series of oscillations here between presence and absence, between Dublin and California, between Miłosz and Oedipus, between appearance and disappearance, and between the act of seeing and that of being seen recalls the couple in the Etruscan sculpture staring at something that they can see but that is not revealed in the artwork, and Heaney goes on to quote the scene in the words of Sophocles's messenger when he reports the incident that, while mysterious, had the ring of common truth about it:

He was gone from sight:
That much I could see . . .
No god had galloped

His thunder chariot, no hurricane
Had swept the hill. Call me mad, if you like,
Or gullible, but that man surely went
In step with a guide he trusted down to where
Light has gone out but the door stands open.
                                        (Heaney 2004c, 4)

The image of the door is culturally significant. Paul Ricoeur suggests that "thresholds, doors, bridges, and narrow pathways" correspond to the "homologous kinds of passage which rites of initiation help us to cross over in the critical moments of our pilgrimage through life: moments such as birth, puberty, marriage, and death" (1976, 62). Doors and thresholds symbolize a movement out of the present immanent state to somewhere else, so that the climax of this quotation should involve a door is hardly surprising, as for much of his career, but especially in the case of his later poetry, Heaney had been interested in the complexity of the interaction between the immanent and the transcendent, between the quotidian and the numinous, between the past and the present, and between the conscious and the unconscious. In this chapter, I will trace his use of the door as a symbolic trope that allows for the opening of each of these aspects to the other. Like the dashes in Dickinson's poetry, the doors in Heaney's later work stand open to allow access from this world to the next, from the seen to the unseen, from the conscious to the unconscious. I will also make connections between Heaney's ongoing and deepening use of the door as a trope and similar connections made by European aesthetic thinkers Martin Heidegger, Jacques Derrida, and Giorgio Agamben. All of these writers question the borders between worlds and perspectives; as Derrida puts it, "We must leave these questions open, like doors" (2007b, 85), for through these doors comes Heaney's "revealing light."

From an early stage in his career, doors were an important image for Heaney as a way of seeing different perspectives. Writing about his second collection, *Door into the Dark* (1969), he tells of wanting to "gesture towards this idea of poetry as a point of entry into the buried life of the feelings or as a point of exit for it," and he goes on to say that "words themselves are doors; Janus is to a certain extent their deity, looking back to a ramification of roots and associations and forward to a clarification of sense and meaning" (*P*, 52). One could see Janus as a personal god for Heaney's work because doors, as portals, limens, passageways, and points of distinction and connection, have always been important to his worldview. He tells us that one of his early memories is of carrying "a can of fresh milk in the evenings from our house to the next house down the road from us." Heaney goes on to explain that his "journey from home to the back door of this house" was only a "couple of hundred yards" but that in his "child's mind" he covered "a great distance every time, because between the two doorsteps I crossed the border between the ecclesiastical diocese of Derry and the diocese—or more properly, the archdiocese—of Armagh" (*FK*, 53). The door is crucial to Heaney's sense of home, and in this he is allied to the ideas of Jacques Derrida, who similarly sees that in order to constitute "the space of a habitable house and a home, you also need an opening, a door and windows, you have to give up a passage to the outside world." He stresses that there is "no house or interior without a door or windows" (Derrida and Dufourmantelle 2000, 61). For Derrida, one's own identity, subjective or political, is differentially constituted, and thus some form of connection with, and separation from, the other, is necessary. The passage from selfhood to alterity, which is central to any sense of growth, is symbolized by this gap, which is the part of the house that "opens the door to the impossible possibility of what comes about [*arrive*] in its taking place" (Derrida 1987, 103). This sense of an openness to the other is crucial to both writers. As Heaney puts it, delivering the milk was "a genuine expedition into an elsewhere" (*FK*, 53), and this was the first step in a process that he would continue throughout his poetry, but especially in the last five books.

In the second poem of his "Lightenings" sequence in *Seeing Things*, Heaney makes this very clear. He is speaking about shelter and the making of a solid shelter—"Roof it again. Batten down. Dig in"—and the minimalistic, and largely monosyllabic, instructions in the imperative mood stress the basic and almost elemental nature of this shelter that is being constructed: "Touch the cross-beam, drive iron in a wall" (*ST*, 56). Significantly in this solidly constructed and carefully drawn picture of the structure ("verify the plumb. . . . Take squarings from the recessed gable"), Heaney stresses the need to "Relocate the bedrock in the threshold" (*ST*, 56). This is highly significant because the home's center, for Heaney, is in the doorway, which is the point of access to and egress from the home. For Heaney, like Derrida, the border is the signifier of the bounds of one's own identity as well as the point of contact with the other, who may develop and change that identity, and this idea is shared with another European thinker, Martin Heidegger, who also speaks of its symbolic importance: "The threshold is the ground-beam that bears the doorway as a whole. It sustains the middle in which the two, the outside and the inside, penetrate each other. The threshold bears the between" (1971, 201). Heaney has said that one could think of "every poem in 'Squarings' as the peg at the end of a tent-rope reaching up into the airy structure, but still with purchase on something earthier and more obscure" (*SS*, 320), and here again we see his desire to move from the immanent to the transcendent, or more precisely, to access the transcendent through the immanent.

This sense of penetration appears again and again in Heaney's later poetry. He locates himself deeply in language and in the immanent, but is simultaneously searching for a point of access to the transcendent. Thus in "The Golden Bough," Heaney's translation from book 6 of the *Aeneid* (lines 98–148), as Aeneas prays to the priestess to be given access to the underworld so that he can speak to his dead father, his plea is voiced in terms of a door to the underworld: "I pray for one look, one face-to-face meeting with my dear father. / Teach me the way and open the holy doors wide" (*ST*, 1). One of the ways he achieves this in his final books is to use the great sustaining myths of European culture, the *Odyssey*, the *Aeneid*, and various other classical myths, as ways of reframing contemporary experience in a transcendent manner. By the time he wrote this poem his own father had died, and through poetic comparisons like this one he is able to contextualize his personal sense of loss and his hope for a future meeting within the emotions of the Latin poet all those centuries ago. It is a way of seeking the transcendent through poetry, a way of finding an "elsewhere" that allows, as Heidegger would have it, a penetration of an outside by an inside and vice versa.

Later in the same poem, the speaker is told that "day and night black Pluto's door stands open," so reaching the elsewhere is not as difficult as he might have first imagined. However, in Heaney's case, the journey is never one-way. Like his recounting of the childhood delivery of milk, he moves between this sense of distance and elsewhere, and home and back again. Each journey to the other place alters his perspective on the first place, and ultimately he is transformed by such journeys: "But to retrace your steps and get back to upper air, / This is the real task and the real undertaking" (*ST*, 2). This journey through the door between the upper air and the underworld is the significant trope here, as through this process, the inside becomes outside and this process is then reversed. Giorgio Agamben has also explored this idea and makes the point that the "threshold is not, in this sense, another thing with respect to the limit; it is, so to speak, the experience of the limit itself, the experience of *being-within* an *outside*" (1993, 68; italics in original).

In so much of Heaney's later poetry, this experience of the threshold, and this passage through the door that stands open and almost invites such a passage, is transformative. Thus, in "Markings," a poem about one of the most grounded of childhood experiences, the impromptu game of football in a field, the concrete quality of the experience is foregrounded. It opens by describing the physical scene, with a sense of "this-worldness" and "the dead-on and the head-on-ness" that Heaney saw and admired in Robert Frost (*SS*, 453): "We marked the pitch: four jackets for four goalposts, / That was all," and the pitch itself is far from even: "the bumpy thistly ground" (*ST*, 8). However, once the structure of the pitch is marked out, and once the boys have "crossed the line our called names drew between us," a door is opened to an elsewhere of experience as another mode of experience is accessed:

> Some limit had been passed,
> There was fleetness, furtherance, untiredness
> In time that was extra, unforeseen and free.
>   (*ST*, 8)

Here a door has been opened, and the perspective of the poem has moved from the adjective- and noun-driven "bumpy thistly ground" into the abstractions of "fleetness, furtherance, untiredness." The alliteration of the first two words, allied to the pararhymes of all three

words, connects them at the level of sound and gives them an almost in-
cantatory quality, thereby validating the passing of the limits from the
physical into a realm that is "extra, unforeseen and free." Here we see
Heaney embodying a point made by Roland Barthes about poetic lan-
guage, which "initiates a discourse full of gaps and full of lights, filled
with absences and over-nourishing signs," and which is opposed to the
social function of language because "to have recourse to a discontinu-
ous speech is to open the door to all that stands above Nature" (1978,
48–49). In this case "description is revelation" (*N*, 71) because the de-
scription is nonutilitarian and attempts to access an unknown world of
feeling, sense, intuition, and the transcendent. The glimpses are occa-
sional, through the chink of a door that stands open, as one stands on
the threshold.

The idea of crossing the threshold as a transformative experience
has a long history in European aesthetic thinking, and it is an idea with
which Heaney has engaged positively. He has noted that between what
is "going to happen" and what we "would wish to happen"—in other
words, between the actual and the wished-for, or the immanent and
transcendent—poetry "holds attention for a space, functions not as dis-
traction but as pure concentration, a focus where our power to con-
centrate is concentrated back on ourselves"; and he goes on to voice this
oscillation through the imagery of the door and the threshold: "Poetry is
more a threshold than a path, one constantly approached and constantly
departed from, at which reader and writer undergo in their different
ways the experience of being at the same time summoned and released"
(*GT*, 108). This idea of poetry as a threshold, as a point of entry and exit
into more than one dimension, is typical of Heaney's poetizing thought,
and it also reflects the idea that identities and notions of place are more
about modes of entry and exit than they are about actual topographical
or physical locations. Such concentration on the self, and such a dy-
namic process of summoning and releasing, "does not limit itself to
distinguishing what is inside from what is outside but instead traces a
threshold (the state of exception) between the two" (Agamben 1998,
19). Heaney similarly views the oscillation of being summoned and re-
leased as transformative: "All these things entered you / As if they were
both the door and what came through it" (*ST*, 9). Such transformation

is imagined later in the poem in an image where two men sawing with a "cross-cut" saw are described as keeping the saw "swimming" in the fallen beech tree so "that they seemed to row the steady earth" (*ST*, 9). The earth has been transformed by this activity, as has our conception of what *rowing* means as a verb, and it is this plural and transformative perspective that Heaney's poetry of the threshold can voice so evocatively.

Immanuel Kant often spoke of the idea of borders between different disciplines or modes of identity, and as Agamben has explained, in Kantian terms, what is in question in this bordering is "not a limit [*Schranke*] that knows no exteriority, but a threshold [*Grenze*], that is, a point of contact with an external" (1993, 65). Agamben thematizes the threshold in *The Coming Community*, where he talks about "the event of an outside" (1993, 66). Through this liminal border the belonging of an entity to a set, or its identity, is determined. This limit does not, however, open on to another determinate space: "The outside is not another space that resides beyond a determinate space, but rather, it is the passage, the exteriority that gives it access" (1993, 66).

Poetry is just such a passage. It is a "point of contact with an external space that must remain empty" (Agamben 1993, 63), and for both Agamben and Heaney it is the emptiness of the space that is important, as the interaction of points of contact, and the summoning and releasing process, will allow new levels of meaning to be created through the crossing and recrossing of this threshold. Agamben notes that notions of outside have been expressed in terms of a door in many languages, and he cites the two seminal languages of the European intellectual tradition to reinforce his point, where "the notion of the 'outside'" is expressed by a word that means "at the door," as "*fores* in Latin is the door of the house," and "*thyrathen* in Greek literally means 'at the threshold'" (1993, 66). For Agamben, both the outside space and the mode of access to it are conveyed in the term *threshold* (Murray and Whyte 2011, 190). Thus when Heaney's father is running on the "afternoon of his own father's death / The open, black half of the half-door waits" (*ST*, 15), and again this is a symbol of the passage between worlds that poetry can access.

Up to this, the examples have all pertained to one of the most seminal passages between worlds, that between mortality and death, but the door and threshold imagery also refers to other passages between worlds or states. In "Lustral Sonnet," Heaney tells us that his "first impulse was never / To double-bar a door or lock a gate" (*ST*, 35) because he was always looking to probe that further shore of experience, even if the consequences could be problematic. In "A Retrospect," he speaks of an old road that was "lover country," where each parked car "played possum in the twilight" as lovers had illicit sex in this out-of-the-way place: "And there they were, / Astray in the hill-fort of all pleasures / Where air was other breath." This sense of breaking a boundary and of flouting convention left the lovers feeling "empowered but still somehow constrained." For others, this transgressive love was a thing of the past:

> Young marrieds, used now to the licit within doors,
> They fell short of the sweetness that had lured them.
> No nest in rushes, the heather bells unbruised,
> The love-drink of the mountain streams untasted.
>
> > (*ST*, 43)

Here, the door serves as a border-limit that is closed, as habit has dulled the tingling excitement of love on the "old road," and the use of the unusual positive of illicit, "licit," underlines through litotes the habitual humdrum nature of the sexual relations between the young marrieds. What is interesting is the grammatical voicing of the door in this poem, as the phrase used is "within doors," which closes off the passage to new experience and to a different world. The final word in the poem, *untasted*, enacts the attenuation of experience that results from doors not standing open but remaining closed, and from allowing a different world to come into being only in retrospect.

This is very much not the case in "Lightenings i," where the door is very much standing open, and new ideas and sensations are flowing in and out through it:

> Shifting brilliancies. Then winter light
> In a doorway, and on the stone doorstep
> A beggar shivering in silhouette.
>
> > (*ST*, 55)

The shifting light, a revealing light, in the doorway is a portal to a new knowledge: "Just old truth dawning: there is no next-time-round. / Unroofed scope. Knowledge-freshening wind" (ST, 55). As well as the light on the doorstep, the structure of the house is unroofed and so is open to the sky, and what this brings to mind is a sense of the immediacy of life and of mortality. This is something that we rationally and cognitively know but that attains a deeper truth when it becomes felt, when the "bastion of sensation" has been secured (ST, 56). Heaney tells of how the term *lightening* can mean the "flaring of the spirit before death" but also notes the attendant meanings "of being unburdened and being illuminated" (SS, 321), and indeed, the poem's genesis was just such an illumination, as it was after he had been working in the national library on an introduction to a selection of poems by Yeats that the first lines "came" to him (1997b, 108). The genesis of the poem is how the unconscious can see something from a slanted perspective, which casts new light on the normative one. Such an altered perspective is often not comfortable: "knowledge-freshening wind" does not sound like a balmy summer breeze; however, it does bring new clarity, and this is at the core of his openness to the new and the different in these poems.

Through the door of perception comes the experiential intuition of mortality, and in "Settings xii" we see a parallel process as the door becomes a portal through which new knowledge can be accessed. Through the shimmer of "Athletic sealight on the doorstep slab," the speaker of the poem is now able to acknowledge the "presence" that he "sensed withdrawing first time round" (ST, 69). This oscillation between presence and absence allows those slanted glimpses of a knowledge that is not rational but rather intuitive, and this knowledge is to be found in the space, the threshold, between them: "The minute the question concerning the essence counts as settled, a door is opened to unessence" (Heidegger 2009, 19). Indeed, the conflation of "sea" and "light" achieves the same effect, suggesting that the sea is a source of light, while also suggesting metonymically that the light is personified with the liveliness of a seal, as it shimmers on the doorstep, transformed, with the single "l" being made to do the work of two.

A parallel transformation can be in "Settings xv." The speaker attempts to preserve a childhood memory in an ekphrastic "Rembrandtgleam" (*ST*, 71) as he conjures an image of his father thrusting his hand into a barrel filled with salt, trying to find the bacon contained there to inspect it. For the child who is watching, the scene is one of biblical splendor ("that night I owned the piled grain of Egypt") as he is privy to his father's careful hoarding and saving of food: "I watched the sentry's torchlight on the hoard. / I stood in the door, unseen and blazed upon" (*ST*, 71). Here his threshold-dwelling eye sees the reality of the need to salt away the bacon for the winter, but also sees that his father is very much the hearth-keeper. This vision of his father, or rather this revision of him, is the dis-place, or Agamben's empty space; it is that space at which the two figures in the earlier image of the Etruscan sarcophagus were gazing. It is an image of the numinous in the immanent. Of course, it is also a site of transfiguration, as the eye of the poet will be recalled by the mature poet, the I, who will gradually bed his own "locale / in the utterance" (*WO*, 25), but an utterance that is transformed and hugely influenced by the locutions and locations of classical Greece, and once again, it is a door that allows these two worlds to interact.

We have already noted the symbolic significance of one journey from Heaney's own back door to a crossing of a border into a new dispensation, and also the fact that it was the repeated crossing of this border from the self and the *Heimlich* to the other and the *Unheimlich* that was retrospectively important to him. In the opening passage of *Preoccupations*, he describes another movement between different perspectives on his own home and locutions: "I would begin with the Greek word, *omphalos*, meaning the navel, and hence the stone that marked the centre of the world, and repeat it, *omphalos, omphalos, omphalos*, until its blunt and falling music becomes the music of somebody pumping water at the pump outside our back door. It is Co. Derry in the early 1940s" (*P*, 17). What is happening here is that opening out to a new world in the same place, as locution has transformed location, and the door of memory has connected the physical place with the center of the classical Greek world. Appropriately, for a poetic mode of thinking, this is done through adequations of sound, as the sound of the pump's plunger going up and down is merged with the sound of the Greek word in an onomatopoeic fusion. The location of this pump is significant: "It stood immediately outside the back door" (*SS*, 8). This retrospective image is also connected with the traveling between the back door and the place of the other that has already been cited, and in both journeys, what is happening is that the *Heimlich* aspects of home are being contrasted with its *Unheimlich* aspects. In an essay published in 1919, Sigmund Freud probed the intersections of signification that took place in the play of the words *Heimlich* and *Unheimlich*. He attempted to explore and ultimately break down the opposition between the *Heimlich*, the "intimate" or "domestic," and the *Unheimlich*, the strange or "uncanny." He begins by stating the seemingly obvious binary opposition that exists in language between the two terms, but a careful etymological excursus leads him to conclude that "among its different shades of meaning the word '*Heimlich*' exhibits one which is identical with its opposite, '*Unheimlich*.' What is *Heimlich* thus comes to be *Unheimlich*" (Freud 1955, 224).

Through the doors of retrospection, Heaney conflates two words: his home place and the ancient center of the classical world. This allows him to offer parallel readings of Ireland though the lens of classical myth, which provides aesthetic distance through which he can speak of atrocities and pain that are too close to him. Thus in *Burial at Thebes* Heaney foregrounds the sense of humanity that requires the burial of the dead in a proper manner, regardless of their crimes against the polis: "You have forbidden burial of one dead, / One who belongs by right to the gods below" (*BT*, 46). For Antigone, there is a deeper law, beyond that of politics and its visible system of reward and punishments. She speaks of "Justice, justice dwelling deep / Among the gods of the dead" (*BT*, 21). The use of the rhetorical device of epizeuxis means that the repeated term *justice* is foregrounded, though it is an elusive concept as it dwells among the dead. Later in the same passage, Antigone will further refine her sense of the location of justice—"Unwritten, original, god-given laws" (*BT*, 21)—and the fact that such laws dwell among the dead is stressed when, later in the play, the chorus sees her return to this place of death in terms that are now familiar to us:

> Steadfast Antigone,
> Never before did Death
> Open his stone door

To one so radiant.
You would not live a lie.
(*BT*, 37)

The sense of seeking that further space beyond the practical, political, and pragmatic fudges that are part and parcel of daily life has been an ongoing factor in Heaney's later work. He seeks that space, that displace, that *non-lieu*, where truth can be glimpsed from that slant perspective that he is so skilled at providing. The notion of the right to a burial, to be remembered in a place and for that place to have a special significance for one's loved ones, is at the core of Antigone, and even more so of Heaney's translation. This common humanity transcends the political and ideological aspects of conflict, as Heaney would see it.

There has been much debate on whether Heaney has been too political, or not sufficiently political, in his career. To me this is very much to miss the point. He is a poet: his role is to inhabit the aesthetic, something symbolized by that space on which the Etruscan couple gaze, and this space can provide a different perspective on the real world in which we live. In "Route 110 IX," this becomes very clear, as this poem refers to two people who died in the Troubles, both of whom were known to Heaney. In the aftermath of the peace process, there has been a tendency to avoid speaking about individual deaths, as a political narrative is set out that sees everyone as casualties of a war, with no, or few, actions deemed more culpable than others. The actuality of the deaths has been occluded in their numerical recounting—to speak of some 3,600 deaths is to avoid the space that sees each death as involving family, relatives, neighbors, friends, all connected in a web of loss and lamentation. In this poem two individuals are called to mind, and the truth of their death is set out clearly:

And what in the end was there left to bury
Of Mr Lavery, blown up in his own pub
As he bore the primed device and bears it still
Mid-morning towards the sun-admitting door
Of Ashley House? Or of Louis O'Neill

In the wrong place the Wednesday they buried
Thirteen who'd been shot in Derry? Or of bodies
Unglorified, accounted for and bagged
Behind the grief cordons: not to be laid
In war graves with full honours, nor in a separate plot
Fired over on anniversaries
By units drilled and spruce and unreconciled.

(*HC*, 56)

Significantly, the two men singled out and commemorated in the poem were murdered by bombs planted by paramilitaries. Michael Parker has explained how both were also personally known to Heaney and died at a critical juncture in his and the province's history. Respectfully referred to as "Mr Lavery," John F. Lavery was a "sixty-year-old Catholic, who owned a pub on a junction of the Lisburn Road in south Belfast, a mere twenty yards or so from the Heaneys' house at 16 Ashley Avenue." He died in 1971 "while trying to remove from the premises a 20lb bomb which had been deposited there in all probability by the Provisional IRA" (Parker 2012, 237). One year later, a friend of Heaney's, Louis O'Neill, "who had initiated the poet into eel-fishing," and who had been "drinking in the Imperial Bar in Stewartstown, Co. Tyrone," in the week following Bloody Sunday, was blown to pieces by the "blast from a 15lb bomb, planted by loyalist paramilitaries" (Parker 2012, 327).

Like Antigone and her brother Polyneices, Heaney is unwilling to allow conflict to desecrate the memory of the dead. While both Lavery and O'Neil were buried, they were not buried whole, as "what in the end was there left to bury / Of Mr Lavery . . . / . . . / . . . Or of Louis O'Neill" (*HC*, 56). The irony is that the killers of these men would be buried with paramilitary honors:

In war graves with full honours, nor in a separate plot
Fired over on anniversaries
By units drilled and spruce and unreconciled.

(*HC*, 56)

However, in the dis-place of writing, these bodies have a memorial—a grave of sorts, a place of memory, a space where they are honored and where their humanity and their human being are remembered. Far more than the "volunteers" and paramilitaries who have volleys fired over them, we will remember Mr Lavery (note the honorific title—he is not given a first name but the formal title) and Louis O'Neill, that "dole-kept bread winner" of *Field Work*. They, like steadfast Antigone, have found their memorial, not in a physical space or a political space, but in the space of writing, the space of literature, which is accessed, as are many others, by a "sun-admitting door" (*HC*, 56).

This bright and illumined space, while unable to act directly in the political realm, was nevertheless able to offer another type of memorial to these victims, and by keeping this door open it allowed them to achieve some form of transcendence with respect to the violence in Northern Ireland. While each side of the paramilitary divide was keen to memorialize their own dead, very often the innocent victims, people who happened to be in the wrong place at the wrong time, remained anonymous. They appear in lists of victims, but just as names in a list. In this poem, Heaney memorializes two people very much as people, as human beings who lived and then died brutally. That their deaths were caused by the strong identification of two different traditions with two very different ideologies of place is important, as the reposition-ing and resignification of place has been an ongoing trope in Heaney's work from the very beginning. His early poems of home, dealing with his childhood, have always been written in terms of a poetic relocation of that place by being written in the context of Greek myth. From the connections between the sound of the pumping of water with the voic-ing of the Greek word *omphalos*, to "Personal Helicon" (*DN*, 57), where the wells of his own townland are written in the context of the rivers of Mount Helicon, home of the muses, and the poet is compared to "big-eyed Narcissus" (*DN*, 57), the achievement of this dual perspective on place is to conflate the writing of place with the place of writing. As Heaney puts it: "If one perceptible function of poetry is to write place into existence, another of its functions is to unwrite it" (*PW*, 47), and this unwriting is part of his creation of that space into which the figures gazed in the Etruscan sculpture.

Maurice Blanchot sees this as one of the seminal functions of litera-ture and the aesthetic. For Blanchot, it is the transformative potential of art that brings this about. He points out that while in the real world things are viewed as objects in order to be grasped, classified, and categorized, in imaginary space "things are *transformed* into that which cannot be grasped. Out of use, beyond wear, they are not in our possession but are the movement of dispossession which releases us both from them and from ourselves" (Blanchot 1982, 131). In Blanchot's mind, literature is primarily an interrogative discourse that poses questions of the political and ideological: "Literature begins at the moment when literature becomes a question" (1981, 21).

In his Nobel lecture Heaney spoke about his own poetic "first place," Mossbawn (*P*, 18), but again in a way that opened it up to a different reading. He questioned the solidity of that place by recalling how the memory of place is interpenetrated by notions of space. The "air around and above us was alive and signalling too," as the wind stirred an "aerial wire attached to the topmost branch of the chestnut tree" (*CP*, 9). The wire came into their kitchen and into the radio, where the voice of a "BBC newsreader" spoke "out of the unexpected like a *deus ex machina*" (*CP*, 10): "I had already begun a journey into the wideness of the world beyond. This in turn became a journey into the wideness of language, a journey where each point of arrival—whether in one's poetry or one's life turned out to be a stepping stone rather than a destination" (*CP*, 11). At this point, Heaney is very close to Blanchot and his sense of *The Space of Literature*, where literature is seen as a point of nullity: "If literature coincides with nothing, for just an instant, it is immediately everything, and this everything begins to exist" (Blanchot 1982, 22). The "short bursts of foreign languages" and Heaney's encounter with the "gutturals and sibilants of European speech" are important signifiers of this widening of Mossbawn as a place and space of poetic and philosophical origin, for as Agamben says there is an experience of language "for which we have no words, which doesn't pretend, like grammatical language, to be there before being," and he terms this "the language of poetry" (1995, 48). It is an experience of language as other, as a form of communication that we cannot understand, even though we know it is signifying on some level. It is an alternative understanding of language, a feeling, a sensation, of difference through language; it is a conceptual displacement from any claim that our own language is the only way in which to speak or say the world. Poetic language has an ability to express and access aspects of experience that are silenced in normal discourse, as it belongs "neither to the day nor to the night but always is spoken between night and day and one single time speaks the truth and leaves it unspoken" (Blanchot 1982, 276). Writing about the spaces that are part of the stepping-stones, Heaney makes the point that poetic language has allowed him to uproot from the appetites of gravity, and the next line in *Crediting Poetry*, after the piece quoted above, validates this point: "I credit poetry for making this space-walk possible" (*CP*, 11). The foreign words are the spaces between the stepping-stones that access the transcendent.

This trope is carried on in his last book, in the sequence entitled "Loughanure." This ekphrastic poem, which begins by looking at a picture sold to the poet by the dedicatee of the sequence, Colin Middleton, and his "painting of Loughanure" that he had sold to the Heaneys for "thirty guineas / Forty-odd years ago" (*HC*, 61), tells how Middleton, who died in 1983, often looked at the picture when he came to the Heaneys' house. The second section of the poem goes on to equate this piece of art with a form of afterlife for Middleton:

> So this is what an afterlife can come to?
> A cloud-boil of grey weather on the wall
> Like murky crystal, a remembered stare—
> (HC, 62)

He proceeds to look at two other writers who discuss transcendence, Dante ("This for an answer to Alighieri"), who wrote about the afterlife in his *Divine Comedy*, and Plato, who concluded *The Republic*:

> And Plato's Er? Who watched immortal souls
> Choose lives to come according as they were
> Fulfilled or repelled by existences they'd known
> Or suffered first time round.
> (HC, 62)

This story about Er, a soldier who dies in battle but whose body remains undecomposed some ten days later, gives credence to the idea that there is a beyond, an open, some form of space, which transcends this world. Whether that is a place or a space is what is being questioned by Heaney here, just as his memory of Mossbawn was of both a place and the sounds that came from the surrounding space through the aerial. In his introduction to the Cambridge edition of *The Republic*, G. R. F. Ferrari (2000, xlvii) explains "the myth of Er, describing the rewards and penalties that await us after death (614a). The souls of the dead meet on a meadow to discuss their experiences of reward and punishment (614c); they travel to a place from which they can view the whole cosmos (616b); they choose their next lives (617d); they are reincarnated (620c)." In other words, Heaney is thinking about the aesthetic as a form of afterlife, as a mode of access to a form of transcendence, to that becoming space of which he spoke in his commentary on the Etruscan sculpture. Our access to such ideas is, of course, through literature and philosophy, symbolized in this poem by Dante and Plato respectively. In literature, the real and the imaginary, the immanent and the transcendent, appear together, and interestingly, given that this poetic sequence concluded with a car journey ("As I drive unhomesick, unbelieving, through / A grant-aided, renovated scene"; *HC*, 65), the path to such a reborn life, in *The Republic*, is also imaged in terms of a "journey from here to there and back again"; this journey, according to Er, "will be along the smooth, heavenly road, not the rough, terrestrial one" (Plato 2000, 343, 619e). The anaphoric parallelism of "Er" and "Errigal" adds to the associative narrative train that is set up in the poem.

The fusion of terrestrial and heavenly journeys comes to fruition in the next lines of the poem, where Heaney is in his car, looking at "Mount Errigal / On the skyline" as the "one constant thing," and he speaks of "trying / To remember the Greek word signifying / A world restored completely . . ." (*HC*, 65). The word in question, I would suggest, is *apokatastasis*, a doctrine propounded by Origen of Alexandria that means the final restitution of all things, a restoration to a primordial condition. It refers to a time when, at the appearance of the Messiah, the Kingdom of God shall encompass the whole earth—an idea extended by Origen to imply the final conversion and salvation of all created beings, the devil and his angels not excepted. It is a suggestion that ultimately the transcendent and immanent will fuse completely and that the latter will shine through the former. One could see much of Heaney's later poetry as attempting to describe and create such a moment, in an ephemeral condition. It has currency in philosophy and theology and interestingly is used by Heaney's great friend and mentor, and the person with whom this chapter began, namely Czesław Miłosz. In the final section of his long poem "Bells in Winter," Miłosz proclaims:

> Yet I belong to those who believe in *apokatastasis.*
> That word promises reverse movement,
> Not the one that was set in *katastasis*,
> And appears in the Acts, 3, 21.
> It means: restoration. So believed: St. Gregory of Nyssa,
> Johannes Scotus Erigena, Ruysbroeck and William Blake.
> For me, therefore, everything has a double existence.
> Both in time and when time shall be no more.
>
> (Miłosz 1978, 69)

In the list of avatars, we see the discourses of mystical religion, philosophy, and poetry, all of which promise such a reinstatement of a sense of place that is brimful of imagery of space and the transcendent. All of these writers speak of a return to a heightened form of life, and in his later poetry, as we have seen, Heaney captures instances of such plenitude. This double existence is what Heaney has prized in Miłosz's work, and for each aspect of existence to animate the other, there needs to be a form of access and egress between them both—and there needs to be a form of openness: "between the vocation of poet and the behaviour of a reasonable man, between the call to open the doors of one's life to the daimonic and prophetic soul and have one's destiny changed by it, between that choice and the temptation to keep the doors closed and the self securely under social and domestic lock and key" (*FK*, 360). For Heaney, as we have seen, those doors always stand open.

WORKS CITED

Abbott, Claude, ed. [1935] 1972. *The Correspondence of Gerard Manley Hopkins and Richard Watson Dixon*. Oxford: Oxford University Press.

Abrams, M. H. 1953. *The Mirror and the Lamp: Romantic Theory and the Critical Tradition*. Oxford: Oxford University Press.

Agamben, Giorgio. 1993. *The Coming Community*. Minneapolis: University of Minnesota Press.

———. 1995. *Idea of Prose*. Translated by Michael Sullivan and Sam Whitsitt. Albany: State University of New York Press.

———. 1998. *Homo Sacer: Sovereign Power and Bare Life*. Stanford, CA: Stanford University Press.

Agamben, Giorgio, and Daniel Heller-Roazen. 1999. *The End of the Poem: Studies in Poetics*. Stanford, CA: Stanford University Press.

Ahmed, Sara. 2004. *The Cultural Politics of Emotion*. New York: Routledge.

Allen, William S. 2007. *Ellipsis: Of Poetry and the Experience of Language after Heidegger, Hölderlin, and Blanchot*. Albany: State University of New York Press.

Arendt, Hannah. 1968. Introduction to *Illuminations*, by Walter Benjamin. New York: Harcourt.

Aristotle. 1941. *De Poetica (Poetics)*. In *The Basic Works of Aristotle*, edited by Richard McKeon, translated by Ingram Bywater. New York: Random House.

Arthur, Chris. 2012. "Relics." In *On the Shoreline of Knowledge: Irish Wanderings*, 106–20. Iowa City: University of Iowa Press.

Auden, W. H. 1945. *The Collected Poetry of W. H. Auden*. New York: Random House.

———. 1979. *Selected Poems*. Edited by Edward Mendelson. New York: Random House.

Auerbach, Eric. 1984. *Scenes from the Drama of European Literature*. Minneapolis: University of Minnesota Press.

Auge, Andrew. 2003. "'A Buoyant Migrant Line': Seamus Heaney's Deterritorialized Poetics." *LIT: Literature Interpretation Theory* 14 (4): 269–88.

Bachelard, Gaston. 1969. *The Poetics of Reverie: Childhood, Language, and the Cosmos*. Translated by Daniel Russell. Boston: Beacon Press.

———. 1994. *The Poetics of Space*. Translated by Maria Jolas. Boston: Beacon Press.

Barthes, Roland. 1975. *The Pleasure of the Text*. Translated by Richard Miller. New York: Farrar, Straus, and Giroux.

———. 1978. *Writing Degree Zero*. New York: Hill and Wang.

Batten, Guinn. 2008. "Heaney's Wordsworth and the Poetics of Displacement." In *The Cambridge Companion to Seamus Heaney*, edited by Bernard O'Donoghue, 178–92. Cambridge: Cambridge University Press.

Beckett, Samuel. 1986. *The Complete Dramatic Works*. London: Faber.

Benfey, Christopher. 2008. *American Audacity: Literary Essays North and South*. Ann Arbor: University of Michigan Press.

Bennington, Geoff, and Jacques Derrida. 1993. *Jacques Derrida*. Chicago: University of Chicago Press.

Blanchot, Maurice. 1981. *The Gaze of Orpheus*. Edited by P. Adams Sitney. Translated by Lydia Davis. New York: Station Hill Press.

———. 1982. *The Space of Literature*. Translated by Ann Smock. Lincoln: University of Nebraska Press.

Bleakney, Jean. 2006. "Gear and Tackle and Trim: *District and Circle*, Seamus Heaney." *Fortnight* 445 (June–July): 29.

Bloom, Harold. 1973. *The Anxiety of Influence*. Oxford: Oxford University Press.

———. 1988. "The Freshness of Transformation: Emerson's Dialectics of Influence." In *Emerson: Prophecy, Metamorphosis, and Influence*, edited by David Levin, 129–48. New York: Columbia University Press.

Brandes, Rand. 2009. "Seamus Heaney's Working Titles: From 'Advancements of Learning' to 'Midnight Anvil.'" In *The Cambridge Companion to Seamus Heaney*, edited by Bernard O'Donoghue, 19–36. Cambridge: Cambridge University Press.

Brandes, Rand, and Michael J. Durkan. 2008. *Seamus Heaney: A Bibliography, 1959–2003*. London: Faber and Faber.

Brearton, Fran. 2008. "Heaney and the Feminine." In *The Cambridge Companion to Seamus Heaney*, edited by Bernard O'Donoghue, 73–91. Cambridge: Cambridge University Press.

Bredin, Hugh. 1984. "A Language of Courage and Love of Objects: Seamus Heaney, *Station Island*." *Fortnight* 209 (November): 18, 20.

Brock, Geoffrey. 2012. *The FSG Book of Twentieth-Century Italian Poetry: An Anthology*. New York: Farrar, Straus, and Giroux.

Brown, Bill. 2001. "Thing Theory." *Critical Inquiry* 28 (1): 1–22.

———. 2004. *A Sense of Things: The Object Matter of American Literature*. Chicago: University of Chicago Press, 2004.

Brown, Terence. 2009. "The Irish Dylan Thomas: Versions and Influences." *Irish Studies Review* 17 (1): 45–54.

Buttel, Robert. 1975. *Seamus Heaney*. Lewisburg, PA: Bucknell University Press.

Caedmon. 1979. "Caedmon's Hymn." In *The Norton Anthology of English Literature*, vol. 1, edited by M. H. Abrams et al., 20–21. New York: W. W. Norton.

Campbell, Joseph. 1949. *The Hero with a Thousand Faces*. Princeton, NJ: Princeton University Press.

———. 2006. "The Mythmaker: Nobel Prize Winner Seamus Heaney Talks to James Campbell." *Guardian*, May 27. www.guardian.co.uk/books/2006/may/27/poetry.hayfestival2006.

Carey, Roane. 1999. "Republic of Pain." *Nation*, July 12, 30–34.

Carpenter, Bogdana, and Madeleine G. Levine. 2002. Introduction to *To Begin Where I Am: Selected Essays*, by Czesław Miłosz. New York: Farrar, Straus and Giroux.

Carson, Ciaran. 1975. "Escaped from the Massacre?" *Honest Ulsterman* 50 (Winter): 183–86.

Casey, Edward. 1987. *Remembering: A Phenomenological Study*. Bloomington: Indiana University Press.

Constantine, David. 1999. "Finding the Words." *Times Literary Supplement*, May 21, 14–15.

Constantine, David, and Helen Constantine. 2009. "Editorial." *Modern Poetry in Translation* 3 (12): 1–3.

Corcoran, Neil. 1998. *The Poetry of Seamus Heaney: A Critical Study*. London: Faber.

———. 2013. "Seamus Heaney Obituary." *Guardian*, August 30.

Cornell, Drucilla. 1999. *Beyond Accommodation: Ethical Feminism, Deconstruction and the Law*. New ed. New York: Rowman and Littlefield.

Coughlan, Patricia. 1991. "'Bog Queens': The Representation of Women in the Poetry of John Montague and Seamus Heaney." In *Gender in Irish Writing*, edited by Toni Johnson and David Cairns, 88–111. Milton Keynes: Open University Press.

Critchley, Simon. 2008. "Original Inauthenticity: On Heidegger's *Sein und Zeit*." In *On Heidegger's "Being and Time,"* by Simon Critchley and Reiner Schürmann, edited by Steven Levine, 132–51. New York: Routledge.

Czarnecka, Ewa, and Aleksander Fiut. 1987. *Conversations with Czesław Miłosz*. Translated by Richard Lourie. New York: Harcourt Brace Jovanovich.

Dante Alighieri. 1939. *Inferno and Paradiso*. Translated by John Sinclair. Oxford: Oxford University Press.

Derrida, Jacques. 1976. *Of Grammatology*. Translated by Gayatri Chakravorty Spivak. Baltimore: Johns Hopkins University Press.

———. 1987. "Living On: Borderlines." In *Deconstruction and Criticism*, edited by Harold Bloom, Paul de Man, Jacques Derrida, Geoffrey Hartman, and J. Hillis Miller, 75–176. New York: Continuum Press.

———. 1993. *Aporias: Dying—Awaiting (One Another at) the Limits of Truth*. Translated by Thomas Dutoit. Stanford, CA: Stanford University Press.

———. 1995. "Deconstruction and the Other." In *States of Mind: Dialogues with Contemporary Continental Thinkers*, edited by Richard Kearney, 139–56. Manchester: Manchester University Press.

———. 2005. *Sovereignties in Question: The Poetics of Paul Celan*. Edited and translated by Thomas Dutoit and Outi Pasanen. New York: Fordham University Press.

———. 2007a. *Learning to Live Finally: The Last Interview*. Edited and introduced by Jean Birnbaum. Translated by Pascale-Anne Brault and Michael Nass. Brooklyn, NY: Melville House.

———. 2007b. *Psyche: Inventions of the Other*. Vol. 2. Edited by Peggy Kamuf and Elizabeth Rottenberg. Stanford, CA: Stanford University Press.

Derrida, Jacques, and Anne Dufourmantelle. 2000. *Of Hospitality*. Translated by Rachel Bowlby. Stanford, CA: Stanford University Press.

Dickinson, Emily. 1924. *The Complete Poems of Emily Dickinson*. Boston: Little, Brown.

Donne, John. 1971. *The Complete English Poems*. Edited by A. J. Smith. New York: Viking Penguin.

———. 1994. *Complete English Poems*. Edited by Constantinos Apostolos Patrides. London: J. M. Dent.

Donoghue, Denis. 2003. *Speaking of Beauty*. New Haven, CT: Yale University Press.

Doran, Peter. 2010. "Can Civil Society Succeed Where Elites Have Failed in the War on Sectarianism? Towards an Infinitely Demanding Politics for the North." *Irish Journal of Sociology* 18:126–50.

Dorgan, Theo. 2013. "Seamus Heaney." *RTE News Now*, August 30.

Draaisma, Douwe. 2006. *Why Life Speeds Up As You Get Older*. Translated by Arno and Erica Pomerans. Cambridge: Cambridge University Press.

Dunn, Douglas. 2001. "Quotidian Miracles: Seeing Things." In *The Art of Seamus Heaney*, edited by Tony Curtis, 205–27. Dublin: Wolfhound Press.

Dunn, Seamus. 1999. "Northern Ireland: A Promising or Partisan Peace?" *Journal of International Affairs* 52:719–33.

Eagleton, Terry. 1999. "Hasped and Hooped and Hirpling: Heaney Conquers *Beowulf*." *London Review of Books*, November 11, 15–16.

Eco, Umberto. 1986. *Art and Beauty in the Middle Ages*. Translated by Hugh Bredin. New Haven, CT: Yale University Press.

Eliade, Mircea. 1971. *The Myth of the Eternal Return*. Translated by Willard R. Trask. Princeton, NJ: Princeton University Press.

Eliot, T. S. [1918] 1976. "A Review of *Georgian Poetry, 1916–17*." Reprinted in *A Map of Modern English Verse*, edited by John Press. Oxford: Oxford University Press.

———. [1924] 2013. "A Neglected Aspect of Chapman." *New York Review of Books*, November 11, 62–64.

———. 1933. "Critical" [Introduction]. In *The Collected Poems of Harold Monro*. London: Cobden-Sanderson.

———. 1953. *Selected Prose*. Edited by John Hayward. Harmondsworth: Penguin.

———. 1957. *On Poetry and Poets*. London: Faber and Faber.

———. 1963. *Collected Poems, 1909–1962*. New York: Harcourt Brace and World.

———. 1967. *The Complete Poems and Plays, 1909–1950*. New York: Harcourt Brace.

———. 1970. *The Complete Poems and Plays of T. S. Eliot*. London: Faber.

Emerson, Ralph Waldo. 1982. *Selected Essays*. Harmondsworth: Penguin.

Erickson, Jon. 1995. *The Fate of the Object: From Modern Object to Postmodern Sign*. Ann Arbor: University of Michigan Press.

Ettinger, Bracha L. 1995. *The Matrixial Gaze*. Leeds: Feminist Arts and Histories Network, Department of Fine Art, Leeds University.

———. 1996. "Borderlinks and Borderspace." In *Rethinking Borders*, edited by John C. Welchman, 125–59. London: Macmillan.

———. 2006. *The Matrixial Borderspace*. Minnesota: University of Minnesota Press.

Feeney, D. C. 2000. "History and Revelation in Vergil's Underworld." In *Why Vergil? A Collection of Interpretations*, edited by Stephanie Quinn, 1–24. Wauconda, IL: Bolchazy-Carducci.

Ferrari, G. R. F. 2000. Introduction to *The Republic*, by Plato. Edited by G. R. F. Ferrari. Translated by Tom Griffith. Cambridge: Cambridge University Press.

Ferry, Anne. 1988. *The Art of Naming*. Chicago: University of Chicago Press.

Fitzpatrick, Maurice. 2010. *The Boys of St. Columb's*. Dublin: Liffey Press.

Foster, John Wilson. 2009. "Crediting Marvels: Heaney after 50." In *The Cambridge Companion to Seamus Heaney*, edited by Bernard O'Donoghue, 206–23. Cambridge: Cambridge University Press.

Freeman, C. E., ed. 1918. *Virgil: Aeneid VI*. Oxford: Oxford University Press.

Freud, Sigmund. 1955. "The 'Uncanny.'" In *An Infantile Neurosis and Other Works*, vol. 17 of *Standard Edition of the Complete Psychological Works of Sigmund Freud*, edited by James Strachey. London: Hogarth Press.

Frost, Robert. 1978. *Selected Poems*. Harmondsworth: Penguin.

Fuit, Aleksander. 1990. *The Eternal Moment: The Poetry of Czesław Miłosz*. Translated by Theodosia S. Robertson. Berkeley: University of California Press.

Gardner, W. H. 1985. Introduction to *Poems and Prose of Gerard Manley Hopkins*, xiv–xxxiv. London: Penguin.

Garfitt, Roger. 1979. Introduction to *Gravities: A Collection of Poems and Drawings*, by Seamus Heaney. Newcastle-upon-Tyne: Charlotte Press.

Garland, Patrick. 1973. "Poets on Poetry." *Listener*, November 8, 629.

Gasset, José Ortega y. 1968. "On Point of View in the Arts." In *The Dehumanization of Art and Other Essays on Art, Culture, and Literature*, translated by Helen Weyl, 105–30. Princeton, NJ: Princeton University Press.

Gilligan, Chris. "Introduction: Instability and the Peace Process." *Global Review of Ethnopolitics* 3 (2003): 3–70.

Glob, P. V. 1977. *The Bog People: Iron-Age Man Preserved*. Translated by R. L. S. Bruce-Mitford. London: Faber.

Guillevic, Eugene. 1979. "Herbier de Bretagne." *Étier: Poèmes 1965–1975*. Paris: Gallimard.

———. 1999. *Living in Poetry: Interviews with Guillevic*. Translated by Maureen Smith. Dublin: Dedalus.

Gussow, Mel. 2000. "An Anglo-Saxon Chiller (with an Irish Touch): Seamus Heaney Adds His Voice to 'Beowulf.'" *New York Times*, March 29, 2000.

Haffenden, John. 1981. *Viewpoints: Poets in Conversation*. London: Faber.

Hamilton, Ian. 1987. Review of *The Haw Lantern*, by Seamus Heaney. *London Review of Books*, October 1, 10–11.

Hamilton, Saskia, ed. 2005. *The Letters of Robert Lowell*. New York: Farrar, Straus and Giroux.

Harington, Sir John. 1991. *The Sixth Book of Virgil's "Aeneid."* Edited by Simon Cauchi. Translated by and commented on by Sir John Harington (1604). Oxford: Oxford University Press.

Harries, Karsten. 2009. *Art Matters: A Critical Commentary on Heidegger's "The Origin of the Work of Art."* Dordrecht: Springer.

Harrison, Robert Pogue. 2003. *The Dominion of the Dead.* Chicago: University of Chicago Press.

Hart, Charles. 1931. *The Student's Catholic Doctrine.* London: Burns Oates and Washbourne.

Hart, David Bentley. 2003. *The Beauty of the Infinite.* Grand Rapids, MI: Eerdmanns.

Hart, Henry. 1989. "History, Myth, and Apocalypse in Seamus Heaney's *North.*" *Contemporary Literature* 30 (3): 387–411.

———. 1992. *Seamus Heaney: Poet of Contrary Progressions.* Syracuse, NY: Syracuse University Press.

———. 1994. "What Is Heaney Seeing in *Seeing Things?*" *Colby Quarterly* 30 (1): 33–42.

Hayward, Katy, and Claire Mitchell. 2003. "Discourses of Equity in Post-Agreement Northern Ireland." *Contemporary Politics* 9:293–312.

Heaney, Seamus. 1966. *Death of a Naturalist.* London: Faber; New York: Farrar, Straus and Giroux.

———. 1969. *Door into the Dark.* London: Faber; New York: Farrar, Straus and Giroux.

———. 1972. *Wintering Out.* London: Faber; New York: Farrar, Straus and Giroux.

———. 1974. "Summoning Lazarus." Review of *The Mound People: Danish Bronze-Age Man Preserved,* by P. V. Glob. *Listener,* June 6, 741–42.

———. 1975a. *North.* London: Faber; New York: Farrar, Straus and Giroux.

———. 1975b. "Polish Sleepers." *New Yorker,* January 17, 79.

———. 1978. "The Poet as a Christian." *Furrow,* October, 603–6.

———. 1979a. *Field Work.* London: Faber; New York: Farrar, Straus and Giroux.

———. 1979b. "An Interview with Seamus Heaney." By James Randall. *Ploughshares* 5 (3): 7–22.

———. 1979c. "Kavanagh of the Parish." *Listener,* April 26, 577–78.

———. 1980a. *Preoccupations: Selected Prose, 1968–1978.* London: Faber.

———. 1980b. "Treely and Rurally." *Quarto,* no. 9 (August): 14.

———. 1981. "Current Unstated Assumptions about Poetry." *Critical Inquiry* 7 (4): 645–51.

———. 1982. "Unhappy and at Home: Interview with Seamus Heaney" [1977]. By Seamus Deane. In *The Crane Bag Book of Irish Studies,* 66–72. Dublin: Blackwater Press.

———. 1983a. "From a Common Bed of Feeling." Review of *The Modern Poetic Sequence,* by M. L. Rosenthal and Sally Gall. *New York Times Book Review,* November 29, 3, 31, 32.

———. 1983b. *An Open Letter.* Derry: Field Day.

———. 1983c. "Poet of the Bogs." Interview by Francis X. Clines. *New York Times*, March 13, 12.

———. 1983d. *Sweeney Astray.* Derry: Field Day.

———. 1984. *Station Island.* London: Faber; New York: Farrar, Straus and Giroux.

———. 1986a. "An Interview with Seamus Heaney." By June Beisch. *Literary Review* 29 (2): 161–69.

———. 1986b. "Place, Pastness, Poems: A Triptych." *Salmagundi* 69 (Winter): 30–47.

———. 1987. *The Haw Lantern.* London: Faber; New York: Farrar, Straus and Giroux.

———. 1988a. *The Government of the Tongue: The 1986 T. S. Eliot Memorial Lectures and Other Critical Writings.* London: Faber.

———. 1988b. "An Interview with Seamus Heaney." By Rand Brandes. *Salmagundi* 80:4–21.

———. 1989a. "'Calling the Tune,' Interview with Seamus Heaney." By Tom Adair. *Linen Hall Review* 6 (2): 7.

———. 1989b. "The Convert." *Alpha*, June 8, 15.

———. 1990. *The Cure at Troy.* London: Faber.

———. 1991a. "Interview with Seamus Heaney." Interview by Melvyn Bragg. *The South Bank Show*, October 27, London Weekend Television.

———. 1991b. "Seamus Famous: Time to Be Dazzled: Interview with Blake Morrison." *Independent on Sunday*, May 19, 26.

———. 1991c. *Seeing Things.* London: Faber; New York: Farrar, Straus and Giroux.

———. 1992. "The Flight Path for Donald Davie." *PN Review 88* 19 (2): 31–32.

———. 1995a. *Crediting Poetry.* Oldcastle, County Meath, Ireland: Gallery Press.

———. 1995b. *The Redress of Poetry.* Oxford: Clarendon.

———. 1996. *The Spirit Level.* London: Faber; New York: Farrar, Straus and Giroux.

———. 1997a. *Commencement Address, University of North Carolina, Chapel Hill, May 12, 1996.* Chapel Hill, NC: George S. Lensing and Weldon Thorton.

———. 1997b. "Interview with Seamus Heaney." By Henri Cole. *Paris Review* 39 (144): 88–138.

———. 1998a. *Opened Ground: Poems, 1966–1996.* London: Faber.

———. 1998b. "Unheard Melodies." *Irish Times*, April 11, 57.

———. 1999. *Beowulf.* London: Faber.

———. 2000a. "The Dearest Freshness." *Threepenny Review* 80 (Winter): 7.

———. 2000b. *The Midnight Verdict.* Oldcastle, County Meath, Ireland: Gallery Press.

———. 2000c. "Seamus Heaney." Interview by Mike Murphy. In *Reading the Future: Irish Writers in Conversation with Mike Murphy*, edited by Mike Murphy and Clíodhna Ní Anluain. Dublin: Lilliput Press.

———. 2001a. *Electric Light.* London: Faber; New York: Farrar, Straus and Giroux.

———. 2001b. "Interview with Seamus Heaney." By Nigel Farndale. *Telegraph*, April 5, 20–25.

———. 2001c. Introduction to *William Wordsworth: Poems Selected by Seamus Heaney*, vii–xii. London: Faber and Faber.

———. 2001d. "Lux Perpetua." *Guardian*, June 16.

———. 2002a. *Finders Keepers: Selected Prose, 1971–2001.* London: Faber.

———. 2002b. "Seamus Heaney." Interview by John Brown. In *In the Chair: Interviews with Poets from the North of Ireland*, 75–86. Cliffs of Moher, County Clare, Ireland: Salmon.

———. 2002c. "The Whole Thing: On the Good of Poetry." *The Recorder: A Journal of the American Irish Historical Society* (Spring): 5–20.

———. 2003. "'Eclogues in Extremis': On the Staying Power of Pastoral." *Proceedings of the Royal Irish Academy. Section C: Archaeology, Celtic Studies, History, Linguistics, Literature* 103C (1): 1–12.

———. 2004a. *"Anything Can Happen": A Poem and Essay by Seamus Heaney with Translations in Support of Art for Amnesty.* Dublin: Town House with Art for Amnesty and Irish Translators' and Interpreters' Association.

———. 2004b. *The Burial at Thebes: Sophocles' Antigone.* London: Faber; New York: Farrar, Straus and Giroux.

———. 2004c. "In Gratitude for All the Gifts." *Guardian*, September 11, 4.

———. 2005. "Polish Sleepers." *New Yorker*, January 17, 79.

———. 2006a. *District and Circle.* London: Faber; New York· Farrar, Straus and Giroux.

———. 2006b. "Pangur Bán." Translation. Dublin, February 7. Privately printed pamphlet welcoming the Notre Dame leadership group to Dublin; designed by Caroline Moloney and Kevin Whelan.

———. 2007a. "The Pathos of Things." *Guardian*, November 24, 21.

———. 2007b. *The Riverbank Field.* Oldcastle: Gallery Press.

———. 2008a. "David Hammond: A 'Natural Force' for Good in Irish Life with a Gift for Television Film-Making and Song." *Guardian*, August 28.

————. 2008b. "Holding Patterns: Arts, Letters and the Academy." In *Articulations: Poetry, Philosophy and the Shaping of Culture*, edited by Seamus Heaney, Paul Muldoon, and Jane Conroy, 11–23. Dublin: Royal Irish Academy.

————. 2008c. *Stepping Stones: Interviews with Seamus Heaney*. Interviews by Dennis O'Driscoll. London: Faber.

————. 2009a. "The Kite." Translation of Giovanni Pascoli's "L'aquilone." In *Auguri: To Mary Kelleher*, edited by Fergus Mulligan, 4–6. Dublin: Royal Dublin Society.

————. 2009b. *Seamus Heaney: Out of the Marvelous*. Documentary. Directed by Charlie McCarthy. Produced by Clíona Ní Bhuachalla. Dublin: Icebox Films Production for RTÉ Television.

————. 2009c. "Three 'Freed Speeches' from *Aeneid* VI." *Modern Poetry in Translation* 3 (12): 58–61.

————. 2010. *Human Chain*. London: Faber; New York: Farrar, Straus and Giroux.

————. 2011. "Seamus Heaney on Czesław Miłosz's Centenary." *Guardian*, April 7.

————. 2012. "The Kite." Griselda Online: Portale de Letteratura. www.griselda online.it/sonde/heaney-kite-pascoli-aquilone.html.

————. 2013a. "Du Bellay in Rome." *New England Review* 34 (2): 6.

————. 2013b. "In a Field." *Irish Times*, October 26, 1.

————. 2013c. "On the Gift of a Fountain Pen." *Beall Poetry Festival Brochure*, March 4, privately printed.

————. 2013d. "'Poets Are Always Young Poets When We Get Together': Nobel Laureate Seamus Heaney Talks to Erica Wagner about the Future of Northern Ireland, His Love for His Fellow Poets and How They Can Still Change the World." Interview by Erica Wagner. *Times* (London), January 28, T2, 2–3.

————. 2013e. "Suffering and Decision." In *Ted Hughes: From Cambridge to Collected*, edited by Mark Wormald, Neil Roberts, and Terry Gifford, 221–37. Basingstoke: Palgrave Macmillan.

————. 2014. "The Latecomers." *Poetry Ireland Review* 112:122.

Heaney, Seamus, and Stanislaw Barańczak, trans. 1995. *Laments*, by Jan Kachanowski. London: Faber.

Heidegger, Martin. 1971. *Poetry, Language, Thought*. Translated by Albert Hofstadter. New York: Harper and Row.

————. 1996. *Being and Time: A Translation of Sein und Zeit*. Translated by Joan Stambaugh. Albany: State University of New York Press.

———. 2009. *Logic as the Question Concerning the Essence of Language*. Translated by Wanda Torres Gregory and Yvonne Unna. New York: State University of New York Press.

Heiny, Stephen. 2013. "Virgil in Heaney's *Human Chain*: 'Images and Symbols Adequate to Our Predicament.'" *Renascence* 65 (4): 305–18.

Hodder, Ian. 2014. "The Entanglements of Humans and Things: A Long-Term View." *New Literary History* 45 (1): 19–36.

Hofmann, Michael, and James Lasdun. *After Ovid: New Metamorphoses*. London: Faber, 1994.

Homem, Rui Carvalho. 2009. *Poetry and Translation in Northern Ireland: Dislocations in Contemporary Writing*. London: Palgrave Macmillan.

Hopkins, Gerard Manley. 1961. *Poems of Gerard Manley Hopkins*. Oxford: Oxford University Press.

———. 1985. *Poems and Prose of Gerard Manley Hopkins*. Selected with introduction and notes by W. H. Gardner. London: Penguin, 1985.

Howard, Ben. 2014. "One of the Venerators: Seamus Heaney, 1939–2013." *Sewanee Review* 122 (1): 164–67.

Hughes, Ted. 1957. *Hawk in the Rain*. London: Faber and Faber.

Hunt, Maurice. 2012–13. "Naming and Unnaming in Spenser's *Colin Clouts Come Home Againe*." *Connotations: A Journal for Critical Debate* 22 (2): 235–59.

Hyde, Lewis. 2007. *The Gift: Creativity and the Artist in the Modern World*. New York: Vintage.

Jameson, Fredric. 1981. *The Political Unconscious: Narrative as a Socially Symbolic Act*. Ithaca, NY: Cornell University Press.

Johnson, Barbara. 2008. *Persons and Things*. Cambridge, MA: Harvard University Press.

Johnson, Samuel. 1975. *Lives of the English Poets: A Selection*. London: J. M. Dent.

Johnston, Maria. 2010. "Review of *Human Chain*." *Poetry Matters*, October. https://mariajohnstondotcom.files.wordpress.com/2015/01/heaney_human -chain_johnston_oct-2010.pdf.

Joyce, James. 1976. *Dubliners*. New York: Penguin.

———. 1986. *Ulysses*. New York: Vintage.

———. 1992. *A Portrait of the Artist as a Young Man*. Harmondsworth: Penguin Books.

Jung, Carl Gustav. 1967. *Alchemical Studies*. Translated by R. F. C. Hull. London: Routledge.

———. 1977. *C. G. Jung Speaking: Interviews and Encounters*. Edited by William McGuire and R. F. C. Hull. Princeton, NJ: Princeton University Press.

Kay, Magdalena. 2010. "Belonging as Mastery: Selfhood and Otherness in the Poetry of Seamus Heaney." *New Hibernia Review* 14 (1): 78–95.

———. 2012. *In Gratitude for All the Gifts: Seamus Heaney and Eastern Europe.* Toronto: University of Toronto Press.

Kearney, Richard. 1988. *The Wake of Imagination.* Minneapolis: University of Minnesota Press.

———. 2006. *Navigations: Collected Irish Essays, 1976–2006.* Syracuse, NY: Syracuse University Press.

Keats, John. 1990. *John Keats.* Edited by Elizabeth Cook. Oxford: Oxford University Press.

Kennedy-Andrews, Elmer. 1988. *The Poetry of Seamus Heaney: All the Realms of Whisper.* Basingstoke: Macmillan.

———. 1991. Review of *Seeing Things*, by Seamus Heaney. *Linen Hall Review* 8 (4): 27–29.

Kinsella, Tina. 2013. "Bracha L. Ettinger's Matrixial Theory and Aesthetics: Matrixial Flesh and the Jouissance of Non-Life-in-Life." PhD diss., National College of Art and Design, Dublin/Graduate School of Creative Arts and Media.

Kopytoff, Igor. 1986. "The Cultural Biography of Things: Commoditization as Process." In *The Social Life of Things: Commodities in Cultural Perspective*, edited by Arjun Appadurai, 264–91. Cambridge: Cambridge University Press.

Lacan, Jacques. 2006. *Écrits: The First Complete Edition in English.* Translated by Bruce Fink with Héloïse Fink and Russell Grigg. London: Norton.

Larkin, Philip. 2012. *Philip Larkin: The Complete Poems.* Edited by Archie Burnett. London: Faber.

Latour, Bruno. 2000. "The Berlin Key or How to Do Words with Things." Translated by Lydia Davis. In *Matter, Materiality, and Modern Culture*, edited by P. M. Graves-Brown, 10–21. London: Routledge.

Lennard, John. 1991. *But I Digress: The Exploitation of Parentheses in English Printed Verse.* Oxford: Oxford University Press.

Lipking, Lawrence. 1981. *The Life of the Poet.* Chicago: University of Chicago Press.

Liu, Jiong. 2010. "Catholic Predilections in the Poetics of Gerard Manley Hopkins and Seamus Heaney." *Religion and the Arts* 14 (3): 267–96.

Lloyd, David. 1993. *Anomalous States: Irish Writing and the Post-Colonial Moment.* Dublin: Lilliput Press.

Lloyd, John. 1998. "Ireland's Uncertain Peace." *Foreign Affairs* 77 (5): 109–22.

Longley, Edna. 1986. *Poetry in the Wars.* Newcastle: Bloodaxe Books.

Luck, Georg. 1973. "Virgil and the Mystery Religions." *American Journal of Philology* 94 (2): 147–66.

Lynch, William. 2004. *Christ and Apollo: The Dimensions of Literary Imagination.* Wilmington, DE: ISI Books.

Madden, F. J. M., and Thomas Bradley, eds. 2004. *Seeking the Kingdom.* Derry: St. Columb's College.

Mahon, Derek. 2010. *An Autumn Wind.* Dublin: Gallery Press.

Mandelbaum, Allen, trans. 1971. *The Aeneid of Virgil.* New York: Bantam Books.

Marchant, Fred. 2011. "Windfall: Seamus Heaney's Human Chain." *Salamander* 16 (2): 4.

Martz, Louis. 1954. *The Poetry of Meditation: A Study in English Literature of the Seventeenth Century.* New Haven, CT: Yale University Press.

Mauss, Marcel. 1990. *The Gift.* Translated by W. D. Halls. New York: W. W. Norton.

McCrum, Robert. 2009. "Seamus Heaney: A Life of Rhyme." *Observer,* July 18.

McDonald, Peter. 2012. "'Our Lost Lives': Protestantism and Northern Irish Poetry." In *The Oxford Handbook of Modern Irish Poetry*, edited by Fran Brearton and Alan Gillis, 473–91. Oxford: Oxford University Press.

McGreevy, Ronan. 2013. "Tributes Paid to 'Keeper of Language' Seamus Heaney." *Irish Times,* August 30.

McKittrick, David, Seamus Kelters, Brian Feeney, and Chris Thornton, eds. 2007. *Lost Lives.* Edinburgh: Mainstream.

Merleau-Ponty, Maurice. 1964. "Eye and Mind." Translated by Carleton Dallery. In *The Primacy of Perception and Other Essays on Phenomenological Psychology, the Philosophy of Art, History, and Politics*, edited by James M. Edie, 159–90. Evanston, IL: Northwestern University Press.

Merton, Thomas. 1961. *Seeds of Contemplation.* Wheathampstead: Anthony Clarke.

Meyer, Kuno. 1913. *Selections from Ancient Irish Poetry.* London: Constable.

———. 2010. "My Hand Is Weary with Writing." In *The Penguin Book of Irish Poetry*, edited by Patrick Crotty, 36–37. London: Penguin.

Miłosz, Czesław. 1953. *Captive Mind.* New York: Vintage.

———. 1978. *Bells in Winter.* Translated by Lillian Valee and Czesław Miłosz. New York: Ecco Press.

———. 1981. "A Separate Notebook." Translated by Robert Hass and Renata Gorczynski. *Ironwood* 18:186.

———. 2001. *New and Collected Poems, 1931–2001.* London: Penguin.

Molino, Michael. 1993. "Flying by the Nets of Language and Nationality: Seamus Heaney, the 'English' Language, and Ulster's Troubles." *Modern Philology* 91 (2): 180–201.

Morgan, George. 2008. "Interview with Seamus Heaney." *Cycnos* 15 (2). http://revel.unice.fr/cycnos/?id=1594.

Morisco, Gabriella. 2013. "Two Poets and a Kite: Seamus Heaney and Giovanni Pascoli." *Linguæ: Rivista di lingue e culture moderne* 1:35–45. www.ledonline.it/index.php/linguae/article/download/313/287.

Morrison, Blake. 1982. *Seamus Heaney*. London: Methuen.

———. 2013. "Seamus Heaney: An Appreciation." *Guardian*, September 6.

Muir, Edwin. 1962. *The Estate of Poetry*. Foreword by Archibald MacLeish. Introduction by John Haines. Cambridge, MA: Harvard University Press.

Muldoon, Orla T., Karen Trew, Jennifer Todd, Nathalie Rougier, and Katrina McLaughlin. 2007. "Religion and National Identity after the Belfast Good Friday Agreement." *Political Psychology* 28:89–103.

Muldoon, Paul. 2013. "Paul Muldoon on Seamus Heaney: The Mark of a Great Poet." *Daily Beast*, August 30. www.thedailybeast.com/articles/2013/08/30/paul-muldoon-on-seamus-heaney-the-mark-of-a-great-poet.html#url=/articles/2013/08/30/.

Murray, Alex, and Jessica Whyte. 2011. *The Agamben Dictionary*. Edinburgh: Edinburgh University Press.

Nagy, Gregory. 2010. "Ancient Greek Elegy." In *The Oxford Handbook of the Elegy*, edited by Karen Weisman, 13–45. Oxford: Oxford University Press.

Nishitani, Keiji. 1982. *Religion and Nothingness*. Translated by Jan van Bragt. Berkeley: University of California Press.

Northern Ireland Peace Agreement. 1998. April 10. Conflict Archive on the Internet. http://cain.ulst.ac.uk/events/peace/docs/agreement.htm.

O'Brien, Eugene. 2002. *Seamus Heaney and the Place of Writing*. Gainesville: University Press of Florida.

———. 2003. *Seamus Heaney: Searches for Answers*. London: Pluto Press.

O'Brien, Flann. 1974. "My Hand Has a Pain from Writing." In *The Faber Book of Irish Verse*, edited by John Montague. London: Faber.

O'Donoghue, Bernard. 1994. *Seamus Heaney and the Language of Poetry*. Hemel Hempstead: Harvester Wheatsheaf.

———, ed. 2009. *The Cambridge Companion to Seamus Heaney*. Cambridge: Cambridge University Press.

O'Driscoll, Dennis. 2002. *Exemplary Damages*. Greenwich: Anvil Press.

O'Hagan, Andrew. 2013. "Seamus Heaney: My Travels with the Great Poet." *Guardian*, September 2.

"The Order of Mass." New English translation of *The Roman Missal*, 3rd ed., in use as of November 27, 2011. www.Catholic-resources.org/ChurchDocs/Mass-RM3.htm.

O'Toole, Fintan. 1998a. "A Radical Deal That Lets You Pick Who You Are: The Northern Ireland Agreement Recognizes How All Has Changed, Changed Utterly in Both the Republic and the North in the Past 30 Years." *Irish Times*, April 13, 16.

———. 1998b. "A Vote That Shattered Our Age-Old Ideologies." *Irish Times*, May 29, 14.

Parker, Michael. 1993. *Seamus Heaney: The Making of the Poet*. London: Macmillan.

———. 2007. *Northern Irish Literature*. Vol. 1. *1956–1975: The Imprint of History*. Basingstoke: Palgrave Macmillan.

———. 2012. "'His Nibs': Self-Reflexivity and the Significance of Translation in Seamus Heaney's *Human Chain*." *Irish University Review* 42 (2): 327–50.

———. 2013. "'Back in the Heartland': Seamus Heaney's 'Route 110' Sequence in *Human Chain*." *Irish Studies Review* 21 (4): 374–86.

Pascoli, Giovanni. 2009. "The Kite." Translated by Seamus Heaney as "A Kite for Aibhín." In *Auguri: To Mary Kelleher*, edited by Fergus Mulligan, 4–6. Dublin: Royal Dublin Society.

Patterson, Henry. 2012. "Unionism after Good Friday and St. Andrews." *Political Quarterly* 83:247–55.

Plato. 2000. *The Republic*. Edited by G. R. F. Ferrari. Translated by Tom Griffith. Cambridge: Cambridge University Press.

Poirier, Richard. 1992. *Poetry and Pragmatism*. London: Faber.

Potts, Abbie Findlay. 1967. *The Elegiac Mode: Poetic Form in Wordsworth and Other Elegists*. Ithaca, NY: Cornell University Press.

Ramazani, Jahan. 1990. *Yeats and the Poetry of Death: Elegy, Self-Elegy, and the Sublime*. New Haven, CT: Yale University Press.

———. 1994. *Poetry of Mourning: The Modern Elegy from Hardy to Heaney*. Chicago: University of Chicago Press.

———. 2009. *A Transnational Poetics*. Chicago: University of Chicago Press.

Regan, Stephen. 2007. "Seamus Heaney and the Modern Irish Elegy." In *Seamus Heaney: Poet Critic Translator*, edited by Ashby Bland Crowder and Jason David Hall, 9–25. Basingstoke: Palgrave Macmillan.

———. 2014. "'Things Remembered': Objects of Memory in the Poetry of Seamus Heaney." *Eire-Ireland* 49 (4): 320–36.

Ricks, Christopher. 2010. "Five Easy Pieces." *The Essay*, BBC Radio 4, broadcast May 17–21.

Ricoeur, Paul. 1976. *Interpretation Theory: Discourse and the Surplus of Meaning*. Fort Worth: Texas Christian University Press.

Robert, William. 2010. *Trials of Antigone and Jesus*. New York: Fordham University Press.

Rolston, Bill. 2013. "Dealing with the Past in Northern Ireland: The Current State of Play." *Estudios Irlandeses* 8:143–49.

Romer, Stephen. 1999. "Introduction to Eugene Guillevic, *Carnac*." Translated by John Montague. Newcastle-upon-Tyne: Bloodaxe.

Russell, Richard Rankin. 2010. *Poetry and Peace: Michael Longley, Seamus Heaney, and Northern Ireland*. Notre Dame, IN: University of Notre Dame Press.

———. 2014. *Seamus Heaney's Regions*. Notre Dame, IN: University of Notre Dame Press, 2014.

Schwartz, Alex. 2012. "Symbolic Equality: Law and National Symbols in Northern Ireland." *International Journal on Minority and Group Rights* 19:339–58.

Scott, Nathan A., Jr. 1971. *The Wild Prayer of Longing*. New Haven, CT: Yale University Press.

Shakespeare, William. 1965. *Measure for Measure*. Arden ed. London: Methuen.

———. 1972. *King Lear*. Arden ed. London: Methuen.

Shaw, George Bernard. 1984. *John Bull's Other Island*. Harmondsworth: Penguin.

Smith, Stan. 1997. "The Distance Between: Seamus Heaney." In *Seamus Heaney: New Casebook*, edited by Michael Allen, 223–51. Basingstoke: Palgrave.

Stevenson, Jonathan. 1998. "Peace in Northern Ireland: Why Now?" *Foreign Policy*, no. 112: 41–54.

Stewart, Susan. 2002. *Poetry and the Fate of the Senses*. Chicago: University of Chicago Press.

Sullivan, Barbara Stevens. 2010. *The Mystery of Analytical Work: Weavings from Jung and Bion*. New York: Routledge.

Sullivan, Moynagh. 2005. "The Treachery of Wetness: Irish Studies, Seamus Heaney and the Politics of Parturition." *Irish Studies Review* 13 (4): 453–68.

Tell, Carol. 2004. *Part-Time Exiles: Contemporary Irish Poets and Their Migrations*. Dublin: Maunsel.

Temin, Christine. 1994. "Harvard's Talking Trees: David Ward Parks His Art in the Yard." *Boston Globe*, May 13.

Tennyson, Alfred Lord. 1901. *In Memoriam A. H. H.* Boston: Knight and Millet.

———. 1969. *The Poems of Tennyson*. Edited by Christopher Ricks. London: Longman.

Thomas, Dylan. 1966. *Collected Poems: 1934–1952*. London: Dent.

Tobin, Daniel. 1998. *Passage to the Center: Imagination and the Sacred in the Poetry of Seamus Heaney*. Lexington: University of Kentucky Press.

———, ed. 2007. *The Book of Irish American Poetry*. Notre Dame, IN: University of Notre Dame Press.

Todorov, Tzvetan. 1988. *Literature and Its Theorists: A Personal View of Twentieth-Century Criticism*. London: Routledge and Kegan Paul.

Toibín, Colm. 2010. Review of *Human Chain*, by Seamus Heaney. *Guardian*, August 21.

Tyler, Meg. 2005. *A Singing Contest: Conventions of Sound in the Poetry of Seamus Heaney*. London: Routledge.

———. 2008. "Paths and Aftermaths: Some Thoughts about Seamus Heaney's and Michael Longley's Recent Sonnets." *Journal of Sonnet Studies* 1 (1): 20–31.

Underhill, Evelyn. 1999. *Mysticism*. Oxford: Oneworld.

Vendler, Helen. 1995. *The Breaking of Style: Hopkins, Heaney, Graham*. Cambridge, MA: Harvard University Press.

———. 1998. *Seamus Heaney*. Cambridge, MA: Harvard University Press.

Virgil. [1916] 1999. *The Aeneid*. Loeb Classical Library 63. Translated by H. R. Fairclough. Revised by G. P. Goold. Cambridge, MA: Harvard University Press.

———. 1951. *The Aeneid*. Edited by Charles Knapp. Chicago: Scott Foresman.

———. 2006. *The Aeneid*. Translated by Robert Fagles. London: Penguin Classics.

———. 2007. *Aeneid*. Translated with notes by Frederick Ahl. Introduction by Elaine Fantham. Oxford: Oxford University Press.

———. 2008. *The Aeneid*. Translated by Sarah Ruden. New Haven, CT: Yale University Press.

Waterman, Andrew. 1992. "The Best Way Out Is Always Through." In *Seamus Heaney: A Collection of Critical Essays*, edited by Elmer Kennedy-Andrews, 11–38. London: Macmillan.

Waters, John. 2010. *Beyond Consolation*. New York: Continuum.

Welch, Robert. 1996. "Sacrament and Significance: Some Reflections on Religion and the Irish." *Religion and Literature* 28 (2–3): 101–13.

White, Timothy J. 2007. "Civil Society and Peace in Northern Ireland." *Peace Review* 19: 445–51.

Wieseltier, Leon. 2004. "Czesław Miłosz, 1911–2004." *New York Times Book Review*, September 12.

Williams, Kristen P., and Neil G. Jesse. 2001. "Resolving Nationalist Conflicts: Promoting Overlapping Identities and Pooling Sovereignty: The 1998 Northern Irish Peace Agreement." *Political Psychology* 22 (2001): 571–99.

Williams, Mary Francis. 1999. "Seamus Heaney's *Exposure* and Vergil's *Aeneid*." *Classical and Modern Literature* 19 (3): 243–56.

Winspur, Steven. 2004. "Transposing a Meadow's Silence (Ponge and Guil-levic)." *French Forum* 29 (2): 55–68.

Wirzba, Norman. 2003. "Placing the Soul: An Agrarian Philosophical Principle." In *The Essential Agrarian Reader: The Future of Culture, Community, and the Land*, edited by Norman Wirzba, 80–100. Washington, DC: Shoemaker and Hoard.

Witherspoon, Alexander, and Frank Warnke. 1982. *Seventeenth-Century Prose and Poetry*. 2nd ed. Fort Worth, TX: Harcourt.

Wordsworth, William. 1967. *The Prelude* (1850), book 12. In *Poetical Works*, edited by Ernest de Selincourt. Oxford: Oxford University Press.

———. 1984. *William Wordsworth: A Critical Edition of the Major Works*. Edited by Stephen Gill. Oxford: Oxford University Press, 1984.

———. 1994. *William Wordsworth: Selected Poems*. Edited by John O. Hayden. London: Penguin.

Wordsworth, William, and Samuel Taylor Coleridge. 1994. "Preface to *Lyrical Ballads*, with Pastoral and Other Poems" (1802). In *Selected Poems*, edited by John O. Hayden. London: Penguin.

Yeats, William Butler. 1965. *Collected Poems*. London: Macmillan.

———. 1983. *The Collected Poems of W. B. Yeats*. Edited by Richard J. Finneran. New York: Macmillan.

CONTRIBUTORS

ANDREW J. AUGE, Professor of English, Loras College, USA.

RAND BRANDES, Martin Luther Stevens Professor of English, Lenoir-Rhyne University, USA.

NEIL CORCORAN, Emeritus Professor of English Literature, University of Liverpool, UK.

HENRY HART, Mildred and J. B. Hickman Professor of English and Humanities, The College of William and Mary, USA.

MAGDALENA KAY, Professor, Department of English, University of Victoria, Canada.

ELMER KENNEDY-ANDREWS, Professor of English, Arts and Humanities Research Institute, School of English and History, University of Ulster, UK.

MICHAEL R. MOLINO, Associate Professor and Chair, Department of English, Southern Illinois University, USA.

EUGENE O'BRIEN, Department of English Language and Literature, Mary Immaculate College, University of Limerick, Ireland.

BERNARD O'DONOGHUE, Common University Fund Lecturer and Tutorial Fellow, Wadham College, Oxford, UK.

MICHAEL PARKER, Visiting Professor at Oxford Brookes University, UK, and part-time tutor at Oxford University's Department of Continuing Education.

STEPHEN REGAN, Professor, Department of English Studies, Durham University, UK.

Richard Rankin Russell, Professor of English, 2012 Baylor Centennial Professor, Baylor University, USA.

Moynagh Sullivan, Lecturer, School of English, Media and Theatre Studies, National University of Ireland, Maynooth, Ireland.

Daniel Tobin, Professor and Interim Dean, School of Arts, Emerson College, USA.

Meg Tyler, Associate Professor of Humanities, College of General Studies, Boston University, USA.

Helen Vendler, Arthur Kingsley Porter University Professor, Department of English, Harvard University, USA.

INDEX

EUGENE O'BRIEN is senior lecturer in the Department of English Language and Literature and director of the Institute for Irish Studies at Mary Immaculate College, University of Limerick. He is the author and editor of numerous books, including *Seamus Heaney as Aesthetic Thinker: A Study of the Prose* and *Seamus Heaney: Creating Irelands of the Mind*.